A CARNIVAL OF REVOLUTION

A CARNIVAL OF REVOLUTION

CENTRAL EUROPE 1989

PADRAIC KENNEY

PRINCETON UNIVERSITY PRESS

PRINCETON AND OXFORD

Library of Congress Cataloging-in-Publication Data

Kenney, Padraic, 1963–

    A carnival of revolution—Central Europe 1989 / Padraic Kenney.

      p. cm.

    Includes bibliographical references and index.

    ISBN 0-691-05028-7 (alk. paper)

    1. Europe, Eastern—History—1989–   2. Revolutions—Europe, Eastern—

History—20th century.   I. Title.

DJK51 .K465 2002

943'.0009'048—dc21   2001036866

British Library Cataloging-in-Publication Data is available

To IMZ-K

CONTENTS

A CARNIVAL OF REVOLUTION

INTRODUCTION: STREET THEATER, CONCRETE POETRY

T UESDAY, February 16, 1988. It was Mardi Gras, the eve of the Lenten season. The weather in Poland was sunny and unseasonably warm, with the temperature reaching the mid-60s in the southeastern city of Wrocław. It was a perfect occasion for a traditional Rio de Janeiro–style carnival, smoothly transposed into a communist setting: a "ProletaRIO Carnival" (*Karnawał RIObotniczy*), in fact. The crowd that gathered around the clock on Świdnicka Street in the center of this city of six hundred thousand was estimated to be three to five thousand.

"Let's make our city outshine Las Vegas," read the flyer posted on the streets and distributed in high schools and colleges. "Dress for a party. This time the police won't touch us. We'll say a magic word and either they'll disappear, or they'll join the carnival."[1] Even the deejays on popular Radio Three called on their Wrocław listeners to join in the fun—until the authorities realized whose carnival it was and rescinded the invitation.

Thus began another "happening," called into being (not to say "organized") by the Orange Alternative. The guru of this guerrilla street-theater collective, 34-year-old Waldemar "Major" Fydrych, couldn't make it: The police detained him and his orange-highway-cone megaphone as he approached the crowd. But the show went on anyway. Everyone seemed to have whistles or horns. There was a guitarist, Krzysztof "Jakub" Jakubczak, stirring up the crowd with children's songs, communist ditties, and nationalist hymns. There was a skeleton, and a makeshift orchestra with a giant drum. Were those Ku Klux Klansmen, waving a sign reading "Open the borders, we'll run to Calgary!"? There were Smurfs, a miner handing out lumps of coal, and a Jaruzelski puppet. There was a Red Riding Hood, arm-in-arm with a wolf, and a bear wielding a machine gun.

The crowd chanted, "The police party with us!" and "Hocus-pocus!" But the police did not disappear. Instead, they grabbed revelers and hauled them to waiting vans. The boisterous crowd freed those detained as quickly as the police could round them up; Jakubczak himself was liberated four times. Many police found themselves trapped inside their cars by the crowd. Finally, several dozen police linked arms and swept down Świdnicka Street. "This was a scene," wrote an underground weekly, "to make any surrealist's head spin."[2] Was this blue-helmeted kickline a late entry in the festivities? Apparently not. By five o'clock, the happening was over—except at the police station, where Jakubczak led sing-alongs on his guitar while the several dozen who had been detained waited their turn to be reprimanded and sent home.

According to the stern reprimand in the communist press, this was just a bit of student foolishness that had to be shut down lest it paralyze the afternoon commuter hour. That was one version. Another saw a political maneuver, in reaction to the price hikes announced at the beginning of February, and to the failures of the regime's multistage economic reform program. After all, one sign promised imminent belt-tightening: "Second stage of reform: Carnival. Third stage: Ash Wednesday."

The report on the happening in *Tygodnik mazowsze,* Solidarity's largest underground paper, ran alongside an article by Solidarity strategist Jacek Kuroń with an ominous opening line: "The specter of a societal eruption is haunting the country."[3] Kuroń feared the destabilizing costs of such an explosion and wondered if the result would be a massive conflict between state and society. After the "Karnawał" happening, the Wrocław authorities would probably have agreed that Kuroń's fears were coming true. But really, how much political baggage can a Red Riding Hood carry?

One year later, Kuroń and the rest of the Solidarity elite would be sitting down to negotiations with the communist regime. Those negotiations, which were unimaginable to anyone in February 1988, led to the legalization of Solidarity, to semi-free elections, and, ultimately, to the fall of communism in Poland and all of Central Europe. A regime wavering between reform and repression sat down to talk with an opposition that feared the power of society's pent-up rage.

So why were the people of Wrocław on the street that winter day, and how do they fit into the story of the revolutions of 1989? We can start to put the pieces together by recognizing that the road from the fears of 1988 to the triumphs of 1989 is an improbable one. A world turned upside down in the space of a few short years. Red Riding Hood did come to embrace the wolf (despite that armed bear nearby). The story, we shall see, must take us through the streets of Wrocław and the peculiar world of Orange Alternative. But it will travel also through the streets of dozens of other cities and towns, accompanied by numerous other movements, and across events usually left out of the standard narratives of the greatest revolutionary event of our lifetime.

The year 1989—the moment when the Cold War, and communism, lost out to democracy, the free market, and nationalist aspirations, in Central Europe and across the world—was a year of dramatic, and immediately evident, beginnings and endings. Communist leaders shook hands with dissidents only recently out of prison; a philosopher was elected president; everywhere, flags with their communist-symbol centers cut out flew above triumphant crowds.

But revolutions are not just turning points; the Russian Revolution and the French Revolution are fascinating not only for the new worlds they wrought, but also for their atmosphere of limitless possibility and colorful aspiration. Both 1917 and 1789 were stages on which politically aware urban societies and movements pursued raucously diverse programs, in elaborate public rituals, celebrations, and (sometimes) battles. Though once the image of unruly mobs manipulated by crafty leaders may have dominated historical memory, we know now that the story is a lot more interesting than that.

Perhaps because Central Europe is a little out of the way, and because the events moved so rapidly across half a dozen countries, descriptions of 1989 often mystify more than they reveal. Even scholars who know the region very well resort to a bit of the supernatural to explain how democracy and freedom emerged from the communist bloc. It was a "year of miracles" (or *annus mirabilis*) in which "people power" "lit the night."[4] Accounts of sudden miracles should make any historian suspicious. Enormous shifts like that of 1989 do not—cannot—appear out of nowhere; miracles rarely occur. The throngs that appeared on the streets or in the voting booths emerged—we must assume, if only by analogy with other revolutionary moments—onto a stage already prepared for them and by them.

The carnival that is the subject of this book played for about three and a half years, from the post-Chernobyl demonstrations in Poland in the spring of 1986 to the Velvet Revolution in Prague. Over these years, new issues, new movements, and a new generation altered the relationship among state, opposition, and society. The stage of this carnival was Poland, Czechoslovakia, Hungary, and the German Democratic Republic (East Germany, GDR), as well as parts of neighboring countries: Slovenia, the northernmost republic of Yugoslavia, and the western part of Ukraine, in the Soviet Union.

This Central Europe* is a region with a common past in Western empires (the Austro-Hungarian Empire, the Kingdom of Poland, and the Kingdom of Prussia). Since World War II, it has evolved shared traditions of nonviolent political engagement. Long before 1989, the people of this region developed ways of resistance to communism—though active participants were rarely more than a small minority. Beyond Central Europe, the events of 1989 and their aftermath looked dramatically different. The bloody fall of Romania's Nicolae Ceauşescu, the horrific wars and genocide in Croatia and Bosnia, and the communist-led disintegration of the Soviet Union belong, in some ways, to an entirely separate story.

* I use the term "Central Europe" in contrast to "Eastern Europe," which refers to all of the former non-Soviet communist countries in Europe, plus the former western republics of the Soviet Union. To assign some countries to the East and some to the West or the Center is a tricky and controversial thing. Readers may draw their own conclusions about common pasts after reading this book.

I call the era of revolution a carnival for several reasons, each of which separates those years from the opposition of the previous decades. First, there was variety, an almost bewildering pluralism of movements. Where once one could safely catalog most opposition as either nationalist/conservative or Marxist/socialist, now so much opposition defied any categorizing. Radical environmentalists, hippies, performance artists, and pacifists crowded onto the scene; they often mixed strands of anarchism, nationalism, liberalism, conservatism, and postmaterialism in idiosyncratic ways.* Most had as their goal the end of communism, but often it was just as important to articulate a new style, and thus to change the social or natural environment. Certainly, some of this variety had appeared earlier: in Poland during Solidarity's first legal existence in 1980–81, or in the much freer Yugoslavia. But in 1986–89 it seemed as if activists' common assumptions and inhibitions simply disappeared.

Second, this revolution was joyful. Opposition had until this time been a weighty business, to match the grimness of life in the slowly decaying Soviet bloc. And for good reason: older generations of opposition remembered the horrors of war and Soviet liberation; of stalinist show trials, prisons, and back-breaking labor; and of Soviet tanks, in East Germany in 1953, Hungary in 1956, and Czechoslovakia in 1968. The road to brave opposition was long and hard. For the most part, one engaged in opposition for philosophical reasons, or as a consequence of one's writings or scholarship, to save the nation's soul. In the carnival years, the new opposition could also be thoughtful: reading Gandhi was their answer to those who preached Lenin. But this opposition never took itself, nor the regime, too seriously. This opposition had a soundtrack (sometimes reggae, sometimes punk, sometimes the rhythms of Mardi Gras). Musicians, too, were not just another cause to write about, but part of the carnival itself. Demonstrations were neither angry nor desperate (though that style would reappear at the end, in 1989), but entertaining; they were as much celebrations as anything else.

The reader with a taste for literary theory will already have wondered: did the Orange Alternative read Bakhtin? Some probably did: Russian theorist Mikhail Bakhtin's writings about "carnival" as a literary trope arrived in Poland in the 1970s, not long after they had begun appearing in English. But whether or not literary critics were on the streets in Wrocław, Bakhtin would have found much that was familiar in Central Europe.

A carnival (Bakhtinian or otherwise) breaks down borders of all kinds. It forces a suspension of the usual rules in society, issuing a challenge to the existing order and reversing social and political hierarchies. And in-

---

* Each of these ideologies meant something quite different to a Central European, compared to a Westerner, as will become clear.

deed, social movements in Central Europe in the second half of the 1980s appeared to disregard the fear that held so many others back, and to act almost with impunity. It didn't matter to them if the police detained participants in a demonstration, because that was part of the game, too. In fact, they were exhibitionists who wanted attention and knew that their antics were threatening to the established order without being dangerous.

Meanwhile, the iron curtains melted away. No longer did Central Europeans fight their national demons alone. These new movements, instead, paid a great deal of attention to one another. When possible, they visited one another, regardless of communist border guards and Kafkaesque passport restrictions. This interaction is a central feature of the carnival story.

These social movements also broke the rules of politics. Anticommunism did not mean, to them, waging war against the regime, or even engaging in dialogue with the communists (though some did). In place of loathing of the regime, or the desire to reform it, came indifference. For decades, the communists had ignored society; now some turned the tables on the state (even as their performances were staged in part for the authorities to view). Opposing the regime, they ignored it. Some movements were even ready to deride their elders in the "senior opposition." Discarding the old politics, they broke free of the usual opposition sites: shop floor, church hall, national monument, underground text. In this revolution, opposition could take place anywhere, on almost any grounds.

Where else but the communist world should we expect (in hindsight, anyway) an opposition we can call "carnivalesque"? To live in Central Europe before 1989 was to be on the receiving end of an incessant monologue. How could one interrupt the regime's stranglehold on communication and force it to listen to society? Years of patient attempts to initiate dialogue (by reformers within the party, or nonparty intellectual dissenters) had not succeeded. But the carnival ruptured this monologue—not with persuasive argument, but with a cacophony of insistent and derisive voices. And the result, if we look at Central Europe after 1989, was a dialogue between state and society that continues today.[5]

This suspension of the rules blurred the boundaries between citizens and opened up borders of all kinds. Ultimately, the fear of communism simply dissipated. From the perspective of grassroots social movements, then, we can look in a new way at the revolutions of 1989.

In September 1986 I arrived in Poland to begin a year's study of the Polish language and the history of early communist Poland.* I chose to live

---

* This was not my first trip behind the Iron Curtain; I had lived for four months in Moscow (on a college study-abroad program) in 1984 and spent ten days in Yugoslavia that same year.

in the city of Wrocław. There was someone there I wanted to see again; I also thought I would learn Polish better if I were far from Warsaw. It was a lucky choice: two years later, Izabela and I were married in Wrocław's cathedral, and the city became my second home. And Wrocław in 1986 was also about to become the most lively city in Central Europe.

The movements that flourished there are among the ones described in this book. They include Orange Alternative; Freedom and Peace; Polish-Czechoslovak Solidarity; and various movements in high schools, universities, and churches. The students and teachers at Adam Mickiewicz Lyceum 3, where my fiancée taught Russian, and my fellow students at Wrocław University, in Prof. Tadeusz Marczak's fifth year class on the history of communist Poland, included many central characters in the Wrocław opposition scene.

I, unfortunately, knew little of this. I wish I could tell of my daring courier missions, clandestine meetings, demonstrations, pilgrimages, and underground seminars. But I was there (I thought) only to learn as much as I could about Polish history before starting a Ph.D. program. So for ten months I worked in the library and read a lot of books and old newspapers. In my free time, I traveled a little around Poland and made brief trips to Hungary and Czechoslovakia. Along the way, I decided that the game of opposition was not for me; after all, I reasoned, it was not my struggle, and anyway I would have an unfair advantage over the Poles, in that my passport would extricate me from any scrape (though possibly with a one-way ticket out of Poland, too). So other Americans could claim to be intrepid underground couriers or Jacek Kuroń's drinking buddies; I would keep my distance.

The real reason, of course, was probably the anxieties of a 23-year-old trying to master a language and choose a graduate career while falling in love at the same time. I attended just one demonstration that year (on April Fool's Day, 1987); when pictures of me hovering at the fringes showed up on the History Institute's bulletin board, I half believed my friends' ribbing that I was in real hot water.

I would not come much closer to participation that year. Careful to the last, I never asked what my friends were doing, and they never asked me to help. Nevertheless, even I could see their attitude of utter indifference toward the communist regime, and toward ideology. I suppose that feeling has colored my writing on the Polish People's Republic ever since.

It was journalism that pushed me to pay more attention. When my parents came to Wrocław for the wedding in the summer of 1988, I arranged some interviews for my father, a journalist at *The Boston Globe*. I was rather surprised to discover that I knew some very interesting people. Then in August, as Izabela and I returned from our honeymoon, strikes broke out in several cities. Just at that time, Boston Mayor Raymond

Flynn arrived in Kraków to attend an opposition-organized International Human Rights Conference there. With strikes raging, no *Globe* reporter could get a Polish visa (Flynn had gotten one only by promising not to tip off the press corps), so I was pressed into service as a stringer. In the space of a week, at the conference and on a trip to Gdańsk with Mayor Flynn, I met opposition leaders like Adam Michnik, Tadeusz Mazowiecki, and Zbigniew Romaszewski; I talked to striking steelworkers and miners in Kraków and Jastrzębie; and I tried to figure out just who was calling the shots. My strongest impression from that summer (which also included an Orange Alternative demonstration in Wrocław in June) was that Solidarity was no longer in charge of the Polish opposition. Western and Eastern observers alike wrote as if "opposition" and "Solidarity" were the same thing. But in truth, even I could see that the opposition was now simply too varied, and the old rules of dissent had disintegrated.

To the perspectives of friend and journalist, finally, I added that of historian. Three years after my first encounter with Poland, I returned for a year's stay to collect material for my dissertation, on Polish workers during the communist revolution of 1945–49. I arrived as Mazowiecki's government took power; posing as a journalist, I managed to bluff my way into the parliament to watch the swearing-in. Many times, as I hurried to the archives in the morning, read Michnik's *Gazeta wyborcza* over lunch, or looked up from dusty folders in the late afternoon, I thought to myself: "Here you are, studying a society in revolution. But there's a revolution happening right now, outside! Chuck aside this research, grab a notebook, and record history as it happens!"

I didn't do that, except for an occasional story filed with the *Globe*. I followed the blistering pace of change in the newspapers (and in my wallet, as the new government's shock therapy reduced my graduate-student stipend to 20 percent of its former buying power in just a few months), and I watched the changes in friends' lives. But I began to think about this revolution in historical terms, as a product of society that could be examined as I was examining the dynamics of 1945. While no one (myself least of all) predicted the revolution, it also could not seem utterly miraculous to anyone who had lived in and studied Poland in those last years. The question, of course, was how to capture that story, as a historian who was also close (and yet not so close) to the events and the participants.

Over the intervening years, I have found that what I read about the revolutions of 1989 does not match what I saw, felt, and experienced. As scholars have moved past the "miracle" story of 1989, they have proposed many different explanations for the swift collapse of communism, and equally swift victory of democracy.

There are three common explanations. The first—and I think, most widely known—centers on the accession to Kremlin leadership of Mikhail

Gorbachev, which emboldened liberalizing and democratic impulses throughout the Soviet empire. Indeed, if we want to understand why communist leaders gave up the ghost so rapidly, even in Eastern Europe's darker corners, Gorbachev is quite important. He was the first Soviet leader of the postwar generation, a man who thought pragmatically about Soviet-style socialism and the communist world. Within a short time after becoming Communist Party general secretary (*gensek*) in early 1985, he initiated sweeping reforms (and, what is more important for Central Europe, talked boldly about those reforms) in the economy, and then in politics and international relations (including a series of meetings with U.S. President Ronald Reagan).

From Gorbachev, economic reformers and democratic thinkers got the signal to push their ideas, while hard-liners found they could no longer rely on Soviet tanks, or Soviet subsidies, to prop up their policies. Central European communist leaders, still accustomed to following Kremlin signals slavishly, offered echoes of Gorbachev's slogans: restructuring the economy (*perestroika*), openness in the media (*glasnost*), and democratization. Gorbachev used visits to Central Europe, and also to the West, to pressure those leaders to rescue socialism according to his plan. The irony is that communism fell sooner on the periphery of empire than in the core, where reform ideas had originated. But the fact that even the hardest-line regimes (Romania, Bulgaria, the GDR) experienced change in 1989 can be credited in part to Gorbachev's pressure.

The "Gorbachev factor" does not take us very far in Central Europe, though. After all, in Mikhail Gorbachev's first two years in power, he was primarily concerned with reviving the Soviet economy. Perestroika meant modestly ambitious plans to introduce competitive mechanisms and decentralization of management. Not until a party plenum in January 1987 did Gorbachev and his allies emphasize glasnost—by which time, as we shall see, social movements in Central Europe had already pushed openness farther than Gorbachev ever would. We shall return to Gorbachev's influence briefly in chapter 4.

One of the taboo subjects Gorbachev addressed—though not until 1987–88—was the Soviet Union's relationship to Eastern Europe. Economic strictures drove this exploration: the Soviets needed to de-emphasize the military's role in foreign policy if they would craft a more manageable budget. Subsidies, too, ought to be scaled back. This meant, ideally, that the countries of the bloc would evolve toward a more trustworthy relationship with their dominant partner. And since trade with the bloc accounted for over half of all Soviet foreign trade, a relationship built upon trust and self-sufficiency rather than coercion and subsidies would benefit perestroika at home.

This leads us to the second explanation of communism's fall: as an economic system, it was fatally flawed. Economic policy tended to be dictated by political necessities, such as the communists' desire to prove that socialism was more powerful than capitalism, or their fear of individual enterprise. The result was a tightly centralized, inflexible planning system that could not respond to popular desires or technological innovation. Meanwhile, a growing familiarity with the West (as more people traveled, or as they encountered Western media and Western products at home) made the citizens of Central Europe more impatient to experience the benefits of Western-style markets. The socialist economies attempted to provide what people wanted but eventually went bankrupt under the strain, and people simply chose a system that they hoped would improve their standard of living.

This explanation, too, helps us to understand why communist leaders (outside of the Balkans) gave in so easily. The widespread assumption, shortly after 1989, that the communists were only surrendering what they had already ruined was not entirely fanciful. Few had expected a peaceful end to communism; after all, the Central European regimes had their own firepower if Gorbachev would not come to their aid. But leaders in Poland and Hungary in particular knew the game was up and had already experimented a little with free-market mechanisms. Indeed, many communist bureaucrats relinquished their hold on political power only to find security in the new economic system (the so-called nomenclaturization of the economy).

Nor were communists the only ones who saw the economic failure. Mass emigration, largely for economic reasons, played a crucial role in the fall of East Germany. If the revolution had an imagined end-point, it was, for many people in Central Europe, the prosperity and economic security of the West. On the other hand, slogans demanding economic change were rare (if they appeared at all) in the protests of 1989. For that matter, Gorbachev's name was usually invoked ironically, to draw a contrast to his supposed faithful minions in Prague, Berlin, and elsewhere.

To understand the ideas that often motivated people in 1989, we can turn to the intellectuals. This third explanation was at one time the most compelling but is now sometimes overlooked. A small group of intellectuals, who drew in part on Western ideas but also upon national traditions, formulated powerful humanist critiques of the state-socialist regimes and then disseminated these ideas by means of *samizdat.** With the Helsinki Accords signed by nearly all European countries in 1975 as their platform, they argued incessantly for the respect of basic human rights. They also gave voice to national and religious traditions. Over the course

---

* "Self-published" (Russian). A companion term is *tamizdat:* literature published "over there," in emigration.

of a decade and a half, these ideas reached more and more people—especially after one Central European intellectual, Archbishop Karol Cardinal Wojtyła of Kraków, became Pope John Paul II in 1978. By 1988 or so, this argument runs, these ideas were second nature to those who took to the streets, or who cast ballots.

This idea becomes clear when we look at postcommunist Central Europe. Those countries where democratic practices and respect for human rights appear to have successfully taken root are also those countries where those ideas were most strongly articulated before 1989 by dissident intellectuals. Ideas about human rights, democracy, and European values entered the national consciousness through samizdat, the demonstrations of 1989, and the attention that former dissidents enjoyed in the first year or so of freedom. Even when civil or human rights have come under attack in those countries, the language of the former dissidents is familiar, and irrevocably part of the national discourse. And finally, the movements whose stories make up this book did not spring from nowhere; most owed a great deal to the ideas and practices of their elders, even when they tried to keep their distance.

Since the older generation of opposition was often a point of departure for many of the movements in the Central European carnival, a brief road map of dissent might be helpful here. "Dissent" itself is a controversial term,* encompassing many different types of resistance or opposition. First, there is reformist dissent within the Communist Party. This was important in Czechoslovakia (and indeed throughout the region) before and during 1968; the Prague Spring of 1968 was reformism's finest hour. Some in the region continued to look to Marxism through the 1980s.

Second, there is the "civil society" dissent pioneered by Václav Havel and Charter 77 in Czechoslovakia, by the Workers' Defense Committee (KOR) in Poland, and by the Democratic Opposition in Hungary, all in the late 1970s. The ideas articulated by these groups and thinkers centered around how the communist system curtailed the independence of the individual; these dissidents countered with advice to "live the truth," as Havel put it. KOR's strategy included close cooperation with opposition-minded workers: at first by defending workers put on trial, later by working with them to develop underground trade unions and newspapers. Their model of "antipolitical" concrete action, and their understanding of the importance of publicity as a safeguard for dissent, would be influential for the next generation of opposition.

A third source of opposition was from within the churches. The most famous case is Poland, because of Pope John Paul II. But the underground

---

* Some former dissidents claim it implies essential agreement with the system and thus is appropriate only for socialist opposition. I will use it as roughly equivalent to "intellectual opposition."

Catholic Church played an important role in Slovakia, while František Cardinal Tomašek of Prague enjoyed great moral authority. In Western Ukraine there was a second secret church: the outlawed Uniate Church, which followed a rite not dissimilar to that of Russian Orthodoxy while maintaining allegiance to Rome. In Slovenia and Hungary, both predominantly Catholic, the Church was one of the ingredients of opposition culture, as was the Lutheran Church in the GDR.

A fourth type of opposition came from the counterculture. The communist regimes did not for the most part ban rock music, but not all of it was acceptable. In Czechoslovakia, home of the most famous underground rock group the Plastic People of the Universe, every musician had to have a license to perform, granted at yearly auditions. Through milieux like the Jazz Section—a semi-tolerated branch of the official musicians' union—many Czechs drifted from alternative culture to alternative politics. Music outside the accepted mainstream existed in a literal underground: it spread by word-of-mouth and spawned samizdat publications and informal associations. Punk music, which was most articulate in Poland and Slovenia, was the most powerful example. Underground music was in a way like the Church: it was not a form of opposition in itself but was a milieu where some people would discover opposition, and a resource (of contacts, and of strategies) for that opposition.

Finally, there was nationalist opposition. This was the oldest of them all, usually with roots stretching back to the 1940s and the communist takeovers. Nationalist opposition focused its attention on sovereignty as a first order of business, or on the salvation of national cultural traditions. The former was an impractical dream until very late in the communist period; the latter was often the work of exile communities, which were an important resource for each of the nations of Central Europe. Nationalist opposition was particularly important in Ukraine, where the work of the Ukrainian Helsinki Union blazed a trail for others to follow, and in Slovenia, where a group of intellectuals in 1981 founded a journal, *Nova revija,* that would set the parameters for opposition based upon Slovene national culture.

All of these strands of dissent came together in one event that would have a great impact on the entire region: the creation of the Solidarity trade union in 1980. Widespread strikes in July–August 1980, and the close cooperation between KOR intellectuals and workers, especially on the Baltic coast, led to negotiations between the Polish government and shipyard workers in Gdańsk, led by Lech Wałęsa. The result was a sixteen-month period in which the regime tolerated an increasingly independent-minded body that grew to nearly ten million members (or close to half the adult population of Poland). Solidarity was a dramatic illustration of the alternative to total communist control: independent organization of society from below. As such, it captured the imagination not only of the West, but also of independent thinkers throughout Central Europe.

Such, in barest detail, is the state of wisdom on the fall of communism at a remove of just over a decade. Each of these explanations contributes much to the story, for no event as epochal as the revolutions of 1989 could possibly be captured by one theory. But if Soviet reform, economic collapse, and dissent are each essential to grasping some part of the complexity of 1989, they are together incomplete without the story of the social movements of the 1980s.

This should become obvious if we try to imagine why people would come out onto the streets in 1989. Even after we take into account such important reasons for the massive support for change, we still need to understand why people felt they could behave as they did in Wrocław, Prague, or Leipzig. Dissidents, no matter how famous in the West, could no more be an instigator of that popular upheaval than was Mikhail Gorbachev. Would most people risk repression because of a text by an imprisoned playwright or a speech by a communist leader? Hardly—no more than it was likely that crowds in Petrograd in 1917 had studied Lenin or Marx. Ideas—even those about freedom and oppression, or about economic deprivation—do not translate automatically into action.

We also don't know why 1989 looked and felt the way it did. For example, a crowd newly and suddenly liberated should be vengeful, even violent. It ought to show distaste for compromise and (at the ballot box) be eager to endorse quick fixes. Anyone familiar with Central Europe will note these attitudes are common today; they were not so in 1989. Instead, gentle, triumphant irony was the order of the day. From the Solidarity election poster showing Gary Cooper in *High Noon* brandishing a ballot, to the Prague banner reading "Well, you've knocked communism out of our heads, comrades . . . ," to the Hungarian poster showing Leonid Brezhnev and Erich Honecker kissing, the sense of the ridiculous ameliorated the gravity of the change. The people of Central Europe preferred ironic protests to slogans promising extermination of the communists (and there were such voices). They accepted protest that was not only about political and economic power, but about environmental and other issues. Protest became a ubiquitous part of everyday life in the major cities. The social movements that are the main actors in this book created this revolutionary style.

To most observers, both inside and outside Central Europe, the revolutions were completely unexpected, in their pace and in their popular nature. Participants in the grassroots activism were less overwhelmed, as the style, mode, language, and goals of society's mass participation in 1989 were an outgrowth of what they had been enacting for several years. For the most part, neither dissident leaders nor reform communists sought to mobilize society (in strikes or demonstrations); the new movements, in contrast, brought the carnival to town. They created the framework, and the language, of the revolutions. People voted, or demonstrated, in part because they had learned how to do so from these movements and accepted (for the moment) their goals. As we pay attention to the carnival, we can learn to think about 1989 without resorting to "miracles," "people power," and "surprise."

Some of the social movements in this story are rather well known; most are now nearly forgotten. As I began this project in Poland, I was interested in examining any and all oppositional activity in the last half-decade of communism. The rough-and-ready distinction that I came to adopt in selecting stories to pursue was one employed by many of my Wrocław friends. They would say that an activist they were recommending to me was "*konkretny.*" As I came to understand, these were the kind of people I wanted to meet. *Konkretny* meant focused on reality: on everyday problems and on realistic, effective means of overcoming, or at least exposing, them. *Konkretny* meant someone who knew how to organize a demonstration, or to use the media, and who could implement ideas effectively. The opposite—and I talked to many of these, too—would be someone who enjoyed analyzing the communist system or the opposition and believed in the power of a devastating critique. Truth—about the workings of the communist system or the promise of, say, liberalism—was for such activists the prerequisite to opposition. It became clear, though, that by the mid-1980s the time of the "truth-tellers" had passed, giving way to what I call the *konkretny* generation.*

The *konkretny* activists matched support of the practical with a new attitude toward pluralism. This was not simply a tolerant pluralism of parties or movements, in which one person might be a socialist and another a conservative, or one person focused on environmental problems while another worried about nuclear war. I think of it as *internal pluralism:* one mixed and matched identities, and issues, as necessary, depending upon what was necessary to defeat the communists. A nationalist pacifist, or a promarket green, was not an uncommon species. One might even support ideas one didn't believe in (by helping at a demonstration, or giving space in one's publications), as long as those ideas furthered the destabilization of the communist system.

---

* The distinction between *konkretny* and *niekonkretny* is not the same as between active and passive, however. A devotee of underground resistance would not be considered *konkretny*. The terms might be translated as realist and idealist, except that "realist" can imply, as *konkretny* does not, a certain defeatism or pessimism. "Pragmatic" is also not a good translation: the demonstrations and protests that the *konkretny* activist organized were hardly the pragmatic thing to do.

A signal tactic of the *konkretny* activist was to exploit issues that laid bare surprising weaknesses of the communist regimes. This owed a great deal to the intellectual dissidents of the earlier generation (Václav Havel, Jacek Kuroń), who had proposed that opposition to the communist system could come in many different forms. Precisely because the communists aimed to control every aspect of society (even if that was impossible), they said, any independent activity, no matter how apolitical it seemed, weakened the regime's hold on power.

But it had always been easiest to attack the communists on the question of national sovereignty, or repression of free speech, or the falsification of history. The new opposition, by contrast, spread into areas on which there ought not to have been any disagreement: a temperance movement in Warsaw, a celebration of folk traditions in Lviv, a march against nuclear holocaust in Budapest, a campaign to clean up Bratislava. Precisely because they were so evidently innocuous, they backed the regimes into uncomfortable corners. They also were, for the same reason, more accessible to those who had not participated in opposition before. These were not intimidatingly subversive ideas, and it was not obvious why the state would arrest anyone for taking part. Such conflicts, then, sharpened the distinctions between state and society, while lowering barriers to participation.

These distinctions held in every country in Central Europe. The generation born between roughly 1957 and 1970 differed from its predecessors in just this way. The strikers in Poland in 1988; the students who demonstrated, then went on strike, in Prague; the spectacularly successful Association of Young Democrats (Fidesz)—a party that barred membership to anyone over 35—in Hungary; the aggressive journalists of the Slovene youth weekly *Mladina;* and the young nationalists in Lviv: none of these remembered 1968 (still less 1945) nor pretended to fight those old battles. They opposed the communists, of course, but did not propose another ideology to take its place.

In each case, of course, there were older opposition leaders who supported (or joined) their younger *konkretny* colleagues; some movements, like the Polish temperance campaign, were made up entirely of people over forty. But the distinction generally held. Even when I turned West, looking at activists from democratic countries who came to Central Europe, I found a roughly similar contrast: there, too, were people who believed in "doing something" and chafed at the bit while their elders talked theory.

The actors in this play—decidedly not a drama, though many would object to calling it a comedy—are social movements: groups of people, sharing a collective identity (and sometimes a lifestyle, too), who seek to mobilize others around a set of issues. But (as my search for the *konkretny* indicates) the individuals who made up these movements can best help us to understand what the movements were like, where they came from, and how they connected with other movements. So, at the risk of making the stage altogether too crowded, individuals from most movements will make their appearance as well.

Though I draw extensively on samizdat and personal archives, this book is in large part an oral history of 1989. It is worth recognizing the pitfalls of this approach. That memories can fail is but the contemporary historian's least worry. Of greater concern is that participants will embellish their roles, intentionally or not, and cast their movement's activities in the benevolent light of a successful revolution. A story told to a "neutral" third party is also an opportunity to settle old scores with movement rivals. Each of these biases is no less true for any written source and must be accounted for by the conscientious historian. For example, I have for the most part disregarded all the less flattering stories interviewees have told me about others, while taking stories of personal valor with a grain of salt.

There are also murky questions of spies, secret funds, and police manipulation. It seems that every movement, every key event in Central Europe trails in its wake rumors of informers or ambiguous ties to one regime or another. These stories can neither be proven nor be disproven in the foreseeable future, if ever, and I have chosen to leave them aside. When, toward the end of the next decade, a few relevant records in Moscow and Washington, as well as in Central European capitals, are released, we may discover that the successes or failures of this or that movement or activist appear in a quite different light. For the meantime, I think, we can safely start by appreciating a spectacle without wondering too much about the pulleys and wires that may or may not make our characters dance.

To write about opposition to communism in the 1980s, one must begin with Poland. The Poles were the only ones ever to stage repeated challenges to communist rule, with major uprisings in 1956, 1968, 1970, 1976, and 1980. Solidarity, the last of these, was a more credible alternative to communism than anything else produced in Central Europe. Its influence throughout the region was incalculable, even after General Wojciech Jaruzelski ordered in the tanks and riot police and installed martial law on December 13, 1981. As a result of the Solidarity experiment, there were far more people in Poland than elsewhere with experience in independent political activism—perhaps by a factor of 100. For this reason, the first chapters of this book will focus mostly on Polish movements. We will then see how the remarkable variety and potential of Polish opposition inspired the rest of the region up through 1989.

What started as just a carnival became a revolution. This story of 1989's revolution is quite different from what others have written. Rather than beginning in Moscow, or perhaps in Gdańsk, and cascading outward, it moves back and forth across borders, searching for parallels and influences. There are no miraculous events here, but many years of concerted action. The actors are not the famous dissident intellectuals and the ruthless communists, but hundreds of lesser-known individuals, most of whom, as I write, have yet to reach their forty-fifth birthday. Nor, finally, is this a pessimistic story of desperately poor societies demanding a better standard of living and turning nasty when their hopes turn sour. Instead this is a story of people who began by trying to change what they could (or believed they could). As they succeeded, their "concrete" efforts contributed to a revolution.

As the years have passed, the term "revolution" often disappears; people even in Central Europe speak of the "changes," the "transition," or just "1989." But the scope of change—political, economic, social, cultural—plus the speed at which it took place make any other word a strange and even tendentious fit. We shall see that many of the hopes of the participants in that raucous time have not been fulfilled. But it is enough to interview them a decade later—in parliamentary offices or in isolated mountain huts, in spacious company headquarters or in Internet cafes (or even over the Internet) to realize that Central Europe has changed utterly and irrevocably. And it is a world that, at least in part, they themselves have made.

Central Europe in 1989

Timeline I: 1975–1987

Year	Poland	Czechoslovakia	Hungary	GDR	Slovenia	Ukraine	East/West
1975							August: Helsinki Accord signed
1976	June: Price hikes and strikes; KOR (Workers' Defense Committee) formed					November: Ukrainian Helsinki Group forms, Kyiv	
1977	Samizdat publishing develops	January: **Charter 77** forms	January: **Democratic Opposition** becomes active				
1978	Underground unions form in Gdansk	October: Václav Havel writes "Power of the Powerless"		Government loosens restrictions on Protestant churches			October: Pope John Paul II begins pontificate
1979	June: Pope John Paul II makes first pilgrimage		Trial of conscientious objector József Merza SZETA (Committee to Help the Poor) forms				December: NATO announces deployment of Cruise and Pershing missiles in Western Europe
1980	August: Solidarity trade union forms in Gdansk				May: Josip Tito dies **Laibach** forms		April: **European Nuclear Disarmament** publishes "END Appeal"
1981	September: Solidarity's 1st National Congress December: Martial law imposed	Slovak greens active	Gábor Demszky visits Poland, founds *Beszélő*		Crackdown on punk begins Nationalist intellectuals found *Nova revija*		
1982	**Fighting Solidarity** forms Regime lifts ban on employee councils, passes law on student self-government	*Náboženstvo a súčasnosť* founded	Summer: **Peace Group for Dialogue** forms December: crackdown on dissidents	First peace protests within churches			June: **Moscow Trust Group** forms
1983	Pope John Paul II's 2nd visit Summer: **Polish–Czechoslovak Solidarity** becomes active August: **Sobriety Brotherhood** active July: Martial law lifted	Exchange of letters between Charter 77 and END	October: István Bibó Special College opens		**Peace Movement Working Group** forms Mile Šetinc becomes editor of *Mladina*		October: Mass protests in West Germany and Netherlands against NATO missile deployment
1984	July: **"Wole być"** appeal **Christian Workers' University** opens October: **Committee for Intervention and Legality** forms November: Fr. Jerzy Popiełuszko killed		Spring: Bibó College exchange visit to Poland September: **Danube Circle** forms				**Network for East-West Dialogue** forms in Perugia

	Poland	Czechoslovakia	Hungary	GDR	Yugoslavia	Ukraine	USSR
1985	April: **Freedom and Peace** forms Summer: Solidarity show trial	Spring: "Prague Appeal" July: Velehrad demonstration Dec: John Lennon demo	Multicandidate elections Opposition meets at Monor and Szarvas		*Information Booklet: Peace Movement in Yugoslavia* debuts		March: Mikhail Gorbachev chosen Communist Party general secretary
1986	May: First Wrocław happening September: final amnesty of political prisoners	September: crackdown on **Jazz Section**		**Initiative for Peace and Human Rights** forms	May: Chernobyl demo August: Franci Zavrl succeeds Mile Šetinc at *Mladina*	April: Accident at Chernobyl	"Helsinki Memorandum" October: Reagan-Gorbachev summit at Reykjavik
1987	March: School boycott May: Peace Seminar June: **Orange Alternative** celebrates Children's Day June: John Paul II's 3rd pilgrimage	April: Gorbachev visit June: Charter 77's environmental forum June: *Bratislava/nahlas* published July: Polish-Czech border meeting November: Navratil petition begins to circulate	January: Democratic opposition issues *New Social Contract* March: Zsolt Keszthelyi on trial September: Party, nationalist opposition meet at Lakitelek October: Peace seminar	February: Honecker spurns Gorbachev-style reform June: Reagan visits Berlin wall	Youth relay scandal	Thaw begins: senior activists return from prison July: **Tovarystvo Leva** forms September: inaugural demo of **Dovira** in Lviv	January: at CPSU plenum, Gorbachev pushes glasnost May: Mathias Rust lands plane on Red Square

PART ONE

ACTORS

STAGES

REPERTOIRES

Chapter One

EATING THE CROCODILE WITH A SPOON, OR, A CAREER GUIDE TO THE UNDERGROUND

THE AMNESTY TRAP

WHAT can an underground hero do when he gets out of prison? Consider the ordeal of Władysław Frasyniuk in Poland. A 25-year-old Wrocław bus driver in August 1980, he rose rapidly to become head of the Lower Silesian regional Solidarity, and a rising star (along with Zbigniew Bujak in Warsaw and a few others) among younger union leaders. When General Jaruzelski declared martial law in December 1981, Frasyniuk was one of the few top unionists to escape internment, thanks to a dramatic escape from a moving train and the help of a friendly railroad engineer. When he was finally captured in October 1982, he was sentenced to six years in prison—one of the longest terms anyone received. And few stayed in prison as long as Frasyniuk; with two additional sentences imposed during his incarceration—one for "insulting a prison official"—he was finally released in the amnesty of July 1984.

Frasyniuk found himself alone when he arrived back in Wrocław. With one of the most famous faces in Poland, he could hardly return to the underground. Even if he were successful in eluding the police* and disappearing again, anyone still in hiding would think twice about arranging a meeting with him, for fear of being captured. On the other hand, he thought, famous faces were just what the opposition needed. Anonymity gave the underground activist a certain security and dulled the edge of resistance as it reinforced the everyday ritual of secrecy. The post–martial

---

* There were three kinds of police in the communist world. The ordinary police were often called the militia; interestingly, many citizens came to associate the term "police" with a democratic, rule-of-law state. I use this latter term for convenience. Second is the security apparatus (SB or UB in Poland—hence the nickname "ubek"; StB in Czechoslovakia; Stasi in the GDR; KGB in the Soviet Union, etc.), employees of the Ministry of Internal Affairs. Though the term is somewhat misleading, I will call them the "secret police," as their role was in part covert, and this term is already a popular one. Finally, Poland in the 1980s also boasted the ZOMO (Zmotoryzowany Oddział Milicji Obywatelskiej, or Motorized Division of the Civil Militia), the shock troops of martial law, especially loathed by most citizens. I have translated this throughout as "riot police."

law underground—like its counterparts in the World War II resistance—used pseudonyms in its appeals to Polish society. But without recognizable names, who would listen? Anonymous declarations could even get Solidarity into trouble: the secret police could (and did) issue false declarations to look like the real thing.

In the factories, meanwhile, frequent arrests had eliminated Solidarity leadership several times over; the infantry, as Frasyniuk put it, was all used up. He arranged a meeting with Marek Muszyński, a chemist at the Polytechnic who now led Solidarity's Regional Strike Committee of Lower Silesia. Muszyński told Frasyniuk he was tired of the underground and planned to get out. But Muszyński was virtually the only recognizable name Solidarity had left in the region. Without him it wouldn't make any difference if the underground was anonymous or not, since no one would know the names anyway. Frasyniuk persuaded Muszyński to stay but wondered what his own role should be.

Frasyniuk was caught in a trap, from which, in 1984, there was no obvious escape. He had hoped to create an "aboveground representation of underground structures"—that is, faces who could represent the union while necessarily covert work (dues-collecting, publishing) continued out of sight. For Muszyński, aboveground meant politics with a capital "P"; the real union work was underground. Frasyniuk felt they were both necessary, but his dream was not easy to realize. In the factories, where such openness would have done the most to ease the fears of workers who had seen their hopes of 1980 dashed and knew they had nowhere else to go, it was impossible: an activist who stepped forward into the light would quickly be fired or arrested.

Barely a month after his release, Frasyniuk was himself back in prison, for attempting to lay flowers by a plaque at his old bus depot on Grabiszyńska Street, which commemorated the founding of Wrocław's Solidarity. This was an important ritual, a public affirmation of the continuing struggle, but only Józef Pinior, his deputy in 1981, accompanied him that year. Out of jail again two months later, Frasyniuk tried to push the openness idea with Solidarity's national leadership. He contacted other experienced unionists who were also blocked from a return to covert work. The few who would listen agreed to meet in Gdańsk in February 1985.

Now Frasyniuk would discover how difficult openness would be: it required either the regime's tacit permission, or enough care so that arrests would happen *after* the statement had been made or the deed done. And Gdańsk was a charmed city: Lech Wałęsa's Nobel Prize in 1983 had rendered him unarrestable, and it seemed to Frasyniuk as if everyone in the city felt they, too, could conduct politics as usual. Thus the meeting was common knowledge; having shaken his police tail, Frasyniuk arrived at the designated house to find it surrounded by police. "I was furious," he recalls, but he went in anyway. He, Bogdan Lis, and Adam Michnik were arrested and, in a show trial that spring, were sentenced to three and a half years.

It is difficult to imagine how things could have turned out differently at that moment. It was not simply that Frasyniuk faced a determined communist regime, but rather that his plan to reactivate Solidarity from above was precisely what the regime expected and could prevent. The Gdańsk affair allowed the regime to portray Solidarity as just a few isolated radicals cut off from society. Government press spokesman Jerzy Urban mocked opposition efforts as pathetic at his weekly press conferences. Frasyniuk's few months of freedom in 1984–85 were the worst time to be in the Polish opposition since at least 1978. The extra-legal procedures of the Gdańsk trial, and the accompanying rhetoric, seemed to hearken a return almost to the stalinist era.

Repression in communist countries has seemed part of the ordinary way of doing business from the very beginning. To cut off debate and protest, communist regimes have imprisoned, beaten, and killed their opponents, both prominent and insignificant. Yet the abduction, torture, and murder of a well-known Catholic priest was different, almost unimaginable since the death of Stalin in 1953. Father Jerzy Popiełuszko was the best-known practitioner of "Fatherland masses," in which the liturgy, and especially the homily, became an expression of political opposition and national pride. Support for Solidarity and human rights suffused Popiełuszko's sermons, which also called upon his parishioners (and pilgrims from all over Poland) in his north Warsaw church to engage in civil disobedience. In late October 1984, three rogue secret police officers—acting apparently with the knowledge of their immediate superiors—intercepted Father Popiełuszko's car on a lonely stretch of highway, tied him up, stuffed him into their trunk, and eventually dumped him, unconscious, into a reservoir, where his body was found almost two weeks later.

Such a brazen act, and the outrage and grief at the loss of such a beloved figure, forced Poland's opposition to rethink its priorities. Did the calculus of resistance still hold? Did Popiełuszko's murder mean that any open activity—even from behind a church pulpit—was too dangerous? Or did it mean that the communists had gone too far and must now be opposed even more strenuously? Should such violence be met with equal reprisals, or with nonviolent resistance? Led by Lech Wałęsa, Solidarity took the high road, mourning its loss instead of plotting revenge. At Popiełuszko's grave, Wałęsa urged Poles to refrain from demonstrations. An article in the leading underground weekly, signed by four Solidarity leaders, even proclaimed, "We are all guilty"; the authors argued that more could have been done to foresee and prevent such an attack.[1] Meanwhile, the nation watched transfixed as the authorities took care of their own, in a spectacular televised trial of the accused murderers.

In the communist world, regime leaders papered over each major confrontation with society with what they called *normalization*: a combination of repression of recalcitrants plus rewards—consumer benefits and nationalist rhetoric, mostly—for those who conformed. In addition, the regimes built new democratic facades so they could affirm to the people and to the world that they had listened to the criticisms raised during the earlier unrest—and would, with the assistance of so-called healthy elements in society, now address them in proper, civilized fashion. In a way, normalization was more sinister than old-fashioned brute force. The latter bred resentments, but the former drove a wedge between opposition and society.

Normalization was effective in Hungary after 1956, in East Germany after the building of the Berlin Wall in 1961, and in Czechoslovakia after 1968. The question was whether it could work in Poland after martial law. Amnesties of political prisoners were an important part of the communist strategy, allowing the communists to appear benevolent, even toward ungrateful dissidents. From the formal lifting of martial law in 1983, the Polish communists staged several amnesties and discovered that it was often better to have former dissidents free but impotent, rather than in prison and a symbol of communist repression. After the last amnesty, in September 1986, many in Solidarity wondered if opposition could even survive.

If the costs of conspiracy were revealed by Popiełuszko's murder, so Solidarity proved to be limited in other ways, too. Since the declaration of martial law, the union's message was "Solidarity lives!"—spraypainted on walls, posted on the mastheads of underground papers, or flashed on TV screens by pirate broadcasters during the evening news. But did Solidarity live? In February 1985 the government announced price hikes to take effect shortly. While these price hikes were not of the magnitude of those that had provoked uprisings in December 1970, June 1976, or August 1980, they were a sign that little had changed: normalization or not, the regime would force painful economic remedies after only a charade of "consultation" with society. In response, Lech Wałęsa and the Solidarity leadership called for a brief nationwide work stoppage to take place February 28 at noon. This was the first attempt since 1982 at any national coordinated action, and factory activists throughout the country began to prepare feverishly for this test of workers' commitment to the union.

The night before the strike was to take place, Wałęsa called it off. The government had agreed to ease some—but not all—of the price hikes. Surely, this was a success for Solidarity: the union had forced the government to back down, and thus implicitly to acknowledge Solidarity's influence on society in spite of continued attacks on its activists. But Solidarity had in a sense echoed the government's methods by calling off the strike without consulting its membership (admittedly a near impossibility). Highlighting the gap between leadership and rank-and-file, the union squandered an opportunity to discover the depth of support and commitment it still enjoyed, and to reveal this power (should it still exist) to society and to the communists. Indeed, in the context of the Gdańsk arrests that same month, the abortive strike raised the question of whether the opposition still existed at all.

It was this kind of hesitation that drove Paweł Kocięba crazy. Kocięba, a student activist in Wrocław, mocked his elders in Solidarity as "old farts without vision." He was as merciless toward his contemporaries. In 1986 he tried to organize a protest in support of Frasyniuk, who had been beaten in prison: "I go to someone," he complained to a local student paper, "and tell him 'Look, brother, Władek has been beaten, so . . . we should do something more concrete, with names, with a face.' And this guy says that's great, but he can't do it because 'hmm,' and that 'hmm' means that he is active in the production of *bibuła* [samizdat]. And here there comes to mind a very simple question: what the hell, then, is *bibuła* for?"[2] The rigors of the underground, Kocięba believed, actually provided an excuse to avoid the dilemmas of public action, as one hid under a cloak of impeccable valor. On his own, Kocięba found a few friends who would march up and down with a sandwich board and leaflets demanding freedom for Frasyniuk.

At about the time that Frasyniuk was on trial in Gdańsk, four Kraków union leaders returned from prison into their own amnesty trap. Stanisław Handzlik, Edward Nowak, Jan Ciesielski, and Mieczysław Gil were "the Four": legends of 1980–81, now a bit inconvenient. They were no longer welcome in the Lenin Steelworks of Nowa Huta, where they had worked and organized until martial law. With some forty thousand workers, a majority of whom (I frequently heard the unverifiable claim of 70 percent) still paid their Solidarity dues, Nowa Huta was a neuralgic point in the Solidarity-regime conflict. Many there believed that coming above ground was a dangerous tactic that could only drive wedges into the union's carefully tended unity.

Edward Nowak saw weakness behind that strength. Sitting in prison in the summer of 1985, he recalls, he felt "ten times worse than during the year and a half in prison right after martial law was introduced. It was more difficult: the feeling of isolation, of being deserted, a feeling of a certain helplessness, a feeling that—well, for whom are we doing this?" The average person was more than just indifferent to Solidarity's struggle, no matter how passionate it might still be inside factories like Nowa Huta. Nowak even sensed enmity: he could hear people thinking, "Why are they doing this? Who asked them to?" The noble struggle had become once again a quixotic, lonely fight, despite the millions of dues-payers the union had once boasted.

To quit, after long months in prison and years in the underground, made as little sense to Nowak as it did to Frasyniuk. Denied his job at the steelworks, he found the door to the underground union closed, too. So he and the rest of the Four formed the Provisional Steelworkers' Council and began to appear publicly at demonstrations and rallies. They hoped in this way to put a human face back on Solidarity, and to demonstrate that personal courage in the face of repression was still possible. The most common argument for demonstrations was that they were necessary to show that "Solidarity Lives." While this made sense in 1982, by 1986 "it had come to this," admits Nowak, "that we were convincing ourselves of how wonderful, great, and heroic we are. But this had no effect on those around us. None." And the police were easily able to contain the Four. Nowak was followed constantly and detained before most demonstrations; having found a job in a semiprivate firm, he couldn't easily ask for a few days off to evade the police. Not that it really mattered, for this was not the real union work he believed in.

Nowak wanted Solidarity to do more than survive. In the tradition of nineteenth-century nationalists who advocated opening schools and cooperatives over storming fortresses, he called himself a positivist, balancing Handzlik's principled idealism. While Handzlik and others pushed for more strikes and more demonstrations, hoping to provoke revolution, Nowak called for pragmatism. He wanted people to think about the economy, to develop new concrete programs, to build independent structures. But when the Four polled the ninety-two members of the Solidarity leadership at the steelworks, they found not one to follow them (though the two sides continued to cooperate).

In programmatic terms, then, Solidarity was by 1985 deeply divided. The dividing line between Nowak and his former colleagues at Nowa Huta was similar to less dramatic conflicts in other cities. Both approaches may have been necessary, or so most in the union deeply believed at the time, but they had little common ground. So what was Solidarity in 1985–86? At the bottom, there were the millions of faithful or once-faithful: workers still paying dues, students making a living at underground printing, grandmothers treasuring photographs of Father Popiełuszko, and anyone still glancing at the occasional underground newspaper. At the top, there were the famous faces—Lech Wałęsa, Adam Michnik, Bronisław Geremek, a few others. These meant most to the Western press, perhaps: even if they were in prison, they kept their voices and their contacts with the West. But for the average Pole, they might as well have been in Siberia.

The task was somehow to connect these two worlds. When Władysław Frasyniuk or the Kraków Four returned home from prison and continued their activism, they revived Solidarity in ways no underground work (nor the essays of leading intellectuals) could. A few slogans painted on walls, a glimpse of an underground leaflet, or a hurried demonstration could not make the point that "Solidarity Lives" as could a familiar face returning to the battle. Though at the time their efforts seemed pointless, their presence—and the new aboveground networks they created—would prove to be magnets for a new generation that could not find its way into the underground. Without them, the opposition would have had to start from scratch.

POLITICAL CHARITY

The question of how one should engage in opposition to a regime that both allowed political murder to take place and put its perpetrators on trial (the defendants in the Popiełuszko trial were sentenced to fourteen to twenty-five years) continued to divide Solidarity up until the moment it took power in 1989 (and may even be at the heart of political quarrels today). On the eve of Popiełuszko's murder, human rights activist and physicist Zbigniew Romaszewski declared in a provocative interview that it was time to return to aboveground work. "I intend to do what I did before [in the years before and during Solidarity's legal phase] . . . to operate openly." Romaszewski argued that the rule of law needed to be defended actively: simply publicizing repression made the underground press read like "a chronicle of martyrs" or a telephone book. And indeed, with hundreds of people in prison, being detained, beaten, or fined, such lists became even counterproductive: why would anyone want to join the ranks of the martyrs, just for a line of smudged agate type? Romaszewski and others in KOR had pioneered the strategy of open opposition over human rights back in the late 1970s; now it was time to return.[3]

The Popiełuszko murder could only confirm Romaszewski's fears. The trial, in fact, showed that the state had a monopoly on the enforcement of legality and would defend its parameters. This monopoly ought not to go unchallenged. Moreover, Romaszewski knew that most repression took place far from the limelight. The point was not to publicize the dreary state of affairs in Poland, but to lighten burdens by helping individuals cope with the regime that targeted them.

Across Poland, especially in cities where opposition was strong, those who shared Romaszewski's thinly veiled frustration with underground strategy established a loose network of intervention committees. Zofia Romaszewska worked to coordinate them. She established firm guidelines: no one's identity would be compromised by seeking help; proper budgets would be drawn up and maintained; no one would be refused help as a result of their political views or because money ran out. The political charity work of the Romaszewski committees was a concrete answer to the problem of how to pursue meaningful opposition in an era of normalization. For individual activists, it was a path from the underground, and out of the amnesty trap.

The most renowned underground was in Wrocław. Two of that city's Solidarity leaders—Frasyniuk and Józef Pinior—had escaped the mass internment of martial law. Pinior had even managed to save the union's eighty million zlotys by withdrawing it days before the crackdown. Another Solidarity advisor, Kornel Morawiecki, waged an underground struggle until 1990. In 1982 Morawiecki created Poland's premier underground unit, Fighting Solidarity, which proudly saw itself as the successor to the underground partisan forces of World War II. Bound together by military order and deep conspiracy, it was emblematic of Poland's active resistance. Wrocław, perhaps along with Gdańsk, was the birthplace of the *zadyma*, or "blizzard," clashes between politicized youth and the militia.

In Wrocław, then, each activist would confront the advantages and the limitations of underground work. One who tried to bridge the two worlds of partisan warfare and positivism was Marek Jakubiec. A Wrocław engineer in his mid-30s, Jakubiec spent four months in a martial law prison. Searching for contacts upon his release, he found Fighting Solidarity and began to produce literature for them. He admired Fighting Solidarity's discipline and clear goals, which he contrasted to the endless discussions that paralyzed the rest of the underground. But by 1984 Jakubiec felt that the formula was wearing out: "it was somehow harder [for underground colleagues] to find the way to clandestine meetings; it was harder and harder to find people, because they were simply tired. People were tired, they ceased to see any sense in this activity. . . . The thing that bothered me most—though I never responded to this question—what bothered me most was when an *ubek* [secret police] would say [mocking the group's secrecy]: 'Well, then, you're such a fighter, yet you're embarrassed to admit to it.'"

Caught in a police roundup of Fighting Solidarity in early 1984, Jakubiec lost his anonymity; he had been "outed" and could no longer do underground work. He looked for a new outlet and heard about the work of Romaszewski's Committee for Intervention and Legality. This was the answer. With a large, comfortable house and a stable family situation, Jakubiec felt lucky, and obligated to help those less fortunate. The house had long been a place where people across the splintered political landscape of the opposition felt welcome, so he was in a position to offer assistance. And most of all, he could hold his head up with pride. Perhaps he would even be safer: despite the death of Father Popiełuszko, Jakubiec maintained that "it's a lot harder to shoot someone who stands out." Helping others who were in trouble brought activism safely back home, too: Ewa Jakubiec, his wife, had been active in Solidarity in 1980–81 but had stepped into the background to care for their young children during martial law. For the next five years, Ewa and Marek would be a team, audaciously handing out their business cards (surely an underground impossibility!) at demonstrations, dispensing money and legal advice, and relaying every report of repression to the Western media.

Work was similar in Kraków, where the Committee for the Protection of Legality brought together lawyers and former underground union activists who reached out beyond their political circles to help those wronged by the police or the courts. Many in the group—like its spokesman, Zygmunt Łenyk—had ties to the underground nationalist party Confederation for an Independent Poland (KPN). Party politics, however, were secondary: the important thing, they claimed, was to find something for the frustrated Solidarity unionist to do—and to keep out of jail. Advocacy work resocialized the outed activist, as it were, keeping the political struggle alive by other means.

For Ryszard Bocian—like Łenyk from the KPN—Kraków's committee was a cover for his conspiratorial work. It was not just a pretext, though: Bocian, who also had legal training, could advise the parents of a beaten student, or a worker thrown out of his or her job, of their rights. In this way, Bocian hoped, society would not only recover and use its legal rights, but also return to the hopes he had at Solidarity's birth. "We'll stick our necks out, they'll beat us hard, but really it doesn't hurt that much," was the lesson Bocian hoped his open activism would convey. As Bocian recognized, every example of courage or activism might spark a conversion in someone else who experiences or observes it. Thus "Piotr," a chance passerby who was injured at a demonstration in the winter of 1985, became an active member of the committee and eventually joined KPN.*

The steps taken into social work in Wrocław, Kraków, and elsewhere were certainly important, as these committees stretched out a hand to people isolated from Solidarity. But we can imagine an alternate characterization of this brave work. Perhaps it was easier to find a path between civil war and surrender simply because the regime was easing up? After all, arrests and trials had become less common, and the numbers of political prisoners declined precipitously after the amnesties, especially as the authorities replaced prison sentences for most politically motivated

---

* Bocian remembers him only by his KPN pseudonym; ironically, a contact made aboveground was then effaced by their common work in political conspiracy.

transgressions with fines. The display of the rule of law at the Popiełuszko trial also had to count for something. Perhaps this was not just normalization, but a long-awaited liberalization?

Things looked bleaker from within the ever-shrinking opposition. The fines were in fact much harder to bear than the prison sentences, for most. In 1987, with the average monthly salary between fifteen and twenty thousand zlotys, a typical fine for participating in a demonstration or distributing underground literature was fifty thousand zlotys.* Few could spare two months' wages. Fines were levied by a summary court, after a brief hearing before a judge; standards of proof were lower, and conviction more likely. Typically, the only witnesses called were the arresting officers. If one refused to pay—and many did—wages were garnished; even if a jail term was offered as an alternative, the courts were reluctant to grant that option, so that the regime could continue to claim there were no political prisoners. It was easy for students to scoff at uncollectible fines. One young woman who monitored demonstrations for the committee was believed to have the record, with around a half-million zlotys in unpaid penalties. But for a worker, even one fine could mean ruin. Money given to pay a fine was like insurance that made opposition possible.

The regime had other ways of stifling the opposition or limiting it to the fanatical few. For example, at a time when one might wait ten years or more for one's turn to purchase a car, the state began to confiscate cars found to be carrying underground literature. Marek Jakubiec realized, however, that precisely because the regime was pretending to show its human side, it would be vulnerable to legal arguments. Unlike their American counterparts, Polish courts preferred not to recognize collective guilt (so as not to imply that the opposition was anything but isolated individuals). So spouses could demand their cars back. The first time he helped win such a judgment, Marek Jakubiec found that the car had already been auctioned off, to a secret policeman. The family had kept a spare set of keys, so they simply repossessed the car from the street in front of the policeman's house, then hid it until the furor over the "theft" died down. In another case, an underground courier lost his Syrenka (a two-cylinder relic from the 1960s). This time, his wife demanded not the right to the car, but her share of the forty thousand at which the police had valued it (in hopes of extorting that amount for its return). She received her twenty thousand, and the police sold the car for thirteen thousand.† Shortly thereafter, the practice of confiscation ceased, at least in Wrocław.

* Ewa Jakubiec showed me her accounting of fines she reimbursed in 1987. The list may not be complete; it contains over 120 fines, of which 49 were for 50,000 and another 22 for 40,000 or 45,000.

† At the time, this was equivalent to about twenty dollars on the black market.

But the fines continued, dozens of them every month. People lost their jobs, and sometimes their homes (if they lived in student dormitories or workers' barracks). Without a registered address, no one could find work. Money proved to be a powerful weapon, though. Every month, Marek and Ewa Jakubiec received anywhere from one thousand dollars to as much as four thousand dollars from Warsaw, where the Romaszewskis distributed the substantial funds coming from the West (such as a one hundred thousand dollar prize they received in 1987 from the Aurora Foundation for their human rights work). The money was carefully exchanged on the black market. Then each applicant needed to be verified: was the applicant thrown out of work for distributing Solidarity leaflets, or for drunkenness? In an odd semblance of normality, Ewa Jakubiec not only kept account of the money disbursed but required recipients to sign receipts. Eventually, the Jakubiecs could offer three months' compensation for those who lost their jobs; they became almost like a trade union.

This was a union for everyone. A glance at Ewa Jakubiec's ledgers, miraculously preserved through four years of constant house searches, reveals a cross section of society, from workers in the copper mines of Lubin to students and union leaders in Wrocław. Wrocław's Solidarity was at the time deeply divided over tactics and personalities. It boasted two rival organizations, Władysław Frasyniuk's Regional Executive Committee (aboveground) and Marek Muszyński's Regional Strike Committee (underground). Both men show up in Ewa Jakubiec's account books and could often be found debating long into the night at the Jakubiecs' open house on Kochanowski Street. People who, as Marek Jakubiec put it, might not even acknowledge one another on the street felt safe in this pluralist, tolerant atmosphere.

But as much as they helped prominent people like Frasyniuk, the Jakubiecs could do most for the "Jaś Kowalski, who carries five leaflets, like an insignificant ordinary guy. He's the one," recalled Jakubiec, "who really needs protection. If he's detained, then you have to make such a fuss, so they let him go quickly, so that they don't dare to think of harming him. We taught people that if they even get a scratch, they should go straight to the doctor, get it examined, file a complaint."

Listening long enough to these stories of attempts to frame Marek Jakubiec, of constant arrests, beatings, and harassment, the temptation to think of this period as the "Gorbachev years" of liberalization and glasnost simply evaporates. Whether one's limit of tolerance was one visit by the police or a constant harassment through detentions and fines, those limits were tested. Most people did not risk their lives, and relatively few ruined their careers—or so it seems today, now that so many (like Marek Jakubiec himself) have regained their jobs or found better ones—but the uncertainty never left.

Given all this, what is most striking is that people like Marek and Ewa Jakubiec found the whole thing comical, too. During one demonstration, Marek received a report that "it looks as if the entire Wrocław militia is chasing demonstrators on Świdnicka Street." As he relayed this information to Warsaw by phone (their line was rarely cut, so that the police could find out what they knew), a voice broke in: "That's not true, because I'm here on the wiretap!" With the regime's control that brazen, one could either cower or laugh it off. Heading to Warsaw for meetings with the Romaszewskis, Jakubiec sometimes took his small children along. Sure, they'd be surrounded by police, but the kids got to see the big city, too. Some in the underground did not see their families for four or five years; Jakubiec and others showed one could lead a normal, happy life while engaged in the opposition.

This was serious work, of course, but if one wanted to stay sane one simply could not take the regime as seriously as dissidents once had. This was not because it was less threatening, but because its ideological pronouncements now seemed empty and pathetic. The regime had shown its worst in December 1981, and nearly everyone in the opposition spent some time in prison over the next few years. It was thus ludicrous to hear the communists still spouting slogans of brotherhood and patriotism. During the strike wave of August 1988, I asked Stanisław Handzlik whether he feared that the communists might respond once again with tanks, curfews, and mass detentions under the guise of national defense. "No," he replied. "You can only scare the people that way once. The second time, it would only be funny."[4]

CHURCH AND OPPOSITION

A peek beyond Poland is now overdue. Where could the ordinary sufferer of wrongs turn, if she or he did not live in a society rich with opposition traditions like Poland? If there was any hope at all, it came from churches. Absent a legal opposition, the churches of Central Europe were the only official institutions with any independence from the regimes. In Christian doctrine, after all, the "Church" means not simply the hierarchy nor the clergy, but a community, a social space where faith is shared and nurtured. "Community" makes one think of openness and self-governance—and sometimes, in Central Europe, it was so. Each embattled church resolved questions of social activism, openness, and self-government in different ways, depending on the nature of the community as well as on the personalities of the clergy who served it. Nowhere did the churches' engagement in opposition even remotely approach that in Poland. But before we return there, a quick survey of the rest of Central Europe will show what was, and was not, possible.

The Lutheran Church in East Germany—the only major Protestant church in a communist regime—was closely controlled by the state. Most bishops and clergy chose to concentrate only on ministering to their small communities of believers. Some, however, sought to foster critiques of the shortcomings of socialism. Particularly after 1978, pastors in many major cities opened their doors to citizens who wanted to discuss change. This often took the form of peace seminars or "peace prayers." Like the Polish Church (as we shall see), this sometimes meant that nonbelievers, even atheists, found a safe haven in the Church—and is not providing shelter to the outcast or marginal one of the most important things a church can do? But in the highly repressed GDR, these conversations would not move outside church walls until 1989.

Hungary's Catholic Church had also made peace with the regime, provoking an even stronger reaction from below. So-called base communities of believers, resistant both to the national Church bureaucracy and to the communists, flourished after the Second Vatican Council, and especially in the 1970s. One network of these communities was the "Bush" movement, led by the charismatic Father György Bulanyi, who promoted ideas of nonviolence and noncooperation with the communist regime. Despite rebukes from the regime (which suspected ties to Czechoslovakia's Charter 77), Hungary's bishops, and even the Vatican, Bulanyi's movement thrived. One participant, József Merza, a mathematics professor, was called up to the army at the age of 47, in 1979. He refused and was sent to prison. His case galvanized the Bush movement, and other conscientious objectors followed. In the 1980s "Uncle Jóska" would be an inspiration for a new generation of student activists.

Nowhere was the Catholic Church under greater scrutiny than in Czechoslovakia. Since the late 1940s, bishops, priests, and lay activists had been imprisoned, often for a decade or more. The officially permitted Church was run by a hierarchy thoroughly vetted by communist officials. While the less religious Czechs tolerated this state of affairs, the Slovaks rebelled. There, alongside the official Church, was a secret church, which by the 1980s had developed an impressive network of undercover clergy and samizdat. For most Slovaks, the two did not meet: faith in the Church was of necessity accompanied by conformity. A small minority maintained obstinate resistance, often inspired by what they knew of Poland. Two lay activists in particular knew Poland well. Ján Čarnogurský, a lawyer, spent a week in Poland in 1976 and returned home deeply impressed. František Mikloško studied mathematics in Warsaw in 1975. Though "those mountains [between Poland and Slovakia] are very high," as Mikloško himself said, Slovaks were closely attuned to the Polish Church, especially after Pope John Paul II's election in 1978.

Quite abruptly, the underground faith exploded into view at a ceremony at Velehrad in July 1985. The occasion was the 1,100th anniversary of the death of St. Methodius, who had brought Christianity to Slovakia. Papal representative Agostino Cardinal Casaroli was there, along with František Cardinal Tomášek of Prague. But a local politician welcomed the crowd to something more secular: "the peace festival of Velehrad." To everyone's astonishment, the crowd hooted and whistled this lame attempt at censorship. "From that moment on," recounts František Mikloško, "neither he nor the minister of culture . . . was allowed to say anything that the people didn't agree with. The faithful shouted 'We want religious freedom! We want the Holy Father! Long Live the Church!' Cardinal Casaroli only smiled, and Cardinal Tomášek later told the young people, 'This is not real, but a dream!'"[5]

In retrospect, the Velehrad demonstration had an effect on Slovaks not unlike that which Pope John Paul II's first return home in 1979 had on the Poles. At this moment, the secret church came aboveground, if only for a moment, before some 150,000 people. In particular, Velehrad energized young Catholics. Eva Klčovanská, a philosophy student at Bratislava's Comenius University, was in the crowd at Velehrad. By the time the fall semester began, she had formed a discussion group (*spoločenstvo*) in her school. It was one of many that Catholic students across the city were then joining. Klčovanská and her friends met clandestinely in private apartments to read the Bible, to discuss their faith, and to exchange samizdat; they also went on trips together.[6] These were not unlike student circles in Poland, except that the risk involved even in praying together was rather greater.

The sense of numbers, however, gradually lessened the fear. Klčovanská shortly joined the *Centrálko*, which coordinated the discussion groups and supplied both samizdat and religious literature. She began writing for Slovakia's leading samizdat journal, *Náboženstvo a súčasnosť*. Finally, a meeting in the small mountain town of Vrútky in December 1987 brought together students from across Slovakia with leaders from the underground church like Mikloško. Out of that meeting came a new journal, *Príloha mladých* (Youth supplement); Klčovanská was one of the editors. This small step marked a certain maturing of the Catholic opposition, as it diversified to reach new constituencies.

Those constituencies are difficult to measure. Numbers of pilgrims on annual trips to Slovakia's most important shrines—Levoča, Šaštin, Nitra, etc.—were one way to gauge Catholic opposition, and indeed the numbers climbed sharply in the mid-1980s. But to take part in a pilgrimage was not necessarily a political act. Until the end of the communist era, petitions were the most popular way for Czechoslovaks to express their dissent, in the way that Poles could by paying their dues to Solidarity. The underground church movement had not yet sponsored a petition, but everyone knew this would have to be the next step after mobilizing students and expanding samizdat. Even as they debated this strategy, in December 1987, came word of just such a petition, prepared by a Moravian farmer, August Navratil. The petition—not Navratil's first; earlier ones had landed him in psychiatric wards and prison—contained no less than thirty-one points.* Navratil appealed for the freeing of the Catholic Church from state control (in which the state could, for example, deny ordained priests their right to practice), the filling of empty bishoprics, a Catholic press, seminaries, lay organizations, and more.

The petition appeared on the first Sunday of Advent; six weeks later Cardinal Tomášek lent his support, advising that "cowardice and fear are unworthy of a true Christian."[7] No more encouragement was needed. Priests began to collect signatures after mass, while high school and university discussion groups passed the petition around. By the end of January 1988, there were 200,000 signatures of an eventual total of about half a million. Almost 300,000 of these were from Slovakia, or something close to 10 percent of the adult population there.

Fear, obviously, had ceased to hold the Slovaks back. But after the Cardinal's letter—which read almost like a dare—did one's signature really mean much? Perhaps the half-million signatures were simply a sign that the communist authorities had decided to allow activism on religious grounds, as a limited concession to glasnost, while keeping a tight lid on political dissent.

This is all true, in a way; many Czech political dissidents looked upon the new retail opposition of Navratil's petition, and the enthusiastic Slovak response, with condescension. However, a petition is not just words and signatures on a page. By signing a petition (especially in a communist state), its supporters could gain a sense of belonging to a public community many thousands strong, sharing a clearly defined (and enumerated) set of beliefs and a minimal level of public bravery. That the percentage of signers in Slovakia was about three times greater (in proportion to population) than among the Czechs tells us that the Slovaks, though overall showing much less activism, did possess a potential public, in the community of followers of the Catholic Church. Navratil's petition awakened this community, well before the same thing would occur in the Czech lands. In 1988, in fact, the Slovaks would be first to manifest their community in a public demonstration.

* The lengthy petition is also a Czechoslovak tradition. This was far from the record: the manifesto of the reform communist group Obroda, issued in 1988, contained eighty-six points.

If the opposition anywhere could find shelter within the Church, it would be in Poland. But the Polish Catholic hierarchy's relationship with opposition was always ambiguous and hesitant. Though individual priests like Father Popiełuszko supported Solidarity throughout its legal existence and martial law, Church leaders like Primate Józef Cardinal Glemp had grave misgivings about left-wing tendencies in the opposition, and about the damage violent confrontation would do to the nation. This history of an arm's-length relationship is a painful one, but it is incomplete. Nor is it enough to focus on the feisty priests of martial law—Popiełuszko, or Henryk Jankowski of Gdańsk—whose rousing sermons tested the limits of state repression and censorship, keeping the image of Solidarity alive. The Church was also a home for the positivist activism that inspired Edward Nowak or the Jakubiecs.

Father Ludwik Wiśniewski is undoubtedly one of the most overlooked figures in the history of Polish opposition. He was what sociologists call a movement entrepreneur—a kind of venture capitalist, willing to invest his time and his church's resources in anyone whose activism might bring social profit. In the 1970s his presence in Gdańsk helped inspire the Young Poland Movement, a group of young conservative thinkers who have had a great influence on Polish politics over the last two decades. He was then in Lublin in the summer of 1980 when strikes began there before spreading to Gdańsk. His transfer to the Dominican Church in Wrocław in the fall of 1981 was fortuitous for that city, helping it to become one of the liveliest corners of Poland for the next eight years. Under his influence, Wrocław evolved from violent confrontation to constructive, positivist activism, especially among students.

Father Ludwik's first concern, in the winter of 1981–82, was the fate of the talented, tireless "blizzard boys" (*chłopcy od zadymy*), the heroes of many a clash with police in the days when Wrocław was the site of the fiercest street conflicts. They weren't really experts at anything, he contended, and he tried to convince them that they would not win any victories through violence. In the end, he told them, "you won't matter" without a specific contribution to society. Poland needed economists and educators, not rock throwers. Unlike other clerics (such as Primate Glemp) who simply counseled peace, Wiśniewski offered a concrete alternative in his ministry, Dominik. If in every city in Poland there was a pastor* who gathered politically aware youth around him, Father Ludwik went further, harnessing them to the positivist cause. Thus Jarosław Obremski, an underground "laborer," as he called himself, became the leader of Dominik and came to believe that the student ministry was better than "all

---

* The word in Polish is *duszpasterz*, or "pastor of souls." *Duszpasterstwo*, however, I have translated as "ministry."

that running around" as a samizdat courier; Henryk Feliks, who had spent six months in prison for samizdat, felt he could "play all the pianos" through the ministry*; and even a determined socialist like Zuzanna Dąbrowska found Dominik an interesting place to be, where it seemed that others thought the way she did about social issues and activism. Father Ludwik had real street credibility, too: he was one of the few to answer Paweł Kocięba's call for sandwich-board protesters to support Frasyniuk in 1986.

Once the university students were gathered into one place, Father Ludwik's investment bore fruit. Out of the Dominik milieu grew a quasi-self-government at Wrocław University. Student self-government was a perverse showpiece of normalization. The law, enacted in 1982 but based upon a draft prepared before the martial-law crackdown, was actually quite liberal. But the regime generally ignored it in its battle to bring rebellious universities and students to heel. Even the most optimistic in the opposition gave up after Parliament gutted the law in 1985, returning ostensibly student powers to the rectors and giving the Ministry of Education more power over university policies. Kocięba, Obremski, Feliks, Dąbrowska, and several others (including Krzysztof Jakubczak of Orange Alternative) resolved to bring together two strands of youth activism, public protest and spiritual awakening, to create a novel form of independent politics. This was the Twelve.

As pretentious as the name sounds, the Twelve were not meant to be apostles. They represented four of the five schools of Wrocław University; had the Law Faculty joined them, they would have been the Fifteen. They announced their existence with a letter to the rector in the winter of 1986. By that fall, they had become the de facto student representation. Students knew to look for Twelve flyers to get information on university politics, and the rector even sent representatives to participate in a public dialogue on "The University of Our Dreams." Pressure from the Twelve, in the form of student surveys, letters, and meetings, resulted in greater freedom for student clubs, student input on university regulations, repairs in dormitories, and even the reversal of a decision to convert new dormitories (highrises nicknamed the Pencil and the Crayon for their sharp roofline) into housing for the police.

These are small steps indeed—and really, each step might just as well be one toward collaboration, not freedom. But each reminded students of their ability to resolve specific, concrete problems. As Kocięba put it in a typically combative interview: "The communist system very often acts as an alibi for laziness and indolence."[8] While everyone in Poland might read the underground press, there were plenty of excuses not to take on the en-

---

* Feliks here quotes Jacek Kuroń.

trenched institutions that made everyone's life a bit more difficult. Instead of adapting to the strict rules of the self-government facade, the Twelve forced self-government from below, normalizing the university on their own terms. In this way, they avoided both the superficiality of regime-sponsored participation and the helpless anger of the underground.

Unlike others in the Church, Wiśniewski promoted a genuine pluralism. Specific political and even religious beliefs were less important than a willingness to search for constructive answers. The Social Concerns Weeks he organized annually drew leading opposition intellectuals from across Poland, and youth from across Lower Silesia, to intense discussions and debates in the churches of Wrocław. There was a similar intensity and openness in Dominik itself. In discussions of Gandhian philosophy—a theme important to Father Ludwik—agnostics like the poet Leszek Budrewicz might as easily take part, or even lecture, as anyone else. Father Ludwik himself admitted that Dominik's activities—camping trips, lectures, etc.—were not particularly religious. However, "it is enough," he said, "to find oneself within the Church's tradition. The point is not a formal program, but to ensure that there is a gathering."[9] Wiśniewski's ministry was a place "where [the students] could be themselves . . . and have their say." Of course, it was more than this: it was a meeting point between philosophy and concrete activism.

The weakest pillar of normalization was the promise that the state would take care of its obedient citizens. Nothing made the holes in the Polish safety net more obvious than martial law, during which almost ten thousand were interned for many weeks or months. In Poland, at least, not even the communists could object if the Roman Catholic Church would minister to prisoners. From the very first days of martial law, with the tacit approval of Cardinal Glemp himself, priests and lay people brought food and clothing to internment camps and offered prayers and medical assistance. For the most part, this was the work of the lay elite: actors, professors, and writers close to the Church hierarchy. Their work—which presaged and paralleled that of the Romaszewskis' committees—was essentially reactive, and (unlike the Romaszewskis) they steered clear of encouraging activism.

A few churches found their way toward a more active role. They became social service centers, dispensing the most varied assistance and advice. One could join a housing cooperative, take classes in history, find a plumber or a lawyer, or go on a pilgrimage. The most famous of all such ministries was in the Nowa Huta district of Kraków. Churches were few and far between among the 300,000 or so residents of the Nowa Huta district; the church at Mistrzejowice was just the second, in fact (the first, known as the Ark, was built with the guidance of then-Bishop Karol Wojtyła). The church's pastor, Father Kazimierz Jancarz, was one of the fieriest orators in Poland, who drew huge crowds of the faithful and patriotic to his Thursday evening masses. This church was also the place to which transports from the West (donated by Dutch churches, or French workers, or German schoolchildren) came to Kraków. It was thus the place where a "human" (Edward Nowak's term) organization, a symbiosis of the political and the pragmatic, could take shape. Unemployed steelworkers and elderly patriotic widows alike found work sorting the food or manning the distribution points.

One among them was Kazimierz Fugiel, a lathe operator at the Lenin Steelworks who discovered, in August 1980 at the age of forty, a talent for organization. During subsequent strikes at Nowa Huta, he learned how to coordinate and distribute food and supplies sent in by the Church, by private citizens, or by Western trade unions, and to see that everyone was fed. His martial law experience showed him that there were two ways of doing this, though. When he saw imprisoned activists fighting for an equal distribution of cigarettes, he realized how much he despised the "socialist" division of goods. He created—in prison, and then upon his release—a food bank, which people would both contribute to and draw upon for help. Thus was born the Social Fund for Workers' Self-Help. When Father Jancarz received a gift of twelve hundred dollars in 1983, Fugiel bought a truck (whose purpose had to be concealed from the police) and also—since a dollar still went quite far in those days—began sending workers' children to summer camp. At first they went to the home of Father Jancarz's mother; later, Fugiel found other destinations, for as many as two hundred children a year.

What these ministries actually did—the summer camps, the help for the ill and the imprisoned, the Christmas parties—broke down the isolation and fear bred by martial law in Polish society. Above all, this work showed that one did not have to rely upon the state alone for help. After forty years of state socialism, there was little the state did not promise to provide (and usually did, though one might wait months or years). But now the Church—or, more precisely, one's colleagues and neighbors—could also provide vacations for the children; a box of food or needed cash at Christmas, or when a family member was ill or in prison; legal advice; even plumbers, roofers, and electricians. This idea of self-help dates back to the founding of KOR in 1976, but not until after 1981 would it reach such a massive scale.

For a while at least, this activism could replace Solidarity as the core of an independent society. When Zbigniew Ferczyk, a newly retired white-collar worker from Nowa Huta, proposed in another church a ministry just for mill workers, he recalls, his friends were skeptical. "But what will we do?" they asked. "Maybe we'll breed rabbits," Ferczyk replied. "It doesn't matter. Only that we're together." In other words, Ferczyk knew that just like the Romaszewski committees, a ministry could be a place for the activist, burned in the underground, to nurse his or her wounds and keep the motor running. Both to give and to receive helped to outline the limits of the socialist economy and showed how easily one could in fact pass the state by. There was a political message delivered along with the tickets to summer camp: Solidarity was still alive and had a role to play in people's lives.

THE WORKERS' DILEMMA

One of Solidarity's fondest dreams from its very beginnings was *samo-rząd*—"self-government." In Polish, the term implies more than just "governing"; also personal or group responsibility and autonomy. It is a positivism for those left of center, placing one's fate in one's own hands. Solidarity itself had helped to invest the term with such power. In 1981 unionists had envisioned a "workers' democracy" and a "Self-Governing Republic," in which a Self-Government Chamber in parliament would give voice to representatives of factories, cities, and villages and exercise control over the national economy. From 1985 to 1989 a group of Warsaw journalists published a bi-weekly underground paper, *The Self-Governing Republic,* which debated theory and highlighted attempts by workers, students, and neighborhood or village residents to take control of their public lives.

Though the benefits of such self-empowerment may seem obvious, they were anything but that to most of the opposition. Every move looked somehow more sinister in the dim light of normalization. In the communists' hands, self-government was key to new democratic facades, as the old rituals of communist pseudo-democracy (like prearranged elections) lost some of their luster. For example, some 30 percent of voters (by Solidarity's estimate) chose to boycott the parliamentary election of October 1985. When the communists began enthusiastically to promote worker and student self-government in 1983–84, the opposition was deeply suspicious. Joining a self-government council, no matter what its powers, seemed not far from collaboration with the enemy.

A sizable minority of activists in the Solidarity trade union in 1980–81 had advocated worker self-government and lobbied communist authorities for its legalization. In the spring of 1981, representatives of the largest factories came together in the Network of Leading Factories. This quickly became a channel of communication, parallel to Solidarity, for activists throughout the country. Its members were champions of self-government initiatives, which were not always popular with Solidarity leadership.

Edward Nowak—one of the staunchest advocates of the idea—points to self-government's contradictions: on the one hand, everyone knew one another in a factory and thus could presumably trust that an elected representative had not become a communist collaborator. On the other hand, the temptations of power were very real in a factory. The employees' council could not remain pure if it was meeting and negotiating with factory administration, yet purity was one of the most precious attributes of underground opposition. If just one Solidarity unionist ran for an employees' council, did that not question the judgment of the hundreds of others who refused to touch anything tainted by the regime?

Debates along these lines raged in Solidarity circles from the moment the regime lifted its ban on employees' councils in 1982. Factory directors were, not surprisingly, able to set the terms and rules of elections. In most cases, it was impossible for a Solidarity member even to stand as a candidate. Little changed over the course of the decade: even in 1987 only 5–15 percent of all employee councils showed any real independence from the party and the director.[10] Especially where Solidarity was strong, like the Lenin Steelworks at Nowa Huta, the employees' councils seemed to be nothing more than a threat to the underground union.

But Marian Kania, an engineer at Nowa Huta, believed in philosopher Mirosław Dzielski's dictum that you had to "eat the crocodile with a spoon": that is, to "enter every crack" in the system and nibble away at the beast from within. He feared that Solidarity was doing nothing to prepare workers for the economic changes that would have to take place eventually. He convinced his Solidarity colleagues to vote for him in the 1985 council election in his division and was not only elected but was then chosen council president, though he was one of the few with a Solidarity pedigree.* At least in Nowa Huta, though, this was too early; after just one year, Kania resigned and left the steel mill. "The possibilities for action were very small," he recalled: the director swamped him with bureaucratic detail, and he felt isolated from and unable to influence the employees as well.

A different way to resolve the collaboration question was to treat the councils as simply an extension of underground work. Ryszard Majdzik tried this, unsuccessfully, at Kraków's Elbud construction materials factory in 1983. Majdzik was known as one of the most radical in Solidarity in the city, having staged a well-publicized hunger strike during his martial-law internment. He and his underground colleagues took advantage of unexpectedly liberal election rules—to this day, Majdzik can't explain why the director allowed the election that swept him and his comrades briefly into power. He intended to use the position to denounce the

---

* In a factory as large as Nowa Huta, there were separate councils in individual workshops, as well as one for the entire plant.

communists and raise Solidarity's banner, but the election was annulled and Majdzik returned to his underground opposition.

Perhaps because she had not been a front-line member of Solidarity in 1980–81, Anastazja Konieczna fared somewhat better at the River Shipyard in Wrocław. She had stepped in to lead the union during martial law, after all the leaders had been fired. With the arrests, the shipyard's union paper had ceased, too. Konieczna, a welder, borrowed a friend's typewriter and began producing one herself; many of her colleagues assumed she was just the courier from whom they bought the paper, and not the sole editor. Then, in 1984, the shipyard director announced elections to the employees' council. It was obvious to Konieczna that there needed to be aboveground as well as clandestine work; someone would have to represent workers before the administration while she carried on collecting dues and distributing the paper. But there was no one else, so Konieczna herself ran and won a seat. For a year she led a double life, fighting for workers' pay and benefits officially while keeping Solidarity alive in her spare time. A search of her apartment in the summer of 1985 exposed her secret journalism and cost her her job. Two years later, though, she was back at the shipyard and this time was elected chair of the employees' council. For Konieczna, there really was no difference between her two functions; both were ways to help people, and to call one of them "collaboration" simply didn't make sense.

Elsewhere in Wrocław, the Polar factory (which built large home appliances) was one of the more militant bastions of Solidarity. The underground leadership, as elsewhere, consisted of the union's second or third string, after the internment, arrests, firings, and emigration of leaders from 1980–81. When elections were announced in 1984, feelings were so strong that the only possible response was a boycott, which the Secret Factory Committee called for in November:

> After careful examination, and listening to the voices of employees, we affirm that at the present time, when [secret police] are murdering innocent people [this was just days after the discovery of Father Popiełuszko's body], when in this factory a merciless drive continues to sign people up for the crow's unions,* it isn't possible to create a real self-government. The ongoing preparations for the formation of a self-government are directed by the PZPR [the Communist Party], and the people on the electoral commissions absolutely do not have the confidence of the work force. In light of these facts, we appeal to the work force to boycott completely the elections to the employees' council.[11]

Przemysław Bogusławski had another idea. Earlier that year, he had spent three months in prison for Solidarity activity, so he was under no il-

---

* A reference to the OPZZ, a state-run union created during martial law; the acronym for the governing body of martial law, WRON, is close to the Polish word for crow, *wrona*.

lusions about the regime. But he found a crack. In a letter to the Electoral Commission, this enameling oven operator proposed some slight changes to the election rules. There were seven proposals in all; the most important was number four, which would allow new candidates to be proposed for any unfilled seats after the first round of voting.[12] No doubt the electoral commission assumed the changes were innocuous in light of the call for a boycott; with the help of a Solidarity sympathizer on the commission, the amendments were accepted.

Solidarity thus found a way to have its cake and eat it too. In the first round, thanks to a near-total boycott in most shops, only seven of twenty-nine seats were filled. Now the union moved in for a knockout punch. Dozens of new candidates were proposed, and there was no time (or procedure) to vet them; in the second round, 75 percent of the workers voted. Bogusławski himself was elected, as was Krzysztof Zadrożny, who had initiated the first Solidarity strike back in August 1980; Andrzej Kowalski, a welder who would, with Zadrożny, be jailed and fired for organizing a Solidarity rally in front of the factory in 1987; and Grzegorz Socha, the chair of the very same Secret Factory Committee that had urged a boycott.

Over the next four years, members of three successive Solidarity-dominated councils would oppose the factory director on worker pay issues and on company strategy (opposing the formation of a holding company in 1985, for example). In 1986 the council gave the director a poor evaluation and called for his resignation. Along the way, there were half a dozen court cases and a few strikes. In August 1988, with the support of a council resolution, Polar's Solidarity attempted to register officially.[13] And in 1991 the chair of the first independent council, Stefan Nowakowski, was elected factory director. It is difficult to imagine how a legal Solidarity representation could have done more. The council essentially functioned as a trade union; workers approached Bogusławski or Zadrożny with the problems they might ordinarily have taken to their union. In resolution after resolution, the council attempted to fill just that role.

In the end, some poor personnel decisions, and perhaps a work force that had become accustomed to the ambiguous status of Solidarity, left the legal activists of Polar behind when the revolution accelerated in 1988. Perhaps, muses Zbigniew Kostecki, chair of Polar's council in 1987–90, Solidarity might have done more to take over employees' councils in the 1980s. Solidarity could then have boasted a more informed, empowered work force and would be stronger today (as it still is strong in Polar). Certainly, notions of compromise and negotiation would have been easier for workers to accept. In Polar, the charge of collaboration with the communists would have seemed ludicrous, while underground union leaders drafted official resolutions calling for the director's resignation. Whether the confrontation was advisable economically is another matter, of course; from the workers' perspective, this was Solidarity by other means.

Solidarity activists at the Lenin Steelworks—which was not only one of the largest factories in Poland by any measure, but also one of Solidarity's two strongest (with the Lenin Shipyard in Gdańsk) redoubts—would not have been impressed. They had a viable alternative system of social welfare, a powerful underground media (plus a courageous aboveground paper, the Catholic weekly *Tygodnik powszechny*), and a vibrant culture of anticommunist demonstrations. A worker self-government was at best superfluous, at worst quixotic. Kania's failure had only proven this point.

Normalization, again, was an insidious beast. While Solidarity leaders like Nowak, Handzlik, or Frasyniuk were barred from their factories and kept under constant vigilance, and local activists like Bogusławski, Majdzik, or Konieczna faced frequent detentions and searches, the other 98 percent of the Polish population was enticed with, among other things, the promise of participation and influence. Logically, these were "healthy elements" who would learn to make the right choices. There was every reason for the communists to be confident that the Solidarity member who joined a council *would* in fact become co-opted.

There was a new element in Nowa Huta by 1986, however. Father Kazimierz Jancarz—at whose Mistrzejowice church Kazimierz Fugiel distributed food and clothing—founded the Christian Workers' University (ChUR)* in 1984. The idea was to give the faithful activist something more than fiery sermons: a solid grounding in history, economics, and politics, along with appropriate lectures on literature and religion. Students would get more than just a lecture series: the two-year program (during which attendance was taken, and slackers were dropped from the rolls) ended with an examination and a certificate. Workers from the steel mill made up most of the first class of about forty. They studied everything from Solidarity themes in great literature to techniques of printing and note-taking, from economic theory to legal advice. And as a place to meet other worker activists, it was radically different from a demonstration, a jail cell, or a factory cafeteria.

Among the first graduates, in 1986, were Marek Szczupak from the hot rolling mill, Janusz Pura from the cold rolling mill, and Andrzej Marciniak from the coking plant. None of the three was of Solidarity's old guard. They had not participated in the birth of the union, though of course they all belonged. In martial law, they found their calling in Fugiel's social work at Mistrzejowice; the church, and not the street, was their enclave of freedom. From there, it was but a short step to ChUR. The ques-

* The name suggests choir (*chór*) in Polish.

tion of using the system, and not just attacking it, returned again and again in their study at ChUR. Armed with their diplomas from the Christian Workers' University, Pura, Marciniak, and Szczupak ran for the employees' councils in their shops—in which a majority of the seats were taken by Solidarity members—in the next election, in late 1987.

Even if these workers are confident that they escaped the clutches of normalization, we should again play devil's advocate. These activists (and those at Polar and elsewhere) could just have been beneficiaries of liberalization without even realizing it, part of a master plan by the regime to prepare its citizens for democracy. This scenario would seem unlikely, if not an insult, to those who battled for respect and concessions in the more independent employees' councils. As for the lessons of Father Jancarz's ChUR, while they might have been lost on the factory directors and the police, they produced a crop of savvy unionists. ChUR was a successor to the underground trade unions of the 1970s on the Baltic Coast, where workers like Lech Wałęsa learned the crafts of politics.

Still, the "right wing" of Nowa Huta's Solidarity opposed the councils, though some top Solidarity leaders in Warsaw were supportive. The gamble turned out to be worth it; the councils could do a great deal that was still impossible for Solidarity. First, they had access to information about the factory's budget and financial situation. This information was essential to the preparations for the strike of April 1988, and councilors like Pura, Szczupak, or Marciniak could, and did, pass it on to their underground colleagues in the factory.

Second, the councils created a new way for the work force to speak to, and oppose, the factory administration. For example, the council headed by Andrzej Marciniak at the coking plant passed a resolution, in January 1988, calling for the dismissal of three upper-level administrators for their violation of some eighteen work code regulations on work safety and environmental protection.[14] The point was not whether or not the director responded, but that the council's was a voice the director had to hear. The stage was set for the labor conflict of 1988: the employees' council, rather than blurring the points of contention, actually helped to make them clearer by multiplying the points of disagreement with factory administration and the communist regime. With the council's help, Solidarity would mobilize not only its loyal membership, but entire workshops and factories as well.

In Nowa Huta (the neighborhood and the factory) circa 1987, one could find many niches in the opposition: in the Solidarity underground or in Nowak's aboveground politics; in Fugiel's or Ferczyk's committees; in Father Jancarz's ChUR; in the employees' councils; or (as we shall see) in the youth underground. This is a key to Solidarity's strength there throughout the 1980s, culminating in the strike of 1988. Certainly all these "pianos" were not playing together—indeed, the cacophony was hard to interpret, and there was no conductor—but Solidarity had at least taken over the concert hall.

VENTS OR ACCUMULATORS?

Though it might be easy enough to forget, there were problems in communist states other than the political and economic conflicts. Ordinary social problems are hardly unique to communism. In the minds of most in the opposition, they were not priorities. Simply to speak about them might provide fodder for more ridicule of the system but would not change people's lives. But some activists turned away from standard political contention to discover that social campaigns became political, too.*

Three examples from Poland—a temperance campaign, the opening of homeless shelters, and a group of pensioned miners—show both the limitations and the potential of this work. Many who were deeper in the political opposition called such campaigns "vents" (*wentyle*), which simply directed the anger or activism of a few people away from the regime and into harmless directions, thus relieving pressure on the communists. Those within these movements saw it differently. They believed that they had eroded a small corner of state authority and created unexpected spheres of social autonomy, in the same way as Kazimierz Fugiel and others in Church ministries had shown working families that someone other than the state-run trade union could offer them assistance. Some also found that their social concerns opened up a way back into the strictly political world as well.

When martial law was declared, Marcin Przybyłowicz had just been elected director of a small firm producing technical supplies for scientific researchers. Instead, he found himself interned for six months, and fired. After his release, working in various private firms, he participated in the ministry for former internees in the seminary church on Krakowskie Przedmieście in Warsaw. Discussions there turned more and more to the moral degradation of communist society, and in particular to the problem of alcohol.

The Catholic Church, of course, had always spoken out against alcoholism. Solidarity had added the observation that since the communist state had a monopoly on alcohol production and distribution, it was dou-

* One important early example was SZETA, the Committee to Help the Poor, established by Gábor Demszky and Ottilia Solt in Budapest in 1979. SZETA focused on the plight of the poor and homeless to raise questions about the equality and progress that socialism supposedly offered. It also provoked urban society into thinking more about others by, for example, sponsoring a charity auction to raise money for its work.

bly in the state's interests to see its citizens drink and lose their will to stand up to the regime even as they enriched the treasury. August—the month of the Warsaw Uprising of 1944, of the birth of Solidarity in 1980, and of pilgrimages to Poland's holiest shrine at Częstochowa—symbolized these multiple meanings of alcohol and abstinence. In the words of an appeal issued during a June 1986 pilgrimage: "August without vodka: this is our modest sacrifice to the memory of all those who gave their lives for the Homeland in August. August without vodka: this does honor to the workers of August, who were the first to raise the banner of sobering up (*otrzeźwienie*).* August without vodka: this repays God for those who in their drunkenness degrade human dignity, and is an act of our solidarity with those harmed by vodka."[15]

The first Sobriety Brotherhood was a group of Catholic intellectuals in several Warsaw parishes who, on the eve of Pope John Paul II's second Polish pilgrimage in June 1983, organized rituals in which they swore oaths of sobriety. With the support of Father Popiełuszko, the nascent movement found a home at St. Stanisław Kostka Church. This was an elite movement, dedicated to the good of all Poland. "The future of the Nation," wrote Przybyłowicz in 1987, "depends on the Polish *inteligencja,* union leaders, social and political activists, whom one can expect to understand that in the sobriety project the issue is not just vodka."[16] That purpose was the same as in the Kraków ministries: to influence social behavior without recourse to official channels, while delivering a message both moral and political.

For Przybyłowicz, however, appeals and oaths were not enough: after all, whether one kept one's oath was in the end a private matter, so the movement lacked a legible public dimension. On his suggestion, the brotherhood began to picket liquor stores in central Warsaw in August 1985. They held signs reading "Drink! You'll turn red!"; "Don't drink—In Gdańsk [i.e. during the 1980 strike] they didn't"; or "Sobriety" written in the familiar red letters of the Solidarity logo. Many of the picketers were older and retired; Przybyłowicz, in his late forties, was among the youngest. Their campaign provoked a kind of absurdity that Orange Alternative mastered a few years later; police looked foolish arresting older men and women peacefully asking people to drink less. More importantly, the picketing delivered a message of self-sufficiency and independence: "What we want to do," one picketer told a reporter, "is, under the pretext of telling people not to drink, to teach them to open their minds to reality and to the ideals of Solidarity."[17]

The humor and modesty of the protest balances the evident bravery of

---

* *Otrzeźwienie* literally means "sobering up," as here; elsewhere it will be translated as "sobriety." It also connotes waking up, in the sense of political awareness.

the few participants, who received no support from Solidarity leaders. They and the regime engaged in a war of numbers: how many had abstained in August, and how much had consumption fallen (or risen, as government press spokesman Jerzy Urban maintained)? Successful or not, the protest was a real challenge precisely to the myth of liberalization. The Polish regime (like the Soviet one, where anti-alcoholism was one of Mikhail Gorbachev's first campaigns) allowed the official press to pursue drunkenness much more intensely than was imaginable even a few years earlier. Newspapers were full of earnest discussions with sociologists and doctors who made the magnitude of Poland's alcohol problem quite plain. This could be interpreted as another sign of Poland's own glasnost—until the Sobriety Brotherhood took to the streets. Their signs and their presence exposed the hypocrisy of a glasnost that stopped at words while the state depended on alcohol revenues.

To change Polish behavior, then, one did not need the firm hand of the state, but personal determination and consistency. Magda Góralska, arrested in the pickets of August 1986, was fined fifty thousand zlotys or fifty days in jail. She insisted on the latter, but it was a year before the authorities reluctantly consented. In prison, Góralska took to counseling the homeless, alcoholic women with whom she shared cells. Perhaps wishing to avoid similar confrontations, the militia in August 1987 did not detain picketers, but only checked identity cards.[18]

Whether this action affected social practices is impossible to gauge. Writing for the underground press in 1985, "Gabriel Szum" claimed to see "something of great scope . . . truly invincible." Among the *inteligencja,* for whom drinking into the wee hours had been the indispensable mode of political discussion, Szum now encountered parties where "more and more often one hears: 'No thanks—the opposition does not drink,' said with a certain feeling of pride. Really, no one expected that snobbisms would turn around so quickly and so radically."[19] Besides the Church (whose attitude, Szum felt, was rather ambiguous) and the legend of the Gdańsk strike, Szum located the roots of this new attitude in the example of Gandhi. And indeed, though he didn't mention it, Szum and the *inteligencja* surely also had in mind Gandhi's famous boycott of British-taxed salt. As in India, the Polish campaign consisted of nonviolent civil disobedience (Szum mentions peaceful blockades of trucks transporting alcohol), moral exemplary leadership, and an appeal to the individual conscience. Probing the enemy's weakest points, such campaigns made violent repression seem absurd.

As a means of bringing down communism, a moral movement would have to be one for the long march. As other strategies promised swifter change, the temperance movement, which lacked the prominent leadership of someone like Wałęsa or Bujak, waned and disappeared after 1987.

While the Sobriety Brotherhood remained largely an elite movement of moral national renewal, a similar group of middle-aged Catholic intellectuals in Wrocław turned to another social problem: homelessness. There had always been homeless people in communist Poland: people who lost their way in the reshuffling of populations after the war, or those released from jail with nowhere to turn. The problem was particularly evident in Wrocław, a city where no one's roots reached farther back than its acquisition from Germany in 1945. And the fate of the homeless in a communist state, where proof of residence was generally a requirement of employment, was especially cruel.

Not until 1981, however, did Father Jerzy Adam Marszałkowicz receive permission for a shelter, which opened for ten homeless men on Christmas Eve, barely a week after martial law was declared. For Father Marszałkowicz, and for many in the Brother Albert Society,* the purpose was simply to attend to the needs of the homeless. Tomasz Wójcik saw in the group nothing less than the continuation of Solidarity by other means. An engineer at the Wrocław Polytechnic, interned three times during martial law for his underground work, Wójcik wanted to keep alive what he saw as Solidarity's great legacy, the awakening of popular sensitivity to social and political problems. The Brother Albert Society, he believed, would not have been possible without Solidarity; now, as the union tried to survive underground, the society was one way to maintain that sensitivity and reawaken Poles to the harmful effects of the communist regime. As with alcoholism, homelessness was a problem the communists could not, or would not, address. Jerzy Urban (who announced that the Polish government would send a shipment of sleeping bags to New York City for the homeless there) declared even in 1986 that there was no homeless problem in Poland.[20]

The door was thus left open to "do something to spite the commies," as Marek Oktaba put it. Oktaba, then a student at the Polytechnic, had helped to form the Maitri Movement, a ministry bringing together students concerned about poverty in Poland; it was inspired by a trip Wójcik and others had taken to India. In the idea of a shelter, Maitri found a "space not yet taken over by the communists." It was both a moral calling and an adventure: "our girlfriends," Oktaba recalled, "would push us out the door when we had duty" at the shelter. In 1983 or 1984 they began to collect money for the shelter, standing at the entrance to cemeteries as people visited relatives' graves on All Souls' Day. As they thus edged into politics through public mention of their work, they were protected from government repression. Their charges were unlikely to become politically

---

* Named after a nineteenth-century monk in Kraków, Adam Chmielowski, founder of the Albertine order, who has recently been canonized by Pope John Paul II.

engaged, after all. But the society was in reality a shelter in more ways than one: for people like Wójcik, who would in the 1990s succeed Frasyniuk as head of Lower Silesia's Solidarity, and for the idea of an independent civil society that helped those in need.

It was not difficult to find such metaphorical shelter in Warsaw intellectual circles or under the wing of the church in Wrocław. Even far from the eyes of foreign reporters and the underground press, social activism offered a toehold in politics. In every city and most towns there was at least one church to which people could turn for some kind of help. Sobriety Brotherhood activist Piotr Wojciechowski recalled hearing about a poor village in southeastern Poland, in which brotherhood members took over the village council and even gained seats on the county council. "Brother Albert shelters" began to appear all across Poland in 1987–88. But still, a Warsaw intellectual or a clergyman enjoyed a level of security of which others could only dream.

No one was as defenseless as retirees and invalids. They could not go on strike, were dependent on their small pensions, and often lived in factory-owned housing. In and around Jastrzębie Zdrój, a coal-mining region developed in the late 1960s, though, a group of retirees organized themselves to demand greater rights. Relative to their low level of security, these were surely among the bravest activists in Poland.

Solidarity initially attracted a lot of enthusiasm from retired workers like Paweł Gross. He had come to Jastrzębie at 25, when the mines were still young themselves. Barely five years later, a work accident left him confined to a wheelchair. For the next decade, until Solidarity came along, he says, he simply "existed." He threw himself into union work, on Solidarity's National Retirees and Invalids Committee, and was a delegate to Solidarity's National Congress in 1981. Solidarity's Silesian Region delegated Bazyli Tyszkiewicz, a technical translator, to organize the retired workers. Most of Gross's retired colleagues, though, got a good scare from martial law (though none was interned) and withdrew from politics. When Tyszkiewicz returned to underground organizing after his martial-law internment, he found that in all Poland, only the Silesians remained determined.

The mid-1980s were especially cruel for people on fixed pensions. Under the pressure of Poland's massive foreign debt, inflation began to creep upward at the beginning of the decade and accelerated in 1984–85. Workers might receive some cost-of-living adjustments, but pensions were not indexed at all. Those who had retired long before found their income simply vanishing. In the dramatic words of one Jastrzębie proclamation: "To become elderly or crippled is unfortunate. To become elderly or crippled in our country is a tragedy."[21]

They began meeting in late 1984, at the garden plot of Henryk Wojtała in Wodzisław Śląski. Wojtała was a repatriate from Belgium, scraping by on a disability pension since a head injury at the May First mine ten years earlier. Others in the group included Renata Szumowska, a retired journalist, and Józef Bujoczek, a native Silesian from Piekary Śląskie. Together, they formed the Committee for Assistance to Retirees, Pensioners, and the Disabled.

Their activism passed almost without comment from the mainstream underground press; we know who they are because, unlike virtually every other opposition group at this time, they signed their names to every document (helpfully supplying addresses and phone numbers for the historian's benefit). First from the garden plot, and then from a room offered them by Father Bernard Czernecki, whose Fatherland Masses at the "Church on the Hill" were the political heart of Jastrzębie, they issued declarations, petitions, and open letters decrying the plight of those who could not work.

Individual committee members could always be seen at the fringes of May Day parades or at demonstrations on the anniversary of the bloody suppression of the strike at the Wujek mine.* Some even picketed social security offices. Mostly, however, they produced letters. These quirky documents have a certain dark humor about them. A letter to Jan Dobraczyński, a popular author and president of the Patriotic Front for National Renewal (PRON, a vehicle of Jaruzelski's normalization), announces the signatories' intent to boycott the 1985 parliamentary election. Noting the recent harassment of the group, they conclude almost wistfully: "Taught by these regrettable experiences, we can expect, with a large dose of probability, that our fates shall be such that, even if we were to want to very much, we won't be able to go to the voting booths on October 13. We simply won't go anywhere that day. Maybe, at most, on a twenty-minute stroll." Addressing Dobraczyński personally, the authors become more hopeful:

Honored Sir: You are now an aged man. The lot of the aged in our country is very precarious. We swear to you that if your situation should demand it, we will come to you with all the assistance that (as you'll understand) we are able to offer. [Signed] The sincerely faithful readers of your wonderful books, and now the members of the Committee of Assistance to Retirees and the Disabled in Katowice.

P.S.: We are also releasing this letter—like all those we are sending—to the public. We hope that you will accept this [fact] with full understanding. After a certain age, one begins to understand everything. And to understand all is to forgive all.[22]

---

* Nine miners were killed on December 16, 1981, in martial law's bloodiest clash.

One can imagine how easy it must have been for Solidarity leaders in Katowice or Warsaw—not to mention the regime itself—to dismiss these writers as crackpots, and no doubt some of them were. But the symbolic weight of their letters cannot be overlooked. From a decade's distance, Bazyli Tyszkiewicz comes to their defense. First, he argues, they helped to rescue the honor of the elderly, whom some in the younger generation blamed for the sorry state of the economy and accused of being more willing to praise the achievements of People's Poland than to see its faults. Now these retirees, at least, could say that they, too, had stood up. Second, the communists shared the same expectations about pensioners and thus did not expect conflict to erupt along this front. Opposition was not supposed to proliferate like this under the conditions of normalization. A "handful of extremists" (the standard epithet applied to any Solidarity demonstration) was becoming dozens of handfuls.

Like that of the anti-alcohol picketers in Warsaw, this was opposition difficult to combat. The committee members' frequent reference to age and infirmity disarmed the regime. Therefore, they could publish their names and addresses and remain relatively unharmed. Not that their opposition was without risk: Józef Bujoczek's son, also a miner, was beaten up by the police as a warning to his father. Whether this activism made an impression on the miners of Jastrzębie who were their sons, nephews, and neighbors, or on those waiting in line to buy bread or collect a social security check, is impossible to gauge. On the other hand, Paweł Gross was a legend in Jastrzębie particularly among miners who struck in 1988. In the wake of the committee's lobbying, discussion of the problems of retirees and the disabled did begin to appear in the official press. The last communist governments even began to index pensions (albeit too little, too late). It would be absurd to attribute this solely to the letters of a dozen lonely people far from Warsaw, but in a society kept under close surveillance, their activism did not go unnoticed.

Three communities, three issues, three movements. Each trod the gray zone between political activism and social work. In each, some individuals were closer to the former, others to the latter. Most of those involved would say that, ultimately, to raise these moral or social issues was more important than the politics. But one can hardly say that these movements merely existed alongside the politics, either. For some, these movements were a way station back to politics. Marcin Przybyłowicz became a member of Parliament in the 1990s; Paweł Gross was twice asked to run and declined. Others in each of these movements have continued their activism in the Church. And the issues they raised have become central to political discourse in the postcommunist era. Rather than vents or pressure valves, these were accumulators, where issues and their champions gathered power.

These examples help us to understand how and why movements could emerge in the most unlikely spaces in the years during and just after martial law. None of them was inevitable, after all: only the Warsaw Sobriety Brotherhood moved outside the Church onto the streets; there was no active retirees' group beyond Silesia; and Wrocław homeless activists themselves often wondered why other cities (like Kraków, home of the Albertine Order) did not follow suit. In each case, a few determined individuals, cut off from the union underground, sensed the political power of social or moral issues. Alliances with individual maverick clergy were crucial: Popiełuszko in Warsaw, Marszałkowicz in Wrocław, Czernecki in Jastrzębie. At the time, neither the Church hierarchy nor Solidarity was prepared to embark upon public campaigns around these issues. For those involved, the movements were little corners of freedom.

Those who left the underground, wholly or in part, in the mid-1980s accomplished two profound changes, without which subsequent developments are difficult to imagine. First, they effectively deconstructed some of the pillars of communist language and ideology. Amnesty, as Władysław Frasyniuk showed, did not mean to retire from political activity, but in fact to increase it, in defiance of regime expectations. So-called vents like church-allied social work did not relieve pressure on the regime but actually raised it and focused it in new directions. Student or worker councils did not become mouthpieces of the authorities, but rather mouthpieces of opposition. Normalization, finally, was a doomed beast where so many people were prepared to jump down its throat and tear it apart from within.

Activists in the gray zone demonstrated the validity of individual rights in Polish society. True, the concept of rights had been a core idea of Solidarity from the beginning. But these campaigns made those theoretical rights palpable. If your car was confiscated or you were beaten, Marek Jakubiec or Ryszard Bocian showed that you were not powerless against the police and might even beat them in court. In classes at ChUR or discussions at Dominik, students and workers met others like themselves and formulated ideas of self-government as a right and as a means to freedom. They learned to use the rules and regulations of the communist bureaucracies to empower rather than to contain, and to face authority without fear.

Solidarity's first goal had always been to help people in concrete ways. During martial law, it sometimes seemed as if, in Edward Nowak's words, "the fight with the communists was more important than to help people, than the economy, and so on." Now help for the student, worker, or high school teacher beaten or fired reaffirmed the ideals of social work that lay at the heart of Solidarity. To help a person in need had multiple meanings in late communist Poland. It might be a way to propagate the ideas of Solidarity and opposition, drawing in new people, or at least reminding them of Solidarity, as they collected food or money. But at the same time, it was a testing of the limits. The great unknown, no matter what direction one wanted to see the opposition pursue, was what one could get away with. These first steps would soon lead to more overt opposition.

Chapter Two

COME WITH US! THEY AREN'T BEATING TODAY!

THE ART OF THE BLIZZARD

The Ballad of Marek Adamkiewicz

EVERY young Polish male, at the start of his obligatory military service, pledged his loyalty in a parade-ground ceremony. In this oath, a soldier not only pledged to serve the Polish nation but vowed "to guard unshakably . . . the Polish People's Republic from the wiles of imperialism, to stand unbendingly in defense of peace, in a fraternal alliance with the Soviet Army and other allied armies."[1] Marek Adamkiewicz was about to complete his college degree in Szczecin when he was called up to the army. Adamkiewicz, 26, had been involved in student opposition for years. On November 8, 1984, he refused to take the military oath.

Over the years, one pacifist or another—as well as dozens of Jehovah's Witnesses—had refused the oath. Roland Kruk, a hippy from Warsaw, had objected in 1980, as did Leszek Budrewicz, a Wrocław poet and literature scholar, in 1981. Both received alternative service; Adamkiewicz, who knew them both from the Student Solidarity Committee and the Independent Students' Association, may have expected similar treatment.

However, the Supreme Military Court had ruled, just days before Adamkiewicz's protest, that to refuse the oath was equivalent to refusing military service and was thus a crime. Adamkiewicz was hauled before a military tribunal and, in December, sentenced to two-and-a-half years in prison. Coming as it did just a month after Father Popiełuszko's body was found, this was a clear signal to the opposition that the regime meant business.

Budrewicz in particular felt an obligation to act, since he had gotten off so lightly three years before. He traveled to Warsaw for Adamkiewicz's appeal and ran into another colleague from the student opposition, Jacek Czaputowicz of Warsaw. Someone needed to speak out, they agreed. This case could fall under the purview of the Romaszewskis' Committee for Intervention and Legality, but it was important that Adamkiewicz's peers themselves take action.

A case like Adamkiewicz's was a problem for the communists. Everyone knew there were many rights the regime promised (in constitutions, for example) and did not deliver. As KOR and Charter 77 had shown long before, the communists were thus an easy target, even if they never really backed down. The ambiguous communist position on peace was an equally promising case. Given the regimes' evident failure to provide a higher standard of living, the most fundamental difference between capitalism and communism was supposed to be their attitude toward war. Capitalist regimes, according to Leninist theory, were driven by their hunger for profit to violent conflict among themselves and against their ideological enemies. Communists, by contrast, were naturally peace-loving. One side built up arsenals to enrich the bosses of industry and sent the proletariat to battle as cannon fodder. The other pledged its support to workers across the world in their "struggle for peace." Sporting contests, folk festivals, kindergarten education, and even military alliances were saturated with the symbols and language of this campaign. The military, in this fantasy world, existed purely for defense of socialism and of the nation.

The oath refusal was an uncomfortable case for Solidarity, too. Its overtones of hostility to the Soviet Union threatened to pull the opposition into dangerous waters. Moreover, in Polish culture, the military is rather sacred; most Poles regard military service as either a national obligation or a test of manhood, or both. During the virtual civil war of the martial-law winter of 1981–82, angry crowds frequently held their fire of rocks or Molotov cocktails when army tanks came by: they were "our boys," unlike the riot police for whom Poles reserved their greatest hatred. Thus to question the army's role—or even the absurdity of swearing allegiance to a foreign power—provoked resistance and incredulity from within the opposition.

Czaputowicz decided to hold a protest fast (during the upcoming Lenten season) in the church of Father Leon Kantorski in Podkowa Leśna, a Warsaw suburb. Budrewicz couldn't go, but his fiancée, Krystyna Surowiec, participated, as did Roland Kruk. Other fasters included Marek Krukowski, a medical student from Wrocław who had refused service in 1983; Barbara Malak, a Warsaw psychology student who became the fast's spokesperson; Piotr Niemczyk; Konstanty Radziwiłł, a young doctor; and Maciej Kuroń, the son of Solidarity's Jacek Kuroń. The elder Kuroń, in fact, had been thinking about the idea of a peace-oriented protest and had once suggested as much both to Budrewicz and to Stanisław Handzlik of Kraków.

The protest lasted one week, during which the fasters issued communiqués and letters demanding Adamkiewicz's freedom and a change in the laws on military service. They took part in seminars on the theology of peace, on morality and patriotism, on Poland's military traditions, and on the theory and practice of civil disobedience. They sang songs like the "Ballad of Marek Adamkiewicz," which ends with the lines: "You knew him, after all, so why do you salute? / You drank beer with him, but you turned out a scoundrel / I, too, just sing and play / We're here together, and he is alone."[2] There were concerts, art exhibits, and even comedy acts, as the entire Warsaw artistic-intellectual elite, it seemed, descended on the church.

Meanwhile, the network of student opposition veterans extended also to Kraków, where the Committee for the Protection of Legality organized a six-week rotating protest fast in the church at Bieżanów. Handzlik was one of the participants, as were his colleague from the committee, law student Jan Maria Rokita; young nationalist activist Radosław Huget; and many others. They, too, were visited by opposition leaders from across the country.

This Lenten season was a turning point, as the fasts provided an opportunity to reflect on what seemed a troubling increase in repression. Especially in Kraków, the need for a new opposition movement became quite clear. The oath problem made the fasters think about parallels between internal state violence and external military violence. Huget pointed out that the communist regime had often taken advantage of Western peace protests in its propaganda; a Polish equivalent would weaken the image of the peace-loving communists. Rokita suggested the name Freedom and Peace, as a way of linking human rights and support for international peace.[3] On April 14, 1985, after a mass at a Kraków church, the Founding Declaration of Freedom and Peace, signed by eighteen Kraków students, was read to the congregation. Within a few days, another twenty—mostly from Warsaw and Wrocław, participants in the Podkowa Leśna fast—added their signatures.

Freedom and Peace (Wolność i Pokój, or WiP—pronounced "veep") would grow to become the most important new opposition movement in Eastern Europe since the birth of Solidarity. Though its participants were a decade or more junior to Solidarity's leaders, WiP developed impressive influence and reputation both east and west. By forcing discussion on several completely new issues, it would ultimately win significant concessions from the communist regime, while helping to provoke opposition among the youngest generation of Polish students as well as in other Central European countries.

Conservative Pacifism, Anarchist Nationalism

Freedom and Peace never sought accommodation with the communists. The movement spoke to the regime, demanding explicit changes in laws, but did so on issues that offered no room for compromise. WiP's position was unequivocal, a shrewd calculation rooted in firm principles. Faced with determined protesters like Adamkiewicz, or the conscientious objectors who would soon follow, the communists either had to lock them up—and thus tarnish their normalizing image—or allow them to go free, and thus make a mockery of compulsory service.

One could hardly refuse military service anonymously. So WiP, like most of the movements already encountered in this book, was defiantly aboveground, yet with a stance as radically oppositional as anything underground. Like the pensioners in Jastrzębie, WiP's participants both defended people suffering persecution and joined them, too. The problem of military service faced every Polish man; the same could not necessarily be said about other violations of human rights, for most people were never arrested nor beaten. WiP's campaign had that much greater impact as a result; they would become familiar to those who knew little about the exploits of, say, Fighting Solidarity.

Wacław Giermek, now a computer salesman in Wrocław, thoughtfully explored his road to resistance in an open letter at the time of his refusal to take the oath, in June 1986, and again in a lengthy interview ten years later. Born in 1960, he had just graduated from the Polytechnic with a degree in applied physics when he was called up for the obligatory two-year service. He too was a veteran of the student opposition of 1980–81 and had helped organize assistance for martial law internees thereafter. He was a leader of the Catholic student community in Wrocław, a participant in the nonviolence movement inspired by Father Ludwik Wiśniewski, and an early signer of WiP's founding declaration.

"No one has the right," Giermek's letter begins, "to demand that an adult, mature person should retreat from his moral or religious values. No one can force another person to act against his conscience. Meanwhile, people's conscience is violated in Poland in many different ways. Obligatory military service is one of these ways." Regarding the oath, he points out that alliances change, and thus swearing allegiance to the Soviet Union is absurd. "If General W. Jaruzelski had sworn allegiance to allies in 1942, . . . he would today have to be loyal to Ronald Reagan, President of the United States." Giermek then cuts through the question of whose responsibility it is that he is now imprisoned (he eventually received a sentence of eighteen months): he lists the options available (transfer to reserves, service without the oath, etc.) and stresses his willingness to serve: "The fact that I have been arrested is directly thanks to the command of the brigade. . . . The decision was up to the command. . . . There are many ways to respect the views of people who, like I, refuse to swear an oath which conflicts with their conscience. Whether they are taken advantage of is entirely up to those who determine the conditions of military service."[4]

Giermek's refusal was as much a challenge to the conscience of the regime as it was about his own. At every demonstration in the spring of 1986—and then again after his release following the amnesty that September—he talked about his decision, both to encourage others to consider this step and to reduce his own isolation in jail. The most important thing, he knew, was that such cases not be forgotten or ignored, either by the communists or by society. Even while in his military unit, in the weeks of training before the oath was administered, he talked over his decision with roommates (one of whom was a party member). In this way, he felt, he would have a greater chance to influence the many people who might witness his determination and the punishment he received.

Giermek's protest was unquestionably anticommunist. This was a position all in WiP shared. Many, like Giermek, or Kraków's Rokita and Huget, would today call themselves conservatives. Some, like Czaputowicz and Rokita, even suggest that the issue of military service did not concern them that much: it was simply an excellent instrument with which to beat the communists. This may seem a postmodern cynicism, but the line between communists and opposition remained very real. Underneath the issues chosen lay a genuine national consciousness and Catholic faith. The discussion of military service and human rights, or the references to Pope John Paul II's teachings on peace in WiP's founding document, offered a firm foundation on which to contest the regime and awaken activism among a certain part of Polish society.

Leszek Budrewicz's involvement reveals yet another side of Freedom and Peace, equally crucial to the movement's success. Budrewicz is an agnostic and a pacifist, as well as a passionate political intellectual. He had to swallow hard before signing the movement's founding text, with its prominent reference to Church teachings and its specific condemnation of only one war (the Soviet invasion of Afghanistan). Years of discussion in Father Ludwik's student ministry, however, had cultivated a tolerance for diverse views, as they read Gandhi and Martin Luther King. He and others in Wrocław came to recognize that the goal—of peace, and an end to the communist regime—was more important than the compromises one might make along the way, the badge one might wear, or the purity of one's companions. It was necessary only that all accept some basic principles, above all that of nonviolence.*

Budrewicz, in turn, inspired students nearly a decade younger, like Zuzanna Dąbrowska. She came from a family of prewar socialists (her great-grandmother had been a political exile in Siberia); at fourteen, she chaired the self-government in her high school and organized contacts with other schools in the province. Only fifteen when martial law was declared, she soon began contributing to the underground press. Arrested in 1984 for monitoring a voting station, she had to leave the underground. Though not a strong believer, she became involved in the Catholic student min-

---

* The English term was often used in Polish, always spelled "non-violance."

istry at Wrocław University, until Budrewicz encouraged her to join WiP. The military oath did not seem to Dąbrowska a men's issue, though she would never be called to swear it; it was simply an anticommunist cause, a logical continuation of her work in the opposition.

All those who made their way to WiP shared this same open attitude. Each had recognized that the ethics and practices of the underground strictly limited what could be accomplished. The underground, they felt, wasted too much time worrying about spies or collaborators, and maintaining ideological unity. WiP's forty-odd original signatories were an eloquent expression of this new pluralism. Solidarity, too, was pluralist, welcoming people of all ideological stripes. In Solidarity, though, the different politics were united behind one unified campaign. There was no room for some to strike for wages, others to march for peace, and still others to negotiate for power. Only a few union leaders, like Jacek Kuroń, articulated a similar idea of pluralist activism. Most feared that such diversity was a weakness that would allow the communists to divide and thus conquer the opposition. Freedom and Peace embodied the internal pluralism I described at the beginning of this book.

The limits of WiP's pluralism were tested by the campaign to support those who refused service altogether. Wojciech Jankowski of Gdańsk was the first well-known case. He was a teacher—ironically enough, of defense preparedness—in a technical school, and a committed anarchist. Back in 1983, at the age of 19, he and several friends founded the Alternative Society Movement (RSA). They rebelled against the domination of Gdańsk's nationalist, Catholic opposition elite. It was more difficult in Gdańsk than anywhere else for a young would-be dissenter to break into the underground. RSA promoted a free lifestyle and indifference to politics, whether of the communist or nationalist variety; it became famous for staging a violent battle with Gdańsk police during the 1985 May Day parade. When the official press attacked RSA as "anarchists," the group sought out the writings of Bakunin, Kropotkin, and nineteenth-century Polish anarchist Edward Abramowski and decided the appellation fit.

From the beginning, Jankowski—known as "Jacob," pronounced as if in English—had thought about refusing military service as the logical consequence of his participation in RSA. This step, which culminated in a three-and-a-half-year sentence, imposed in December 1985, meant breaking with the RSA underground, though. He began to search for new allies. Jankowski's inquiries led him, ironically enough, to Father Ludwik, who pointed him back to Gdańsk conservatives, who directed him, in turn, to Jacek Czaputowicz in Warsaw.

An anarchist like Wojciech Jankowski had little in common with Jacek Czaputowicz. Yet Czaputowicz and WiP worked hard to publicize Jankowski's case even though he disagreed with Jankowski on the role of the military. The key, for Czaputowicz, was the legal argument. Polish law did theoretically allow for conscientious objector status, though this was almost never granted; as with the oath (which was not technically required in the exact wording quoted earlier), protesters thus had legal justification behind them. Petitioners could also point to the Polish constitution's protection of the freedom of conscience, and they frequently based their request on religious grounds—pointing to the dozens of Jehovah's Witnesses who preceded them into jail. Many petitioners also emphasized their desire to work in health care or social work in place of military service. Even more than the military oath question, the conscientious objector issue invoked the spirit of the Helsinki Accords of 1976.

Jankowski's argument, of course, was not a patriotic one, but it was both deeply moral and clearly anticommunist. In a letter to the State Council, written from his prison cell in August 1986, "Jacob" confronted the irony of a teacher of a military subject becoming a conscientious objector:

> The Naval Court stated that pacifist views are not compatible with my occupation, a teacher of defense preparedness, and that "the special duty of inculcating the youth in my charge with the lofty ideals of love for one's Fatherland and its defense in the case of invasion or menace" fell especially upon me as a teacher and pedagogue. So, first: there is a basic difference between defense preparedness and the science of killing, which is what military service is. . . . Indeed, I did not teach them to kill. I taught them how to save a person's life, health, and property from the weapons of mass destruction in modern arsenals. . . .
>
> Second: the development of civilization means that today humanity is one family, linked by the common interest to live in peace and freedom. Violating human rights in one country or in a bloc is a threat to all the residents of our planet. . . . Freedom and peace are general human values, and the politics of militarizing entire societies, carried out in countries with compulsory military service, threatens those values. Compulsory military service is barbaric, in the full sense of that word. . . .
>
> "Defense of the Fatherland" is but a pretext for actions which in reality aim to maintain the state's socialist status quo, the essence of which is the ruling of a privileged class over the overwhelming majority of society. The goal of the army and the militia in 1956, 1970, and 1981 was not "defense of the fatherland." Nor did "defense of the fatherland" guide the tanks invading Czechoslovakia in 1968. They did not balk at murder, and the goal of their actions was, and is, one: to force slave's fetters upon people who fight for their rights. These fetters are all the more repulsive in that they are covered up with revolutionary, workers' slogans.[6]

A close look at Jankowski's rhetoric suggests that the distance between him and, say, Wacław Giermek is not so great. His deeply felt pacifism is tied not only to the idea of human rights, but also to opposition to the communist regime in Poland and the Soviet bloc. That Giermek is a devout Catholic, while Jankowski reviled his more famous Gdańsk namesake, Solidarity pastor Henryk Jankowski, naturally meant that they did not share all the same causes. (They disagree, for example, on the right to abortion and on the legalization of marijuana.) But it also meant that their common opposition to the Polish regime would be based not on the abstractions of ideology, but on the defense of specific human rights.

A month after Jankowski wrote his letter, General Jaruzelski's regime announced a third and final amnesty of all political prisoners. Jankowski, however, remained in prison, as did another WiP participant, Jarosław Nakielski of Warsaw. Jankowski began a hunger strike. To Jacek Czaputowicz and others in WiP, it was obvious that the amnesty was a fraud. Their elders in Solidarity, and contacts in the Church, counseled caution: this could be, they argued, a first step toward valuable dialogue with the regime. It was one thing to minister to those in prison, and another thing entirely to demonstrate for their release.

Nevertheless, Czaputowicz organized a WiP sit-in. A dozen or so participants from Wrocław, Kraków, and Gdańsk, as well as Warsaw, occupied the sidewalk in front of a department store in central Warsaw, linking arms and chanting for their colleagues' release. They carried slogans like "Refusal of military service is the right of every person," and "Freedom and Peace (and love) for everyone," on T-shirts, banners, and sandwich boards. Czaputowicz had made sure Western cameras would be there; he stood to one side, recalled one of the demonstrators, orchestrating the protest, exhorting his colleagues to "Turn this way—toward the cameras, over here!" Though all participants were detained and fined after about half an hour, Jankowski was released from prison the next day (in time to come to Warsaw to thank his friends), and Nakielski two weeks later. Thus was won the first of a string of impressive victories by this small band.

IDEALS AND INSTRUMENTS

WiP today is sometimes recalled as a group of media-hungry students who grabbed the spotlight briefly from Solidarity. There is no shame in that, for this is precisely what was needed in mid-decade, when Solidarity was generating little news of note. The media were a key to WiP's success. Solidarity (and KOR before it) had used the media, too, but not until Freedom and Peace did a movement build itself through publicity. Every protest, no matter how small, reached Warsaw and Radio Free Europe immediately. This was standard practice in Solidarity as well, but WiP was, for a time, the only opposition producing newsworthy events.

The publicity helped the movement to grow. This rankled the communists: when Jacek Czaputowicz and Piotr Niemczyk were put on trial in the spring of 1986, prosecutors reminded them of one such publicity success, as evidence of WiP's antisocialist character. In the provincial town of Gorzów, members of the small underground Independent Youth Movement heard about Marek Adamkiewicz's protest and WiP on Radio Free Europe. This inspired two members of the group to refuse the oath; one of them even circulated a petition among his fellow soldiers demanding permission to go to Sunday Mass, or at least to listen to Mass on the radio.[6] After the predictable arrests, their co-conspirators Marek Rusakiewicz and Kazimierz Sokołowski considered the movement's options. Their little circle had been able to withstand the usual police repression (better than most: they had been working in the underground since 1982), but these arrests overwhelmed them. They decided that Sokołowski would go to a Freedom and Peace gathering on the Baltic coast. There, Sokołowski met Budrewicz, who put him in touch with Czaputowicz; the Independent Youth Movement became the Gorzów circle of WiP.

The media was WiP's connective tissue, because, unlike Solidarity, Freedom and Peace could not be called an organization, and it had no "members." Those in WiP insisted on the term "participants," to underscore their belief that goals should take priority over ideological allegiance.* The only structure was a foundation based in Warsaw, with representatives from each circle who dispersed money received from Solidarity or Western sources. WiP also boasted a network of nearly thirty publications. Even set against the two thousand or so periodicals published in the Polish underground between 1981 and 1989, WiP was quite prolific. The periodicals, which ranged from one-page bulletins to sizable booklets, drew readers to the movement, as every issue included names and addresses of people to contact.

The journals—with titles like *Dezerter* and *Without Violence*—were also manuals for action. They went beyond the standard reports of repression to issue specific suggestions for the reader. The second issue of the Gdańsk circle's periodical, *A cappella,* exhorted, in mock military language:

CIVILIAN!
    If political, religious, or any other kind of beliefs won't permit you to perform military service; if you would prefer to fulfill that service with work, THEN START DEMANDING IT!
    One of the ways to get the authorities' attention in this matter is to send your

* Estimates of active participants in the movement range from two hundred to five hundred, with major circles in Kraków, Wrocław, and Gdańsk, large ones in Warsaw, Gorzów, and Szczecin, and scattered adherents across the country.

military booklets to the Ministry of National Defense.* This act is not the same as refusing military service. You can later claim your booklet. The Military Draft Board (WKU) gives you 14 days for that; if you don't claim it in that time, the matter is turned over to the Misdemeanor Board, where you will be punished for this "crime" with—as the experience of WiP-ists shows—three months in jail, which may or may not be convertible to 50 thousand zlotys.

The most important thing will be the fact that you have not feared to present clearly your position on the matter of compulsory military service.

Not everyone has an uncle on the WKU.

Not everyone has enough money to buy himself Category "E."

Not everyone can arrange for a false doctor's certificate.

But everyone has a military booklet, which he can send to the following address.[7]

Dozens of young men did so, taking their first step to conscientious objection, and, often, to participation in WiP. They became *kaloryfery,* or "radiators," a nickname derived from the fact that the initials "c.o." in Polish stand not for "conscientious objector" but for "central heating." Because WiP was an aboveground movement, its doors were wide open to anyone who would seek it out and follow its path.

The pluralism of Freedom and Peace did, as I suggested earlier, embrace diverse attitudes toward movement issues. Some circles—especially the "Kraków-Gorzów axis"—were quite conservative on social issues. The Gorzów group even attempted to get movement support for an anti-abortion protest, with no success. With that exception, they (as well as the more liberal but politically astute activists in Warsaw) saw the issues instrumentally. Anticommunism remained the central focus of their activism.

Idealists, in turn, dominated in Wrocław and Gdańsk. In those cities, many saw self-improvement as a means to broader social change; peace was a part of a holistic agenda. Such activists embraced vegetarianism, explored Eastern religions, or became interested in animal rights. Still, each circle contained a spectrum of views. Moreover, because Freedom and Peace was not an organization, it was difficult to demarcate, say, WiP and the RSA in Gdańsk, or WiP and the Twelve in Wrocław. This is another mark of WiP's pluralism: one could "work for different companies" (so the slang went, with a hint of corporate culture!) without compromising one's credentials as a Freedom and Peace participant.

Freedom and Peace became known among the 15-to-25 age group as the new élite. They were fearless, they were determined, and they had, so

* Each male adult was given a military booklet, roughly equivalent to a registration card, in which was recorded his military status (deferments, health category, etc.).

it was said, the best parties.* For some, their community defined the best of activist culture in the late 1980s. After the first gathering, in late 1985 in a hut in the mountains south of Wrocław, WiP met nearly every summer for camping jamborees that lasted for days; eventually, they organized these gatherings into full-blown festivals, christened "Hyde Parks"; some of the best-known reggae, punk, and postpunk bands joined the raucous festivities. Though the "Ballad of Marek Adamkiewicz" did not catch on, other songs did—like "Rotting Carcass" (*Padlina*), which became WiP's unofficial anthem. The movement's camaraderie and trust were nurtured by long hours on trains (quite cheap then for students or teachers, which most participants were), traveling to demonstrations called by WiP circles in other cities.

With the partial exception of Wrocław, WiP was a man's world. Most of the women involved were the wives or girlfriends of other participants. WiP did not break out of the accepted gender divisions in opposition established by Solidarity. It was difficult, recalls Urszula Nowakowska, now director of Warsaw's Women's Rights Center, to work against stereotyped roles. Women made the sandwiches while men made politics. These women were then, and now, as determined in their opposition as were the men, but someone, it seemed, had to take care of the children. There was no serious push to upend this hierarchy and get women out of the back room. When men in the Wrocław group proposed setting up a feminist discussion group sometime around 1988, the response was muted (and, by women, unremembered); most likely the proposal sounded too much like just another anticommunist tactic rather than an evolution in movement culture.

That assumption was probably correct: women's images were in Freedom and Peace a valuable commodity. One year after the first protest fast, a new one took place in the same Podkowa Leśna church. This time, all nine fasters who gathered for a week of prayer, study, and protest were women. There were Wrocław WiP-ists Anna Gawlik and Gosia Krukowska, whose husbands were also active in the movement; socialist Zuzanna Dąbrowska; and Małgorzata Gorczewska from the Gdańsk circle that produced *A cappella*. For Anna Gawlik, this "great family" of politically committed women from across the country was a consciousness-raising event.

The women's communiqués did not raise feminist perspectives but rather insisted that the "boys" now in jail—including Czaputowicz, Niemczyk, Adamkiewicz, and three others—would not be forgotten by the nation. Historical discussions during the fast drew parallels with the

---

* An Orange Alternative participant in Wrocław carefully distinguished for me between the "pot" scene of that collective and the "vodka" scene of WiP.

struggles of the nineteenth century: "In contrast to our eastern and western neighbors," wrote the WiP women, "in Poland the woman's role has been much greater, both in the area of upbringing and in social issues. . . . The absence of fathers, caused by uprisings, wars, and exile, has forced mothers to take on most responsibilities, including the passing on of models of patriotism and democracy." These women, some of them on the left, spoke here as representatives of the nation and of the family, since "the most essential matter for a child is the presence of, and constant warm contact with, both parents."[8] These weapons of nation and family were carefully aimed; against them, the communist regime was most helpless.

Even as Freedom and Peace exploited national traditions, participants also sought to refashion the meaning of nationalism, questioning its limits and placing peace and human rights at its core. For this campaign, they turned to the figure of Otto Schimek. Schimek was an Austrian soldier in World War II who refused to participate in executions of civilians. At the age of 19, he was himself executed by order of his commanding officer and buried in the village of Machowa, near Tarnów. Just like all other WiP weapons (if that word is not inappropriate), Schimek as a symbol put the communists in a difficult position. After all, he had refused to shoot Poles: wasn't he then a national hero, even if he were a soldier in an enemy army? The problem for the communists was not that he was an Austrian, but that he had disobeyed explicit orders from his commander. To honor Schimek implied that morality and human rights should take precedence over the rules of a regime. This was precisely the position that Freedom and Peace advocated.

Leszek Budrewicz proposed, at that first gathering in the mountains, that participants visit Schimek's grave. The first trip in November 1985, for the forty-first anniversary of his death, ended with the detention of fourteen participants; six months later, some fifty marchers were detained as they attempted to mark Schimek's birthday. These twice-yearly visits were a peace-march version of Catholic pilgrimages to the holy shrine of Częstochowa. If a movement as varied as Freedom and Peace had a spiritual center, it was the grave at Machowa.* When participants in the Wrocław WiP circle created a Peace Ministry at St. Dorothy's Church in 1988, they naturally christened it with Schimek's name.

"RADIATORS" ACROSS THE BLOC

Building on the Schimek story, it was natural that Freedom and Peace should begin to pay attention to conscientious objectors (COs) in other

---

* There was an early rival for the role of WiP patron, proposed by the Kraków circle: Lech Zondek, an Australian Pole who died fighting the Soviets in Afghanistan.

countries. As a human rights movement, it was already attuned to an international network, and the refusal of military service lends itself easily to transnational protest. To the pacifist, the conflict between draftee and military establishment is everywhere the same. The instrumentalist knew that support of other COs undermined the regime's argument that WiP was in alliance with the Western powers. WiP publications began to write about *kaloryfery* from Greece, France, Norway, Yugoslavia, the Soviet Union, Czechoslovakia, and the United States and invited readers to send letters of protest to appropriate authorities. One case that Freedom and Peace championed was particularly close to home: that of Zsolt Keszthelyi of Hungary.

Zsolt Keszthelyi was precisely the kind of student who in Poland would be a participant in WiP. He began his studies in the provincial town of Szeged, where he had some contact with the Dialogue peace group there (see next chapter). He was interested in peace issues, but also in Hungarian national traditions: his father, a teacher of history, was a prominent intellectual figure in his small town of Baja. Dialogue's public stance impressed Keszthelyi; he felt it was important that "a civilian movement is doing anything at all." At the same time, he feared the "trap of all-out pacifism" and decided that Dialogue was not confrontational enough.

Keszthelyi's other interest was Poland: after moving to Budapest in 1983, he tried unsuccessfully to add Polish studies to his English and French major. He admired Poles' anticommunist opposition (which he followed on Radio Free Europe). A friend in Dialogue gave him Polish contacts: first in Paris, where he visited in 1983, and then in Gdańsk, where in 1984–85 he stayed with future WiP participants Gosia Tarasiewicz and Adam Jagusiak. They had gone to Budapest the previous summer and begun to meet Hungarian students interested in opposition. Their apartment in Sopot soon became a place where students from all over the bloc stayed and met each other. They talked about anarchism, about militarism, and about the tarnished traditions of Polish-Hungarian friendship.

In Budapest, Keszthelyi helped to start a samizdat journal, *Vox Humana*. The Vox Humana Circle was a semi-official student discussion group, like many in Budapest at the time. The discussions, and the journal, moved deeper into taboo topics of Hungarian national consciousness, such as 1956, or the plight of the Hungarian minority in Romania. Poland, peace issues, and Hungarian nationalism: a complex mixture that reminded Gosia Tarasiewicz of some of her colleagues in WiP. It was therefore not surprising that Keszthelyi would decide to refuse to serve. He knew just what to do. "I got the recipe," he says. "Write your ideas, write openly what you think, and send it to the military together with your [military registration] book. And this is what I did."

Keszthelyi's letter of February 18, 1987, explained his reasons in WiP language. "I don't have trust in the 'popular-democratic' army, which is subordinate to a government that was not chosen by a popular vote based upon competing political programs. I think that by this refusal, as in my fight for a free press, I can contribute to the creation of a society free from fear, in which the administration of public affairs will be based upon responsibility and individual conscience, and not upon uncritical faith, or on fear."[9] Arrest and sentencing were virtually certain; in April—at a trial attended by hundreds of Hungarian opposition figures—Keszthelyi received a three-year sentence.* The trial, in fact, became one of the most public events of Hungarian opposition to that date. Dissident writer Miklós Haraszti covered the trial for both *Beszélő* and *The New York Times.* At his appeal hearing, Keszthelyi connected his fate directly to the Polish cause: hearing about the bravery of Father Jerzy Popiełuszko had made him feel like a Pole, he declared; now, he was being sentenced by representatives of the same system that had murdered the Polish priest as well as the leader of 1956, Imre Nagy.

Even before the trial, WiP participants took up Keszthelyi's cause. In Warsaw they hung a banner on a downtown building in early April, demanding the release of Keszthelyi and a Czech prisoner, Petr Pospíchal (whose case we will encounter in the next chapter). Thousands of leaflets explaining their cases came fluttering down as well. That same month, WiP picketed the Hungarian Embassy in Warsaw. In September over eighty WiP participants staged a protest fast—the movement's third—in a church in Bydgoszcz. They were joined by Keszthelyi's fiancée, Olga Dioszegi, who was also a member of the Vox Humana Circle. The Hungarian CO became a focal point of the fast; the fasters sent letters of protest in his support, as well as in support of other prisoners of conscience identified by Amnesty International. Though this fast, like the others, was allowed to go on, its organizer, Sławomir Dutkiewicz, was shortly thereafter in prison himself.

There are many other CO cases—like that of Ivan Čečko in Slovenia (chapter 4) or Petr Obšil and Vladan Koči in Czechoslovakia (whose cases would be championed by WiP's counterpart in Prague, the Independent Peace Association). None of these came quite as close to WiP's orbit as Keszthelyi's story. And there was no other movement in Poland that could have responded as quickly to the news of a young Polonophile going to jail in imitation of its own campaigns. Solidarity itself never staged such a public campaign in defense of a foreign movement. Solidarity was in general slow to react to external events, though reporters on some underground papers covered foreign events well. Nor did WiP limit its ac-

---

* Later reduced to two and a half years on appeal. Unlike his counterparts in Poland, Keszthelyi served most of his sentence. He was released on January 10, 1989, having missed, as he says, the entire "time of ferment."

tions to a formal protest or petition. The banners and leaflets, the protest fast, and the frequent discussion of the Keszthelyi and Pospíchal cases also gave Freedom and Peace an international legitimacy that most other movements in Central Europe (except Solidarity and Charter 77) could not aspire to. In a society where information was limited and gatherings were restricted, it was difficult to act quickly. WiP could because it was at the same time decentralized, informal, and media-savvy.

ŻARNOBYL

One year and twelve days after Freedom and Peace's founding, a new opportunity galvanized the movement and allowed it to reach beyond students. This was the explosion of the nuclear reactor at Chernobyl, a remarkable event whose impact on the revolutions of 1989 is still underestimated. The April 26, 1986 catastrophe posed a unique challenge to a regime built upon control of information: full disclosure was preferable to censorship if the regime hoped to maintain order. Mikhail Gorbachev quickly realized this and offered full access to Western and Soviet reporters within a week. Polish media, too, began to relay the full story, but only after May 1 parades had been completed.

The everyday corruption and mismanagement of the communist economy, and the slow deterioration of the environment, could easily be covered up or put to the back of one's mind. Not so a radioactive cloud: Western scientists quickly established that the cloud originated from northern Ukraine, and satellite photos confirmed the damage. While Polish media at first followed the Soviet lead in saying little or nothing, millions of Poles heard detailed information (some of it quite exaggerated) on foreign broadcasts and began to panic.

Chernobyl represented an immediate threat to personal safety and the well-being of families, a threat quite evidently the result of communist social policy. Poles woke up abruptly to this unexpected danger. "Julia," a writer in the underground press, saw this change among Polish women, who, she admitted, had acquired a reputation for political passivity, even apathy. After Chernobyl, the pulse quickened:

> the voices of women could be heard in every shop and on every Polish street. They didn't sound like jokes, or like gossip. They sounded like a threat. Little groups of women—strangers to one another—in front of stores, on the sidewalks, all talking about one thing. This was more important than a possible shortage of butter.
>
> This time, there were no explanations in the [regime] press that "terrorists under Solidarity's banner" or "the cynicism of capitalist powers" threaten the

safety of our children. Communist propaganda, which has striven to terrify society with a vision of atomic extinction . . . has achieved a complete success. Finally everything is clear, and we know whom to blame.

One price hike after another came along, food supplies worsened, and the women in the lines kept silent. They had already learned how to make ends meet, though much was wanting. . . .

And only on that Wednesday [April 27] did they begin to speak. Not in the newspaper, not at rallies, but in line, they loudly spat out phrases no worse than those on [underground] leaflets: a boycott of the communist parade [May 1], and refusing to support a regime which takes care only of itself and its militia. We haven't heard such boiling among women since the start of martial law.

No longer do they say: "as long as things are calm." They have understood that here the welfare of their children is at stake. They don't really know much about politics; they don't understand what the regime in the PRL has to do with the reactor near Kyiv. But they know that the communist regime threatens their greatest treasure: the welfare of their children. We mustn't waste the strength which comes from the anger of these women.[10]

The women's fast just six weeks earlier positioned Freedom and Peace to make use of women's anger. By the time Julia's words appeared, women in Wrocław associated with WiP had already staged two protests, on May 2 and May 9. Both were staged during the afternoon rush hour, at one of the city's busiest intersections. The first one was silent: about twenty-five people sat on the ground, holding signs. About a thousand people watched, and some came to join the demonstrators. When the police detained only a few participants, the organizers planned another one for the following week. This time, following a plan apparently proposed by Budrewicz, all the participants were women. Anna Gawlik was one who marched, with her infant in a stroller. The women and children marched up and down the street, carrying signs demanding more information about the dangers to their health. They found that a march kept passersby at bay. These were Freedom and Peace's first forays onto the street, and marching techniques were as yet unmastered—or perhaps the punk hair and clothes of some of the protesters evoked negative reactions. But eventually a crowd gathered around them, and an intense discussion of Chernobyl ensued.[11] The police's reluctance to intervene—probably both because of the regime's evidently awkward position and to avoid arresting women—made an impression on participants and observers alike. Gawlik felt that she "hadn't risked much," but that, of course, was the point.

In Kraków, a group of women had been planning an ecological demonstration for Children's Day (June 1) for some time; the radioactive cloud gave the protest greater urgency and brought Freedom and Peace's involvement. The protest began with a noon Mass in the Marian church on

Kraków's Rynek.* Many of the women, styling themselves the "mothers of Kraków," came holding dried flowers to symbolize the death of nature. As they left the church, Freedom and Peace banners greeted them. Singing nationalist, religious, and Solidarity songs, the group marched through Kraków's old town to the castle on Wawel Hill. Just as in Wrocław, the police made no attempt to break up the demonstration.

Ecological issues had appeared in Freedom and Peace's "Ideological Statement," drawn up in the fall of 1985 by Budrewicz and the Krukow-skis. At the time, nuclear energy was not a pressing issue. In fact, the authors concluded that "Poland is not threatened by dynamic growth of nuclear power." The popularity and relative safety of the Chernobyl demonstrations made ecological disaster a WiP priority. Even as the move-ment's political focus, and international reputation, remained focused on peace and conscientious objection, its ecological demonstrations would gain it more notoriety at home. And just as in the case of COs, those in WiP who did not consider the environment to be their cause recognized its value in exposing regime hypocrisy.

In March 1985—even as the protesters fasted in Podkowa Leśna and Bieżanów—work began in earnest on Poland's first nuclear power plant, at Żarnowiec, northwest of Gdańsk. First to take note were the anar-chists of RSA. Not until after Chernobyl did an issue that had seemed rather distant to most Poles suddenly become very frightening. The Żar-nowiec marches attracted support from an even younger generation of high school students. Protests against what WiP quickly dubbed "Żarno-byl" soon took on a theatrical flavor. Darek Paczkowski, then just 16 and commuting to demonstrations from a town two hours away, recalls being stopped by police with friends from RSA and WiP on the way to one demonstration; the police questioned why everyone had mushroom cos-tumes in their backpacks and were reassured to hear they were for a school play.

WiP's clearest environmental victory came in Wrocław, with the clos-ing of a metallurgical plant at Siechnice, upriver from Poland's fourth-largest city. Leszek Budrewicz came across information about Siechnice and Wrocław's water supply in an official publication; he realized that "there was something here" for Freedom and Peace. Radek Gawlik (then a mathematics teacher and—in part because of his engineering studies in Czechoslovakia in the early 1980s—a committed environmentalist) pro-posed that WiP organize demonstrations to close Siechnice.

The first took place at noon, Sunday, January 10, 1987, on the Rynek in Wrocław's old town: "Snow, freezing temperatures, and in every door-way one or two policemen. Secret police everywhere. And a caravan of

---

* *Rynek* (also *rynok*, in Ukrainian) is usually the main square in a city, near the town hall.

police wagons circling Town Hall." Marek Niedziewicz (19 years old) had come out of curiosity to see what a "March against Siechnice" could be. Before he could approach the tiny group of demonstrators sitting in the snow with arms linked, he was hustled off to prison. In jail, Niedziewicz met the "intellectual elite" of WiP and joined in planning the next marches. Thus the police helped WiP to recruit.

Even this inauspicious beginning—there could be few observers of any protest during the worst cold snap in years—had unexpected effect. That same month, the provincial government announced that the plant would not be expanded and would close within five years. A year and a half later, with no change in sight, WiP initiated a series of monthly "Black Marches" to demand cleaner drinking water. The marches featured WiP's trademark, gently chiding slogan: "Come with Us! They Aren't Beating Today!" About a thousand marchers turned out for the first, in June 1988; the last one, in late November, saw nearly ten thousand on the streets of Wrocław. That same month, Prime Minister Mieczysław Rakowski somewhat deviously announced that in the spirit of economic reform he would close two plants: Siechnice and Solidarity's birthplace, the Lenin Shipyard in Gdańsk.

No other campaign better highlights the local power that environmental protest had than one that took place in the small town of Międzyrzecz, twenty-five miles south of Gorzów in western Poland. When half a dozen participants from WiP's Gorzów circle climbed onto the roof of a Międzyrzecz grocery store on Wednesday, September 2, 1987, and unfurled their banners protesting the building of a nuclear waste dump nearby, they were in uncharted waters. "Leave the bunkers to the bats!" they proclaimed. To store radioactive waste in a ten-kilometer system of bunkers built by the Germans just before World War II was dangerous, they argued, both to local residents and to wildlife—including several protected species of bat. For two hours that afternoon, they avoided arrest, throwing leaflets from their perch and urging onlookers to participate in a march on Sunday.

A successful protest in a provincial town—Międzyrzecz has less than twenty thousand residents—was qualitatively different from what WiP had attempted before. This was far from the usual centers of opposition power. Międzyrzecz has no important industry, and a large percentage of the population was then directly or indirectly employed by the military. It was, from a political standpoint (even today the region stalwartly supports the communist successor party in elections), an ideal place to store radioactive waste, much of which would come from a nuclear plant to be built in the area.

The road to protest involved both long-time activists and some new faces. That spring of 1987, Stanisław Bożek, a Międzyrzecz farmer active in the Solidarity underground and a leader of the Individual Farmers' Solidarity, had been invited by a friend to attend meetings of an ecological seminar—scientists, engineers, and activists—at the Dominican church in Poznań. There, Bożek heard for the first time details of the government's nuclear program, including the dump at Międzyrzecz. He organized a protest march for Sunday, May 3. Several hundred showed up, but at successive monthly marches, the numbers dwindled rapidly; Międzyrzecz began to return to its small-town isolation.

The Freedom and Peace activists could have expected to be ignored, or even denounced. "In this critical moment," wrote one Międzyrzecz participant, "the WiP boys from Gorzów helped us enormously. They started organizing pickets, which really emboldened people. . . . [Thanks to them] the issue took on momentum, and something in people began to crack."[12] (The "boys" included Barbara Hrybacz, whose role, as the one person from Gorzów's WiP with Warsaw contacts, was to get the story out to Western media. She stayed safely out of reach of police.) Marek Rusakiewicz explained WiP's intentions: "to show people that they could be strong . . . that was our goal. . . . We, as a small group, determined—very determined . . . would create an uproar." This, says Kazimierz Sokołowski (then 21), is what happened on September 2. "People saw that we are not afraid, [and] they stood up in our defense."

When the six finally climbed down to await the police, the crowd refused to allow them to be arrested. In consternation—for they feared that the expected arrest might frighten the less savvy residents of Międzyrzecz—they led an impromptu march to a nearby church, where Marek Rusakiewicz made a brief speech thanking the crowd for its support. Then they escaped their admirers through the church, coming out a side entrance to allow the police to arrest them with as few onlookers as possible.

Rather than rejecting this scruffy band of students (most with jail terms behind them), the people of Międzyrzecz adopted their methods—and won. Four days later, three to four thousand people marched through Międzyrzecz, a level of mobilization, proportionate to population, unmatched anywhere else in Poland between 1981 and 1989. Soon the townspeople were performing acts of civil disobedience previously unthinkable. When the authorities cracked down after the march with detentions, beatings, and large fines, Międzyrzecz responded with a protest fast in the church, and one more march even more massive than that in September. The result was the first significant defeat of communist government policy in Poland by a group of citizens since the fall of Solidarity in 1981. The town council (hitherto a rubber stamp) met during the hunger strike and voted unexpectedly against the dump; over the winter, Warsaw quietly shelved the idea. The bunkers are now a tourist attraction and a nature reserve.

In its environmental campaigns, Freedom and Peace discovered the truth of the maxim that all politics is local. Defense of imprisoned conscientious objectors—or of colleagues arrested for demonstrating—was a national affair, involving the entire WiP community speaking with one voice in a common protest. Environmental protests, in contrast, were generally local: as Wrocław organized the Siechnice protests, so Gdańsk coordinated the Żarnowiec campaign, and Gorzów and Poznań organized the protests at Międzyrzecz. Yet each of these causes received support—publicity in WiP papers or attendance at local demonstrations—from other circles. The broad acceptance of overarching goals and a generally common culture meant that, within limits, any member might propose an issue and count on local and even national support in carrying out protests.

THE BLUE AND THE GREEN

The great folly of the communist environment was the leaders' gigantomanic imagination. Reversing rivers, sculpting mountains, irrigating deserts, building large cities and industrial complexes overnight: communists could imagine these superhuman feats because they were in the service of humanity's progress. They could also believe that the consequences (like the consequences of storing radioactive waste in damp, crumbling bunkers) were irrelevant, or at least were outweighed by the enormous benefits that socialist planning would bring.

This is the only way to explain the enormous chutzpah of the project to dam the great Danube River between Hungary and Czechoslovakia. The slow-moving Danube is not suited for hydroelectric power, only for drinking water and transport. The two communist neighbors, with the assistance of Austrian government and business, thus planned to divert water into a fifteen-mile-long canal on the Czechoslovak side of the border, leading to a power plant on the Hungarian side at Nagymaros; a series of barrages on the Danube's main channel would complete the scheme. The project, a planners' dream for decades, was approved in the mid-1970s in the wake of the international oil crisis, which hit the Soviet Bloc especially hard.

Objections to the project were quite fundamental. The system of dams and canal would flood riverbank communities of historical and ethnographic significance. It would destroy valuable wetlands, habitats of endangered species, and prime farmland. It would threaten the supply of drinking water, mar the landscape, and limit the shipping industry. All this for a supply of approximately 3 percent of Hungary's energy needs, in a country where energy use far exceeded the ratio to GDP of capitalist countries, meaning that minimal conservation would have a comparable effect at virtually no cost.

This was the kind of issue—at once economic, health-related, and profoundly nationalist—that would, after Chernobyl, energize opposition throughout the bloc. Hungarian biologist János Vargha first outlined the dangers in a 1981 article, "Ever Farther from the Good." This article, and subsequent coverage in *Beszélő*, the samizdat journal of the democratic opposition, awakened interest but did not spur any protest. Opposition circles mustered a few petitions, but these were years when the opposition was virtually invisible to the Hungarian public, and signatures numbered in the dozens.

Then in January 1984 Vargha accepted an invitation to participate in a discussion at the Rakpart Club, a popular meeting point on the banks of the Danube. It was supposed to be a debate with proponents of the dam, but the other side didn't show up. Everyone in the room agreed about the problem; as they talked late into the night, they began to search for a solution. By the early morning, a new petition campaign, asking only for the project to be suspended while its impact was examined, took shape.

Such a campaign was difficult, though, without the structure that Polish, or even Czech, opposition relied upon. Judit Vasarhelyi recalls having to type the petition on carbons (a technology the Polish opposition had discarded at least five years earlier) while student volunteers waited with outstretched hands. And soon it turned out that there was no way to gather the forms, which had included no address to which they should be sent. Even so, more than ten thousand people signed the petition, giving their names, addresses, and occupations. Vasarhelyi, a sociologist, noticed that most of the signatures came from beyond Budapest, which had always supplied the lion's share of public dissent. Even more interesting, as she scanned the sheets that had come back from small towns and villages, one occupation surfaced over and over: teachers. Like no other issue since 1956, the Danube problem had awakened the small-town intelligentsia, the backbone of both traditional nationalism and regime stability.

When the authorities ignored the petition, its authors felt compelled to take the next step and form a group, the Danube Circle, in September. The eleven founders—including both Vargha and Vasarhelyi—now created their own samizdat and looked for new ways to spread the word and mobilize discontent with the Nagymaros project.

They found a perfect opportunity when the communist leaders announced a limited experiment with multicandidate elections to Parliament in 1985. Nomination meetings were highly orchestrated and tightly controlled; for example, the majority of the participants might be party members from a nearby factory, bused in for the purpose. For Vasarhelyi, standing up (in the back of the hall) at such a meeting, to nominate ichthyologist János Tóth, was far more risky than the petitions. While the latter circulated from hand to hand along extended networks of family and friends, the meeting was full of utter strangers, disposed to be hostile, hearing such opposition for the first time. But in this case, the strategy was effective. Toth was excluded (though he won a seat from another district), but the regime's favored candidate also lost, as a straw candidate began giving fiery speeches on the dam issue and was elected, to eventually join eight other Danube Circle–supported members of Parliament in voting against the dam.

There were setbacks, too. Flush with the success of a leaflet campaign in the fall of 1985, the more radical wing of the Circle—which came to be known as the "Blues"—organized a "walk along the Danube" for February 1986, and invited Austrian greens to join them. But even as a small crowd gathered on Batthyány Square, pressure from city authorities moved organizers to call off the event. It would be more than two years before opposition to the dam again went public.

The Danube Circle, even before the Chernobyl accident galvanized Freedom and Peace, had located a sensitive problem with enormous potential for mass discontent. The obstacle to motivating those ten thousand who had signed the 1984 petition, and the tens of thousands more who learned the story since, was not state repression alone. Hungary was definitely not Czechoslovakia, nor even Poland, in this respect. The problem rather was the enervating complacency that suffused Hungarian society by the 1980s. Within the formulae of intellectual opposition, there was probably no way to remedy this. Not until 1988 would society awaken and mobilize around the Danube issue and others, thanks to the new oppositional forces emerging that year. It would then be possible to say that, more than anywhere else in Central Europe, environmental opposition contributed directly to the downfall of Hungarian communism.

BRATISLAVA SPEAKS UP

The emergence of environmental protest everywhere helped transform anticommunist dissent from an intellectual pursuit into focused contestation. Though the Chernobyl cloud never really reached Czechoslovakia, the accident in neighboring Ukraine jolted citizens as it did in Poland. While the calculus of risk was rather different, ordinary citizens began to speak up on environmental problems outside of official channels. As Brno environmentalist Yvonna Gailly explained to me, residents of communist Czechoslovakia could easily imagine the fantastic mess that could spawn such a disaster like Chernobyl, because they had already lived a nightmare like it every day.

The year and a half after Chernobyl saw a proliferation of local initiatives to resist the worst excesses of developed socialism, such as a Grand Prix auto race through fragile Moravian forests, the planned destruction of a well-known castle at Jezeří, the construction of a giant mountaintop ski resort, or the erection of a huge statue (at the expense of trees) in Brno's Lužanky Park. Each of these, and others like them, brought small numbers of concerned citizens together. Though they might first attempt to work through official channels and seek support for their cause, the indifference of the regime would finally lead them to a more reliable source of information and support: samizdat and the opposition.

Environmental causes were not necessarily anticommunist; for many, though, they were a first step in precisely that direction. In the northern Bohemian industrial town of Chomutov, a handful of young people and a few local Chartists had attempted in 1985 to organize a legal environmental group; they were threatened with long prison sentences if they did not desist. Two years later they tried again, this time circulating a petition protesting the region's air quality. They collected 162 signatures, quite a few for a small provincial town. Not only Chernobyl, but the worsening economy worked in their favor: "Citizens who had come to the region with a vision of better financial and social conditions were suddenly faced," writes historian Miroslav Vaněk, "with the prospect of living in what was then the most devastated area of Czechoslovakia, without the advantages which had still been evident in the first half of the 1980s." In the spring of 1987, some three hundred residents signed a letter inviting Prime Minister Ladislav Adamec to come experience the air of Chomutov for himself.[13]

On the other side of the Czech lands, in Opava, Jaromir Piskoř was reading Polish samizdat and Czech émigré literature, which filtered not through Prague (where Piskoř occasionally traveled to participate in underground seminars), but across the nearby border at Cieszyń/Český Těsín and the small Polish minority on the Czech side. In May 1987 Piskoř founded *Against Traffic* (*Protějši chodník*—literally "The Sidewalk in the Opposite Direction"), one of the first samizdat titles outside Prague, Brno, or Bratislava, and the first to focus on environmental problems. The environmentalism owed a lot to what Piskoř learned from the Poles, particularly Janusz Okrzesik, a WiP participant and journalism student from Kraków. It was Okrzesik who alerted Piskoř to the danger posed by a giant coking plant to be built at Stonava, not far from Opava. Not only was it cynically placed so as to blow all the emissions across the border to Poland, but it was being constructed in a mining town, where underground tunnels could cause it to collapse, wreaking horrific local damage.

If a giant factory built to crash down on the city is not impetus for protest, then nothing is, surely. Somewhat belatedly, the Czech opposition tried to develop an environmental strategy. Celebrating its tenth anniversary in January 1987, Charter 77 issued one of its most important statements: "A Word to Our Fellow Citizens." One Chartist historian-member called this a landmark in the Charter's history, as it signaled new strategies as well as a new activist tone in Czech opposition.[14] Gorbachev, interestingly enough, did not receive any attention at this key juncture; instead, the Charter implored Czechs and Slovaks: "Let's stop waiting to see what others do, and do something ourselves! Let's wake up from our apathy, avoid the feeling of frustration, and overcome our fear!" The appeal outlined ways to overcome that apathy and create freedom. Alongside the predictable Havelian echoes (speak the truth, and demand respect for human rights), there was also this: "We can all create, in various places, informal political fora," where views could be exchanged freely. One area for discussion should be the environment: "We all know how catastrophic is the ecological situation in our country. Why do we speak about it only in private?"[15]

For the Czechs, this was indeed a departure. Words, no matter how brilliant, should be matched by public action. Ivan Dejmal, an original signer of Charter 77, helped to organize the Charter's first forum, a semipublic exchange of views and ideas on the topic of Czechoslovakia's environmental nightmare, in June 1987. Charter 77 had just issued its first major statement on the environment, "So That One Could Breathe." The forum brought together more than fifty Chartists and others who wanted to answer Charter's tenth-anniversary call to speak up in public about the ecological hardships everyone faced. Those at the forum spoke of "assisting in the creation of new initiatives . . . and generally stimulating and activating independent movements."[16]

Dejmal and a small group of other Chartists founded *Ekologický bulletin* to pursue the problem. In an essay in the third issue, Dejmal opened a debate that exposed the problems and frustrations of Czech opposition. "Begin, begin, but how?" he asked. He knew what should be avoided in a green movement: the ideological certainties he witnessed among the students of 1968. Ecology, he argued, was not an objective science, and it would not lead anyone to a "radiant future." Nor did it make sense simply to record and condemn crimes, like an ecological counterpart to the human-rights group VONS, because the problem was also one of societal behavior and attitudes. Spreading ecological awareness would allow people to live in a way that seemed right to them. This is standard stuff for green movements in the 1980s, perhaps, but Dejmal wanted to find a niche for ecology within the Chartist tradition. Evoking Václav Havel, he concluded that "every effort to live in truth is, in the end, an ecological endeavor."[17]

To someone in the younger generation like Pavel Křivka, this was all just "dry academic discourse." Křivka had himself been sentenced, in 1985, to three years in prison for criticizing the environmental situation in Czechoslovakia. While the older generations hoped to change society or the land, Křivka simply wanted to change the regime: "Is the idea to shout, to roar, to complain, to defend, to write, and so on, against the unreal arrogance of the technocrats and their industrial civilization over nature, or not?" Praising the campaign against the proposed ski resort, Křivka proclaimed his support for any public action at all. "But where," he demanded, "do we have any other campaigns?"[18]

This discussion of form was quite different from that in Poland. There, to act was obvious; the question was only what the content should be. But Czech dissidents lacked a clear frame for their protests. Despite its relative isolation from society, Charter 77 was an unquestioned authority in defense of human rights—with its sister movement VONS, the Committee for the Defense of the Unjustly Persecuted—and dignity. Like an activist judge moving beyond a strict reading of the constitution to fashion new rights, the Charter gradually expanded its field of interests, from human rights to the environment and economic reform. Charter 77 did not itself fill the new space for decentralized, issue-oriented political opposition. Rather, having framed the questions, it watched as others (some within Charter, others firmly outside it) made that move and created new types of opposition.

Only after the demonstrations of the fall and winter of 1988–89 would there be a model that the Prague environmentalists could borrow. Meanwhile, though, the Greens in Slovakia were having much more success.

Of the fourteen hundred or so signatories of Charter 77 by the spring of 1989, barely thirty were from Slovakia. But Ján Budaj, one of Bratislava's best-known activists of the time, insists this was only an indication that Slovak political energies were directed elsewhere. If someone active in the underground church, or an avant-garde artist, or an independent ecologist, were to sign the Charter (or any other petition before 1988), this might compromise his or her primary cause. In Prague, one's signature on a petition could work in the opposite way, offering publicity, and thus safety. Far from the networks of the Czech capital, the risks—to one's cause as much as to one's person—were greater.

Still, Slovakia's opposition was limited not by diversity, but isolation: the greens, the artists, the Church, and the Chartist intellectuals moved in different circles. "We might have coffee together if we met on the street," says Budaj, "but that was it." Prague and the Chartist tradition of diversity was far away from Bratislava.

Much closer were Budapest—just down the river—and Poland; Kraków was just over the mountains, and the language is close enough to be easily understood by any Slovak. Patterns of protest that emerged in

1987–88 would owe more to Polish models than to Czech opposition. Religious activists were not the only Slovak dissidents visiting Poland. In the late 1970s—after Čarnogurský and Mikloško had already gotten to know Poland—Budaj, himself a liberal Catholic, made the trip for the first time. He visited frequently in the years 1979–81, even attending Solidarity's national congress, until his passport was confiscated just before martial law. On his last trip, Budaj and a Bratislava colleague were the cause of a four-hour delay on the border as guards literally took the train apart until they found the Polish samizdat hidden behind wall paneling in another compartment. "I became," he says, "a political polonophile."

In practice, this meant thinking about society more than about the state, in closer contact with the tiny political opposition around Milan Šimečka and Miroslav Kusý. It also meant that while Budaj continued to go on yearly pilgrimages, for example, to the Catholic shrine at Levoča, he came to see them as political manifestations as much as they were spiritual. Budaj hoped to encourage interaction among the various segments of independent thought in Bratislava. With roots in the artist community, he was one of the few individuals who knew them all. In 1987 he founded the journal *Kontakt,* the first truly political samizdat in Slovakia. The name referred to Budaj's aim to unite the independent communities.

The one community in Slovakia that most approached Budaj's idea of a pluralist, Polish-style politics was the greens. A state-run ecological movement was a key player in Czechoslovakia's normalization. Groups like Brontosaurus in the Czech lands or the Slovak Strom Života (Tree of Life) encouraged "recreational conservation,"[19] a nonconfrontational alternative for the would-be activist. Toward the very end of the communist era, these groups tried to evolve from pressure vents to pressure groups, raising cautious questions about environmental policy. The Slovak Union of Protectors of Nature and the Land (SZOPK) went the farthest, almost accidentally becoming the focal point for opposition and a core of Slovakia's nascent civil society.

Budaj joined Bratislava's SZOPK chapter in 1981 and immediately joined a campaign to rescue two historical cemeteries that the city planned to bulldoze and turn into a park. This was the kind of concrete action Budaj felt was essential; though the campaign was unsuccessful, SZOPK members clearly had the energy to confront the authorities on even bigger stages.

Maria Filková became the secretary of Bratislava's SZOPK in 1987. A passionate environmentalist with a real organizing talent, she recognized that environmental issues were best presented in seemingly apolitical terms. In 1985–86, for example, she successfully mobilized the first graders of the Mudroňova School to save a five-hundred-year-old elm, slated for destruction by a government official who wanted to build a summer house.

A model for this kind of opposition lay close to hand: the Danube Circle in Budapest. One of SZOPK's first brushes with the police had been due to a daringly critical article on the Gabčikovo-Nagymaros Dam published in 1981. Though Slovak environmentalists in the 1980s never became as vocal in opposition to the dam as their Hungarian colleagues, they found other powerful causes. Bratislava had suffered more under the policies of normalization than had any other large city in Czechoslovakia. Air and water quality had declined dramatically, and whole sections of the historic city center had been torn down for road projects or unsightly new buildings. Budaj, Filková, and a collective of scientists, journalists, and architects began to compile data on the multiple threats to the life of the city. When they failed to attract the attention of city officials, they turned, fatefully, to the gray zone of quasi-samizdat.

The result was *Bratislava/nahlas*—literally "Bratislava Aloud," but implying also a link to Gorbachev's glasnost—a sixty-two-page booklet that electrified Slovakia. The editorial collective bypassed their censor by publishing it as an appendix to meeting minutes and ostensibly distributing only a thousand copies for internal use only. In reality, four thousand copies were made; this was samizdat masquerading as a legal publication.

Bratislava/nahlas was much more than a litany of ecological disasters. The first third of the booklet documented poor air and water quality, considered the noise levels caused by traffic, and warned of the hazards of siting a nuclear reactor near the city. The authors then turned to the state of urban planning, industry and industrial safety, transportation, and housing. To each case study, they appended a list of concrete suggestions. And while all the above problems might be categorized—in the euphemistic language of normalization—as the growing pains of developing socialism, other topics were more politically sensitive. *Bratislava/nahlas* exposed the decrepit social infrastructure of the city: the lack of theaters, of shops and restaurants, of parks and playgrounds, and of health clinics. It was a portrait of a city neglected even by comparison with the rest of the country, reduced to decidedly un-European levels of civilization. And the conclusion of the report left no doubt that the fault lay with the communist bureaucracy and its tight hold on information. Though *Bratislava/nahlas* steered away from any discussion of politics, it was perhaps the most comprehensive condemnation of developed socialism published anywhere in Central Europe.

The hundreds of recommendations contained in *Bratislava/nahlas* were a blueprint for new popular activism. Coupons at the end of the book asked for readers to respond; thousands from all over Slovakia did so over the next six months. As a document, *Bratislava/nahlas* became in effect, says Budaj, the Slovak Charter 77. It filled the space in Slovak society that the Charter had failed to fill, and it became a touchstone for opposition for the next two years. It can hardly be a coincidence that just a few months after the sensation caused by the report's release, the largest, most successful petition campaign swept across Czechoslovakia: the Navratil petition, described in chapter 1. *Bratislava/nahlas* was more than just a document; it was a record of real audacity. Bratislava had indeed spoken up.

"I'D RATHER LIVE"

The tactics that worked for Freedom and Peace were clearly impossible in countries without the Poles' traditions of rebellion. Precisely targeted to local concerns and fears, WiP campaigns mobilized Poles against the communist regime. The risk of punishment had come to seem smaller, in the case of environmental campaigns, than the risk of not doing anything and facing extinction. But even within Poland, WiP was an élite, popular among urban students but too daring for those who lived in the normalized world of small towns and villages.

Radek Gawlik of Wrocław's WiP thought there might be a way to reach the provinces. He looked to Wolę Być, a green youth movement started in 1984. For most in WiP, Wolę Być raised serious doubts. It was sponsored by *Na przełaj* (Cross-country), the weekly magazine of the state-sponsored scouting organization. The magazine and the movement (as well as a popular radio show also sponsored by the scouts) were, they considered, the most pernicious of the vents crafted by the regime to lure people away from opposition. They were aimed at the youngest generation, those with no personal memory of Solidarity, whose support was essential if Polish opposition would continue on. This ersatz activism could be a treacherous front in the battle between regime and opposition for the next generation.

Gawlik disagreed. In January 1987, shortly after he had been fined fifty thousand zlotys for his role in the first Siechnice march, he wrote a letter to Wolę Być participants that was published in *Na przełaj*. He offered the movement his expertise on green matters but did not mention his connection with Freedom and Peace (information that the censor would not, of course, have allowed).

Wolę Być can be translated as "I'd rather live," or, more precisely, "I prefer to be." Ewa Charkiewicz, a journalist at *Na przełaj*, published an appeal in a July 1984 issue devoted entirely to environmental problems in Poland and elsewhere. She wrote that modern society had come to believe in technology as a savior, and in consumption as the goal of life. But, she argued, "to be" rather than "to have" was the secret of preserving human dignity. Contact between people on equal terms, and between humans and nature, would realize this ideal. Charkiewicz offered no concrete plans; in fact, neither she nor the magazine's editorial board appeared to expect a social movement. "We want to be a mailbox for the exchange of your ideas and experiences. We want to write about the people and the problems that fit into our formula, and to seek out allies for the idea of Wolę Być. We want to promise the enthusiasts of our idea that we will come to a gathering during this vacation, and then to your communities and schools."[20]

The name, and Charkiewicz's letter, suggest a certain passivity, a focus on self-awareness seemingly at odds with activism, let alone opposition. Participants, who called themselves "sympathizers," interpreted the phrase differently. To "prefer" or to "want" restored their individual initiative, they argued: they preferred to live, to act, to help, to decide about their own lives. In letters to the editors, high school students across the country exclaimed that they had read the appeal "with burning cheeks" and "grabbed a pen" to respond, because "there has never been anything like this."[21] What may have been intended as a passive vent these writers interpreted as a chance for action, and they threw themselves into the pursuit of as yet undefined goals. By late 1987 there were some thousand sympathizers, many in local circles that met regularly on their own.

To their elders who formed Freedom and Peace the following spring, or who were active in the underground, the idea that Wolę Być was something new and daring would have seemed absurd. But out in the provinces, beyond the university strongholds of youth opposition, in the small and medium-sized towns that might not even boast a politically vocal priest, there was nothing like Wolę Być. There were no student ministries or cultural clubs where people would gather informally. The choice was stark: the occasional high school dance, or the rigors of membership in the Union of Socialist Polish Youth or the Polish Scouting Union.

Thus was life in Kowary, an industrial town of some ten thousand people, south of Jelenia Góra in extreme southwestern Poland. Kasia Gierełło grew up there and went to a high school where even an independent student council was impossible to imagine. Kasia joined the scouts "to do something" and read Na przełaj regularly. She was fifteen when she saw the Wolę Być appeal; she says the pictures of dying forests in the Karkonosze Mountains—her mountains, near Kowary—"pissed me off," so she wrote to the address provided. The editors wrote back: Wolę Być would be gathering soon in Kowary, and would she help organize?

The first gathering—jamboree (zlot), in scouting parlance—was on the Baltic coast in the summer of 1985. The forty participants, chosen by lottery, ranged in age from 12 to 24; none was from a university town except for a few from Warsaw. The high point of the camp was a visit to the Żarnowiec building site. Here were all the possibilities and limitations of

Wolę Być in operation: On the one hand, participants could see more of the plant than Freedom and Peace protesters ever could. They could even talk with officials at the site and present their arguments against nuclear power. On the other hand, though, they were there by official permission, as part of what the regime presumably intended to be a charade. It was too easy for the officials to nod politely and dismiss these children.

Like the first gathering, the Kowary camp took place alongside an official scouting jamboree. Among hundreds of scouts, with their morning drills, marches, and reveilles, were forty "Wolębyćki." Kasia Gierełło and her friends pursued ecological protests, including a failed attempt to visit Celwiskoza, one of the most polluting plants in Poland. But they also tried at every gathering to articulate a different model of community, one that was strikingly similar to the style of WiP. They ignored regimen, dressed as they pleased, and took their impromptu protests—holding signs like "I'd Rather Be—and You?" or campaigning for alternative transportation—to the streets of the town. In April 1986 Wolę Być representatives even staged the first Chernobyl march, while returning from a classic normalizing event, a Youth Forum sponsored by PRON; like Freedom and Peace, they used the slogan "Żarnobyl."[22]

Much as others in their generation kept distant from the "adult opposition" while expecting that opposition's support, so Wolę Być participants used the scouts as a foil, without whom their efforts to articulate opposition might have gone unnoticed. At the same time, Wolę Być was *not,* participants believed, like the mainstream opposition, but better. "We didn't shout 'away with factories,'" one participant explained, "but we tried to provoke in people a positive reflection on their behavior and their relationship with the environment."[23] Part of the fun was precisely in subverting official contacts with the regime: the tough questions at Żarnowiec; refusing to accept then Minister of Youth (now President) Aleksander Kwaśniewski's offer of funding (Kasia Gierełło was particularly offended by the minister's arrival at the camp by helicopter); using official status to get out of minor scrapes with the police; or even the opportunity to deliver a speech before General Wojciech Jaruzelski as a representative of Polish youth.* In each of these encounters, there was a small chance to destabilize the authorities. Perhaps, they hoped, such an approach would be more effective too. Many in Poland apparently thought so: by 1987, *Na przełaj* was receiving letters begging Wolę Być to take action on various local issues.[24]

But it is also difficult to separate Wolę Być from the opposition. To return to Radek Gawlik: he took a break from the Siechnice protests to at-

---

* The staff of *Na przełaj,* which always participated in the camps, trod this line in a different way. For example, Dariusz Szymczycha graduated from the magazine to become editor-in-chief of *Trybuna,* successor to the communist daily *Trybuna ludu.*

tend the movement's fourth national gathering, in Gdańsk, in February 1987. That he was at least ten years older than most of the participants gave him an air of authority. Yet he was also one of them and did not hide his role in a movement actively persecuted by the communist regime. After the camp, he urged participants (in another letter published in *Na przełaj*) to form regional circles and pursue concrete goals, while not neglecting national-scale problems. His salutation was jocular, but also deeply subversive: "Greens of the world, unite!"[25]

In the city of Oświęcim, near Kraków, Kasia Terlecka found that Wolę Być and Freedom and Peace were inseparable parts of the same environment. Wolę Być was her entry point into a world of free thinkers. A poster surreptitiously hung in her school announced a meeting of "all those who give a shit." Soon, Kasia Terlecka was traveling all over Poland, meeting deep ecologists and conscientious objectors, to Wolę Być camps, peace pilgrimages, and tours of ecological disasters. In 1989–90 she participated in demonstrations and a hunger strike against Żarnowiec. Wolę Być had recruited her into at least the fringes of the opposition.

The story is a little more complicated than this neat tale of political awakening suggests. For Kasia Terlecka was also the one who gave the speech before Jaruzelski and then found her earnest appeal to movement themes of peace, tolerance, and respect twisted around by the state news agency. And not too long after, the secret police found Freedom and Peace leaflets in Terlecka's dorm room, interrogated her, and forced this teenager to sign a *lojalka*, a promise to disengage from activism and inform on her friends. The line between opposition and cooperation, between change of oneself and political change, was not one the communists were prepared to honor.[26]

The merry parades or "happenings" in the towns where Wolę Być met twice yearly; the bulletin boards on green and peace issues hung in small-town high schools (often immediately torn down by school officials); the campaigns for bicycle transportation, for live Christmas trees, or against a school built with hazardous materials: all this does not add up to an op position movement in the way Freedom and Peace participants would understand it. Yet Wolę Być was in fact a "Freedom and Peace" for those who lived in Oświęcim and Kowary, or who were only 16, or perhaps sought a middle ground between purely contemplative church groups and the public confrontations that WiP offered.

Though it actually took shape slightly earlier, Wolę Być must be understood in the context of Freedom and Peace. The last generation to reach young adulthood before 1989 was also politicized, even where it was out of the opposition's reach. The gravitational pull of Freedom and Peace, or more generally of the countercultural world in which WiP played a central role, proved greater than that of normalization.

In the Future Tense

In every single campaign I have discussed here, Freedom and Peace was successful. The military oath was changed in June 1988; one month later, the Polish parliament amended the law on universal military service and let out WiP's last political prisoners—one of whom, Sławomir Dutkiewicz, had been on a hunger strike for nearly nine months. The Żarnowiec reactor and the factory at Siechnice were scrapped, and plans for other nuclear reactors were shelved, as was the radioactive waste dump at Międzyrzecz. All of these decisions were made, or at least begun, during communist rule. What could the regime have gained from such concessions? Very little, indeed. The retreat on each of these issues cost the regime some dignity—and money, in the case of closed plants. No less a figure than Jerzy Urban, as government spokesman the author of much anti-WiP counterpropaganda, acknowledged to me in a 1997 interview that WiP itself, not some internal liberalization of party or army, was responsible for its key victories.

On a much smaller scale, the student or employees' councils had already demonstrated that one could win concessions from the regime in one's school or workplace. No other movement, however, won a nationwide victory before those won by Freedom and Peace. More surprisingly, they won not through compromise, but confrontation. In fact, their protest responded to what they saw as *increased* repression—or repression on new fronts—and not to relaxed controls. They advanced counter to the regime, moving not deeper into the underground, but onto the surface. The amnesties of political prisoners and other "liberal" actions on the part of the communists only encouraged WiP to intensify its activity. For much of the opposition, amnesty was not an opportunity, but a difficult challenge. Groups like WiP, already operating in the open, were better able to respond than Solidarity leadership. They were a step ahead of the regime, not reacting to it.

Though as irreproachably anticommunist as was Solidarity, Freedom and Peace's attitude toward state power also set it apart. As practitioners of nonviolence—and also, perhaps, aware that the police were unimportant in the face of higher goals—WiP participants did not call the police "Gestapo" or even resist arrest. Years later a secret police captain told "Jacob" Jankowski that WiP had been different from those groups that screamed at their jailers and threatened revenge. Until the end, it was common enough for a demonstration to end with police beatings, and detentions were a matter of course. WiP participants, however, generally reported more polite treatment—and even cooperation or understanding—from the police. At the same time, they also held the police accountable:

in separate cases in 1986 and 1987, Agata Michałek and Jan Maria Rokita of Kraków each won cases against the police for unlawful mistreatment. This strange relationship (which would reach a new stage with Orange Alternative in 1987–88) helped to lessen one of the gulfs that divided Polish society.

Freedom and Peace found the chinks in the armor and exploited issues that were sensitive to the regime and in which—in contrast to, say, democratic elections—victory was conceivable. Looking ahead, one can see that these first victories, though born of confrontation, inched Poland closer to the historic compromise of 1989. Before the communists could decide they could sit at a table with longtime adversaries like Kuroń or Michnik, they would first discover that what the radicals on the streets were demanding was not so impossible to grant.

Even as victory was achieved, the tensions between ideals and instruments began to tear WiP apart. In April 1988 a heated discussion began on the pages of *Dezerter,* WiP's bi-weekly bulletin. While some hoped to transform Freedom and Peace into an organization with a recognized hierarchy, in the end two other points of view prevailed and determined the direction WiP participants would take over the next decade. Some argued that, as the editors of *Dezerter* put it, "the subjectivity of the Movement's participants is the highest value. . . . The differences in world views of participants from many different circles, ranging from anarchists through socialists, hippies, punks, Catholic youth, Buddhists to those with their origins in the KPN, are of value in and of themselves; they teach tolerance and cooperation in actions directed toward precisely defined goals."[27]

Jacek Czaputowicz, informally the movement's spokesman, articulated another position at a protest fast staged in Wrocław in May: "A stage in our activity is coming to an end. WiP's goals are slowly becoming worn out. . . . I am afraid that when the central point that integrated WiP—the problem of refusing the army, and of those who went to jail—disappears, then will the political, ideological, and personal differences not cause WiP to fly apart?" In such a situation, added Leszek Budrewicz, "I don't consider myself a man who has walked away; I simply believe that Solidarity is our common responsibility."[28]

Those who advocated the first option would engage in new campaigns—and old ones like Żarnowiec and the defense of conscientious objectors' rights—under the name of WiP. They would attract, after 1989, a new generation of idealists, some of whom still claim today to represent Freedom and Peace. Those who favored the second path turned back to Solidarity and, after 1989, took their places in parliament, city councils, and government ministries. Most felt that in some way their careers continued to be shaped by the experience of WiP, but the WiP of 1985–88 had surely ceased to exist.

Freedom and Peace's greatest contribution was to the nature of anti-communist opposition in the last years of the Soviet Bloc. There were movements more radical, and there were movements with more comprehensive proposals, but none as active. WiP entertained Poland with an impressive number of demonstrations, sit-ins, "scaffold-ins" (when participants chained themselves to the scaffolding around buildings under renovation), marches, protest fasts, leafletings, seminars, happenings, and conferences. And all of this was produced—mostly in the space of barely two years—by no more than a hundred or so core activists.

Though few in Solidarity would say so openly, a letter from Władysław Frasyniuk to WiP upon his final release from jail in 1986 captures what many in the union knew: the Polish opposition needed Freedom and Peace. "When I heard of 'WiP,' I understood that this means 'Very Important Persons.' And it turned out to be so. This turns out to be the most effective way to organize and act, and the most spectacular as well. Every [activist], sitting in prison, dreams that when he gets out of jail he will find a new initiative, a new group of fighters with a program, with resources, and with a proposal for the future."[29] Leszek Budrewicz would soon join Frasyniuk's Regional Executive Committee of Solidarity. He and many others brought to Solidarity something of the WiP style and strategy: openness, confrontation, and ideological flexibility. Indeed, the atmosphere and language of opposition in Poland from then on would owe a great deal to Freedom and Peace. And as WiP influenced the younger Polish generation, so too its influence spread across borders into the rest of Central Europe. The new politics of 1987–88 was created in WiP's shadow.

Chapter Three

AS IF IN EUROPE: THE INTERNATIONAL WORLD
OF PEACE AND HUMAN RIGHTS

Reticence and Revolutionary Tourism

LYNNE Jones had never been to Central Europe—in fact, she had never really thought of herself as a "European." She was a well-known figure in the British antinuclear movement, as a prominent participant of the Greenham Common protests, a women's peace camp set up outside a nuclear missile site in Britain in 1981, which used civil disobedience methods to try to block missile deployment. This protest was very much a part of the main thrust of British peace activism, focusing on Britain's relationship to NATO and the Cold War.

Jones's focus began to change thanks to the END Appeal. European Nuclear Disarmament, founded in April 1980, was a breakthrough in Western peace activism, and also in the way the British saw Europe. The founding document was the work of eminent historian and famed antinuclear activist E. P. Thompson. Reacting against nationally focused, unilateralist traditions, Thompson implored: "We must commence to act as if a united, neutral, and pacific Europe already exists. We must learn to be loyal, not to 'East' or 'West,' but to each other, and we must disregard the prohibitions and limitations imposed by any national state."[1]

The END Appeal struck at a Cold War mentality that gripped peace activists, accustomed to thinking of the East as different from (and perhaps better than) the West, as much as it did politicians. Reading the appeal, Jones began to think about her commitment to nonviolent protest in a new light. When, in the summer of 1981, another END participant wondered aloud why no one was trying to make direct contact with Solidarity, Jones made an abrupt decision to hop across the Channel and take the train to Warsaw. She would eventually become one of Freedom and Peace's closest contacts in Britain.

To the average politically conscious American in the late Cold War, those who resisted communism in Central Europe were heroes. The workers and intellectuals of Solidarity, the lonely Soviet *refuseniks,* writers in exile like Milan Kundera all somehow represented the best of the American spirit. They longed for freedom, and they spoke without fear. In a country where strongly partisan political convictions are no longer voiced in polite company, it didn't matter that much whether these people were "right" or "left." They were an antidote to post-Watergate cynicism. How could one not celebrate their struggles and welcome their message with open arms?

Western Europeans saw their neighbors differently. While there were those who traveled to Central Europe, and supported dissidents, all throughout the communist era, the general attitude seemed to be, in the words of Václav Havel, "reticence . . . if not outright distrust and uneasiness."[2]

One reason for the Western Europeans' reticence was that Central Europe was closer. If an uprising in Poland thrilled the American, the West European could not help but think about where the invading Soviet tanks might stop, and whether Europe would again be a battleground. Getting along with the Soviets was not just the luxury of a superpower, but a necessity.

A second difference between Europe and the United States is that partisan distinctions still count for a lot in Europe. One's newspaper, trade union, and even the schools one's children attend might differ according to one's party affiliation. So looking east, it mattered whether a dissident was on the right or the left. The distinctions had determined Europe's fate in World War II, when right and left had now and again been in deadly struggle. The bravery of anticommunist opposition was not a sufficient reason to admire it, until one was sure of its ultimate goals.

This reticence was thus strongest on the left. Over the years, activists in groups like Britain's Campaign for Nuclear Disarmament (CND) or (more recently) the German Green Party developed working relationships with official peace organizations in the Soviet Bloc. Insofar as they paid any attention to Central Europe, they were comfortable with the language of Central European reformist communists. To socialists especially, the communist experiment offered hope that the egregious injustices of capitalism could be conquered. It was also clear to them that the arms merchants of developed capitalism most threatened the future of humanity, though of course Soviet nuclear weapons were no less deadly. Thus, they built working relationships with the Soviet Peace Committee and analogous groups in Central Europe, where they found people who also professed dedication to both peace and socialism.

The agenda of the opponents of Central European communism, by contrast, seemed suspicious—not least because they reaped praise from the likes of Ronald Reagan or Margaret Thatcher. In speaking out against the evils that their regimes had perpetrated in their stalinist pasts, Central European activists sounded as if they were opposed to the very idea of socialism (as many were). If so, this smelled, to the Western left, like a return to the semi-authoritarian nationalist regimes of prewar Central Europe. The few well-known socialist dissidents in each country could of course be allies. But even a casual glimpse of Solidarity's religious or nationalist rhetoric, or the antimodernist polemics in Milan Kundera's novels, made the antidemocratic past seem alarmingly close. So West European socialists kept their distance.

Oddly enough, a similar reticence marked the Central Europeans. In the essay quoted above, Havel was responding—by letter, because he was prevented from doing so in person—to an invitation to attend an END conference in Amsterdam in 1985. While Havel had no reason to love the communists, he was not sure that Western peace movements were his allies, either. He entitled his essay "Anatomy of a Reticence"—expressing not enmity, or even distrust, but a curiosity mixed with doubt.

Though today leaders in the region talk about their countries' "return to Europe," as oppositionists they kept Europe at arms' length. Solidarity, for example, hesitated to establish representatives in Western Europe. Since their fight was for a free Poland, Polish unionists reasoned, press releases and visiting delegations would only bring distractions. Visitors unschooled in the ways of conspiracy were more likely to get their hosts in trouble than to help them. Even worse would be if visiting politicians or activists met with officials, for this might unintentionally confer legitimacy on the regime.

So much like Americans in this, Central Europeans by the 1970s were wary of political labels, and especially of the label "socialist." The term seemed to have little meaning after the failure of "Socialism with a Human Face" in 1968's Prague Spring. And the more their own governments publicized the protests of the Western left, the more Central Europeans were suspicious. Furthermore, precisely because peace groups posited the common experience of humanity, and the common threat of nuclear war, they appeared to belittle the radically different lives Central Europeans led.

If some Western Europeans were suspicious of the ends envisioned by dissidents, Central Europeans—having no objection to the goal of peace as such—wondered about the means. Havel's essay quoted above is full of images of earnest Westerners, blind to the daily travails and real fears of Czechs, attempting "dialogue" about peace in ways guaranteed only to jeopardize their hosts' freedom. Havel found it difficult to imagine how peace could be achieved without first achieving basic civil rights and freedoms. And any serious dialogue would have to begin with understanding the fundamental differences between life East and West.

Though the Czech playwright may not have noticed the similarity, the END Appeal of 1980 reflected the same antipolitical bent as, for example, Havel's 1978 essay "Power of the Powerless." The idea that one should "act as if" one were free, or in Europe, regardless of ideologies' straitjackets, was central to Havel's philosophy. But Havel's letter to Amsterdam suggested that if one lived in a Western democracy, one would have to stretch a little harder to "act as if," and understand the real world a little better.

E. P. Thompson agreed with Havel's diagnosis. Thompson followed the appeal with visits to Prague (in 1980) and to Budapest (in 1982). The Prague visit, during which Thompson met both prominent Chartists and official peace representatives, touched off a heated debate over this even-handedness. In Hungary, though he again met with both camps, Thompson's role was rather different: his visit helped to publicize the existence of the Dialogue group (see below). To activists like Lynne Jones, the rise of Solidarity (just months after the END Appeal) suddenly made Thompson's idea of cooperation and dialogue palpable.

In New York, socialist peace activist Joanne Landy felt the same pull: she just had to see how a social movement emerged. In Warsaw (where she connected with Jan Józef Lipski, the socialist from KOR) she felt as if she were back in Berkeley during the Free Speech Movement. Back home, she organized a conference of the left, under the title "Solidarity with Solidarity"; Pete Seeger performed for the gathering, and Michael Harrington and others spoke.

In West Germany, a motley collection of former Maoists and Trotskyites, green politicians, and journalists bucked the German left's traditional suspicions of dissent and formed a Working Group for Eastern Europe, under the umbrella of the Green Party. Berliner Dieter Esche, a civil rights activists and veteran of the student movement of 1968, made his first trip east to see Solidarity: he called it "revolution tourism."

Esche was being a bit cynical, perhaps, but the term is accurate. Just as a Western socialist in 1917 simply had to see what the Russian Revolution had wrought, so too the social movement activist in 1980 could not ignore the largest movement in the developed world in over a decade. In Poland these pilgrims rediscovered that sense of exhilaration which, at least for their generation in the West, was the exclusive property of the left. They sought out, and felt at home in, social movements—the more chaotic the better. In this sense, at least, they found kindred spirits, not only among the prominent intellectuals chain-smoking in cafés, but also among the harried printers in secret basements. And if differences emerged in discussion, these travelers took it in stride: the dialogue itself was what they craved.

There were more than revolutionaries traveling east. Ecumenical church groups, like the Dutch Inter-Church Peace Council (IKV), one of the most powerful peace groups in Europe, were moved by a dream of a truly European ministry of peace and justice. Founded in 1966, the IKV had spent years trying to make Dutch political parties take a stand against all nuclear weapons. The campaign petered out by mid-decade, and in 1983 American Cruise missiles were being deployed in several NATO countries (though not in the Netherlands). Now the IKV began to turn toward international campaigns. Mient-Jan Faber, a mathematician who had been working with the IKV since shortly after the Helsinki Accords, proposed linking peace campaigns with human rights work. These two ideas intersected in Central Europe, which was accessible through church contacts with Lutheran parishes in East Germany, Calvinists in Hungary, and so forth.

Faber's idea was to build trust between people, though always with an overlay of political concerns. Toward the end of a visit to the GDR in 1982, he met with Rainer Eppelmann, a Protestant pastor and opposition activist he had come to know well. They both knew, says Faber, that it would be his last visit for awhile, as the Stasi seemed to be everywhere. Searching for a way to leave a record of their discussions, Eppelmann and Faber created the "personal peace contract." Signing this contract, they pledged to one another to observe and work for peace and nonviolence. This ritual would soon become a standard part of East-West pacifist encounters.

Environmental movements gained strength in Western Europe alongside the peace movements, yet greens were much less interested in exploring the East. Environmental activism thrives on local involvement and local campaigns, which would be hard to stage behind the Iron Curtain. Nor was working with state bureaucracies (or engaging in dialogue with official environmental groups) part of the environmentalist repertoire. With nothing but a notebook full of addresses of semi-official environmental groups, Dutch activist Ed Romeijn set out to build a Central European network in 1985. The result was Greenway, a project that brought together young green activists from Hungary, Czechoslovakia, and Poland to talk about techniques and issues in environmental activism.

Romeijn's task was in some ways easier than that of the peace activists. His contacts were fully focused on environmental issues and needed the technical advice he could offer. The human-rights opposition, for its part, had seen more than its share of empty overtures from the West. It was hard to believe there could be any tangible benefit from such contact anyway. Thanks to the efforts of some Central Europeans living in the West, who could understand the reticences on both sides, and the different languages of peace and activism, attitudes slowly began to change.

Jan Minkiewicz was Solidarity's representative in Amsterdam, helping to publicize the struggles of the trade union and doing what he could to secure material help for the Poles. Unlike other Solidarity representatives, Minkiewicz, a Dutch journalist and union activist, had grown up in the West. It seemed to him that it would be more effective to work with Western peace movements, rather than simply to denounce them as agents of the Soviet Union (as Soviet dissident Vladimir Bukovsky had done in a widely read book). Otherwise, Solidarity would soon have only the support of aging anticommunists.

In the spring of 1985, Minkiewicz wrote a long letter to Jacek Kuroń, urging that Solidarity take a fresh look at the peace movements. True, he conceded, there were some who were tied closely to their communist parties. But others—he singled out END-UK and the Dutch IKV—were determined not to be "fellow travelers" and wanted to reach out to the opposition. In between were many people who were simply "naïve" about the East. If Solidarity were not to be isolated, Minkiewicz argued, it should seize this opportunity to overcome Western indifference (especially among the younger generation) toward Central European opposition.

It wasn't long before Minkiewicz got a call from Konstanty Gebert, a Warsaw journalist active in the Social Defense Committee (KOS) network, proposing that Minkiewicz act as the KOS representative in the West. The next call was from Jacek Czaputowicz, whom Minkiewicz did not know. Freedom and Peace was just forming, and would Minkiewicz represent them as well? Thus began an intense relationship, through which WiP became the best-known group in the "East-West crowd" (Minkiewicz's phrase), and the most zealous for Western contacts.

That July, WiP sent an open letter to the END Convention in Amsterdam, writing with rather more enthusiasm than did Havel. Piotr Niemczyk showed up in Amsterdam shortly thereafter; for some reason the authorities let him and Czaputowicz travel that year. Minkiewicz showed Niemczyk around the Dutch social movement scene, where Niemczyk made a great impression. He looked like one of them in his military-cast-off style clothes and high leather punk boots. Niemczyk was arrested shortly after his return home, as was Czaputowicz. Both were charged, among other things, with harming Poland through their contacts with Western peace organizations. This was for them a sign that they had struck a raw nerve, and it was one they would continue to probe throughout WiP's existence.

For the Czech opposition, the man in the middle was Jan Kavan. Kavan (whose mother was English) had fled Czechoslovakia in 1970, as a student leader facing likely imprisonment, and made his way to London. He founded the Palach Press, and later the East European Cultural Foundation, to publish work by Czech authors and to publicize the work of the intellectual opposition. When Charter 77 appeared, Kavan was one of its most vigorous supporters outside Czechoslovakia. Kavan was also a socialist, however; he remained so even as most of his Czech friends gave up on that idea.

On one side, Kavan labored to convince his Western socialist and social-democratic friends that "this was not a struggle which in the end would help the Reagans and the Thatchers and the right wing circles in the West, but that on the contrary it would, in the long term, create an atmosphere in Europe in which one could discuss socialist ideas without feeling guilty, without having to suppress information about how these ideas were misused in one half of the world." But even more difficult to face was the distrust of his friends in Charter 77. Kavan's task was the same as Minkiewicz's: "I had to spend a lot of my time trying to explain that not all peace activists are the same, that there are people among them who analysed the problem as we did, and that it was important to be patient even with the naïve ones and open their eyes to the reality of the situation."[3] Kavan helped bring about closer contact between Charter 77 and END, resulting in a series of letters published in an END booklet, *Voices from Prague,* in 1983. Meanwhile, he endeavored to awaken contacts among the Polish, Czech, and Hungarian oppositions. One result would be the *East European Reporter,* a key source of information on Central European opposition in 1985–89. Like a few other journals— Peter Rossman's *Across Frontiers* in Berkeley, or the British socialist quarterly *Labour Focus on Eastern Europe*—it would become a way for Central European activists, through their texts, to meet and exchange ideas.

DIALOGUE FOR AN ENDANGERED CONTINENT

If in Poland and Czechoslovakia Western activists searched almost in vain for friendly voices (and perhaps for confirmation of their beliefs) among indifferent or even openly suspicious oppositions, the reception in Hungary was much different. "Europe" was a real idea there: Hungarian intellectuals had come to think of their revolution of 1956 as a fight for Europe. Relaxed travel restrictions beginning in the 1970s had also brought Hungary closer to its neighbors. Even so, international cooperation was never an easy thing.

In the summer of 1982, 25-year-old student Ferenc Köszegi wrote to London, inviting people from END to come to Budapest to meet his new movement, the Peace Group for Dialogue. The group had emerged earlier that year, at the height of the controversial deployment of Soviet and U.S. nuclear missiles in the European theater. The idea was to fight this threat to the survival of Europe as Europeans—in a Europe without borders, following the recipe advanced in the END Appeal.

Hungary was at that moment the most liberal state in the Soviet bloc; as these young peace activists discovered, it was paradoxically the place where it was hardest to make oneself heard and to stake out an active, independent position. János Kádár's socialist consumerism had given Hungarians a reason to play it safe, while the police and the mass organizations silenced any lonely protest. Most Hungarians were unaware of any dissent and did not feel the need.

To become a public activist in Hungary, then, was like trying to attract attention in a crowded shopping mall. When some high school students proposed a protest march against all nuclear weapons for Victory Day (May 9), the Communist Youth League simply stole their idea and organized an official peace parade. The students' voices were lost among the official ritual and the slogans denouncing Western imperialist militarism. It was precisely in public, on the streets, that a Hungarian opposition could easily be manipulated. And popular indifference made their struggle a lonely one.

But Dialogue's strengths would be its personal and international campaigns. That was the power of the nuclear threat: it posed an intensely personal, but also universal, threat to survival, so it naturally invited—even required—cross-border cooperation among "human neighbors, on an endangered continent."[4] For Köszegi, it was a question of honor: "If 'the waves of the peace movement stop at the gates of Vienna,'" he wrote (with István Szent-Iványi), "then, after a time, this will mean that Western movements have been in vain; it will prove that in Eastern Europe there is no genuine desire for spontaneous movements."[5] A peace movement, then, was an obligation Hungary owed to Europe.

Under the comfortable shell of complacency typical of the Kádár regime, the youngest generation, some of whose parents were even too young to have fought in 1956, understood this obligation. Zsuzsa Gille was an avid participant in a Communist Youth League group in her high school. The theme of their meetings was world affairs; Gille, who was learning English as well, once presented a talk on the problem of terrorism. One day in the fall of 1982, her girlfriend suggested they go to a lecture by a famous British peace activist. When they got to the university, they found a crowd waiting outside in the rain; the authorities had denied permission for the talk to take place. At long last, the whole group, now approaching eighty, trooped off to the spacious apartment of György Konrád to hear E. P. Thompson speak on "The Normalisation of Europe."

Gille and her friend were the only two high school students there; most were university students, with a smattering of prominent intellectuals like Konrád and sociologist Miklós Haraszti. For Gille, both these worlds—the luminaries of the democratic opposition and the peace activist from the other side of Europe—were new. The latter seemed closer, however: when Thompson relayed greetings from a peace meeting in Wales (along with some token gifts), Gille was moved. Here were foreign relations made real, and personal, in a genuine dialogue free of the stultifying rhetoric of the regime but also staying clear of the dangerous behavior of dissidents.

Zoltán Rozgonyi, four years older, was a second-year student in electrical engineering at the technical university. Like the vast majority of students, he was not involved in political activity. The Marxist debates of the 1960s and 1970s were ancient history to him; the uprising of 1956, though obviously important, had happened five years before he was born. But the need for debate and discussion was no less great. It brought "Rozi" to the Rakpart Club, on the fringes of legality, where there were regular discussions (or performances) of popular culture and current events.* There, in November 1982, he heard Ferenc Köszegi talk about Dialogue, to a crowd of some four hundred. Mary Kaldor of END and Mient-Jan Faber, who had been invited in the wake of Thompson's visit, also spoke. "I clearly remember my feelings after that meeting," says Rozgonyi. "That's it after all, the thing I've been looking for a long time. . . . I've found it. I think my enthusiasm was partly due to their cautious, non-confronting behavior, partly the very strong almost unquestionable moral foundation of the whole initiative." He threw himself into the movement.

Gille and Rozgonyi were not leaders in the group. The public face of Dialogue was Ferenc Köszegi and Ferenc Ruzsa. Dialogue was a "way toward opposition," says Zsolt Enyedi, another younger member. But just as the movement rejected the Cold War conflict, it also sought a middle ground between state and opposition. Köszegi's characterization was one many accepted: on one side was the Peace Council, trying to "co-opt the initiatives of the young." On the other were the dissidents, who sought to slap labels on Dialogue: "The new peace movement [Dialogue] is called unofficial, non-official, autonomous, spontaneous, grass roots, dissident, oppositionist. These names carry with them a strong flavour of political prejudice, and even the desire to manipulate." The "so-called opposition," Köszegi concluded, cynically "hope[s] to enlarge their base by means of this movement."[6] This fear of infiltration from both sides at times bordered on the paranoid. Such was the cost of fighting for the middle ground. Gille describes Dialogue's position more optimistically than did Köszegi: they wanted, she says, "to exploit a space in which we could maneuver." Advancing the cause of peace, they might make an impact on the world precisely because they enjoyed the regime's toleration.

---

* The guru of Rakpart (and its successor, the Lemon Club) was the late Miklós Horváth. Horváth had the backing of the Communist Youth League (meeting rooms, money for flyers, etc.) and tested the regime's limits. Some compared these clubs to the famous Petöfi circles where the political arguments of 1956 got their start. Both prominent reform communists and quasi-opposition figures like Köszegi and János Vargha of the Danube Circle addressed these gatherings.

Not unlike Freedom and Peace three years later, Dialogue took advantage of the regime's peace rhetoric. But in searching for a space between, Dialogue made the same mistake that some in the West would also make. Seeking to break down hostility between two camps (whether East/West or regime/dissident) they assumed there were only two sides. Trapped in the language of the Cold War, Dialogue saw a battle of opposing forces in which the middle ground had to be fiercely guarded. Where some Western peace activists, as we shall see, recognized the pluralism of voices on either side, Dialogue shrank back. The balancing act would eventually tear it apart and set independent opposition back until a new radical pluralism emerged in 1987–88.

Meanwhile, though, Dialogue pursued Western contacts like no other East European movement ever had. Dialogue's greatest trick was to organize, along with Mient-Jan Faber and IKV, an International Peace Camp for summer 1983. Several dozen Westerners—mostly Dutch, but also Germans, Scandinavians, and a group of women from Lynne Jones's Greenham Common camp—arrived to take part in a week of dialogue and trust-building. When the authorities canceled Dialogue's reservations at several campsites, a decision was made to go anyway, to a small village near Szentendre, just north of Budapest. Thus Dialogue crossed the line into defiance and opposition.

For two days, the hundred or so participants talked about the missiles, and about nonviolence. They learned methods of civil disobedience (such as how to go limp when grabbed by the police) and compared lifestyles and movement strategies. They discussed Gandhi and Martin Luther King and played games to build trust. And on the third day, the police arrived. "When they descended on us in the park," Zsuzsa Gille "realized this was not just a misunderstanding," and that the regime "really [didn't] want us to do this."

It may seem implausible that a police raid could be a shock to anyone in Hungary, fifteen years after the Prague Spring had marked the limits to political independence in the Soviet Bloc. But neither the Hungarian students nor their Western peace friends had tried—they thought—to engage in politics. The space they hoped to liberate was more personal. They believed they could do without ideology, and be agnostic on political affairs.

After the raid on the camp, the Peace Group for Dialogue began to look more like an opposition. Inspired by the Western contacts they had developed, some in the group pushed for more public actions. On October 29, 1983, the group organized a companion to a huge anti–nuclear missile demonstration that same day in The Hague (the home of Mient-Jan Faber's IKV). An appeal handed out to Budapest onlookers asked Hungarians to think of themselves as Europeans:

Today in Holland hundreds of thousands of Dutch people are protesting personally against the preparations for war. They believe that only they themselves have the right to decide about their own lives. You too should have the strength and the will to speak out.

Let us defend Europe together!

If you too feel sympathy and affection towards them, take a flower and bring it personally to the Dutch embassy.[7]

Members of Dialogue were all over the city that day. They marched with placards and flowers, staged a "Burial of the Known Soldier," and everywhere tried to jolt Budapesters out of their apathy.

Though on a very small scale, this protest was remarkably provocative. The coordination with the Dutch protests did make it possible to maneuver in the narrow space that peace rhetoric provided: the date, rather than explicit slogans, articulated a protest against Soviet as well as American weapons. And the "dialogue" was not a formal exchange over the heads of society, but intensely personal and local. "We handed out drawings to people," explained a participant in a "Burial" parade. "It was important for them that they should get something they could take away. It brought them closer to us, and they stopped being bystanders."[8]

But this was a kind of dialogue the regime would not tolerate. In December Zsuzsa Gille and Zoltán Rozgonyi tried another "happening" to commemorate the fourth anniversary of the Pershing missile deployment. They were to dress up as an angel and Santa Claus (respectively) and hand out gifts to passersby: little matchboxes with missiles inside, origami cranes, and flyers explaining the protest. But they were still changing into their costumes inside a university building when the police came to arrest them.

Thus the narrow space Dialogue had occupied collapsed, from both sides. Opposition proved an almost unavoidable path. Though human or civil rights were of course the province of the daring dissidents, "dialogue" required freedom of speech and—if the dialogue would be really international—travel. As the police harassed paraders, or bureaucrats denied groups spaces to meet or withheld passports for travel to the West, the distance between Dialogue and the dissidents—especially those, like Miklós Haraszti, who had long championed the group and urged it toward more risky positions—began to diminish.

Nor could the regime be held at bay. Hungarian communism confounded Dialogue with its combination of aggressive response and mild follow-through. After Dialogue's breakup, some participants found their way back to the Peace Council and used its contacts to continue the work of East-West dialogue. Ferenc Köszegi, for example, started a group within the Peace Council called 4-6-0; the numbers referred to the length of time (in years) of World War I and II and, depending on one's perspective, either the length of time a nuclear war would take or the goal of avoiding World War III.

Others moved toward political opposition: Dialogue veterans would turn up in several of the movements of 1988–89. Looking back, Zoltán Rozgonyi feels that the most important goal had already been accomplished by 1984: that of getting people together and learning how to self-organize. This was "even more important than the issue [of peace] itself." The international contacts, in turn, taught the Hungarians more about difference than about similarities. Meetings with other Europeans, he says, "helped Dialogue to understand its uniqueness." This insight would be necessary in the later struggle to change Hungary.

HELSINKI FROM BELOW

From its roots in the British peace community, the END quickly became the international movement its founders had envisioned. Some eight hundred activists from every country in Western Europe packed its first convention, in Brussels in July 1982.* Indeed, the END Appeal had provoked a Europeanization elsewhere—in France, for example, where the peace movement had been dominated by the Communist Party for decades. CODENE, France's answer to the appeal, would become one of the most active participants in the East European program, along with the Dutch IKV and the German Greens.

From the beginning, though, there were quarrels within END over the relationship with official peace organizations in the communist bloc. In communist terminology, these organizations were "weapons" in the workers' struggle for peace. They attacked only "Western imperialists" and ignored their own countries' military establishment. Few in END believed that these were authentic voices of socialism. As E. P. Thompson put it, these organizations "stand in the place where, if they didn't exist, a spontaneous independent peace movement would spring up."[9] But dialogue was the way to create a free, peaceful Europe; therefore, argued some, it was essential to talk with anyone who would listen. And while the Soviet Peace Council might speak in the dead bureaucratese of their party masters, others seemed much more reasonable and European.

The Hungarian Peace Council was the most approachable. Today, END

* "END" here means the loose coalition that participated in the yearly conventions, which were organized by a Liaison Committee made up of representatives of various national groups. One member of this coalition was END-UK, which, among other things, published the *END Journal*.

veterans pronounce the name of council chair Miklós Barabas with distaste; then, he and his colleagues were friendly faces who spoke the language of peace and offered a window into Central Europe. They didn't hesitate, too, to offer gentle criticisms of the division of Europe. And like all the official peace committees, these Hungarians could travel to the West. At the first several END conventions, Central Europe was represented primarily by the officials, not by dissidents.

Independent groups like Charter 77, Dialogue, or Solidarity might at best be represented by a letter (like Havel's to the 1985 convention), or by an émigré spokesperson like Kavan. Only rarely would an intrepid individual, out on a tourist visa, risk exposure by appearing in public. One Hungarian remembers her terror at the 1986 convention in Paris, to which she had brought greetings from other peace activists who could not attend. At a reception, a prominent END-UK activist grabbed her hand and led her over to where a Soviet peace official was standing. To the END activist, this was a perfect opportunity to further East-West dialogue and remove barriers of mistrust. To the Hungarian, this was a perfect opportunity to end up in deep trouble when she got home. So she shook hands with the Soviet, mumbled her name incoherently, and slipped away.

For the official Central European groups, the conventions were a platform to push their propaganda, not to root out pacifists, so the threat of exposure was limited. The real danger, for the opposition, was that this form of ersatz dialogue might satisfy END and leave the fledgling independent groups in Central Europe even more isolated than before.

This, at least, is how Dieter Esche saw it. In 1983 Esche began to circulate a proposal to cast END's lot exclusively with the independents. At the END's third convention, in Perugia, Italy, in 1984, Esche and a small group of allies felt things had gone far enough: there were again dozens of peace bureaucrats from Central Europe, "all sitting in the front rows," and just one representative from Hungary's Dialogue. "We decided," Esche says, "that our piece of paper [the earlier proposal] was not enough; let's do an action, in typical '68 style." They prepared posters bearing the names and symbols of groups that were "silent" at the convention: Dialogue, Charter 77, the Moscow Trust Group, the GDR's Swords into Ploughshares.* As the first speaker, an Italian delegate, began to welcome the participants, Esche and the others walked up onto the stage. Each wore a red bandanna over his or her mouth; they lined up before the podium, facing the audience and displaying the alternative groups' symbols. The auditorium erupted: East European peace officials all stood up to leave. E. P. Thompson and others in the END leadership gestured furi-

---

* Another featured group—perhaps included to combat the charge that this was simply an antisocialist demonstration—was the Turkish Peace Association.

ously at this rudeness toward invited guests. Half the audience, though, stood and applauded. That very afternoon, the Network for East-West Dialogue was founded.

Esche's account—which includes a dramatic street confrontation with Thompson—casts the Network founders as daring heroes, just like the opposition groups they were reaching out to. The conflict was not nearly so great in reality. Almost everyone in END wanted to talk with the independents; Thompson himself had blazed that trail well before Esche or the others had even encountered Central Europe. The difference was rather one of emphasis. While for END peace was the paramount goal, no matter with whom one had to meet to achieve it, the Network valued the opening of dialogue with the anticommunist opposition even more highly. One could buy the Network's *Bulletin* at END offices in London, and most participants in the Network continued to participate in END conventions and in national peace movements. But the Network—which essentially operated out of Esche's apartment in West Berlin—was now the site of the most vigorous interaction with Central Europe.

The East-West dialogue now became quite vigorous, spilling out of its narrow channels. In 1985 forty-five Charter signatories issued the Prague Appeal, calling for the withdrawal of U.S. and Soviet troops and nuclear weapons from Europe, the dissolution of both Cold War alliances, and the reopening of the question of a divided Germany. A year later, on the tenth anniversary of the Helsinki Accords—which had introduced human rights into international relations—peace activists East and West, from Ljubljana to London, collaborated on a call for "détente from below": a memorandum entitled "Giving Real Life to the Helsinki Accords." The so-called Helsinki Memorandum demanded that independent peace groups gain a voice in the assurance of European security and human rights.

Peace movements East and West have over the years produced reams of appeals and declarations. Most of these proposals and demands, and their uninspiring rhetoric, began gathering dust almost immediately. A decade and a half later, what is most striking about the Helsinki Memorandum is not the text (though there is no neater expression of the argument that social movements should influence international policy), but the list of signatories. In addition to the usual progressive politicians, academics, and activists from the West (who risked nothing, of course, and were for the most part uninvolved in the process of dialogue anyway), there were over two hundred signatures from Poland, Hungary, Czechoslovakia, East Germany, and Yugoslavia. There were famous Chartists, Solidarity leaders, and Budapest intellectuals, but also unknown students, greens, and pacifists.

This was possible thanks to a two-year round of discussions across the proverbial kitchen tables of Central Europe, in which Esche, Mient-Jan

Faber, and others gathered input on the successive drafts. Many of their Central European contacts (the Slovenes especially) contributed passionate critiques of early drafts. The result was a genuinely European forum on peace and human rights, the first ever with such broad participation. Where once there had been token Central Europeans—writing impassioned essays for *END Journal* or other magazines, or open letters to faraway human rights conferences—now there was a remarkable variety of voices in conversation with one another.

Before dismissing such a document as empty symbolism, then, it is worth recalling the strategies that peace groups in Central Europe had already discovered. They had found an effective, even safe, vantage point by pitching their battles on issues crucial to the communist regimes' public image as peace-loving Europeans. This was not really dissimilar from the END's idea of dialogue, which simply challenged the communist regimes to live up to their professed ideals. Arguably, a peace movement had more of a chance to speak truth to power than could, say, a more traditionally anticommunist group.

This was E. P. Thompson's fundamental point. When a Charter 77 correspondent questioned how he could even contemplate attending a peace congress in Prague in 1983 while several leading Chartists—including spokesman Ladislav Lis, who had been in contact with END—were in prison, Thompson promised a boycott. He knew that his presence was of value to the Czech regime, and he believed that only this kind of pressure would work: END would "exact from them one small 'human right' as the price of attendance: let them release Ladislav Lis, and give to him the right to speak from the podium."[10]

Lis was not released then, and some peace activists (not Thompson) showed up in Prague anyway. But campaigns on behalf of peace activists (such as Jacek Czaputowicz) in 1986 and 1987 were more successful, in large part because the web of East-West connections was by then so much denser. The voices of END, IKV, the Network, and others offered a new kind of publicity for dissidents. And that new generation, lacking the fame and international connections of their elders, and so with no other outlets to Western attention, needed support. Their signatures on the Helsinki Memorandum, and the voices raised in their defense, gave them a legitimacy disproportionate to their small numbers.

ON THE FRIENDSHIP TRAIL

To cross a border within the Soviet bloc not only brought the same risk as to travel West-East; it was often a trip burdened by just as much ideological baggage. As Polish, Czech, and Hungarian dissidents encountered each other through the 1970s and 1980s, there was always an implied reference to the crimes their states had committed against one another. Hungary, Poland, and Germany (in different guises) had twice invaded Czechoslovakia: in the wake of the Munich Agreement in 1938, and as part of the Warsaw Pact invasion of August 1968. These invasions were the more troublesome as they were forbidden topics among socialist allies.

In more recent history, no one in Poland could forget the outrage in all the capitals of the bloc when Solidarity's first national congress, meeting in Gdańsk in September 1981, passed a resolution addressed to the nations of Central Europe: "We support all of you who have decided to take the difficult path and fight for free trade unions," the statement read. "We believe that soon your and our representatives will be able to meet to exchange our union experience."[11] Though Westerners always found it odd that it was not much easier for a Pole to visit Budapest than, say, Munich, the regimes' paranoia was thus understandable. The bloc was built according to the pseudo-efficient logic of Stalin's "socialism in one country" thesis; individual movement across borders simply introduced too much uncertainty into the socialist system. And Poles, with their proud tradition of fighting "For Your Freedom and Ours"—not to mention their legions of black-market laborers all across Western Europe—were the most dangerous export of all.

Mirek Jasiński, a 21-year-old university student in Wrocław at the time of Solidarity's international appeal, followed the usual opposition path of his generation, from the Student Solidarity Committee in 1979–80 through the Independent Students Association in the martial-law period. He was studying Polish and Czech literature, in preparation for teaching high school. Tired of the conspiratorial routine, Jasiński decided to try something really risky. With a half-dozen friends (mostly students of history or literature in Wrocław), he formed Polish-Czechoslovak Solidarity in 1983. All they had were a few contacts in Prague, notably VONS/Charter 77 activists Petr Uhl and his wife, Anna Šabatová.

The Poles had a lot to offer their Czechoslovak neighbors. With hundreds of periodicals and several large publishers, some with nearly up-to-date technology, they were light years ahead of the Czechs, where the half-dozen or so clandestine periodicals still used typewriters and carbons. The Czechs were hungry for the Poles' wealth of independent history, political commentary, philosophy, literature, and opposition know-how. Poles had much easier access to the West, too. Jaruzelski's half-hearted economic reforms rested in part on the hard currency brought back by those thousands of black-market laborers. Some of them smuggled back trunk-loads of banned literature from the Czech émigré communities (as well as Polish literature, of course); Poland thus became an essential channel of communication between the post-1968 political emigration and Prague.

Most of this baggage reached Czechoslovakia across the mountains, which reach five thousand feet along the border southwest of Wrocław. Polish-Czechoslovak Solidarity couriers would stuff their backpacks with fifty to eighty pounds of literature and set off through the forests. In the remotest parts of the Karkonosze/Krkonoše Mountains, one could slip across after the border patrol had passed. As long as there was no snow on the ground (winter crossings were rare, lest couriers' tracks expose their trails), there might be two trips monthly. At a prearranged spot on the border, the goods would be handed to a Czech contact; sometimes, the Polish courier would descend to the nearest Czech village and mail packages at the post office. There were larger packages, too: photocopiers, offset printers, and even—in 1989—a laptop computer. These were purchased in Vienna with money from Czech émigré organizations. Marked as in transit to Poland, they simply vanished from the train in Czechoslovakia.

Domestic conspiratorial work in Poland had come to seem almost too easy, but crossing the "green border"* was a challenge worth the effort. There was no thaw, no perestroika, on the Polish-Czechoslovak border. This was a tightly controlled zone—despite the signs that directed one to the "Trail of International Friendship"—until December 1989. In the event of apprehension, the Polish couriers knew to take all the blame on themselves while the Czech got away: a Czech might get several years in prison, while the Pole would face at most a fine plus a few days in jail. With greater risk came irresistible opportunities to drive the Czech authorities crazy. In 1985 a Warsaw-Brno axis (over the rather higher Tatra Mountains) expanded Polish-Czech contacts. Working as if on contract for the Czechs, Warsaw printers composed and published an entire edition of a Brno literary journal, then smuggled it back over the Tatras. The Czech police were stunned to discover that despite all their efforts, Czech samizdat now (apparently) had offset printers of their own.

Around this time, Jan Kavan put Ukrainian émigrés in touch with Wrocław: could they expand their network to the east? Jasiński turned to Paweł Chmiel, who taught English at the same high school as he. As a student in the Catholic Intellectuals' Club, Chmiel had been advocating some kind of rapprochement with Ukrainians, so he agreed to try. He found a customs officer on the Czech border who was willing to look the other way, and soon another channel was open. Ukrainian literature and Bibles thus made their way to Lviv and Kyiv across the Czechoslovak-Soviet border (marginally looser than the Polish-Soviet one).

Polish-Czechoslovak Solidarity destroyed the isolation of the Czech op-

* The term was borrowed from World War II, when it referred to the border between the General-Gouvernement and the Polish lands annexed to the Third Reich.

position. Almost twenty years after the Prague Spring, letters from émigrés or the sounds of Radio Free Europe were almost all that remained,
and they were, after all, themselves reminders of the border that cut the
Czechs off from the world. But Polish students scrambling up mountains,
evading border patrols, and delivering packages: this was an invigorating
change.

In January 1987 the Czechoslovak secret police arrested Brno peace activist Petr Pospíchal, Polish-Czechoslovak Solidarity's main contact outside of Prague. Pospíchal, a poet and translator from Polish, had long been
one of the most active samizdat publishers in the country; a search of his
apartment (ostensibly in connection with a murder case) turned up flyers
celebrating Charter 77's tenth anniversary, and much more. His Charter
colleagues formed a Pospíchal Defense Committee, and petitions demanding his release flowed in from all the usual places. But no sign of solidarity was more powerful than a letter Pospíchal received in prison,
franked with a counterfeit Czechoslovak stamp bearing Charter 77 and
Polish-Czechoslovak Solidarity logos. Polish underground printers had
been turning out high-quality postage stamps for years, to be sold to col-
lectors as a fundraiser; this batch had been spirited over the border on
New Year's Day in time for the anniversary.

All the signs pointed to Pospíchal getting a long prison sentence, perhaps five to ten years. But Pospíchal, hitherto little known outside his
country, became an international case. Freedom and Peace, followed by
the East German Initiative for Peace and Human Rights, sent their own
protest letters. In April WiP and Polish-Czechoslovak Solidarity staged a
small demonstration in Wrocław—the most public demonstration ever in
support of a foreign prisoner. And in May, before he had even had time
to become an Amnesty International prisoner of conscience, Pospíchal
was freed for lack of evidence. By living and acting as if they were in a
democratic Europe, the Poles and Czechs had put into effect the same Solidarity declaration that had seemed suicidal six years earlier.

Poles had a resource even more valuable than the literature they carried: activists with years of experience in organizing anticommunist resistance and protest. If great, cumbersome backpacks could reach the
border, then why not smuggle people as well? After months of planning
in 1987, Mirek Jasiński and Ivan Lamper (a journalist for Prague's underground counterculture mag *Revolver Revue*) brought to the Trail of
Polish-Czechoslovak Friendship some of their countries' best-known opposition figures: intellectuals like Zbigniew Romaszewski, Václav
Havel, Jaroslav Šabata, Adam Michnik, and Jacek Kuroń (who brought
along a large bottle of whiskey to help break the ice); unionists like Władysław Frasyniuk; and others all trekked up the mountain. They announced the formation of the "Circle of Friends of Polish-Czechoslovak

Solidarity," with Anna Šabatová and Józef Pinior, the Wrocław social-ist, as spokespeople.*

This was of course a publicity coup above all: famous dissidents meet-ing with impunity, in a place legally off limits. They posed proudly next to a sign reading "State Border, Crossing Forbidden." For Jasiński, the meeting and the new group were, paradoxically, safety measures. A cou-rier arrested on either side of the border might yet disappear into prison unless the case were well publicized; leaders in Charter 77 or Solidarity could fight for them.

The price paid, though, was a certain theatricality that old hands like Jasiński found a little bothersome. The pictures of Havel, Michnik, and Kuroń cavorting merrily on the mountaintop became famous. Many peo-ple imagined that these were serious planning sessions for the revolution. But while the big names exchanged platitudes about human rights, issued joint declarations, and (most important) got to know each other, Jasiński's conspiratorial work continued. He and Lamper might discuss what Czech samizdat most needed, or who else should come to the next meeting. Then another shipment from Vienna or Wrocław might be arranged, and the circle of mountain climbers might expand. The summit meetings, contin-ued in 1988 and 1989, thus operated at two levels. They were a theater performance for an international public, and they featured a genuine backstage as well.

Polish-Czechoslovak Solidarity in effect helped raise the Iron Curtain ahead of schedule. Two years before Hungarian soldiers walked up to the Austrian border with wire clippers, this group took the fear out of the bor-der. It made the border into a place to have fun—even, perhaps, the place to which one traveled to prove one was having fun. The September fol-lowing the first summit meeting, WiP scaled the Karkonosze Mountains to meet young Czech environmentalists (who were prevented from com-ing); the following summer, Orange Alternative staged a happening there. In 1989 the new generation of Czech activists would discover the border, too. Both Poland and Czechoslovakia got a lot bigger as a result.

BORDERS FALL IN EAST GERMANY

Two hundred Orange Alternative troops stormed up the mountainside in August 1988 (actually, some took the ski lift), staging an unsuccessful twentieth-anniversary reinvasion of Czechoslovakia. Major Fydrych was dressed as a samurai, with a huge sword; Paweł Kocięba had somehow

---

* This was not the first border encounter; KOR and Charter 77 had staged a smaller gath-ering back in 1978.

procured the uniform of an East German officer; the anarchists from Gdańsk were there, waving a black flag. Improbably, they had come to dispel the remnants of mistrust between Poles and Czechs. The events of 1968 in particular weighed heavily on the older dissidents, many of whom had then turned in their party memberships in protest. Orange Alternative's slogan "Long Live Fraternal Assistance!" might exorcise that ghost.

How much heavier than for the Hungarians or Poles, though, was the burden of memory for the East Germans. The communist regime in the GDR acknowledged no need to atone for the sins of the Nazi regime. Still, the German invasion of Czechoslovakia and Poland in 1938–39, and the horrifying destruction wrought during the occupation, slept just under the surface. In East Germany this memory, and that of its own invasion of Czechoslovakia thirty years later, existed alongside a traditional antipathy toward Polish opposition in particular. Striking workers, Catholic processions, and nationalist dissidents made many East Germans uneasy, whether they were dissidents themselves or not.

Ludwig Mehlhorn and Wolfgang Templin are, most probably, the only two dissidents in the GDR who speak Polish. Both discovered Poland in the mid-1970s: Mehlhorn went to study mathematics, while Templin was interested in the Kraków school of philosophy. They both ended up studying KOR instead. This interest did not go unnoticed by the Stasi, who once arrested Mehlhorn for distributing KOR materials in East Germany and eventually forbade both men from visiting Poland. But until 1981 the border between the two countries was relatively open, and Poland was a school of opposition. The main lesson that Solidarity (and Charter 77) had for the East Germans was about the value of acting openly. "When I asked people [in Poland] why they did everything so openly," Templin recalls, "they said they needn't have bothered to study if they weren't going to draw consequences from what they learned. That was the opposite of [Templin's experience in the GDR opposition]."[12]

Traditionally, the GDR opposition focused westward. The Berlin Wall was both the most potent symbol of the GDR's lack of freedom and a reminder of how difficult it was to construct a humane socialist society. As the twenty-fifth anniversary of the Wall approached in 1986, Mehlhorn implored his fellow dissidents in an open letter to think also of their isolation from the East.[13]

Templin, meanwhile, was more impatient with the overly theoretical approach of his Berlin colleagues. Peace was a dominant, almost sacred theme in the GDR opposition. But peace seminars in the few hospitable churches, or discussions of the future of socialism, were not enough. Though originally on the left, he had acquired from the Poles some of their pluralist instincts; he began to cultivate closer ties to the Lutheran Church.

And as Templin learned about Freedom and Peace—through Radio Free Europe, from Dieter Esche in West Berlin, and in the visits of alternative-press journalists from the West—he began to think about emulating the Polish movement's linking of peace and human rights.

The result was the Initiative for Peace and Human Rights (IFM), the first real opposition group in East Germany. Templin, born in 1948, was just about the oldest in the group. Most were in their twenties and represented the GDR's "youthful counterculture."[14] IFM appeared on the scene in January 1986 and soon published the GDR's very first true samizdat periodical. *Grenzfall* ("Borderline Case" or "Fall of the Border") was remarkable for its relentless promotion of an Eastern perspective to an audience that usually thought about only one border, that with West Germany. While the first issue (in June 1986) displayed a cover graphic of a crumbling Berlin Wall, this was changed beginning with the next issue to show a decrepit rural border crossing that appeared to lead off into the (Eastern?) hinterlands.

The first issue also carried a report about Freedom and Peace, with addresses in Poland for those who wished to write in protest of repression against WiP participants. Subsequent issues brought more reports on dissidence in Poland, Czechoslovakia, and the Soviet Union. But Central Europe itself remained off limits for most readers. One *Grenzfall* correspondent, Björn, was able to go east and described his experience in "Impressions of a Trip to Poland, or, a Lesson in Civil Courage."

"Björn" was Bernd Oehler, a theology student from Leipzig and a participant in the Leipzig Working Group for Justice (AKG, closely tied to the IFM), the only thriving IFM circle beyond Berlin. He had, years before, run afoul of the authorities by refusing to serve in the army (he was prevented from attending university for awhile), and he had been a participant in peace seminars for nearly a decade. He also had Polish roots: his mother, though German, had grown up in Warsaw, and Oehler had twice been there as a child. It was Templin who asked him to try to go to Poland again, on behalf of the IFM; to everyone's surprise, he got permission to travel. In just a few short weeks, he visited Warsaw, Wrocław, Kraków, and Gdańsk. As had Templin and Mehlhorn a decade earlier, he returned convinced that the GDR opposition should look to Poland; the Poles were, he recalled years later, "more emancipated than we were."

In his essay, Oehler avoided direct comparisons with East Germany, but the implied contrasts were easy to read. What struck Oehler most in Poland was the intensity of national expression. The ubiquitous Polish flags and national symbols, and the public role of the Church, contrasted sharply with the near-total lack of these in East Germany; Oehler recognized these as valuable resources for the opposition. Looking at the opposition itself, Oehler noted its diversity; unlike the opposition in East

Germany (and especially Berlin), Polish opposition tolerated diversity. He encountered "radicals, *Realpolitiker,* and nationalists" and came to the cautious conclusion that pluralism could be a strength of opposition. He spent much of his time, indeed, not with Solidarity, but with Freedom and Peace. In WiP's public and international stance, cemented by personal peace treaties, he found a model for the IFM. While Oehler noted also problems in Polish opposition—he bemoaned the male-dominated culture of opposition, where women were relegated to supporting roles—his conclusion was unequivocal: "One can learn from this civil courage."[15]

Oehler was part of a network of semi-anonymous East Germans who smuggled literature in both directions across the Polish and, especially, Czechoslovak borders. Leipzig's AKG created a Working Group on Eastern Europe to organize such a network. Thomas Rudolph, a theology student and peace-seminar veteran like Oehler, was one of its coordinators. He traveled to Czechoslovakia as often as he could, though he brought no samizdat with him. He assumed that the secret police were happy to let him go there so they could track his contacts. Meanwhile, he was a useful conduit of information between Prague and Berlin in the late 1980s. Others, much more anonymous than Rudolph, might make two or three trips carrying samizdat, or simply agree to receive mail from Czech opposition groups.

One may wonder about the value of all these trips. Dissidents' apartments in Warsaw, Prague, and Berlin must have been piled high with unread foreign samizdat, an occasional article earmarked for translation for the domestic underground. The short visits and smuggled letters were the equivalent of thumbs-up signs; there was rarely room for real coordinated action or exchange of experiences. The occasional joint declarations did not usually have much effect; protests on one another's behalf only rarely—as in the case of Petr Pospíchal—were heard.

The East German and Czechoslovak cases do offer a clue, though, to the value of East-East contacts. These were societies keenly aware of their borders, and suspicious of their neighbors. In both countries, contempt for lazy and rebellious Poles was common. Even the communist antagonist did not unite the oppositions as much as might have been expected. The breakdown of isolation in these societies is often attributed to Gorbachev, but the means by which the Soviet leader might have contributed to an integrated opposition are obscure, to say the least. Opposition like the Leipzig IFM, or Polish-Czechoslovak Solidarity, broke through these barriers from below. Movements in each country increasingly became coordinated with their neighbors and even began to resemble each other. In doing so, they made it impossible for the communist regimes to contain dissent within national borders. And if the stereotypes and fears that each culture had of each other were dispelled (at least among the most activist section of society), the events in one country could influence those across its borders—as would happen in 1988–89.

That East Germany was not a full-time participant in the transnational carnival was due to the peculiar nature of its borders—specifically, the western one. Every citizen of East Germany knew that he or she was welcome as a citizen of West Germany, if only one could get out. The communist authorities, in turn, were only too happy to get rid of troublemakers by shoving them out the door to West Berlin. Until the 1980s, what kept most dissenters from accepting a one-way ticket out was their commitment to the reform of socialism. Some who joined the opposition, moreover, did so only to provoke enough trouble to be shown the door. The ease and accessibility of emigration is probably the main reason that opposition in the GDR was always much smaller than in the other countries of Central Europe.

The young IFM generation was more troublesome. Most of its members did not care so much for socialism but did not want to leave, either, because of their commitment to human rights. For both these reasons, the regime had much less hold on them. It could still expel them by force, though, and did so in January 1988. Prominent IFM activists, including Templin, Ralf Hirsch of *Grenzfall,* and Bärbel Bohley, along with the independent artists Stephan Krawczyk and Freya Klier, were arrested in the aftermath of an official demonstration commemorating the 1919 assassination of German communists Rosa Luxemburg and Karl Liebknecht. This march was an annual ritual, virtually obligatory for all citizens. IFM activists, along with some from an opposition group focused on the right to emigrate, showed up waving a banner emblazoned with a Luxemburg quote: "Freedom is always the freedom of those who think differently." The regime used this occasion to clean house; the expulsion of Templin, Bohley, and the others effectively silenced the IFM and set Berlin opposition back for some time.

East German participation in the movement against Central European communism would be limited until the very year 1989, then, for two reasons. One part of the opposition was happy to leave the GDR for the West; another could be defused through the simple expedient of expelling its most vocal participants. Given all the reasons why East Germans might look west, that there was any interaction with eastern neighbors at all was the most surprising thing.

COVENTRY CATHEDRAL AND THE CHURCH ON ŻYTNIA STREET

Back in Western Europe, the contacts cultivated by Kavan, Minkiewicz, Jones, Faber, and others bore fruit at the END Convention in Coventry,

England, in July 1987. Coventry, the victim of carpetbombing by Nazi Germany in 1940, was for many a symbol of the consequences of war. In the aftermath of the Helsinki Memorandum, Central European peace groups were ever more assertive and open to transnational initiatives. Now, argued Lynne Jones, they should become full-fledged partners in dialogue, not just token voices. Otherwise, END's democratic values would be damaged. She quoted Mient-Jan Faber: "Opposition is necessary for a truly human society—we have learnt that from Central Europe. Now is the time to put *more* emphasis on opposition groups, because they might actually have more space in which to operate."[16]

Yet to many Western peace activists, Gorbachev's disarmament proposals promised much more to the world than a few opposition activists whose commitment to a program of peace was questionable. They maintained that this was the moment to encourage Soviet bloc officials by inviting representatives from the communist parties to Coventry. "We want to embrace the changes at the top," argued one senior British activist. "It is a process that could be stopped if it is not supported. We are not a league of oppositions."[17]

When END gathered in the new Coventry Cathedral, built beside the one destroyed by German bombers, there were more opposition representatives than in previous years. Konstanty Radziwiłł and Urszula Nowakowska of WiP had come, as had several students from the former Dialogue group, and individuals from Yugoslavia and East Germany. They were overshadowed, however, by official delegates from the Soviet Union, East Germany, and especially Hungary, who bodysnatched roles intended for the more timid independents. END's Mark Thompson watched one Hungarian official modestly introduce himself to the audience as "an independent peace activist from Budapest." Miklós Barabas, general secretary of the Hungarian Peace Council, announced at a press conference that he had signed the END Appeal and promised that the council would provide "an authentic East European voice" in the Liaison Committee as it planned the next convention.[18]

Central European activists and their friends in END were appalled. Joanne Landy of the Campaign for Peace and Democracy/East and West called this a "slide into alignment with the East bloc" and worried that the average Hungarian citizen would now equate END with the empty words of the Peace Council.[19] If END was serious about peace, Network participants felt, it should pay attention to the speech in Coventry by WiP's Radziwiłł. He called on END to "go beyond mere military disarmament. We need political disarmament. This means the elimination of the political reasons for the arms race; of aggression; of hostile images; of cold and hot wars. Such disarmament also includes an end to aggressive propaganda and ideological indoctrination; the dissolution of blocs and military pacts; and education for peace. Only strong and self-governing societies can guarantee the credibility of peace agreements contracted by governments."[20]

Even as Radziwiłł and Barabas spoke, however, the terms of dialogue were changing. In retrospect, the Coventry convention marked an end to the era in which the initiative for transnational contacts came from the West, on the West's terms. Movements in Central Europe were gaining in sophistication and confidence. They still valued their contacts with the West, but they also knew that the Western agenda could easily obscure what they hoped to achieve. The initiative slipped decisively to the Central Europeans themselves, led by Freedom and Peace.

The idea for a gathering *within* Central Europe on peace and human rights grew out of discussions between Freedom and Peace's Jacek Czaputowicz and Dieter Esche of the Network. Though the risks and logistical hurdles were much greater, a meeting in Warsaw could be attended by many Central European activists who had no hope of attending END conventions. No more would Central Europe be represented by a plaintive letter applauded at a plenary session and then filed away, nor by the lucky individual passport holder who had to represent all the complexity of his or her movement while avoiding the gaze of Eastern delegates there on official peace business. Thus would be realized the END Appeal's idea of a Europe without borders—ironically, in that part of Europe where borders were least porous. And the agenda, too, would be quite different.

Central Europe was no longer unfamiliar territory for most of the invited Westerners who traveled to Warsaw in early May 1987. They knew the risks, too. Esche (long persona non grata on GDR territory) made it to Poland by his usual circuitous route, taking the ferry from Copenhagen to Świnoujście. Joanne Landy had no difficulty, since her passport was in her maiden name. Jan Kavan shaved off his beard, donned a wig, and traveled under an assumed name (with passport to match). There was even one representative of Charter 77 there—Jiří Vančura, a historian—and two from the GDR. But dozens of others (including Jan Minkiewicz, Mient-Jan Faber, and Mary Kaldor of END, and almost everyone from the GDR and Czechoslovakia), were denied visas or turned back at the border. Many of those who made it decided to sleep at the church. As Joanne Landy explained, "I didn't spend $1,200 to be detained" by the police.[21] And as for WiP, Jacek Szymanderski had to jump out a window to escape police detention; others, like Jacek Czaputowicz, didn't sleep at home for several days before the seminar began. Twenty-two WiP participants were detained for most or all of the seminar.

Still, some two hundred opposition leaders, peace activists, scholars, and journalists crowded into the basement of the Church of God's Mercy on Żytnia Street (where Czaputowicz was employed as a chauffeur) for three days of discussion, followed by a pilgrimage to Otto Schimek's grave. For WiP, that the seminar took place at all was a major coup in the "game" versus the Polish authorities. "This time we won," Szymanderski told the conference. "We can say that we did it!"[22]

And they had. The seminar laid bare, as no exchange of documents possibly could, both how far East and West had come toward one another in the last few years, but also how much still divided the hosts from most of their guests. The very setting—the church basement's unfinished walls hung with the stations of the cross—challenged the visitors to think about Polish perspectives on peace and human rights. From the opening day panel entitled "Helsinki and Assisi," through the "Peace Mass" celebrated Friday evening, to the visit to Father Popiełuszko's grave Saturday afternoon, the teachings of the Church and Polish traditions of martyrdom were a constant presence. In contrast, a Polish observer at Coventry noted "barely four, maybe five meetings (of one hundred fifty) during the convention contained any sort of religious reference. . . . There was a lot said . . . about the peaceful Europe of the future. No one, however, took up the problem of the roots of Europeanness."[23] This was a question not simply of local styles, but of fundamentally divergent goals and beliefs, masked by similar tactics.

In place of the big international picture of the END conventions, the Warsaw seminar offered a focus on practicality, survival, and personal responsibility. Jan Maria Rokita, always one of WiP's most energetic polemicists, presented a speech entitled "Freedom and Peace, or How to Improve the Chances for Peace in Europe." For Rokita, pacifists (as he understood them) were dangerous fundamentalists. "The pacifist simply falls victim to the same illusion that claims any believer in a social doctrine that does not recognize the radical ontological distinction between a social fact and a social ideal. . . . Antinuclear incantations or antinuclear slogans take the place of rational thinking about the possible means to maintain peace."[24]

To Western activists (pacifist or not) in the audience, this sounded rather out of place, as if Margaret Thatcher were to have hectored them at Coventry. Even Rokita's broadside was nothing compared to an open letter sent from the seminar by WiP to the Afghan forces fighting the Soviets: "Though we live in different conditions and use different methods in our fight for freedom, our goals—the defense of national culture, the return of independence, and the protection of freedom and peace in our countries—are the same. . . . LONG LIVE A FREE AFGHANISTAN! LONG LIVE A FREE POLAND!"[25]

This was not the only current of Polish thought on display during the seminar, of course: Wojciech Jankowski and other Gdańsk anarchists were there, for example. But Freedom and Peace finally had a captive audience and could force upon it awareness of the Polish version of pluralism. The result was something quite different from the kitchen-table encounters that had shaped the Helsinki Memorandum, or E. P. Thompson's sensational visit to György Konrád's Budapest apartment.

The seminar also revealed just how much more open the new generation of Central European activism was. In 1980 Solidarity had, with few exceptions, been hesitant even to address the world beyond Poland's borders (and, when it did, had great difficulty finding a common language, both figuratively and literally). WiP's representatives had no qualms about discussing the nuclear arms race, or any other international affair. This was as true for Rokita as for the many pacifists in the movement. And while a session on feminism conducted by women from END drew mostly smirks from the Central Europeans, the topic certainly hadn't even come up at the Solidarity Congress in 1981. In the broadest sense, a common language had indeed been found.

Hopes were high coming out of Warsaw; the disappointment of Coventry simply spurred more meetings in the East. The next was in Budapest that October (see next chapter). There was no cloak-and-dagger *frisson* this time—though organizers had to threaten a scandal in order to keep the Peace Council at bay—but, coming hard on the heels of the Warsaw seminar, it contributed to the impression that the movements East and West really had become one peace community, uncontained by borders.

It was a little harder to take this traveling peace show to Prague. Jan Kavan and Chartist Jaroslav Šabata tried to organize a similar peace seminar in June 1988. After a few days of furtive meetings in dissidents' apartments, the whole group of visitors—Lynne Jones, Mary Kaldor, Jan Minkiewicz, Joanne Landy, Slovenia's Tomaž Mastnak, and a few others—found themselves in jail and soon were thrown out of the country. There would be no more dialogue this time. Still, something of the sense of impunity experienced in Warsaw had rubbed off. Joanne Landy remembers a hilarious time, with the jailers frequently barking "stop laughing!" at the group. They busied themselves making demands on the police, smuggling news of their capture to Western reporters, and hatching a plan for a "European Citizens' Assembly" to link progressive movements and monitor human rights. This idea would carry the movement through to the revolution. And if they suspected it before, now they knew for sure that "Europe" looked a lot different from a Prague jail cell, or the basement of a Warsaw church, than from a convention hall in Amsterdam, Coventry, or Berlin.

More than one Western peace activist found the journey east required a recalibration of the political compass. What seemed obvious from afar—help the oppressed dissidents, break down walls, engage in dialogue, build peace—was more confused close up. For 22-year-old Neil

Finer, the Warsaw seminar was his first trip through the Iron Curtain. He was there mainly to present a paper by Mary Kaldor. Quickly, he realized that some in Freedom and Peace cared more about the fact of Western contacts than about the agenda he and his colleagues had brought. There was another level of dialogue to which END was not a party: the one between Freedom and Peace and the senior leaders of Solidarity, like Bronisław Geremek or Zbigniew Romaszewski, who were seeing for the first time what their younger colleagues were capable of. Did those tortured debates within END even matter, then?

They did, of course, though not always in ways that were clear to Western observers. Though some may have felt an uneasy sense of superfluity, the Westerners' presence, and East-West contacts in general, were vitally important to the Central Europeans. Beginning with E. P. Thompson, Western observers had been cognizant of their possible value to Soviet-bloc contacts. But some, like Finer, in this new generation of travelers cared rather less about the ideas they brought than about the contacts themselves. As did many of their Eastern counterparts, they understood politics in an instrumental or *konkretny* way, even if this meant that they themselves would be the instrument to be manipulated.

The new movements in the East had greater need of such contacts than did the established opposition. Solidarity, or Charter 77, or the Democratic Opposition in Hungary, spoke from a position of moral authority that did not require this kind of outside legitimation—though time and again, of course, Western publicity helped to free jailed activists or at least made them harder to touch. In other words, the elder opposition drew upon a combination of universally accepted norms (freedom of speech, for example) and national traditions, not upon values they shared with any particular group outside their countries' borders.

Groups like Dialogue or Freedom and Peace, in contrast, based their opposition partly upon ideas that ran contrary to international norms, or to national traditions. Peace itself was a universally accepted idea, of course, but not the breakdown of blocs, nor conscientious objection to military service, nor ecological objections to industrial development. It was also, more than for Westerners, a subversive path that brought one into opposition to the regime; the Central European activists thus needed some external affirmation of their choice. In addition, the younger generation that embraced these ideas lacked the visibility that the writers, philosophers, and union leaders of the older movements enjoyed.

This is where END, and other groups, could help. When a student like Konstanty Radziwiłł of WiP, or Zsuzsa Gille of Dialogue, got an invitation to an END Convention; when Jacek Czaputowicz or Ferenc Köszegi became as well known to readers of mainstream peace magazines as were the older dissident intellectuals; when fifty to seventy Western activists and journalists showed up to a seminar in Warsaw or a peace camp near Budapest; when the carnival, in short, became an international festivity, the new movements gained in authority. By the end of 1987, Western familiarity with the movement scene in Central Europe was so great that newcomers in Hungary or Czechoslovakia had instant credibility, benefiting from the trails blazed by the early birds in their countries.

Contact with the West did change the way young opposition participants thought as well. In December 1985 the Campaign for Peace and Democracy/East and West initiated a statement against the Reagan administration's Nicaragua policy. Joanne Landy decided to get signatures from her new friends in Central Europe, but it wasn't at all easy. In the end, she rounded up a handful of signatures each from Hungary, Czechoslovakia, East Germany, and Yugoslavia, and just two from Poland, where Jan Józef Lipski and Jacek Czaputowicz signed.[26] For Czaputowicz to sign was a radical step, and a necessary one. Had he not done so, Poland would have been represented by one lone signature; this, Landy felt, would only have reinforced stereotypes about reactionary Poles, and further isolated the Polish opposition. Later, Czaputowicz recalled the storm that erupted in the generally pro-Reagan Polish opposition as a result. But that signature signaled the debut of an opposition ready to participate, on its own terms, in an agenda broader than the borders of any one country.

At the Warsaw seminar, the same people who showed their enthusiasm for the Afghan freedom fighters accepted the Westerners' position that Third World conflicts were largely imposed by the circumstances of the Cold War and the whims of the superpowers. Conflicts like those between U.S.-supported forces and the Nicaraguan Sandinistas were still ideological minefields that left Poles feeling "quite confused."[27] But that the subject even came up was thanks to Western pressure.

Still, the gulf remained, deeper than many participants realized at the time. Reflecting on the Warsaw seminar, Lynne Jones wrote: "Perhaps there really is a new beginning here, the possibility of forming some kind of independent and effective cooperation between peace, human rights, and ecology movements that does stretch across borders."[28] Jan Maria Rokita acidly dispels her optimism: his movement's contacts with END were useful simply "to bother the Soviets."* This was an extreme (though not unique) perspective; still, Neil Finer's suspicions were right: the activists of Freedom and Peace, and indeed all the opposition groups of Central Europe, did have another agenda. In their struggle to make themselves heard by the senior opposition, and in their battles with the communist regimes, they found their Western colleagues valuable allies. In the heat

---

* Though this remark was made ten years after the seminar, it is consistent with Rokita's position at the time.

of the moment, they were united in the struggle for peace and human rights. But what was to the Western activists a goal in and of itself was, to most in the East, also (and perhaps above all) a means to another end: a free, safe, and democratic future in their own countries. Each movement, regardless of its international ties, ultimately fought for freedom at home.

Chapter Four

THE NEW POLITICS OF THE
KONKRETNY GENERATION

A Shy Little Wave for Gorbachev

VÁCLAV Havel took his dog for a walk one evening in April 1987 and ran into Mikhail Gorbachev. To tell the truth, Havel wasn't all that sure he wanted to see the Soviet leader, but there was the huge crowd in front of the National Theater, welcoming the "glasnost czar," as Havel called him. Havel was the most famous dissident in Central Europe, but to the Communist regime he was just a repeat offender temporarily between prison spells. Gorbachev was on a series of visits to East European capitals, encouraging leaders to follow his twinned policies of perestroika and glasnost. In Prague he vigorously advocated the virtues of economic reform and openness.

Seeing a typical crowd of Praguers suddenly erupt in enthusiasm for Gorbachev, Havel was ashamed. "This nation of ours never learns. How many times has it put all its faith in some external force which, it believed, would solve its problems? How many times had it ended up bitterly disillusioned . . . ? And yet here we are again, making exactly the same mistake. They seem to think that Gorbachev has come to liberate them from Husák!"[1]

Mikhail Gorbachev has barely made an appearance in this story so far. But before we look for him, we should ask why we are looking. The place of the Soviet general secretary in the story of 1989 depends upon what one is trying to explain, and where one is. If we wish to understand changes in international relations, the cooling of the arms race, or the shifting alliances in Central European politburos as hard-liners lost their Kremlin backing, then Gorbachev is our man. If we are examining the spectacular failure of the command economy before and after 1989, the Soviet leadership will also be a key factor to consider. But our focus is on the streets, and the people who came to fill them. Though he has figured prominently in so many analyses of the revolution, to the protagonists of this book his role looked more ambiguous.

By the time Gorbachev assumed power in March 1985, Polish opposition was not only alive and well but actively exploring new directions in self-government, in creative expression, and in new movements, without a Soviet green light. The protest fasts that would spawn Freedom and Peace were at that moment under way. In Hungary, Dialogue had already come and gone, and the Bibó College students (about whom below) had been to Poland. Other contacts were also burgeoning. European Nuclear Disarmament was developing its Eastern networks, and some activists were already forming the Network for East-West Dialogue to push further. None of these things could possibly have happened because there had been a turnover in the Kremlin.

Wherever in his empire Gorbachev went, the same odd spectacle was repeated: the Soviet leader was welcomed with all the pomp traditionally due the bloc's emperor. Then his hosts sat in uncomfortable silence, or pretended not to hear, as Gorbachev lectured them on the need for change. Gorbachev was saying nothing new, the communist dailies would report; the native leaders had been following such policies all along. In Prague Gorbachev was hardly insistent on change; Havel noted irritably that this herald of glasnost "praised one of the worst governments our country has had in modern times."[2] On the eve of Gorbachev's visit, Charter 77 had sent the Soviet boss an open letter calling on him to demonstrate his commitment to glasnost and democratization by withdrawing Soviet troops and nuclear weapons from Czechoslovak soil; this the Kremlin ignored.[3]

Gorbachev's chronological irrelevance to social movements in Central Europe is matched by a logical limitation, applicable anywhere. The emergence of new social movements is not a chemical reaction, occurring automatically under the right conditions. No matter how liberal, even revolutionary, we may know Gorbachev to have been, how does that affect the would-be demonstrator? After decades of thaws and freezes in the Kremlin's mercurial foreign policy, it would be a foolish Central European who would read the actions of the youthful *gensek* as a signal to act. Gorbachev's ascension, after all, did not bring immediate easing of repression anywhere in Central Europe, even in Poland. Though one can and should put the detentions, fines, and house searches of 1986–88 in perspective—no one received ten-year sentences anymore, and very few were severely beaten—repression was nonetheless quite serious everywhere.

Some dissidents in the older generation felt that Gorbachev was the real thing. Adam Michnik, for example, began trumpeting his excitement at the changes in Moscow to anyone who would listen. Even Havel found himself giving Gorbachev a "shy little wave" as the Soviet entourage swept by.[4] But cautious optimism is far from actually following the Kremlin's signals.

To the younger peace activist or environmentalist, the release of controversial films or reports of a breakthrough summit meeting were hardly relevant; these were performances for Western consumption. Freedom and Peace's Piotr Niemczyk expressed his doubts in a widely read open letter to American peace activist Joanne Landy in 1987. Despite Gorbachev's declarations, he noted, hundreds of dissidents (in particular those who objected to military service) languished in jails and psychiatric hospitals, while the war in Afghanistan raged on. While applauding the idea of disarmament, he cautioned: "Only a sovereign society can be the guarantor of genuine disarmament and peace policy. An individual—even if, like the general secretary of the Communist Party of the Soviet Union, he possesses full power—cannot be such a guarantor."[5] Gorbachev's peace would leave the opposition movements and their concerns again out in the cold; human rights would be no more secure than before.

Turning south from Poland, to countries where the opposition was more isolated and vulnerable, we can see more clearly how movements were interdependent. Dissent was already well developed in each of these countries before 1985. There *was* a change in the style and the goals of opposition at about mid-decade, but the sources of that change had little to do with geopolitics. Instead, Poland's example was a powerful beacon. Sparked by the rise of Solidarity, then dimmed for a while by the imposition of martial law, fascination with Polish opposition contributed to new trends across Central Europe.

Under this Polish influence, Central Europe experienced a shift from the intellectual critiques of the communist system, typical of the older generation, to opposition grounded in concrete concerns. Antimilitary protests, environmental action, and defense of cultural autonomy are common themes after 1985 and are difficult to link to Gorbachev. Instead, the opposition in Poland itself—whether through direct contact, or filtered through Radio Free Europe or mutual Western contacts—spoke to its contemporaries in Central Europe. Not everyone was looking to Poland, of course, but in every country there were activists quite interested in the Polish style of opposition to communism.

THE LION CUBS OF WESTERN UKRAINE

Within the Soviet Union, Ukraine had been remarkably quiet up through most of 1987, in comparison with Moscow, Leningrad, the Baltic republics, or the Caucasus. Ukraine, a "real museum of Brezhnevism," as veteran dissident Viacheslav Chornovil remarked, was still a haven from the excitements of perestroika.[6] Since the late 1970s, repression of dissent in Ukraine had been quite harsh—brutal, even. Opposition had been most tenacious in Western Ukraine, an area joined to the USSR after World War II. In Lviv,* that region's capital, it would rise again. But while older dis-

---

* Transliterations from the Cyrillic alphabet in Ukrainian (and Russian) are given here without the soft signs. "Lviv," for example, is correctly transliterated as "L'viv."

sidents like Chornovil looked hopefully to Gorbachev, they dreamed at most of a return to the brief opportunities of the 1970s, not of any great upheaval. A public movement was yet far from their plans.

There was no niche in the Soviet Union for the nonconformist. The individual who rejected the norms of Soviet life would not simply be out of a job and installed as a boiler-room stoker, as in Czechoslovakia (though that punishment was also in the Soviet repertoire). A labor camp or a psychiatric hospital was a more likely destination. This had been the fate of the nationalist opposition in Ukraine; many never returned from the camps or from forced exile. For the younger generation—those who did not follow the path of the hippies, whom we will encounter in the next chapter—there was university and the Komsomol, the army, and work.

Two things changed in Ukraine with the Gorbachev era. First, the Chernobyl accident had an enormous political impact, especially on those then in university or just beginning careers. Ihor Koliushko, a student of physics at the time, thought about it in just the way his counterparts in Poland did: Chernobyl "forced people to stop fearing." For Ukrainians, fear of the state had been vastly greater than in Poland—but even more fearsome was the environmental threat they now faced. Young scientists like Lev Zakharchyshyn felt the first effects of Gorbachev's liberalization in a relaxed attitude toward ecological research; to them, Chernobyl meant that it was time to act.

A year after Chernobyl, Viacheslav Chornovil and Mykhaylo Horyn returned from prison. They immediately revived their samizdat journal, the *Ukrainian Herald,* dormant since 1974. As the leaders of the Ukrainian Helsinki Union, they were the most prominent dissidents in Ukraine. Chornovil especially was a nearly legendary figure to many in Lviv for the repression he had endured. Young hippy Ihor Copestynskyi was far from opposition politics, devoted to the rock underground. But he went to see Chornovil when he learned that the senior oppositionist was working in the same factory (in the boiler room, in fact), and asked how he too could help the cause. Soon he was helping to compose and distribute the *Ukrainian Herald.* But he wondered about the "normal people" who might be afraid to meet Chornovil, and he wanted to create something for them, too.

Meanwhile, in the Café Yunist (the "Youth Café"), the Nektar Café, and the Writers' Union Club, students and young intellectuals began meeting with some of the so-called moderate nationalists of the older generation, including Iryna Kalynets, editor of the cultural-spiritual samizdat *Evshan-Zille,* and poet Roman Bratun. More discussions took place in the home of Iryna and Ihor Kalynets, an apartment suffused with Ukrainian culture. Ihor was one of the region's best-known poets; Iryna had begun an informal society (the Society of Mercy) to reawaken the banned Uniate Church.

Taras Stetskiw later recalled that the two generations were united "by one thought: one can't exist like this any longer, and something must be done. But what exactly—[we] didn't know. What kept [us] together in those first three months [in late 1987]? Probably the unconscious desire to rescue national culture . . . to find a way out of the stagnant swamp. In this circle (far from the only one in the city) there gradually arose the conviction [that we should] become the laborers of the national awakening." If one allows for the greater emphasis on national survival, Stetskiw sounds much like his counterparts in Wrocław two or three years earlier. They would begin with "concrete practical work, and from there move to the universal."[7]

Many students in Lviv had gotten a glimpse already of new ways of organizing from Ukrainian students from Poland. For decades, the existence of minorities on either side of the border, and the ways each had been treated under communism, had made the border nearly impenetrable. The first students from Lublin, Poland, were allowed to go to Kyiv in 1986. In 1987 they began coming to Lviv. Though any Ukrainian students' movement in Poland still had to keep a very low profile (else they be branded "national chauvinists" and severely punished), they knew the ins and outs of student opposition well. As Polish student Mirosław Czech saw it, the most important thing he and his friends could share was a "positivist" approach to political change. These students would become an outlet for Lviv students to communicate with the West, too.

Stetskiw, and many other students, were members of the Komsomol at the university. It was therefore entirely appropriate that the "laborers'" first action was a *subotnyk*—voluntary labor service, according to the model inspired by Lenin almost seventy years earlier—organized by the Lviv Komsomol that July. Orest Sheika, a senior Komsomol activist and former art student, hatched the idea of using the *subotnyk* to clean and restore some of Lviv's historical landmarks. The *Leninist Youth* newspaper published Sheika's appeal, and several dozen people showed up at the historic Lychakiv cemetery on July 4 to clean gravestones. The idea for a society to promote Ukrainian culture was born; meeting in Sheika's Komsomol office a few days later, a small group of students drew up the statute for the Lion Society (Tovarystva Leva). The name evoked the city (Lviv, the City of Lions), though the inspiration came from a book of poems by a nineteenth-century poet of Lviv. To their elders, the students were the "lion cubs" (*leveniata*).

Sheika was playing a risky game. The *subotnyk* and the organization raised the specter of West Ukrainian nationalism, discouraged even under Gorbachev. The protection of monuments, the purity of the Ukrainian language, and the rebirth of spirituality—all mentioned in the first draft of the statute—were hardly innocent proposals. But the Lviv Communist

Party approved the statute, without the point about language, which reappeared later. Party officials found they could not ban the group nor easily change the statute because Sheika had first gained the support of four official organizations, including the Komsomol. With these patrons, the Lion Society could not be uprooted without a massive crackdown.

This was not another vent, part of a secret plan from above to give restless youth a distraction from real problems. One-time society leader Lev Zakharchyshyn insists it was a spontaneous organization from below that found support from the Komsomol. Each side needed the other. The Komsomol hoped to avoid the isolation that official organizations had already experienced in the Baltic republics. The Lion Society, in turn, needed an umbrella and funding for the concrete projects that it would pursue.

Thus began what Sheika recalled as "the most pure period in the political life of our land"—an era, comments another participant, of "romantic exaltation and selfless work in preparation for the awakening of the future state."[8] If they really thought about independence, the lion cubs were very precocious indeed. It was hard to think about a state when the nation—framed by popular allegiance to Ukrainian culture—was in such disrepair. First, the Lion Society would have to reach out precisely to those about whom Copestynskyi had worried: those who hesitated to celebrate national traditions openly for fear of retribution. It would, in the words of another lion cub, Ihor Koliushko, "build up people's appetite," reminding them of what they had been doing without.

Orest Sheika came regularly to Iryna Kalynets for advice as the society planned its happenings. He met people like Kalynets's co-editor Valentyn Stetsiuk and Bratun at weekly discussions in the Kalynets salon. Through them, the society indeed became the place for those who hesitated to follow a more radical confrontational politics. Many participants described it as the place for people who wanted to get things done; they might have used the word *konkretny.*

Thus, for example, the nearly forgotten Christmas tradition of *vertepy*—a folk theater procession of elaborately costumed figures who visit homes to play out the Christmas story and sing carols. *Vertepy* were not illegal, but the average Lviv resident (even if faithful to the Uniate Church) would be unsure. First, then, Roman Bratun (who by then had been invited to join the society) co-authored an article in the literary weekly *Literaturna Ukraina* explaining the history and meaning of the tradition. Then, one December evening, came the procession of high school and college students—an angel, a King Herod, the three magi, a devil, shepherds, and assorted other figures—winding through the city streets to the simple accompaniment of a traditional reed pipe.

This was a moment at once religious, national, and civic, and it had a revolutionary impact on the city's residents. People were given a chance to rediscover who they were—and not through a nationalism of confrontation and conflict, but by recapturing what it meant to be a citizen of Lviv and of Galicia, Western Ukraine. By the following Christmas, Lviv was a different place. As the *vertepy*—this time multiple processions, singing and playing instruments loudly—walked through the city on their way to homes where they knew they would be welcome, total strangers ran up and begged the carolers to come and perform in their homes, too. The city's appetite had indeed returned.

The lion cubs unearthed other traditions, too, "attracting society's attention," writes Valentyn Stetsiuk, "with a steady stream of actions of a kind not seen before, changing the consciousness of the masses and the stereotypical behavior of frightened people."[9] Some group members traveled to villages in the Havaretsk region, where the distinctive tradition of making black pottery was dying out. Not only did they document this style and collect examples, they learned how to make it themselves and sold their work in Lviv. As they stood in the winter cold in their embroidered peasant shirts, they both saved the tradition and reincorporated it into a contemporary version of the Ukrainian nation.

Another "lost" tradition was the *hayvka*, a May picnic, which the society staged, complete with a samizdat songbook. The people who gathered at the Museum of Ethnography's open-air park, writes Stetsiuk, "cried when they heard the enchanting songs that they had last heard in childhood."[10] Thus the Lion Society became familiar to the city's residents without becoming at all threatening. And if an ordinary regime-sponsored *subotnyk* were a tiresome obligation, a Lion Society *subotnyk* —renamed a "Green *Toloka*" (roughly translated, a "barn raising") to reconnect it to local traditions and rhythms—attracted hundreds of eager citizens. Like Solidarity, the Lion Society became an alternative force in Lviv, and eventually across the region.

For a younger generation that might be indifferent to the fate of black pottery and unfamiliar with farming songs, the task was not to capture what was lost. "It was necessary," asserts Olek Starovoit, "to create a new Ukrainian culture," since the official one was simply useless. Starovoit organized rock concerts—where the music was defiantly Ukrainian, the words Ukrainian—poetry readings, art exhibits. And lest the nationalism become too pompous, the society's journal *Postup* (on which see scene 4) was followed by a satirical version, *Saltseson* (Sausage)—the name challenging readers to consider which, in the end, was more important, Ukraine or a full stomach.

In its first year, the Lion Society's greatest undertaking was a raft expedition. Ecologists had for some time tried to call attention to the devastation of the Dnister River, the largest in Western Ukraine, which flowed to the south of Lviv. Here was another national yet apparently unobjectionable cause: how could communist officials mind a little rafting trip? The organizers, including Valentyn Stetsiuk (who would be the informal leader of the expedition) and Lev Zakharchyshyn, built six catamarans atop oil drums. They made hand copies of secret military maps, since no navigational charts could be had legally. Money had been raised at a benefit concert given by the cabaret satirical group Ne Zhurys (Don't Worry). Some thirty people, almost all from the society, set sail after a ceremonial unveiling of the catamarans on Lviv's Rynok on May 25, 1988. Over one hundred days, the expedition traveled from the Dnister's source near the Polish border all the way to the Black Sea.

One could do a lot of things from a raft floating down river. Some of the participants focused on ecological problems. They took water samples, caught and studied fish, and took note of illegal waste discharge into the river. They advised villagers on ways to sink wells to draw healthier water, and how to dispose of agricultural waste safely. And they compiled an "Ecological Map" of the Dnister, showing major pollution sources: not just factories and farms, but even places where people habitually washed their cars on weekends.[11]

At the same time, the expedition was a vehicle for national awakening. Villagers came forward to tell stories, unspoken for forty years, of their wartime experiences. Expedition members tried to record as many of these as they could. In return, they talked to villagers about glasnost and their hopes for political liberalization. Zakharchyshyn recalls coming to one village in the Carpathian Mountains near Turek, early in the expedition. The villagers listened somewhat impatiently to the environmental information and advice, with the typical distrust of what they assumed was an official visit. Then they began to explain that, more than anything else, they wanted their long-closed parish church back. This was a district where the Uniate Church had been brutally suppressed in the 1940s. There were some on the expedition who knew something of the Church's history: they stood up to offer impromptu lectures. After the meeting, the villagers went themselves to open the shuttered church; then the Dnister explorers and the villagers prayed there together.

No other movement in Central Europe—not even Freedom and Peace —so thoroughly combined local dreams and national politics. But nowhere else in the region had the population been so silenced, either. The Lion Society searched for the micronationalism of everyday practice, underneath the macronationalism of forbidden holidays, banned writers, and violated sovereignty. Micronationalism accomplished the same goals, awakening people's hunger for greater freedom. It was also less directly threatening to the regime. In June 1988, as the expedition entered its second month, KGB harassment of the expedition suddenly ceased. Demonstrations had begun in Lviv (see scene 4), and a few dozen rafters now seemed a lot less dangerous.

But it was no less radical for all that. A new generation of student radicals, indeed, would emerge from the Lion Society. The Student Brotherhood, an underground network organized by journalism student Markian Ivashchyshyn, began in 1988 to protest compulsory military service, demanding also the right to serve only on Ukraine's territory. Before its official founding in 1989, the Brotherhood benefited from links to the Lion Society, which, as an officially registered organization, could rent meeting rooms. And the best way to attract new supporters, Ivashchyshyn found, was at Lion Society concerts.

At its first anniversary conference, in October 1988, the Lion Society demonstrated a mastery of political performance then unmatched in Ukraine. The city authorities seemed determined now to silence the society. Independent movements from across the Soviet Union had been invited to observe the conference. But as activists arrived in Lviv, they were met by city officials at the train station and invited onto a bus that, instead of heading to the conference, circled the city on a surreal sightseeing tour for several hours, making it impossible to attend the meeting. The society itself was denied permission to meet in the hall it had reserved in the National Institute. Police and KGB forces lined up behind cordons, expecting to provoke a violent reaction. As a thousand or more gathered in the square, Lion Society members wearing green armbands expected to bear the brunt of a police assault.

This was a moment to denounce the Soviet regime—perhaps, even, to storm the building and declare a free Ukraine. Ukrainian Helsinki Union leader Chornovil pushed through the crowd to speak, but society members held him back, fearing that he "would certainly ruin everything."[12] Instead, Orest Sheika, speaking from the steps of the National Institute, suggested that the assembly return to the Lion Society's roots and march to the Lychakiv cemetery, where some of them had met the previous July. This time, he said, they would not clean gravestones but dig a grave, for the era of stagnation that perestroika had promised to end. Arm in arm with Rostislav Bratun, he marched off in the direction of the Rynok, toward the cemetery. The crowd followed; the nonplussed KGB officers could only retreat to their cars and follow along. On this day, Lviv still belonged to the Lion Society.

On very different soil from Warsaw or Budapest, the Lion Society developed a political style not unlike that found farther west. It avoided extremes in favor of moderation and pluralism, all the while pushing the cause of anticommunism as firmly as did more prominent nationalists. The lion cubs' sheer variety of ideas, and their constant activity, breathed new life into Ukrainian culture. Though in the end the Soviet context limited what the Lion Society could accomplish, its style and politics was essentially Central European. Ihor Koliushko felt this strongly when, in the summer of 1989, he could finally meet Polish activists. The conversation, he found, flowed on two levels. On one, senior dissident intellectuals talked about the "blank spots" in Polish-Ukrainian history, and how to resolve mutual misunderstandings. This was important, Koliushko knew, but more important for him were the young Polish Ukrainians like Mirosław Czech. They talked about how to publish samizdat, and how to organize demonstrations. Both conversations were important, but only one looked toward the future.

SLOVENIA'S PEOPLE FOR PEACE CULTURE

Beyond Berlin, the birthplace of the Network for East-West Dialogue, there was one other city where paths leading east and west in search of peace actually crossed: Ljubljana, in Slovenia. Yugoslavia was the only major communist country in Europe not in the Warsaw Pact and had the most open borders as well. Contacts with the West lacked the official stigma that they always had elsewhere. Indeed, the position between two camps was a central tenet of Yugoslav socialism; General Secretary Josip Tito was one of the leaders of the organization of nonaligned states in the 1970s. A dialogue between East and West would logically begin here.

But there were deep contradictions between the appearance of relative openness and reality. Nonalignment meant, for Tito and his successors, constant vigilance. A primal fear of Soviet invasion haunted Yugoslavia—which had already endured terrible destruction in World War II—for the better part of a decade after Yugoslavia left the Soviet bloc in 1948, and it never really faded from memory. Departure from the bloc meant a perceived need for greater military preparedness, not less. Only in East Germany did citizens face a comparable barrage of exhortations to vigilance and battle-readiness. Sociologist Gregor Tomc compiled some examples of militaristic propaganda, in a report he sent to the 1986 END Convention: "peace" in Yugoslavia was "the peace of a bullet in a barrel of a gun"; "to go to work is . . . to go to war"; "all actions against self-management are a diversion and sabotage," conducted by traitors.[13]

This language reached a crescendo in the years after Tito's death in 1980, as Yugoslavia celebrated the fortieth anniversary of landmarks in the partisan victory over the Nazis. An impressive military parade in Belgrade in May 1985 completed this commemorative season. For the generations that had grown up after the war, this aggressive neutrality had begun to seem both irrational and unnecessary. "So we began," writes

Slavenka Drakulić, "to assume an ironic attitude towards the War, to the partisans and the communist revolution—to our history as represented in such caricature."[14]

This was the kind of terrain, of obvious contradictions and worn-out propaganda, ripe for exploitation by the *konkretny* generation. In Yugoslavia that task would fall to the Slovenes. For Yugoslav communism had another weakness: the tension between the status of the six individual republics and the unity of the state, dominated from Belgrade. The problem was not that nationalist friction was inevitable, but that Yugoslavia was a federal state without democracy. This lack was felt most deeply in Slovenia, where traditions of democracy and civic activism were strongest. Beginning with the problem of peace, Slovene activists would eventually move on to the contradictions of Yugoslav nationalism.

Slovenia is a difficult place for the student of anticommunist opposition, schooled in the world of samizdat and tamizdat, to understand: there were no underground journals, nor even an "underground" in the usual sense. Instead, opposition emerged from within the League of Communists and the League of Socialist Youth of Slovenia (ZSMS). The latter gave birth to the Peace Movement Working Group in early 1983. Its members were students and young intellectuals in Ljubljana. Some were active in the youth organization; all recognized that the ZSMS could be a foundation for civic activism. Tomaž Mastnak, a social scientist, put it this way: "To me, it was of rather secondary importance that the group was a peace group; I was interested in what we then (rather uncritically) called developing civil society."[15]

We have encountered this instrumental voice before, but here the emphasis is less on defeating communism than on building society. "Civil society," as Mastnak and the others understood it, was both a goal—the creation of autonomous civic activity, fully independent of the state—and the practice of being autonomous. What one actually did was in a way not so important. Though it masqueraded as an exploration of a particular issue, the Peace Group was even more an experiment in reinventing Slovene politics.

The ZSMS actually spawned quite a number of other interest groups, of which the most significant was the Women's Working Group. In 1983 Vlasta Jalušič and Mojca Dobnikar visited West Berlin. The sheer variety of women's clubs, libraries, and organizations amazed them, and they resolved that the same should be possible in Ljubljana. They began with a working group, which in 1985 led to Lilith, one of the few activist women's groups anywhere in the communist world.* Lilith's first action

---

* There were several identity movements in Ljubljana at that time. Another was Magnus, which, beginning in 1984, ran the only gay nightclub in all of Central Europe.

was a women-only disco. Like the Peace Group, Lilith understood civil society in the broadest sense and would be an engine behind some of the important protests of the last half of the 1980s.

Like movements in Hungary or Poland, the Peace Group was marked by its internal pluralism. Its guiding spirit, and first editor of its semi-samizdat, English-language *Information Booklet,* was Marko Hren, a mathematician and pacifist. In high school Hren had traveled to Switzerland to learn about the movement there to abolish the army. In 1981 he refused to bear arms during his military service. He was joined in the movement by Mastnak, who did not consider himself a pacifist; Gregor Tomc, who was not only a sociologist but a member of and the songwriter for Slovenia's pioneering punk band *Pankrti* (Bastards); Janez Janša, at the time something of an anarchist, who specialized in studying the Yugoslav military system; Jalušič; and others.

In tiny Slovenia, which already in the 1980s found its relationship with the rest of Yugoslavia increasingly uncomfortable, the Peace Group had to cross borders to make any sense at all of its ideals. Beginning in 1984 the Peace Group sponsored annual peace camps, bringing together activists from Slovenia and neighboring provinces in Italy and Austria. One could visit the West with ease, and even hope to bring Western ideas home, as Lilith had done. But Yugoslavia was not the West, the Slovenes knew; at least not as long as Tito's version of socialism was in power. They knew they had more in common with their counterparts in Hungary, Czechoslovakia, or Poland, and they found Western attitudes toward communism (of which the Yugoslav version was often supposed to be the most palatable) naïve. Thus Mastnak and Hren were among the authors of a strident critique of early drafts of the Helsinki Memorandum. After "five years of dialogue," they wrote, "easterners" had earned the right to push their concerns about human rights to the forefront, ahead of the talk about disarmament that the Western activists appeared to prefer.[16]

The Slovene search for models of civil society and human rights activism led them straight to Poland. A thick volume of documents on Solidarity was published in 1985. Mastnak, meanwhile, began traveling to Poland. By 1987, when Mastnak was attending the Freedom and Peace seminar in Warsaw, the *Information Booklet* had shed some of its idealism for aggressive stands on human rights and on communism in general.

The basic agenda of the Peace Group—demilitarization of society, the evolution of a peace-based culture, and international understanding—was rather like that of Hungary's Dialogue. Like Dialogue, the Peace Group activists hoped to encourage popular self-awareness, and to discuss the problems that concerned them, more than they sought to change the regime. This reflected the movement's semi-official sponsorship. But unlike Dialogue, the Slovene Peace Group would choose a path leading to greater engagement in politics and confrontation with the regime. To do so, the movement replicated itself: People for Peace Culture, a group that emerged in 1986, was in fact the Peace Group, under another name and affiliated with the student organization at the university. This was, says Marko Hren, simply insurance in case the whims of either bureaucracy (the ZSMS or the university) would change.

But what the Peace Group really needed was independence. It did not even have the meager independent resources that other Central European movements enjoyed; there was no senior opposition or émigré publishing house that might want to help an alternative social movement. So some in the movement decided to create their own umbrella: a private computer firm, Mikro Ada. This company was the creation of four men: Marko Hren, Janez Janša, Igor Bavčar (who, like Janša, had recently been expelled from the ZSMS leadership), and Igor Omerza. "As individuals," Hren explained, "we wanted to be independent . . . and to equip ourselves." They imported and sold computers and software and used some of the profit to launch desktop publishing projects. The first issue of *Information Booklet* (the title later changed to *Independent Voices from Yugoslavia*) came in 1985.

Mikro Ada's biggest publishing venture, in the spring of 1988, was the memoirs of Stane Kavčič, a voice of liberalism among Slovene communists in the Tito era. The first edition sold out in a matter of hours, from sidewalk kiosks the Peace Group set up. It was both a political sensation, raising once again the specter of Slovene separatism, and a great moneymaker for the opposition at what would prove to be a crucial moment. For renting halls or nightclubs, for hiring speakers, or for printing materials, Mikro Ada would be an essential resource.

The Peace Group began with information booths on the streets of Ljubljana—"peace street shops," they called them—that distributed peace literature, posters, and peace sign badges. Then, during the December 1984 "peace street" action, the movement collected signatures on a petition protesting the production of military toys. The idea resonated with a society tired of living the last war; in the essay quoted earlier, Slavenka Drakulić describes the look of horror on her father's face when he saw her hold the gun he had used in World War II. As Christmas 1985 approached, the Peace Group set up a stall offering educational, peaceful toys, in exchange for "unsuitable" military toys. The stall collected some 250 toy guns, which they turned over to a recycling plant, enacting military conversion on a tiny scale.[17]

The conversations that these actions (which took place in Maribor as well) provoked opened up more subversive questions about how the Yugoslav state shaped its citizens' attitude toward the military. Again, the commemoration of war brought the intentions of the state into sharper focus. To celebrate the fortieth anniversary of the partisan victory—in which women fighters had played an important role—the army proposed extending obligatory military training to women. This plan, drafted in secret by army leaders, was leaked to the Slovene peace activists. Together, Lilith and the Peace Group organized a public discussion of this still-secret proposal, followed by a petition protesting this "further militarization of society." They wondered at this antiquated need for vigilance against unknown aggressors; surely it was enough that women could volunteer for military training if they so chose.[18]

At first, the generals railed against Slovene troublemakers; to Belgrade, any protest from Slovenia smelled of secessionist tendencies. But by the end of the summer of 1985, the proposal had quietly disappeared. Quite reluctantly, the Yugoslav authorities had found they could not ignore social protest. Perhaps the most telling argument the peace activists and feminists made was that such obligatory service did not exist in the advanced countries of Western Europe, which Yugoslavia in some ways emulated. It was contradictions like these that made Titoist ideology so easy to undermine.

The campaign for conscientious objectors would be much more difficult. Perhaps only nationalist opposition aroused the anger of leaders of the partisan generation more than an attack on obligatory military service. In Slovenia, Ivan Čečko, a Jehovah's Witness from Maribor, most likely held the modern European record, with a total of fifteen years in prison for refusal to serve. But Čečko was, unlike other Jehovah's Witnesses, willing to talk about his experiences. Upon his release from prison in 1986, he was immediately sentenced to a new term, a practice that no other country in Central Europe employed. When he was briefly released again in 1987, Čečko gave talks on his experiences in both Maribor and Ljubljana. Without Čečko, it would have been difficult to make the conscientious objector issue real for many Slovenes. An issue that had naturally been part of the Peace Group's portfolio from the outset now had a name and a face.

The Yugoslav regime's first response was to allow conscientious objection based upon religious belief. But as the Peace Group pointed out, this was in conflict with the Yugoslav Constitution, which promoted equality of believers and nonbelievers. An atheist, in this communist country, would now have fewer rights than a Catholic or a Jehovah's Witness. Once again, communist rhetoric had provided the Peace Group with a neat irony.

The Yugoslav regime would not budge; military service was still a duty for all young men, and alternative service would "violate the principles of socialist norms." Still, the campaign left its mark. Two years of "peace street" actions and the Čečko case had thrust the problem into the public eye. "Almost every day," the *Information Booklet* reported in 1987, "there are articles on [the] CO issue appearing in all kinds of newspapers. Well, usually in the negative way, but in any case, people [can now] think about it, and that is what is most important."[19]

With the CO issue, the Peace Group became an opposition movement almost in spite of itself. Their powerful opponents labeled the peace activists enemies of socialism and power-hungry national separatists. Evaluating the CO campaign as a participant and an observer, Gregor Tomc saw how ties to the ZSMS limited the movement's autonomy. He foresaw that any real success of an "alternative" movement (in Yugoslavia, the term "opposition" was still taboo) would require both more "concrete" actions like the CO campaign and political action, directed against the system itself.[20]

Politics would come soon enough. But first came a campaign that, unexpectedly, mobilized onto the streets more people than had been seen in decades. As in Poland, the issue was nuclear power. There was only one nuclear power station in Yugoslavia, at Krško in Slovenia. While the fallout from Chernobyl did not affect Slovenia itself very much, and the Krško plant was not of the same suspect model as that in Ukraine, the incident nevertheless aggravated anti-Belgrade, anticommunist instincts. It also awakened environmental fears in a republic whose identity was tied closely to nature.

On May 10, 1986 (two weeks after the accident), some two thousand came out to listen to a declaration written by peace and environmental activists. The crowd then "spontaneously decided" to march to Parliament.[21] Shielded from fallout by Marko Hren's battered umbrella, Juvan Janez read out the Peace Group's declaration; Hren wore a surgical mask. Signs in the crowd called for "More Light in the Heads of Slovene Energy Planners!" and exclaimed "You Praise Nuclear Energy and Harm Our Health."

One year later, Lilith and the Peace and Environmental working groups staged an anniversary march. Vlasta Jalušič's idea was to use the occasion to question also the regime's commitment to women's emancipation. In communist tradition, women were recognized as they passively received bouquets on International Women's Day (March 8). Jalušič proposed an anticelebration of women's political activism, linked to a health issue that, as in Poland, mobilized women in particular.

The crowd on April 23, 1987, was several times larger than the year before as it marched from the university to the Parliament. This was in fact the biggest crowd in Slovenia in at least fifteen years. Ljubljana had woken up, thanks to the Peace Group's campaign, and to the youth weekly *Mladina*, which published a series of provocative articles on ecology and on the Krško plant. The patient wait for information about the accident, and about plans for nuclear energy in Yugoslavia, had been exhausted, and rumor had taken hold. It was easy, for example, to believe that the cheap imported food, suddenly appearing in stores stripped bare by a prolonged debt crisis, were actually radioactive goods priced for dumping on unsuspecting consumers.

The demonstration lasted for hours. Jalušič and other speakers called for the closing of Krško and of Slovenia's uranium mines, and they challenged the government to release information about nuclear energy. Huge banners denounced nuclear energy; one read, in English, "Nuclear Energy—Fuck Off!"

There were more public demonstrations in Yugoslavia by this time. In the spring of 1987, for example, Serbs in Kosovo began demonstrating against Albanians' demands for ethnic rights—a movement that Slobodan Milošević would seize upon to grab power in Yugoslavia. But the organized, peaceful, civic demonstrations of Slovenia were different. The Chernobyl demonstration of 1987 would prove to be a dress rehearsal for the Slovene Spring of 1988.

HUNGARIAN ORANGE APPEAL

At least since 1956, when Polish and Hungarian students followed, and shouted their support for, the revolutionary events in each other's country closely, a real affection developed between dissent in the two countries.* In the decades after the 1956 defeat, the influence was almost entirely in one direction. In the 1960s and 1970s, young Hungarians traveled to the jazz clubs of Warsaw to hear what they could not at home. The late 1970s and early 1980s brought the powerful influence of KOR and Solidarity. Gábor Demszky went to Poland to study Solidarity's samizdat techniques; upon his return, he started what became Hungary's premier underground publishing house on the Polish model.

Tamás Fellegi and István Stumpf were just a few years younger than Demszky. In 1983 Stumpf was a young teacher, finishing a study of the establishment of communism in Poland. Fellegi had recently graduated from law school, with an interest in the political history of the Soviet Bloc. That May they and their wives traveled by car to witness Pope John Paul II's second pilgrimage to Poland. They had a contact, a Polish-Hungarian translator in Warsaw, who introduced them to the peculiarities of martial law Poland.

* The roots go back much further, actually, to the leadership of Polish General Józef Bem during the revolution of 1848 in Budapest. The statue of Bem, near the Buda side of the Margit Bridge, has been an important spot on the political map of Budapest, a touchstone for many demonstrations.

To Hungarian visitors, Poland made no sense. On the one hand, the repressive state was a lot more evident on the Warsaw streets than it had been in Hungary for twenty-five years—though Budapest dissidents were living through a crackdown at the time. But on the other hand, Polish society was freer than anything imaginable in Hungary. Samizdat was everywhere, and Solidarity seemed to have survived. Fellegi and Stumpf attended a papal mass in Warsaw and were deeply impressed by the sight of hundreds of thousands of worshippers, some carrying Solidarity signs or singing forbidden songs. It was not just the level of freedom or the audacity of the people they met: it was the capacity for self-organization that struck them, and stayed with them as they drove back to Budapest.

Stumpf had been given permission, by the rector of Eötvös Loránd University, to form a residential college for law students from beyond Budapest. The idea (as with another older college, the László Rajk College at the Economic Institute) was to integrate the student community and give small-town students the advantages that native Budapesters enjoyed. Innocuous enough—but Stumpf had other ideas. For the Special Juristic Sociological College—later named the István Bibó Special College, after a political thinker and member of the 1956 government who had died in 1979—he designed a program of courses oriented around political questions.

Fellegi was the first official lecturer at the college. He signaled the direction the college would take by offering, in October 1983, a full-year course on the Revolution of 1956. He arrived for the first class to find a line a half-mile long in front of the college on Ménesi Street. Few in the crowd were students (the college itself housed only forty at the time); most were, Fellegi quickly realized, either opposition activists looking for some kind of sensational breakthrough, or police sensing a subversive situation. Perhaps both sides imagined the Bibó College could spawn a youth wing for the established opposition. But as Fellegi understood its role, the college should help a new generation of students to find their own answers to the problems facing Hungary, and not just follow what their elders had discovered. This would be impossible if the college became a cause célèbre and ran afoul of the regime. So Fellegi gave an especially dull opening lecture, and within a few weeks the class was down to manageable size.

Over the next few years, Fellegi presented courses on "The Crises of Communism" and on Marxism. Others offered courses on the culture of Hungarian Transylvania, on contemporary Hungarian society, and so forth. In each course, professors and students tried to unhinge anticommunist opposition from any ideological standpoints. Was Marxism a good idea, badly implemented, they asked, or a bad idea that had somehow managed to survive? What could Adam Michnik, or his Hungarian counterpart György Konrád, have to offer if read with fresh eyes? And above all: what should be done?

One of the first residents at the Bibó College was a 20-year-old law student from Székesfehérvár, southwest of Budapest, named Viktor Orbán. Lászlo Kövér, from Pápa, was a few years older, as was Gábor Fodor. Kövér was a student in 1981 and participated in an attempt to set up a rival student organization to the communist-sponsored one, inspired in part by the experiment then under way in Poland. Orbán, in turn, had had an intensely personal experience of Solidarity: when martial law was declared, he was fulfilling his military service and expected at any moment to be mobilized to invade Poland in support of Soviet troops. Subsequently, Orbán wrote his master's thesis on Solidarity, focusing on the role of self-organizing groups in Poland in 1980–81.[22]

Orbán, Kövér, Fodor, and about twenty other students participated in the Bibó College's first summer retreat, at Visegrad (above the Nagymaros dam site) in August 1983. Step by step, Stumpf and Fellegi were helping to create a student community, and a movement. Their model was Poland, and they hoped that their students would somehow learn from Polish students the ways of independent political activity. The following spring, teachers and students went to Poznań on the college's first exchange program, spending a week in dormitories at Adam Mickiewicz University.

The next year, the Hungarian students added Gdańsk and Warsaw to their itinerary. Now they would really learn Polish opposition culture. In Gdańsk, some of them stayed with Adam Jagusiak and Gosia Tarasiewicz, in the same apartment where conscientious objector Zsolt Keszthelyi had stayed the previous year. Fellegi had met the Polish students, both soon to be participants in Freedom and Peace, in Budapest. Together, the Hungarians and Poles went to lay flowers at the monument to the victims of the 1970 shipyard massacre and were detained there by the police for four hours.

Opposition in Hungary was beginning to emerge from salons and basements. The older opposition gathered at Monor, a campsite just outside Budapest, in June 1985. The three days of discussion brought only short-lived cooperation among the various strands of intellectual dissent. Fresh from Poland, the Bibó students joined representatives of "special colleges" across Hungary at Szarvas in August to try to coordinate some activities. The main product of Szarvas was a collective, semi-official student periodical entitled *End of the Century* (*Századveg*), edited by a team including Orbán and Kövér and published by István Stumpf. The contrast between the two meetings is telling: only the students came away with something moderately concrete and lasting. Kövér saw the Szarvas meeting as a radicalizing event, as the regime's unwillingness to listen to the students, evident then and subsequently, pulled students together.[23]

Orbán, Kövér, Fellegi, and several others made one last trip to Gdańsk, for Pope John Paul II's third pilgrimage, in June 1987. Their friends Adam and Gosia were now active in WiP, writing for the journal *A cappella* and organizing demonstrations. The Hungarian students found the apartment full of people painting WiP banners for the upcoming papal mass and arrived just in time to witness the arrest of their would-be hosts. Control in Gdańsk was tight; Orbán and Fellegi had to be smuggled into the pope's youth mass via a middle-of-the-night rendezvous and a safe apartment.

Thinking back on the Polish expeditions, Fellegi doubts that his Bibó students gained one "big lesson" from the Poles; they knew, after all, that there was no patent for success. The Polish struggle could not be reduced to Michnik's essays, the pope's sermons, or Freedom and Peace banners. Poland, to the Hungarians, was about strategies for survival and techniques of successful activism in a repressive state. The Freedom and Peace approach was to ignore the state, as much as possible; to act according to one's own plan, whatever the police might do. After the police had taken Jagusiak and Tarasiewicz away in 1987, their apartment sprang back to life as if nothing had happened. A half-dozen guests to spirit around Gdańsk were nothing to their implacable hosts. As Fellegi put it, the lesson was to be "proactive and streetwise." Gábor Fodor saw a more direct influence: "We want to follow some of their ways," he thought, for the qualities Fellegi listed had not marked Hungarian opposition for decades.

Everyone noticed one great difference between the two countries, in the enormous power of the Catholic Church. Most in the Bibó College were not particularly religious. Some (like Orbán) came from a Calvinist background; others were nominally Catholic or had no religious traditions whatsoever. But all could see the space for freedom from the regime afforded by religious practice and national traditions. A visit to any Polish church, to a papal mass, or to the shrine at Częstochowa, which the Bibó expedition once visited on the way to Gdańsk, transformed the Hungarians' understanding of religion from something practiced in private to a powerful, cohesive social force. These students were already acquiring a perspective that would differentiate them from their elders back in Budapest.

If there was a specific goal to Polish opposition (beyond the fall of communism, that is), it was, the Hungarians decided, the "self-governing republic." Economic reform could come later (though private property rights were something all at Bibó accepted), but the immediate goal was to encourage society's self-organization. The Bibó College was itself a step down this road.

The next step, the Poles showed, was political pluralism. This was yet a radical idea in Hungary, for it meant that the system must be dismantled. Hungarian dissent had so far scrupulously avoided that program. In its strongest statement yet, the so-called New Social Contract of 1987, the Democratic Opposition had only called for party chief János Kádár to resign. Of course, there were many activists who knew Hungary needed more than this; on the fringes (like Zsolt Keszthelyi's trial), too, one could hear such demands. The Bibó generation would help push this politics into the mainstream.

The international peace network (and its most prominent Hungarian voice, Ferenc Miszlivetz) had a hand in opening direct contact between the students and the Democratic Opposition. Miszlivetz planned the October 1987 peace seminar as a follow-up to the Freedom and Peace seminar in Warsaw, hoping to shake up Budapest a little. He wanted both to move opposition out of the underground, while also reaching out to intellectuals who had kept their distance from overt opposition. The seminar offered such an opportunity. When promised auditoriums suddenly ceased to be available, István Stumpf offered the Bibó College. Ultimately, the college's lecture halls were too small, and the risk of sanctions too great, so Stumpf organized a fleet of taxis to meet participants on Ménesi Street and take them away to a secret location.

The some 150 participants (including much of the Democratic Opposition, and Network for East-West Dialogue activists from Germany, Britain, and the United States) were welcomed by Bibó student József Szajer, one of the few in the college who spoke English well. But the sensation was Viktor Orbán. Though Orbán read a speech that others had translated into English for him, his charismatic presence and provocative speech made a powerful impression on an audience who knew little or nothing about him. He did not say so, but Orbán was recapitulating the Polish lessons of the past few summers. "We got fed up with this half-life" (of consumer goods without basic freedoms), Orbán told the audience. "First, we took back the right to form circles, networks, colleges. Next, as the second step, we gained the right of discussing our views about the problems of the society we live in. And today we reclaim the next piece of the empire of official policy: the field of détente, of East-West contacts."[24] As Orbán stepped down from the podium, some of the older opposition rushed forward to shake his hand and to hug him. At this moment, the Bibó students definitively entered the world of Hungarian opposition. Shortly after the seminar, Miszlivetz and some of the Bibó students formed a Circle of the Network for East-West Dialogue at the college; this would be one steppingstone to articulating that opposition.

In the winter of 1987–88, Professor Wacław Felczak from Jagiellonian University in Kraków came to Budapest to teach Polish history at the university. Felczak was an expert in Hungarian history who had spent World War II in Budapest organizing underground contacts between Poland and the West. One evening Orbán and Kövér came to visit Felczak, to request that he give a lecture on Solidarity at the Bibó College (just across the street from Felczak's office). Interest in the lecture was so great that Felczak came to give a follow-up. It was after this second lecture that someone in the audience asked Professor Felczak what the Polish story of opposition meant for them: what should they do? "Found a party," Felczak advised. "They will probably lock you up for it, but all the signs suggest that you won't be in jail for long."[25]

And indeed, things were getting interesting, and the regime was becoming more vulnerable to pressure. The path the Hungarian communists had chosen—cautious liberalization, symbolized by the multicandidate elections of 1985—was getting words of approval from Gorbachev. In 1987 the praise from the Kremlin grew more direct; now, the Soviets seemed even to suggest that they would be borrowing from the Hungarian model. Since the model did not include political pluralism or a free press, this was hardly exciting news, but it did suggest there would be limits on repression.

March 15, 1988, was the 140th anniversary of the Revolution of 1848. The Democratic Opposition had been organizing demonstrations on that day since the early 1970s, and many students at the Bibó College had been participating ever since they had moved to Budapest. But even in comparison to the previous year, this round anniversary brought a new sense of opposition momentum. It was the first anniversary since the Democratic Opposition's New Social Contract, but it was also the first since Zsolt Keszthelyi had gone to prison. The official press now openly discussed the economic crisis, and the Soviet reforms, but party leader János Kádár had recently denied that there were any problems in Hungary. It was a moment to apply new kinds of public pressure.

Though March 15 was a Tuesday, some ten thousand—at least three times the previous year's crowd—marched to the statue of revolutionary poet Sandor Petöfi. As in recent years, young faces dominated the crowd. A few primitive banners at the front of the crowd called for freedom of speech and civil rights. The protesters chanted "Democracy!" and listened to senior dissident Gáspár Miklós Tamás call for free elections and a new constitution. As in 1987, the police did not break up the demonstration but arrested several well-known dissidents.

The energy of March 15 bore fruit immediately. Just two days later, several dozen intellectuals—mostly from the Democratic Opposition, but including also people from the Danube Circle and from other, more informal groupings such as veterans of 1956, created the Network of Free Initiatives (Network, or Hálózat, for short). Several students also signed, among them István Hegedűs, a 31-year-old sociologist. At least at first, Hálózat promised to link Hungarian opposition as it had not been before;

some hoped it might be the basis for a movement like Solidarity. Soon the Hálózat banner would be visible at demonstrations, offering a name around which opposition-minded Hungarians could rally.

But Hálózat, by its very name, signaled that it was not a political organization. This is the step Felczak had recommended to his listeners at the Bibó College, and they took it on March 30. The founding declaration of the Association of Young Democrats—Fidesz—signed by thirty-seven students and young intellectuals, including Orbán, Kövér, Fodor, Hegedűs, and Stumpf, purported simply to establish a youth organization to rival the official Communist Youth League. However, it was clearly something different: the declaration promised to unite the "politically *radical,* active, and *reform-minded*" toward the goals of a rational market economy based partly on private property; support for Hungarians in Transylvania and elsewhere outside Hungary; and national independence in a "demilitarized and unified Europe."

Fidesz thus staked out a position slightly more radical than the slogans of March 15. But the greatest contrast with previous opposition was a promise of coordinated, targeted action. Fidesz promised "to *take a stand* on every social, economic, political question that concerns the interests of its members"; "to intervene in major political decisions"; to "*influence* young people to spread the intellectual and *political* values it represents"; and to "promote the opportunities of its members in *acquiring political experience.*"[26]

Members, influence, and—nearly always underlined in the declaration —politics: these were strong words on the Hungarian opposition scene. Two days later (April Fools' Day, but with no irony intended), Fidesz signers held a press conference of sorts, meeting samizdat and international reporters in the Ma Chèrie Café. Within six weeks, Fidesz was climbing toward a thousand members in several cities.

The police took immediate notice of Fidesz. A week after the Ma Chèrie press conference, they summoned five Fidesz members and advised them that their activities were illegal. The official press condemned the new organization and imposed a virtual blackout on mention of its activities, lasting until August. And when Viktor Orbán, among others, chose to protest on the anniversary of June 16, the date when Prime Minister Imre Nagy was executed in 1958 for his role in the 1956 revolution, he was arrested.

But these were law students, after all. Responding to the summons, they came armed with citations from the Hungarian Constitution— specifically, paragraph 65(2), which guaranteed the right to form political organizations by citizens' initiative. They pointed out that they were not required to register the organization, and that, in fact, the right to association was left suspiciously vague in Hungarian law. They even instituted a case against Hungarian media for calling Fidesz "illegal."*

All over Budapest's political map, political parties were reemerging. But Fidesz, though not yet a party, pushed the boundaries of the possible more insistently than did any other. This was in no small part thanks to the experience that so many of its leaders had gained in Poland, and also through contact with Western activists. The latter would prove a valuable resource; this, too, they knew from Poland. Soon after the founding declaration, Fidesz leaders mailed their résumés to Amnesty International, so that they would not be anonymous should they be imprisoned. Fidesz had a great advantage over their Polish friends: the borders in Kádár's Hungary were the most open, after Yugoslavia, of any in Central Europe. As early as the fall of 1988, several Fidesz members, including Orbán, would begin traveling to the West, to stipends at British and other European universities, to END conventions, and to meetings of the Network for East-West Dialogue.

Comparisons with Freedom and Peace come immediately to mind. Fidesz came from the same university milieu as did WiP in Poland. The movements shared an impatience toward both communist ritual and the verities of "adult" opposition. Unlike WiP, Fidesz carved out a distinct political-organizational profile that has survived (though dramatically altered) until today. Autonomy was a choice, but also a necessity. Until the advent of Hálózat a scant two weeks before Fidesz's birth, there simply was no entity that could serve as umbrella and resource the way Solidarity could in Poland (or Charter 77 in Czechoslovakia). By 1988 it was probably too late for Fidesz to become a youth alternative within a larger opposition movement, as was partially true of Freedom and Peace. As if to underscore its independence, Fidesz banned membership to anyone over the age of 35.

At least through its first two years, Fidesz also shared with its Polish counterpart a tolerance for diversity. It attracted people from a variety of political directions: nationalist, liberal, social democratic, anarchist, green. Fidesz accommodated this variety through the formal creation of internal groups. The Alice Madzsar Group, a women's circle, took its name from the woman who had once owned the house that the Bibó College now occupied. Madzsar was a leader in the artistic and literary avant-garde of interwar Budapest. The idea of the group was to raise focus on women's issues, such as abortion and family policy. Another circle, the 56 Strawberry Group, took its name from the address where its members met.

---

* The case ultimately failed, but it forced the regime to draft legislation on freedom of association. The climate was sufficiently changed, by the time the law was passed, that Fidesz's original demands were incorporated into the constitution.

After a lengthy debate among partisans of various fruits, this group formed the nucleus of the Fidesz press, publishing a journal titled *Hungarian Orange* (*Magyar narancs*).

A third faction was the Workers' Group. Its members were mostly not students, but workers, some from the famed factory district of Csepel. They rode the radical edge of Fidesz. For example, they staged a demonstration on October 23, 1988, the anniversary of the revolution of 1956. All other opposition (including Fidesz) had decided to heed official warnings and stay at home; the demonstration ended in a clash with police. Soon after, the Workers' Group forced a confrontation with the regime in the most unlikely way: inspired by Radio Free Europe accounts of Orange Alternative, they staged a happening of their own on November 7, the Russian Revolution anniversary. Though it was a national holiday, a handful of participants showed up on Vörösmarty Square (the heart of Budapest's pedestrian zone), ready to work. They carried brooms and wore work aprons and cardboard hats adorned with slogans calling for the November 7 holiday to be deleted from the calendar and replaced by March 15. In the spirit of Lenin, they proceeded to perform voluntary labor, vigorously sweeping the square and picking up trash. "We are working now," read one sign, "and you [the communists] should work on March 15." The authorities, however, had no more of a sense of humor than in Poland, and they arrested the "workers."

In less than one year, Fidesz had succeeded in forcing itself into the attention of the generation of the 1980s, with a movement promising independent activity based on opposition to the communist system. It also won the attention of the older dissidents; in 1989, Fidesz would be an unquestioned partner in both demonstrations and negotiations. Finally, it won the attention of a regime desperate to outdo Gorbachev's semblance of liberalization. In August 1988, István Stumpf gave an interview to a regime newspaper, and Gábor Fodor was interviewed on the radio. In October Fidesz representatives secured a meeting with Imre Pozsgay, minister of state and leader of the reformist wing of the Hungarian Socialist Workers' Party.

Hungarian politics was also embarked upon a path quite different from that in Poland. Shortly after Fidesz's inaugural congress in October, the Network for Free Initiatives transformed itself into a political party, the Alliance of Free Democrats. This political pluralism would eventually allow Fidesz to become more unified internally than Freedom and Peace had ever been. By November 1988 Fidesz had become an important feature of this political landscape. Programmatic flexibility, organizational discipline, and willingness to test boundaries would give Fidesz, in 1989, its hour of glory.

Towards an Opposition in Prague

The tenth anniversary declaration of Charter 77 (in January 1987; see chapter 2), which had called for more attention to specific issues and new constituencies, sparked a reply from within the Charter itself. Some forty younger Chartists sent an open letter that spring to the spokespeople of the Charter. They called for demonstrations instead of declarations, for public debate on the problems important to Charter 77—in a word, for more politics. The signers included Ivan Lamper of Polish-Czechoslovak Solidarity and Stanislav Deváty, who had recently created one of the oddest groups yet, the Society of Friends of the USA, in his hometown of Zlín (Gottwaldov).

The letter signaled growing frustration with the opposition's isolation from society. Deváty's appointment the following year as the youngest Charter spokesman yet (at 35), and one of the few ever from beyond Prague, was one attempt to bridge this gap.* Even as this middle generation stepped forward into the carefully measured world of dissent, younger generations were developing new repertoires, taking the Czechs much closer to the streets of the Velvet Revolution. One of these, the Independent Peace Association, became the closest thing Czechoslovakia would see to a political, active opposition.

The Independent Peace Association—Initiative for the Demilitarization of Society (Nezávislá Mírová Sdružení—Iniciativa za Demilitarizaci Společnosti, NMS), the most dynamic and exciting movement to emerge in Czechoslovakia in the 1980s, bears a strong family resemblance to Freedom and Peace. Like WiP, NMS started as a coalition of pacifists and opponents of the communist army and then branched out into environmental issues as well (though to a lesser degree). Its participants put a premium on action, staging as many demonstrations as possible. Though there were a few older members in NMS, most were in their twenties and had the same ambivalent relationship with the "senior opposition," enjoying its protection but not accepting its methods. Also like its Polish counterpart, NMS developed a greater samizdat record than any other group of its generation and quickly spawned circles in provincial cities. In just nineteen

---

* Another was Democratic Initiative, a group that emerged among thinkers of the 1968 generation who scornfully rejected the Charter's "antipolitical" approach of issuing statements and demands. Only profound political change, they argued, could both protect national traditions and unleash economic creativity. Formed in September 1987, Democratic Initiative demanded an end to the practices of nomenklatura (in which the party dictated who would fill even minor official positions) and freedom for self-government initiatives. In 1989, as we shall see, Democratic Initiative would provide a bridge between Charter 77 and nascent opposition in the universities.

months of existence, the Czech peace group could not approach WiP's accomplishments; the difference is not just that Poland was a more tolerant place, but that Czech society required tactics quite unlike those familiar to the Poles.

Three currents came together in 1987 to make NMS possible. The first of these were Charter 77 veterans, like Luboš Vydra and Jiří Pavlíček, who felt it was time for much more forceful action. Vydra, for example, had signed the Charter back in December 1977. Ten years later he was among a small group of perhaps twenty Chartists who staged a demonstration—the first to involve so many Chartists—in celebration of International Human Rights Day, December 10, 1987. They rushed out of the metro station tunnel at Old Town Square with banners calling for the release of political prisoners. Their demonstration was brief, before the police detained nearly all the participants, with at most a thousand onlookers. For Vydra, though, this was an important moment in the maturation of Czech opposition (second only to the demonstration of August 1988). At last the ideals that the Chartists espoused existed not only on paper but in the streets, where far more people could see them and realize that some opposition still existed.

A second current was that of young Catholic students, like Tomáš Dvořák and Hana Marvanová. Dvořák, then just twenty, had in 1985 attempted to register an official peace organization, Young Artists for Peace. The idea was a cross between the Jazz Section (Dvořák had consulted with the section's leader Karel Srp) and the followers of John Lennon (see next chapter). Dvořák had thought that the legal route would be the more effective, since an illegal organization would surely end with everyone's arrest. He expected this innocuous application to be accepted; instead—"and I still don't see why," complained Dvořák in 1988—the only answer was long interrogations by the security forces.[27] Reluctantly, he turned toward the illegal zone, and by the end of 1988 he was high on the security police's list of most dangerous opposition figures.

Finally, there was Jan Svoboda, a graduate of the Czech Brethren seminary. In February 1987 Svoboda wrote a letter to the Czechoslovak Parliament, proposing that the system of compulsory military service be changed. He suggested shortening service and allowing for exemptions (or alternative service) for those who objected for reasons of conscience. In keeping with Czechoslovak tradition, the letter became a petition, signed by over one hundred. Charter 77 issued a supporting statement, and Svoboda's wife Alice Svobodová, along with Ruth Šormová—who was also married to a seminarian and would also be active in NMS—sent a second letter in support of the first.[28]

Ruth Šormová began her road to activism in high school, where she started to read theology. She and her high school roommate attended informal seminars at which seminarians, pastors, and lay members of the church discussed spiritual and social issues; many participants were dissidents, including those like Svoboda who had been denied pastorships for their views. These were Šormová's first contacts with dissent, but soon she was introduced to Petr Uhl. She felt drawn to Charter 77 but faced a choice:

> I was thinking a lot about signing Charter 77. I was a bit afraid, but also I wasn't sure whether my signature as a 20-year-old young woman—whether this is the way to do what I would like to do. And then, in the surroundings of Charter 77, I met some more young people who had very similar ideas and similar feelings, hesitating whether to sign the Charter or whether to start something new, discussing what they feel is the problem—and, well, with them we started NMS.

As an education major who had worked with handicapped children, Šormová would lead the NMS campaign against the production and sale of military toys.

Jan Svoboda's letter, along with the model suggested by WiP, crystallized the idea for NMS. Marvanová, Pavlíček, Dvořák, and several others issued NMS's founding declaration in April 1988. Like Polish and Slovene movements, NMS tackled the regime's sacred rhetoric head on: "Peace politics, peace efforts, building peace, the struggle for peace . . . a person in our country hears such terms, and many similar ones, today and every day, all around. One sees them on banners, reads them in newspaper headlines and slogans; peace has become a profaned word, deprived of its content." To inoculate NMS against the charge of undermining the state, the declaration contrasted this rhetorical emptiness to the recent Soviet-American arms talks. Gorbachev had left his mark: NMS would pay much more attention to superpower relations than did WiP. The authors called for glasnost on military issues, the building of trust between nations, an educational system that would teach respect for human life, and for the basic right to refuse military service. They pointed out that shortening military service would "build trust between the state's official structures and the citizens," while boosting society's economic potential (since young people could begin working sooner) and lessening international tension.[29] "Trust" was a key component of their notion of change.

NMS brought an entrepreneurial spirit to Czech opposition, one that clearly appealed to the same constituency WiP had discovered: twenty-somethings who saw nothing to like in the communist regime but who wanted more than the previous generation of dissent had offered. The movement was only a month old when it began publishing its own samizdat. The first issue carried several dozen supporting signatures.

Almost immediately, NMS seemed to be everywhere. Just three days after the declaration, NMS met with visiting peace activists from France's

CODENE, exchanging ideas on the reform of military service. In early May they staged their first protest: a relay fast (one person a day, for eight days) in solidarity with WiP participant Sławomir Dutkiewicz.* And there were more letters to Czechoslovak authorities. In July Marvanová and others from NMS were stars of the abortive International Peace Seminar in Prague. The NMS bulletin reported on everything members did· every letter or proclamation, every new conscientious objector, or activist jailed, tried, or released. This practice had made Freedom and Peace seem a lot larger than it actually was, and increased its impact. The same was true for NMS.

In the midst of the Dutkiewicz fast, NMS leaders were summoned to meet with officials from the Czechoslovak Peace Committee. "[We] were assured," they noted acerbically, "that the official Czechoslovak peace movement had many points in common with this independent initiative, but this was not borne out by further discussion."[30] Many in the movement, like Vydra, harbored serious doubts about being used as empty examples of regime dialogue: the post-1968 purges had excised nearly all genuine reformers or liberals from the party apparatus. But NMS had obviously struck a chord, even though it lacked the name recognition of Charter 77. NMS claimed to have approached its official counterpart almost as an equal—as a true representative of civil society. Though it would not be long before most of the NMS members at the meeting that day would be in jail, they left having established both their independence and their commitment to concrete, measurable change.

Over the next year, there would be more meetings, both with the Peace Committee and with the Union of Socialist Youth (SSM). For an intellectual or political group like Charter 77 or Democratic Initiative to interact with the official world in this way would appear to condone the regime's political façade, which combined "a ritual dance around the magic word 'perestroika' with harsh words about the 'enemies of socialism.'"[31] But on the specific platform, say, of conscientious objection, there was no question of compromising one's radical stance: instead, one could force the regime in this way simply to acknowledge the existence of a problem. And when NMS members staged protest fasts—as they had in May, or when Jiří Štencl organized one to demand the release of nine political prisoners in November 1988—their action implied that negotiation was impossible.

Despite, or perhaps because of, this threat, NMS was able to dictate the terms and pace of its official contacts. For example, representatives of both the Peace Committee and the Human Rights Society (another com-

---

* Dutkiewicz's hunger strike, ongoing since November 1987, had been covered in the first *Bulletin* of Polish-Czechoslovak Solidarity. In August NMS sent letters to Dutkiewicz and to General Wojciech Jaruzelski.

ponent of Czech normalization) attended Tomáš Dvořák's trial in March 1989, hoping in this way still to win NMS to their side. When representatives of the Peace Committee and NMS held a series of meetings in early 1989, the agenda was entirely NMS: conversion of military industries, shortening military service, civilian control of the military, and military toys. Each such contact was reported in the NMS bulletin, where members did not hesitate to criticize their counterparts, as when the Peace Committee did not protest Dvořák's and Marvanová's imprisonment.[32] Through its samizdat, the NMS could speak with two voices at the same time. And a third voice, the voice of demonstrations, would soon become the best known in the NMS repertoire.

In some ways, NMS duplicated Charter 77, even as it resolved the generational crisis that had broken into the open in 1987. The new movement became, in effect, a Charter "88": while acting beyond the scope of the original Charter, it also replicated, for the generation that had no memory of the Prague Spring, the most important functions of its predecessor. Like VONS, it was a reliable voice on violations of human rights, especially for anyone who ran into trouble with the military bureaucracy. It became a vehicle for expressing opposition to the regime and for establishing one's own civic courage.

Because there was no central organization, any new group of people who signed the proclamation could call themselves NMS and begin to act. The strongest local chapter outside Prague was in Brno, where some fifty activists came together, strongly influenced by Jaroslav Šabata, the senior Chartist whose letters on peace in 1983–84 had initiated Czechoslovak contacts with Western peace movements. Others emerged—mostly in the summer of 1989—in northern Bohemia, in Turnovo, Poděbrady, Plzeň, České Budějovice, and Liberec.

NMS was, again, decidedly pluralist, both in views and in issues addressed. Though military concerns had inspired the movement, it quickly started to speak out on other issues, especially the environment. "Ecology is inseparable from peace work; after all, a healthy environment is also one of the conditions of a full and dignified life. Besides this, it is really a supranational matter: ecological problems know no borders. . . . It is one of the ways to bring together nations and build trust between them. So it is necessary to do something." Thus wrote the *Bulletin*'s editors in November 1988, describing a campaign near Liberec, in which fourteen activists, mostly from NMS, cleaned up a clear-cut and fenced in part of it for a tree nursery. While they were redefining the parameters of peace, they were also expanding the limits of opposition. The group was paid for their work that day, and—despite the fact that some were not NMS members—they sent their earnings to the parents of three NMS activists then in jail.[33]

The following spring and summer brought more tree plantings. In June an "Ecological Appeal" announced that there would be protests, too, alongside this "concrete work in nature."[34] That same issue of the *Bulletin* contained an enthusiastic report on a WiP initiative to protest closed borders, and a list of forty basic human rights. NMS was on its way to becoming a comprehensive social movement.

In spite of the disagreements over dialogue with official organizations, or over the movement's relationship to Charter 77, NMS did not splinter in the almost two years of its existence. Instead—in the tradition of Charter 77—its members also worked in, or even helped to found, other movements. The John Lennon Peace Club, the Society for a Merrier Present, and the independent student association STUHA, all of which played an important role in the events of 1989, counted NMS activists among their founders. Peace, ecology, conscientious objection, human rights, and self-government were all part of a shared opposition to the regime and to the stifling culture it had fostered.*

Czech opposition had not changed much for the two decades before 1988. There had been new issues raised—like ecology, or peace—or political programs advanced, but the forms and tactics of dissent remained largely what they had been even before the advent of Charter 77. What Charter 77 added was a platform for new participants and new ideas, and a resource for new opposition. Charter 77 had by no means failed; indeed, it continued to dominate the political scene up through the revolution of November 1989. But if Czechs proved ready to go into the streets and demonstrate, or to sign petitions by the tens of thousands, or to accept an orderly assumption of power, this was partly thanks to the new approach to opposition that NMS introduced. The ideas of constant action, of frequent international contact and relentless publicity, and of using concrete proposals to test the limits of regime liberalization destabilized the uneasy triangular relationship among state, society, and opposition. NMS still held back from a direct political challenge to the regime—but that step would come soon.

WORKERS OF THE LAST HOUR

As he watched the demonstrations of 1988 and 1989 unfold in Prague, Canadian diplomat Rob McRae kept wondering, "Where are the students?" Even just a few weeks before November, McRae—a philosopher who got to know many in the Czech dissident elite—was frankly frus-

---

* The Brno circle created separate working groups for various issues; the division in Prague was less formal. In general, the provincial circles seem to have taken the lead in environmental protests.

trated that students "had once again refused to be in the forefront of change."[35] Many of the speakers at those demonstrations represented Charter 77; they remembered 1968 well, and often World War II. The leaders in the NMS were often of student age, but not students: some had graduated, while others had been denied entry to college for their views, or their parents'. The practice of denying entry to higher education, rare in Poland or Hungary since the 1960s, was still common in Czechoslovakia.

Perhaps for anyone who, like McRae, had witnessed the worldwide protests of 1968, dramatic social change could not be imagined without student radicals. Students could provide fresh ideas and would also have the time to commit themselves fully to revolution. Fortunately for Czechoslovakia, McRae was wrong: the universities were, if not exactly seething, alive with patient, slowly maturing activism. There were many students on the fringes of opposition, searching for the means to give the youth a voice, well aware that their generation would not respond if the risks did not seem worth the trouble. As the year of demonstrations began, they would edge closer and closer to the spotlight.

Martin Mejstřík followed the rise and fall of Solidarity in 1980–81 from a forestry high school in Frydlant, close by the Polish border. He and his friends tried to promote the ideas of Solidarity (like civil rights) in their school, but this was a school for the communist proletariat, and they didn't get far. Mejstřík didn't lose his fascination with alternatives. Arriving in Prague at the age of 20, in 1982, he quickly found the Jazz Section: "for me, an island of freedom in Czechoslovakia. I went there regularly, I got to know Mr. Srp, occasionally I licked envelopes for the section, that kind of thing—but everyone there helped out. While I was at the pedagogical school, the Jazz Section began to run into huge problems. I went up to Srp and asked how I could help—I'm in school, I'm doing this and that, things weren't too bad for me. It astonished me when he replied 'Martin, finish school.'"

In this exchange is a key to understanding the limits on Czech student opposition before 1989 (as we have seen, Slovak students were more likely to be active already, in the Catholic underground). In a country where intellectual dissent so dominated, and where national consciousness was a product of writers and philosophers (not heroic strikers, as in Poland), to finish university was paramount. The young would-be oppositionist in another country might drop out of school, or be thrown out, and earn the admiration of those around him or her, but not the Czech, who should not squander the opportunity to become one of the educated elite. Perhaps more important, a degree might afford a bit of protection, because the graduate would become more valuable and visible, too. Thus Mejstřík—who would become, in the Velvet Revolution, one of Prague's best-known faces—refined his goals: "the point for me was not to overthrow the regime somehow—definitely not. It was enough for me that people would begin to think about where they live, and so on."[36] The regime would fall apart by itself, perhaps, if people began to think freely.

Mejstřík—now at the Drama Academy—founded a student paper, *Kavárna AFFA* (*AFFA Café*), in October 1987. *Kavárna* was published under the aegis of the Union of Socialist Youth. The connection was "to no one's liking," says Mejstřík, "not one of us was in the Union, but we told ourselves, OK, let's try it." The alternative was to go into samizdat, but "the atmosphere at the school was so good there could even be Unionists who were OK."[37] With its daring cultural criticism and frank look at student life, *Kavárna* was a magnet for students both at the drama school and across the city.

Martin Klíma, a whole student generation younger than Mejstřík, found his way to opposition through science fiction. Sci-fi fan clubs were another layer of Czechoslovak normalization—another way to keep the kids quiet—yet, Klíma explains: "our SF community was in a different situation, and was created by a different type of person from in the West. In America, fans are people . . . who would not engage in anything useful anywhere else. . . . Here, on the other hand, [sci-fi] attracted a lot of people who would rather do something more useful, but couldn't. Work in the *fandom* was simply a substitute activity."[38] Klíma—a cousin of prominent Czech writer Ivan Klíma—joined the Villoidus sci-fi club, which published an eponymous mimeographed magazine through the SSM, while in high school. Others in the group, like Marek and Martin Benda, sons of leading Chartist Václav Benda, had grown up breathing the heady air of dissent. For these students, sci-fi (like theater, or the Church, or philosophical debates) were ways to practice their critical voice while, in the proper Czech tradition, keeping to their studies.*

Monika Pajerová was another student who grew up on the edges of the world of Charter 77. Her mother, a psychologist, often took her along to the private seminars at Charter spokeswoman Dana Němcová's apartment; she herself started going to evangelical seminars like the ones Ruth Šormová attended—"but really because this was the opposition, not that I was inclined to some kind of religious feeling." At university, Pajerová studied English, and then Swedish. Returning from a hard-won semester in Sweden in the summer of 1987, she joined a group in her college who edited a wall gazette, *Situace*.† The editor, Josef "Pepe" Brož, described *Situace* as "more philosophical, oriented toward things which the artists [Mejstřík et al.] weren't following. I wanted to avoid the exhibitionism of

---

* Other children of well-known dissidents who were students in 1989 include Jiří Dienstbier, Jr., and Jan Dus, Jr.

† Student papers often began as single-copy posters hung in dormitories or academic buildings, before they received permission to distribute more widely.

Kavárna." But when she first met the *Kavárna* group, Pajerová was shocked: "They were wild—we admired them like crazy. The philosophical institute—we tried hard . . . but we were so moderate, and they spoke out loud what we didn't dare."[39] Thanks to sympathetic college administrators, Pajerová found her own voice: she traveled around Europe interviewing Czech literary émigrés and publishing their recollections in *Situace*.

Tomáš Drábek's family was privileged in another way: his father had been an army officer and his mother, a doctor, remained in the Communist Party until 1989. Drábek was active in the Pioneers (the party's youth organization) and went to an elite high school. And then John Lennon died. Drábek was just 14. He and his friends were among those who began to gather at the impromptu memorial in the Kampa park. There, for the first time, he heard about samizdat and met people from the Jazz Section. Love for music also drew him to the American Embassy, where—after getting past the Czech police who usually blocked the sidewalk—he could read film or music magazines.

Eventually, Drábek began to notice the *International Herald Tribune*, and even CNN, and saw that their coverage of events differed from what the communist papers said. From then on, journalism became his passion. He even published his own samizdat journal in high school: he copied interesting articles from samizdat and added his own photos of rock concerts. This he distributed "among my friends, but mostly to my girlfriend, now my wife, whom I wanted to impress."

Though he chose medical school over journalism—and got in thanks to the right connections—Drábek would soon be back in his hobby, helping to found *EM* (like the other student papers, published under the SSM label) in 1987. Starting with coverage of music, sports, and school news, *EM* grew braver, encouraged by contacts with the other student journalists in Prague. Sometime early in 1988, intrigued by the vitriolic attacks he read in the communist papers, Drábek—who had never had any real contact with dissidents—decided to find out what Charter 77 was. He looked up Václav Havel in the telephone book and went to introduce himself. Havel "peered out at me, a little surprised," and sent him to Saša Vondra, who the following year would become the Charter's youngest spokesperson ever, at 28. The next issue of *EM* featured an interview with Charter spokesperson Stanislav Devátý—"we sent it to the Unionists for approval, and their hair really stood on end from fright"—and an article by Jolana Šopová on Havel, which neither *Kavárna* nor *Situace* would run.[40]

What had changed among the students, so that these two separate worlds—so separate that a well-read 22-year-old knew nothing about the Charter beyond Havel's name—could begin to find each other? As unsatisfactory as it may seem, time is an important factor. The latest generation of students—"workers of the last hour," as the Benda brothers nicknamed students who discovered opposition later than they[41]—was important not for what it knew (about glasnost, for example), but for what it didn't know. The editor of yet another student journal, Pavel Žáček of *Proto* at the School of Journalism, sees 1987, the year he began his studies, as a watershed: "Our class of 1987 was considered to be the first of its kind in twenty years: the first class which had no patience with the loss experienced by our parents' generation in 1968, and which had all the conditions necessary for the expansion of free thinking. School itself was sterile, lifeless, covered by ideological blinkers. So there emerged a good-sized group of activists who wanted to do something."[42] Their choice was to begin with publishing, which they could do best at the edge of legality, and thus build a community of students.

Perhaps these students would have been destined one day to join the elite of Czech intellectual dissent. But that day never came. Until the Velvet Revolution itself, moreover, their elders as yet were not sure they needed the students. Some five years after Mejstřík's encounter with Karel Srp, Tomáš Drábek was on the same quest: what could a student with political interests do? Maybe it was his duty to sign Charter 77. He posed the question to Saša Vondra, who advised against it: finishing university was more important, and anyway one more signature wouldn't mean much.

Whether the students had grown up around the dissidents, like Pajerová or Benda, or discovered it late, like Mejstřík or Drábek, they belonged to a different world. They were separated by generation, but also by a nearly invisible hierarchy. In Poland, with traditions of underground universities and student partisan fighters, a college degree could (and perhaps ought to) take second place to the country's needs; not so in Czechoslovakia. When they finished school, they—like Vondra, a Ph.D. in geography, before them—could join the front ranks of those who risked their names and careers for the cause of human rights, but until then they should work within the system.

But it was possible for students to break this mold. A group of students in Brno, led by Jiří Voráč, went much farther in testing the limits of legality. Brno, the second-largest city in the Czech lands, is large enough to boast a university and a sizable intellectual community, yet small enough (and far enough from Prague) to shrink the distance between those active in dissent and the rest of society. Voráč grew up in a devout family; his father had been a leader in the Catholic Youth Association before the communists disbanded it in 1949. His parents, though, kept their distance from dissent. With his older brother Miloš, Jiří Voráč began attending private seminars and lectures, mostly held in people's apartments (such as

Jaroslav Šabata's home). In Prague, the musical and artistic crowd of which Voráč was a part might have little to do with political or religious dissent; in Brno they were all close, despite divergent world views. Voráč names Šabata as one of his greatest influences, though he did not share the older man's socialism.*

Voráč adopted a stance of strict noncooperation: unlike the other students portrayed here, he didn't join the Union of Socialist Students. He refused to go on student work brigades, and he spent four years faking a psychiatric diagnosis to stay out of the army. So when he was removed from the editorial board of a student monthly and denied permission to publish in another, Voráč joined the nascent *Revue '88*. This would be the only student journal before 1988 that was published in true samizdat. For Voráč and the other editors, "the official student journals . . . are ideologically straitjacketed, and cannot pursue a whole bunch of questions about which young people are concerned."[43] They had two arguments: first, the Helsinki Accords allowed for freedom of the press; second, if *Revue '88* was an *irregular* periodical, it ought not to be bound by the same rules as other student publications.[†]

In the four issues that appeared in 1988–89 (they kept the "'88" in the title because it evoked 1968), the *Revue* tackled all the taboo questions, going further than did the student periodicals in Prague. But most importantly, the *Revue* did not just report on the problems of society; articles on NMS, on Green protests, and on the independent students in Poland offered readers directions on how they could stand up and oppose the communists.

As all these student journals, to different degrees, began to test the limits of censorship and of the communist bureaucracies' tolerance, they began to work together. "There's strength in numbers," says Drábek, "so we tried to create some kind of organization which would give us uniform rules: to what extent the university's permission is necessary, [and] whether the papers could be distributed outside the school."[44] They created a Student Press and Information Center (STIS). Dramaturgy student Jolana Šopová was given the task of organizing STIS, at the White Pony Club on Old Town Square, where every Thursday afternoon students could come and read student papers (as well as sci-fi, and eventually other samizdat). Soon enough, there were lectures, discussion groups, and fi-

---

* Indeed, Brno reminds one of Wrocław, both in its relationship to the capital city and in the close ties among intellectuals. The distance the opposition kept from the regime is also typical of Wrocław.

† Of course, the authorities had never before accepted either of these arguments, which could apply to any samizdat. The fact that a group of Prague Chartists had in late 1987 attempted to register officially their own weekly paper, *Lidove noviny*, encouraged the Brno students.

nally, in the fall of 1989, an independent student organization—and the demonstration of November 17, 1989.

So while Rob McRae was lamenting the absence of students, they were in fact organizing swiftly, continually testing (and sometimes ignoring) the limits of official structures. Still, Jiří Voráč found the Prague students "somewhat terrified" when he visited STIS in the winter of 1988–89. To the Prague students, the visitors from Brno were dissidents whose daring ideas threatened the success of the legal route they were taking.[45]

The students of Prague were indeed facing a choice. To push too fast might perhaps isolate student leaders from the rest of their classmates. Moreover, while Voráč himself was never jailed, many in NMS were facing highly publicized trials, so the danger was still quite real. But Voráč, NMS, and other groups were finding ways to develop opposition just over the edge of legality, and making the communist regime increasingly uncomfortable. The new generation of students (to whom even Mejstřík must have seemed a bit out of touch) were finding their place in samizdat and at the demonstrations.

What was missing was one spark to inspire the students to risk more than they had so far—"a great catastrophe that would radicalize the students."[46] The demonstrations of 1988–89, combined with new ideas from Mejstřík and others, would eventually bring them out on the streets in the thousands.

Chapter Five

HOW THE SMURFS CAPTURED GARGAMEL,

OR, A REVOLUTION OF STYLE

The Elfin Rebellion

"SINCE reality is the oldest and most threatening enemy of man, schizophrenia is an entrenchment of the highest quality. Down with intellectual art. Long live the highest-quality socialism, as a work of comic art. Vivat Sorbovit!"[1] Thus wrote Waldemar Maria "Major" Fydrych of the New Culture Movement in 1981. All hail to a vitamin drink! In a year of black-and-white politics, of Solidarity versus the party, dadaist humor was a distraction from the political battle.

Fydrych, a former art student, would soon dub his movement "Orange Alternative." "Orange" was a rejection of two colors, the red of communism and the yellow of the papal flag.* The movement, born during student strikes in October–December 1981, espoused an ideology Fydrych dubbed "socialist surrealism." Though its absurd language and actions clearly aped those of the regime, its broadsheets were filled with satire of Solidarity's self-importance as well. Wrocław's student leaders even attempted to ban their publication.

Wrocław was a likely place for surrealists. The city was, wrote one independent journalist, "different . . . [with] almost metaphysical characteristics"[2]—by which he presumably meant that no one in Poland could understand what was going on in Wrocław. For nearly twenty years, Wrocław had been a center of alternative culture and theater, like the experimental workshop of Jerzy Grotowski, which pulled audiences into the middle of its emotionally cathartic performances.

Eventually, Orange Alternative's "happenings," a form of guerrilla street theater/performance art ridiculing the communist regime, would captivate just about the entire city and become the talk of Poland; one can see echoes of Wrocław's antics across Central Europe. The movement's fantastic success, and its rapid decline amid scandal in 1989–90, spawned a debate over authorship—and, indirectly, over the meaning of the revolution—which is still quite fierce over a decade later.

* Fydrych enjoyed teasing journalists by inventing alternative explanations of the name: for example, that it evoked the anarchy of *A Clockwork Orange* or had something to do with Dutch artists.

If in 1981 Orange Alternative's satire was ahead of its time, it began to find its place during the martial law period. Suddenly the enemy was clearer, and Orange Alternative took sides. Its participants cared about Poland and feared the "Russification of Polish culture," as Agata Saraczyńska, one of the younger participants at this time, puts it. A beginning art student, she was drawn into the "boys' club" around Fydrych as they searched for a new language.

They began to experiment with graffiti, one of the few public expressions of opposition then possible. When the police painted over Solidarity graffiti, they left misshapen blobs on the walls. A little added decoration, and these blobs became little elves—as if, by Hegelian logic, the synthesis of two opposing ideas (a slogan and its negation) would produce a new idea. But what was the idea? To the police this seemed the secret mark of a partisan band; to Western reporters it was the work of a children's Solidarity. The message was simpler for passersby: they were forced to consider the point of the struggle over wall space, and to wonder why little elves were threatening to the communists.

The game remained anonymous and ambiguous; anyone with a can of paint could join in, but could not thus enter the community of guerrilla painters. Indeed, the ideas of Fydrych and the New Culture Movement were deliberately opaque; their performances were for others to watch. Fydrych and the New Culture Movement supplied the basic ideas of a new movement—the socialist surrealism, the use of official forms of expression, and the elves—but they did not mobilize people beyond a small circle. In 1986 student politicians at Wrocław University—members of the Twelve encountered in chapter 1—provided the crowds. They shared Fydrych's ironic distance from the regime, but not his distance from society. For students like Krzysztof Jakubczak, more important was to reach out to and engage the audience, to help people feel that others thought like them.

Jakubczak, known universally as Jakub, came to Wrocław from a small mountain town to study physics in 1982. His guitar was the way to make himself known: he began to appear at student gatherings to play and sing forbidden songs. He was elected to the student senate, then was one of the founders of the Twelve, and of the Wagant student club, offering independent concerts, lectures, and plays. But "one day the rector began to complain," recalls Jakubczak, "that every one of these events strikes at the system, and proposed that we organize an apolitical event for once—like students from another dorm, 'The Hive,' who rented a bus and toured Wrocław. You didn't have to tell us twice." With this, Jakubczak's forbidden participatory culture hit the streets. This would not be a mere picnic. "We dressed up in various costumes we borrowed from a theater, and took off in Fredruś," an open-top sightseeing bus named after a nineteenth-century satirical playwright, Aleksander Fredro, whose statue stood in the center of the city.[3]

It being May, the students waved red flags and banners and sang communist songs. A banner on the side of the bus claimed the bus had been hijacked and was heading to West Berlin; another read, in letters ominously similar to the familiar Solidarity script: "Solidity Will Win." The bus visited the zoo, where students demanded freedom for the bears, and the house of Władysław Frasyniuk, where students threw flowers at the police.

Of course, before long the police surrounded the bus and detained nearly all the several dozen passengers. But they were not sure what to do with these lunatics in sombreros and other bizarre headgear, singing innocuous songs. The party continued at the police station, where some invited the officers to dance as Jakubczak strummed his guitar. To haul the students to court and fine them would have made the authorities look ridiculous and would also have meant a decisive return to the brutality of the past, as in 1968, when students were beaten by hired thugs and then sent to jail for years. This would not fit with the kinder face of normalization, so the students were let go after, at most, forty-eight hours.

Jakubczak and his colleagues from the Twelve had found the formula that had eluded Fydrych and the New Culture Movement. This style was more satisfying because, says Jakubczak, "it was obvious you were anti . . . but they [the police] couldn't do anything." Though a forty-eight-hour detention was not exactly nothing, this cultural-entrepreneur-turned-politician had found a form of protest both meaningful and accessible. To passersby (and the student passengers themselves, not all of whom knew what they were getting into), Fredruś was an island of perfect freedom, in which free expression was both comprehensible (unlike Fydrych's slogans) and nonthreatening (unlike the freedom of a violent demonstration). The Fredruś prank had resolved Václav Havel's famous problem of the would-be dissident grocer (who finally balks at posting communist slogans in his shop): instead of refusing to ape official ideology, it was more effective to ape it grotesquely.

After Fredruś's journey, "an incredible legend swept the city," says Jakubczak. College students might have been inclined either not to take the escapade too seriously, or to overpoliticize the event—by visiting Frasyniuk's house, for example. But one group in particular was excited by the Fredruś story: high-school students. Jakubczak (with Paweł Chmiel and others) had been active in planning camping trips for high school self-government activists, like the camps organized for first-year university students. These teenagers were politically aware but sought forms—and above all styles—of protest that would avoid the old ruts. They threw themselves into participation.

Of course, city authorities would not let Fredruś out of their hands again. But the following spring both the Twelve and Fydrych's Orange Alternative organized a series of happenings, and Wrocław's Orange era commenced. First, on April Fools' Day 1987, university students were invited to join in a "spontaneous action for the good of Polish scholarship," that is, a communist *subbotnik,* expressing their love for socialism through voluntary labor. A thousand of us, including this reluctantly curious American, showed up (some freed from classes by confused professors who thought the call had come from the rector) armed with toothbrushes, mops, and other implements, and dressed like workers from old stalinist movies. Paweł Kocięba, who has the oratorical style and theatrical manner of an old Bolshevik, delivered a fiery Leninesque speech from a balcony above University Square, as representative of the new revolutionary leadership. We admired the giant portraits of revolutionary hero workers hanging from the windows. And with socialist labor songs on its lips, the crowd set to work cleaning the square. The police rounded up a few participants—especially those with cameras—and the university rector feebly appealed to the pretenders to his rank to vacate the supposedly unsafe balcony. Authority once again proved nearly helpless, and foolish, in the face of absurdity.

Now that socialist surrealism had a ready audience, Orange Alternative took the spotlight. On Children's Day, June 1, Orange Alternative staged a happening that is generally regarded as the catalyst for all that followed. Alerted by invitations in independent high school and university papers, nearly a thousand young Wrocławians showed up on Świdnicka Street. There they donned red caps and became elves—the Polish word is *krasnoludek,* literally "little red person"—the embodiment of the graffiti of a few years earlier. In honor of Children's Day, they handed out candy, sang children's songs, and danced. "Major" Fydrych was detained at the outset, but Jakubczak began to move through the crowd, strumming songs on his guitar. The songs themselves were not important, he explained, "but only that [people feel] they are together in a group, and are not afraid." As the police began to detain individual elves, the crowd began to chant "Elves are real!"[4] Elves waving merrily out of police vans, kissing police officers, throwing candy out the windows as they were taken away—these were the images (soon greatly embellished) that flashed across Poland, symbolizing a kind of surreal immunity from repression through foolishness.

There has been a great deal of bad writing about Orange Alternative, a movement notoriously hard to pin down. To describe and categorize it is to risk, with one misstep, becoming an unwitting victim of its relentless satire. Yet to treat it as mere foolishness is to miss the point.

Agata Saraczyńska comes closest to defining Orange Alternative: it was not a movement, nor a community (*środowisko*), because participants had little in common except that they all "sought something." It was simply a "communal party (*impreza*)." Some, especially younger participants, needed and sought a leader; Fydrych became for them, and for Poland, that leader, while those closer to him laughed at his "leadership drive." Jakubczak sees it slightly differently: at each happening, several different groups—older artists from the New Culture Movement, the Twelve, high school resistance groups, some from WiP—would contribute their ideas and abilities. It was, perhaps, a natural product of the search for new styles of protest, and of Wrocław's unusually vibrant opposition culture.

At the center of the fun were several strong individuals: Jakub with his guitar; Major with his persuasive story lines and guru-like presence; Krzysztof Albin (another member of the Twelve), who eventually became the Alternative's spokesman; Marek Krukowski of WiP, accustomed to pushing confrontation a little farther each time; and Robert Jezierski, an imaginative graphic artist who, like Major Fydrych, wanted to focus on the theater more than the politics. These (and a few others) were first among equals. All were concerned with the crowd and the streets, though they envisioned the Alternative's goals, and the relationship between entertainment and politics, in different ways.

The most successful and famous Orange Alternative happening was that on the eve of the 70th anniversary of the Russian Revolution, November 6, 1987. First came the flyers announcing the happening:

Comrades!!!
The day of the eruption of the Great Proletarian October Revolution is a day of a Great Event. . . . Comrades, it is time to break the passivity of the popular masses! . . . Let us gather on November 6, Friday, at 4 P.M. on Świdnicka Street under the "clock of history." Comrades, dress festively, in red. Put on red shoes, a red cap or scarf. . . . As a last resort, with no red flag, then paint your fingernails red. If you've got nothing red, then buy a red baguette, with ketchup. We reds (red faces, hair, pants and lips) will gather that day, under the clock at about 4 P.M. . . . The festivities will end in the "Barbara" Bar, where participants will sup traditional red borscht, and other appropriate dishes, from one bowl.

Major Fydrych's report on the proceedings is the best (if perhaps not fully reliable) account. Sometimes it is difficult to tell from the surrealist prose whether he is describing a violent battle or a bizarre charade:

Historical materialism appeared at four o'clock, when the Battleship Potemkin appeared. The pride of the Black Sea Fleet is soon surrounded by the traditional blue glow [i.e., the police, or militia]. The ship leans on its side; cops rip the cardboard. . . . A brief, manly struggle and the sailors, pulled from the bow, are transported to the "Nysa" [a police van] where, handcuffed, they get slapped in the face.

. . .

Relief comes in the form of the riflemen from the naval infantry. Comrades from the Kronstadt garrison. They take the department store and move to the attack. There is shooting from the direction of the square—a cannonade of whistles—and a ten-man division spreads out across Świdnicka. But the militia is ready. . . . They swiftly put up a barrier near the post office. Kronstadt, however, charges to the defense of the cruiser. The post office is still in the hands of the Provisional Government, as is the famed Barbara Bar (the Winter Palace), which is closely guarded by cops. . . . The crowd's attention focuses on the Aurora, the Muse of the revolution. The militia surrounds it and boards, preparing for battle. . . .

To prevent further attacks, the SB [secret police] parks its vehicles to block the street. A gentleman is shouting that he won't remove red overalls from his child. The number of detained rises dramatically. Not only people with whistles, but many passersby wearing red are taken to the Nysas. Red scarves, caps, coats, sweaters, and stockings sit in the vans.

A bus approaches; it's quite lively inside: passengers of the Red Guard. Meanwhile, the gathering is ever larger on Świdnicka Street. Socialist surrealism in full display. Shouts of "RE-VO-LU-TION." The Proletariat emerges from the bus; on their shirts are signs reading: "I will work more," and "Tomorrow will be better." These proletarians are comrades from Polar and other factories, armed with rifles.

. . . The militia are disoriented: whom should they arrest first? The dog with a red ribbon? The banners? Or the red comrades running and whistling? . . .

At 4:20, carolers appear near the Hotel Monopol. They jumped from a tram with a huge banner reading "Red Borscht." This culinary revolution is blessed by a red star on a stick. Just a few moments and the carolers are in their proper place, in the proper care. Only the star wanders alone through the pedestrian underpass, to emerge on the other side like the dawn of freedom. . . .

Meanwhile, the Angel of Revolution watches over Świdnicka Street. Near St. Dorota's Church is a kiosk selling baguettes. . . . The crowd demands baguettes. The Angel of Revolution asks only for ketchup. The saleslady apologizes: there's nothing to put the ketchup on, because she was forbidden to bake the baguettes. The Angel stretches out its hand and asks for ketchup. The cops interrupt this pleasant conversation. A red halo falls in the mud.

The remains of the cavalry arrive on Świdnicka. It's nearly 5 P.M. Finally the Barbara Bar is open, but borscht has been taken off the menu. The cavaliers smile beneath their green Budionny caps. They drink strawberry juice. They aren't allowed to finish.[5]

For observers as well as for the police, this was difficult to interpret. Each actor, each slogan—there were also banners supporting Trotsky and Boris Yeltsin—could be read as political, while also scoffing at those who would see political messages everywhere. Thus some Western media reported that Trotskyists had demonstrated in Wrocław. Fydrych himself seems torn, as his report is in equal measure a surreal fable and political report, where each beating and arrest is carefully noted. The October Revolution happening demanded that observers reflect on the meaning of "political" and "opposition." One also needed to consider what freedom meant: freedom to make political statements, to ridicule (or ignore) political ideas, or simply to enjoy oneself.

In an essay entitled "Forward to the Past," Yugoslav feminist Slavenka Drakulić claims that the socialist system rose and fell on its ability to supply basic needs like toilet paper. In another essay, she describes confronting an audience of American intellectuals and producing from her bag a sanitary pad, exclaiming, "This I hold as one of the proofs of why communism failed, because . . . it couldn't fulfil the basic needs of half the population."[6] True as this observation might be, it was hard for an opposition movement to argue seriously for more toilet paper when the communists were guilty of so many weightier crimes. Orange Alternative could, and did, exploit the politics of this everyday problem in happenings on October 1 and 15, 1987.

In place of the ridiculous, this demonstration offered the sublime as a defense against fear. Participants festooned with toilet paper handed out supplies of this rare item, next to a sign reading "RIP Toilet Paper and Sanitary Pads." "Who's afraid of toilet paper?" read one banner. While challenging police to question their repressive reflex, this slogan implied a further question for onlookers: what are we really afraid of, and why? Armed with toilet paper, more and more citizens of Wrocław decided they feared nothing.

To participate, or even to watch a happening was to confront one's own ability and willingness to perform, and to risk punishment in public. Orange Alternative addressed people's fears in a different way from Freedom and Peace, for one conquered fear not through anger and determination, but through laughter. Whether the October Revolution happening and its aftermath was evidence of greater police repression or of Poland's relative freedom depended on one's point of view. To be detained by the police and taken to jail, even for only two hours, for wearing red stockings could be a sign that state repression was crueler than ever. On the other hand, to march down the street with a banner—even one with a meaningless slogan—and only be detained: that had rarely been possible in communist Central Europe.

Earlier street actions, such as the demonstrations that shook Polish cities (particularly Wrocław) in 1982–83, had been framed by participants like Fighting Solidarity (whose symbol, in the shape of an anchor, recalled the emblem of Poland's underground war with the Nazis) as evidence of the state's "Gestapo" tactics. It would not have been difficult for masters of propaganda like Fydrych or Jezierski to plaster the city with posters denouncing the "mass arrests" after the October Revolution happening (when 150 were detained for two hours). Instead, despite Fydrych's chronicling of repression, the real focus was on the freedom of each individual participant and observer. Fydrych remarked in 1988 that there were but three places in communist Poland where one could be free: prison, church, and street. The last had not been fully utilized, he felt, until Orange Alternative, whose happenings made the street appear safe for the free expression of one's self and one's core beliefs.

HIPPIES IN THE HOLY GARDEN

In a photograph of the first public demonstration in Gorbachev-era Ukraine, in September 1987, a small group of young demonstrators sits on the grass in a Lviv park. Oleh Olisevych is in the foreground. The thin band around his forehead, holding his long hair in place, identifies him as a hippy. He stares impassively at the camera, holding a large, hand-lettered sign: "Glasnost."

Olisevych's little group was an unlikely political voice. But hippiedom behind the Iron Curtain did not mean turning off politics. The hippy movement in the Soviet Union had always been rather more political than hippies in the West. Deviation in appearance or lifestyle seemed a threat to the egalitarian conformity that was communism's ideal. At the age of ten, Olisevych says, he was thrown out of school for wearing jeans. In high school he hitchhiked around the country every summer and found his way to the Baltic coast. Tallinn and Riga in particular had become "legendary summer gathering places" for hippies.[7]

Clashes with the police gave the hippy movement a perspective on human rights. In Lviv hippies discovered nationalism, too. The rock group the Vuyky, formed in 1975, became the focal point for the whole alternative scene in West Ukraine; unlike other rock groups in Ukraine, the Vuyky sang in Ukrainian (and English). So too Olisevych, who made a point of speaking only Ukrainian in the Soviet context, while most hippies adopted Russian as a lingua franca; many spoke English as well. Thus language became one criterion of the alternative and national culture in Ukraine.

In June 1976 this alternative scene took over the garden of an abandoned Carmelite monastery near the city center, nicknamed the "Holy Garden" after a hippy, "The Holy One," who camped there. For several evenings in a row, a hundred or so people gathered to listen to the Vuyky, and to play or sing along. Driven deep underground again by the repression of the next decade, hippies looked forward to greater freedom with the rise of Gorbachev—"a beautiful man," says Olisevych.*

The idea for the first demonstration came to Olisevych when he attended a pacifist demonstration in Riga in August 1987. He returned home thinking about making the same statement in Lviv. By this time, demonstrations in Central Europe were unremarkable; one would stand a good chance of encountering some public manifestation somewhere in the region, or in Moscow or Leningrad, on any given week. But Ukraine had so far been utterly quiet.

September 20, 1987, was "City of Lviv Day." The thirty or so demonstrators took advantage of the festive atmosphere, and the streets closed to traffic, to march before the holiday crowd. They waved banners or chanted slogans: "Freedom," "USSR and USA Disarmament," or "Alternative Military Service." The police, unsure how to react, stood watch over the demonstrators as they sat in the park by City Hall, then moved in to check identification cards and brought some of the demonstrators in for questioning; a few of the students were expelled from school.

The group subsequently made contact with the Moscow East-West Trust Group and christened itself Doviria (Trust). Doviria was more active publicly than its Moscow counterpart, which distributed leaflets on behalf of jailed dissidents and maintained a samizdat journal but did not generally demonstrate. The idea to demonstrate, in any case, came not from the East, but from Poland. Olisevych followed the success of the new opposition there via the BBC and Voice of America. The demonstrations of Freedom and Peace and Orange Alternative seemed to him to promote the same kind of radical expression that Doviria could embrace.

The interest was mutual. Jacek Czaputowicz read about the September demonstration in the Moscow Trust Group's bulletin *Den za dnem* and wrote to Olisevych. Return mail brought a long list of proposals for cooperation: Olisevych hoped they might be able to coordinate demonstrations, take part in each other's actions, and support each other's demands. Doviria thus became a conduit into Ukraine for information about new Polish movements, while trying to teach WiP about opposition in the Soviet Union. Not that this was easy: "I tried to send you our official press," wrote Olisevych in January 1988, "but it was sent back to me. There were good articles in those papers . . . about hippies, punks, and pacifists."[8]

---

* For this reason, Olisevych told me, his hippy credentials are sometimes questioned by others in the hippy scene. But he has no doubt himself: for him, the hippy identity is a question of both style and self-awareness.

Closer cooperation would prove impossible until Olisevych visited Kraków in August 1989.

The Lviv pacifists, Olisevych wrote, "are a radical group, and we are for active methods."[9] There were several more demonstrations in 1987, culminating in one planned for December 26, to commemorate the eighth anniversary of the Soviet invasion of Afghanistan. This one was preempted by arrests. There were also protest letters, fasts, and ever more contacts with Poland, the Ukrainian émigré community in London, and the Independent Peace Association in Czechoslovakia.

Back at the first demonstration, a plainclothes policeman had called out in warning: "You can stroll like this, boys, until May."[10] May came and went, and Doviria kept on. About one spring 1988 demonstration, Olisevych wrote to Czaputowicz that "there were theatrical situations, just like you had not long ago in Wrocław."[11] Even if he had gotten his Polish movements confused, assuming that Czaputowicz had anything to do with the escapades of Major Fydrych, Olisevych was right: the Orange style had come east and found a natural home among the nationalist hippy pacifists of Lviv.

The joining of hippy culture and serious politics seems to be simply a strange product of the time warp that was the Soviet Union—until we look west, to Prague. There, on the Kampa Park in the shadow of the Charles Bridge, emerged perhaps the strongest cult of John Lennon outside of the English-speaking world.

In the days just after Lennon's assassination (December 8, 1980), youth from Prague and beyond came to this park, a traditional meeting place for the counterculture, to honor a singer who had come to symbolize the international peace movement. A gravestone was outlined on one wall of the park; people brought flowers and lit candles. Tomáš Drábek, the medical student who would later edit *EM,* remembered those days as "one of the first turning points in my life." Drábek was then just 14, but this "apolitical" encounter set him on a path toward questioning authority.[12]

Some of those who came to the Kampa every December were hippies; most were like Drábek, drawn by a love of the music and a vague feeling of support for Lennon's ideas. Others came from the jazz underground, which had heretofore dominated the Czech counterculture. But just like the hippy gatherings on the Baltic coast in which Olisevych participated, these celebrations eventually fused an antipolitical style with an ever more concrete politics. The Czechoslovak regime could have championed Lennon as an enemy of American imperialism or the like; instead, it turned on his fans and thus helped to politicize these gatherings and turn them into opposition.

By the fifth anniversary of Lennon's death, the gathering had explicitly become a peace demonstration. When police called on the several hundred gathered to disperse, they obeyed, but only to congregate again on the Charles Bridge. Drifting toward the other side of the bridge and the Old Town Square, the crowd gained in numbers and in political momentum. By the time they reached the statue of Jan Hus in the square, they were chanting "We want freedom! We want peace!" Besides the songs of Lennon, participants sang the forbidden songs of Czech bard Karel Kryl. Led by two young women carrying candles and a portrait of Lennon, the crowd moved on to Václav Square, now shouting "Down with the red bourgeoisie, down with the SS-20s [i.e., Soviet rockets]!"[13] With shouts of "To the castle!" the crowd turned back across the river, finally reaching the square before the presidential palace some four hours after they had first gathered on the Kampa. Faced with a police cordon, and an announced curfew, the crowd broke up, but not before almost three hundred had signed a petition against the deployment of nuclear rockets in Europe. Some in the crowd invited the police to sign the petition, without success.

Until the birth of the Independent Peace Association, this loose alliance of musicians, pacifists, and more or less frustrated youth was the only public expression available for the younger generation in Prague. Eventually, there emerged a leader of sorts: Ota Veverka, a writer, musician, and Charter 77 veteran. At the December 1987 gathering—which came just two days before the brief human rights protest generally considered to be the first open demonstration in Prague since 1969—Veverka read a petition "against nuclear weapons, against the fraternal army temporarily stationed in our country (though that temporary period doesn't seem to end), and against other meanness that I don't like. And I guess the rest of us don't like it either. I barely finished when they crowded around, yelling 'Give me that!' 'Let me at it!'"[14] Quickly the petition circled the crowd. When the police moved in, Veverka was detained but got out in time to be detained again at the Chartists' demonstration on December 10th.

Inevitably, what started as little more than a hippies' camp spawned an organization. At the gathering in 1988, Veverka, Heřman Chromý of NMS, and 18-year-old Stanislav Penc announced the John Lennon Peace Club. "Peace" by now meant, in the spirit of Freedom and Peace and the NMS, human rights above all. "Czechoslovakia declares that it is struggling for peace, and meanwhile it imprisons Hana Marvanová, Tomáš Dvořák, Luboš Vydra, and Tomáš Tvaroch, members of the Independent Peace Association," read their statement. "The Czechoslovak government proclaims that world peace is one of the most urgent questions, and meanwhile it exports arms to many of the countries of the world. The Czechoslovak government lives in constant contradiction between word and deed."[15]

In precisely the spirit of their predecessors in Prague and in Poland, the Lennonists sought to use these contradictions to their advantage. Indeed, the gathering on the Kampa had that year been first announced by the Union of Socialist Youth, which hoped in this way to co-opt the popularity of the movement. Instead, this served to give the Lennonists a cover from which they could proclaim that they believed in the same things the regime did.

From then on, the John Lennon Peace Club and its members would be reliable participants in the demonstrations that laid the foundations of the Velvet Revolution. Like the hippies of the Lviv Trust Group, they offered an alternative to the more directly political groups. One could join in search of a lifestyle—the style one heard in the songs of Lennon and Yoko Ono, or encountered at a jazz concert on the fringes of legality. And because in communist Czechoslovakia, just as in the Soviet Union, that lifestyle explicitly rejected the regimentation and politicization of everyday life, it too became political, until it could neither be contained nor co-opted.

THE YOUNG SUBVERSIVE'S HANDBOOK

Marek Niedziewicz's father was a secret policeman—in fact, he was the security police chief for the largest district in Wrocław. For a high school student in the years of martial law, this was a difficult cross to bear. Marek had gone to an elementary school where many police families sent their children. He grew up not only with a deep ambivalence toward the communist regime, but with doubts about Solidarity as well. Perhaps it was difficult to hear about the opposition day after day at home and not lose at least some of one's illusions. An apprenticeship at seventeen in a metal factory—where he hoped to escape the proscribed paths of a child of the elite—didn't help either. "I wanted," he says, "everything to be beautiful, and Solidarity was not as beautiful as one would want." Most workers didn't seem to care very much about politics. When General Jaruzelski came to visit the factory (a "surprise" visit preceded by several days of frantic cleaning), Niedziewicz was chosen to greet the communist leader. He discovered that even if he would rather not take sides, neutrality was impossible.

Like others of his generation, Niedziewicz first encountered the underground by reading the samizdat that flowed through any urban high school in Poland. As he was a good writer, friends soon suggested he submit something to his school's underground paper, *Wyrostek* (Stripling). The editors were anonymous, but one could submit an article by passing it to the courier who distributed or sold the paper. Through his writing,

Niedziewicz began to enter the political subculture of Wrocław's schools. The risks of opposition were great in the hierarchical school system, where to be expelled from an elite lyceum would mean going to a lesser school and forfeiting the chance to get into university. For those who wanted the risk, there was only graffiti-painting and samizdat distribution.

The "adult opposition"—as it was commonly referred to by people of that high school generation—didn't treat the high school underground seriously, though Solidarity might occasionally give them paper or old printing supplies. It was a separate world, cut adrift from the main currents. Youth papers were often started by, in Niedziewicz's words, "boys and girls from the vocational schools, who were impressed by the idea of publishing something, but couldn't write," and thus needed people like Niedziewicz, who attended one of the better high schools.

Generations change quickly among high school students. Until at least 1985, the aura of Solidarity's heroic underground—the dashing exploits of Zbigniew Bujak or Władysław Frasyniuk, who eluded the communists for years while directing resistance—was strong. Those who founded *Wyrostek* had been in high school when martial law was declared. They had thrown rocks at police during the often violent confrontations of 1982–83, when the streets of Wrocław were the most contested in Poland. Youth's goals were Solidarity's goals. By 1986 the last of the martial-law students were finishing high school. In college many would go on to participate in groups like Freedom and Peace. Left behind were those too young to have participated, or even to have strong memories of those clashes. The old political rhetoric fell on deaf ears. From the perspective of teenagers, Solidarity seemed almost as foreign as the party—or, worse, their parents. Niedziewicz recalled how the ways the underground checked whether someone was "clean" struck him as similar to what his father's colleagues were capable of.

Politics aside, who wanted to read Solidarity's grubby, half-legible bulletins anyway? Wrocław Solidarity's *Z dnia na dzień* (From Day to Day) had a noble history, with a longer publishing record than any other underground paper in Poland, but as a high school critic commented sarcastically: "Picasso is turning over in his grave, and Cicero has been struck dumb by the sight of the Wrocław bulletin *Z dnia na dzień*. The excellent articles and the simply perfect graphic design have made the residents of Wrocław go mad reading this once-respected bulletin. If the editors do not wake up soon, the only readers left will be the blind, and on-duty functionaries of the SB."[16]

Szkoła podziemna (Underground School), the paper of the Inter-School Resistance Committee (MKO), which Marek Niedziewicz joined in the fall of 1985, proposed an alternative. In the fall of 1986 it dropped the "underground" from its name. The standard polemics on the duties of conspiracy, diatribes against communism, and solemn observance of historical anniversaries—with titles like "The Last Breath of a Dying Fatherland," or "Communism and Poland's Independence"—disappeared; in their place came a comic strip ("Animal Farm"), dozens of cartoons and illustrations, and interviews with innovative teachers and local opposition leaders of interest to students. *Szkoła* was now about school: vacations, exams, teachers and principals, the problems of different kinds of schools, school subcultures. All of these were political issues too, in an undemocratic society. Yet this was the politics of the everyday and the familiar, not of unattainable heroism. Heroes no longer had a place in *Szkoła*'s pages. The quote chosen for the subtitle of an interview with Orange activist Krzysztof Jakubczak reflected the more flexible standards of the semi-underground *Szkoła:* "I don't like students who are the best at everything."[17]

This was a stylish revolution. As Marek Niedziewicz put it, *Szkoła* became the Polish underground's first newsmagazine, offering "real journalism." It targeted its audience the way *Na przełaj* (ch. 2) had. Instead of dense lines of barely legible text, *Szkoła* offered bright graphics, varied fonts, and—its signature feature—the impish drawings of Waldemar Krass, a student at Lyceum 9, whose chubby, mischievous schoolkids illustrated every issue. They, and the other cartoons, were controversial, though: each drawing took up both space and ink, both of which cost money, time, and the nerves of clandestine printers. "Everyone thought we were nuts," editor Benita Sokołowska recalled, "because after all, it was a waste of space." Few other independent periodicals (and none that was for students) dared to waste these precious resources on nonpolitical content. Nevertheless, *Szkoła*'s editors were proud to have broken through the "wall of pathos surrounding nearly every independent paper [to] become a truly merry periodical."[18] By 1988 *Szkoła* was read across the country and published in press runs of five thousand copies.

Szkoła and the MKO reinvented youth politics, creating an audience and a community not through commercial advertising, but through activist campaigns. High school activism was essential if opposition would survive. The high schools seemed an easy target for the Ministry of National Education, which, having disposed of university autonomy the previous year, announced major changes in high school education in the spring of 1986. The reform introduced ideological subjects like military training, introduction to society, and religious studies* and reintroduced a work practicum as well. Most ominously, the school week would now stretch to Saturday once a month.

---

* Religious studies was a course about world religions; students saw it as inherently hostile to Roman Catholicism.

A reform like this would once have encountered stiff opposition from students steeled in Solidarity's battle. But four years into normalization, those students were gone. In Wrocław, student leaders were people like Barbara Widera, just 15, an enthusiastic member of the student council at Lyceum 12. Her parents had been in Solidarity, but she confesses she had not understood much of it at the time. Now she and other students looked frantically for a way to register their protest. Write letters? Most students were too scared to stick their necks out, and teachers and administrators were only too ready to persecute those who did. Nor could they look to their parents to lead a protest. In the face of a growing economic crisis, most parents hoped only that their children would get a good job or go to university.

From the teenage perspective, communism was not liberalizing but expanding its reach. The reforms of 1986 showed that normalization would aim to conquer this youngest generation. Even to survive the new curriculum, students needed to communicate strategies and ideas. It was nearly impossible for would-be student leaders to gather without arousing the suspicion of parents, teachers, and police. So in April 1986 the leaders of several student councils organized a beauty contest to pick a "Miss Lyceum." The student council representatives themselves would be the jury. While debating the finer points of Wrocław teen beauty, they could get to know one another and tackle the more pressing problem of how to respond to the school reforms. They decided to send a protest letter to Parliament; there was not much more they could do.

The MKO came to the rescue in the summer of 1986. The MKO was much like other youth resistance in Poland, with task forces carrying out courier work for Solidarity or spraying political graffiti. (And where did they get the spray paint, after it was pulled from store shelves? From Slovak priests, naturally. Rudolf Fiby, a Bratislava computer scientist secretly ordained in Poland, recalls that when Polish Catholic groups smuggled south hard-to-get religious literature, they traded it for cans of spray paint.[19]) But they discovered that August, when the security police arrested most of its leaders, that the underground was really a fiction. Many of those who had not been arrested or beaten decided to quit the opposition; Sławek "Sheriff" Sobieszek, one of the few who escaped, now rejected the life of the lonely partisan. He became determined to get the MKO "into the schools," at least halfway out of the underground. Graffiti, leaflets, and monitoring elections were no longer enough. At one district meeting of MKO couriers and school representatives, someone suggested working with student councils.

That fall, the Sheriff contacted student council chairs at several schools and invited them to meet, clandestinely. These were mostly students like Widera, who had no interest in conspiracy and task forces and had kept clear of the MKO. But they were also legalistically minded and knew their rights. They needed the MKO's assistance to do what they felt their schools deserved. Indeed, at schools where there was no student council, the MKO could create one. Thus at the Communications Vocational School, MKO courier Mariusz Zieliński stuffed the ballot box to get elected (the election wasn't really democratic anyway, and "an order is an order," he explained). The council reps began to meet frequently with Sobieszek. He collected information on conflicts, problems, and student attitudes in the schools. In return, he could help arrange, for example, contacts with bands to play at school parties.

Still, the biggest problem was how to respond to the school reform. The first idea, to boycott the religious studies classes, failed, because the classes were only for the first-year students (who most feared to risk expulsion). So did "quiet breaks," in which students walked silently in the halls between classes. Finally, the MKO called for a boycott of classes on Saturday, March 28, 1987. The appeal asked students to send letters to the Ministry of National Education, and teachers to refrain from harassing students who participated.

On the day of the boycott, police patrolled the streets, rounding up truant students. They even surrounded some schools to prevent anyone from leaving. But in the schools connected to the MKO, about half the students didn't show up. In several, including Widera's Lyceum 12, over 80 percent boycotted. Repression was swift: some students lost stipends or were evicted from their dormitories. Others were forced to sign a declaration in which they accepted a failing behavior grade for the year, redeemable only by joining the communist youth organization. There was, of course, little that the MKO could do, other than to collect money to help those students whose stipends were withdrawn. But their action attracted notice from the "adult opposition." Soon Frasyniuk's Solidarity would find money to finance high school periodicals, while students from Dominik would organize summer camping retreats for MKO activists. Rescued from normalization, the high school students were welcomed into the carnival.

The school boycott was a concrete protest organized entirely by students of a new generation, who remembered martial law better than they did a free Solidarity. Had this been purely an MKO action, the repression would likely have driven most students back into conformity. But the schools that participated were those in which the student representatives had learned to act as a link between students and the youth underground. The boycott and subsequent protests, says Widera, showed students that their student councils were their "legal defenders." In Lyceum 12, when the principal summoned seniors (who faced maturation exams and thus might be easily cowed) to report to him with their parents, the entire school staged a twenty-minute silent protest before his office. "We felt that this is one group, one team, and that it won't be so easy to get at one of us." Most of the students of Lyceum 12 felt encouraged to take part in the next boycott, of May 1 parades. This time, principals responded with selective punishments, which only, says Widera, "united us more."

Certainly one could call this cheap opposition, in which the desire to sleep in on Saturday is dressed up as a political act. But to speak out was most difficult precisely for this post-Solidarity generation, which needed first to find its own form of protest, distinct from that of the older opposition. Saturdays in school remained—though the ministry shelved plans to expand them to every week beginning in the fall of 1987—until the end of communism. The protest did, however, introduce yet another set of issues, concerning how, what, and when students should learn.

As much as *Szkoła* energized its readers, so its readers shaped *Szkoła*. In the fall of her junior year, Benita Sokołowska, whose mother was a lawyer, sent a letter to the editors (through the courier at her school) suggesting they run a column advising kids how to behave if detained or interrogated. The next day she received a reply: could she write that column? Under the pseudonym "Tatiana," she submitted "The Young Subversive's Handbook" and then was asked if she would join the editorial board. Soon, this 17-year-old had taken over one of the most visible samizdat publications in Poland. Under her leadership, *Szkoła* became even more focused on school issues, and on humor—such as the fictional series "Memoirs of a Young ZOMO." And *Szkoła* itself was an amusement—albeit one that even Sokołowska's closest friends didn't know she was involved in. The idea was to be relaxed, she explained: "We believed that we're making *Szkoła* because it brings us pleasure. But when we told someone that we're having a great time, pasting up layout or correcting copy, then everyone would go: 'My God, how can you say that? When others have died for these causes, and you are having a great time—how can you?'" Even with colleagues three or four years older, Sokołowska often found she had little in common. Why stay up all night writing stories, she wondered, if it wasn't fun?

It was common for underground editors to title their publications with pathos: "We Are" (*Jesteśmy*) "Survival" (*Przetrwanie*), "Presence" (*Obecność*), "Tomorrow" (*Jutro*). These periodicals sent the message that the underground still lived; *Szkoła* wanted something more: to be a good read. In June 1988 the editors sent out a survey—an enormously tricky thing to do, since these had to be distributed and collected by couriers in each school. (Conspiracy, though, was not the point: respondents were asked to identify their school and home classroom, which would be enough for any principal to identify suspects; not one bothered to leave these questions blank.) "Do you like the graphic design—and if not, how should it look, in your opinion?" "What topics have been raised too frequently in *Szkoła;* what topics too infrequently, or not at all?" "Should *Szkoła* be a school paper par excellence, or should it deal with various issues?" These questions and others turned readers into participants in the still-underground movement that was *Szkoła.*

Dozens sent responses, often with extensive comments. These were engaged reader-consumers who held *Szkoła* to the standards of the official press. "The pictures are really indistinct; do something in color," suggested one reader, a freshman—innocently requesting what was virtually impossible in samizdat. Recalling an article that gave instructions for making one's own spray paint, the reader begged: "Distribute sprays to students, organize a graffiti campaign, do more blizzards (*zadymy*), do the 'Saturday at home' campaign again!" A sophomore asked for articles about the history of Solidarity—as a practical matter, because "in 1980 I was nine years old." A freshman was pleased that though "there were a few boring politicizing articles [reprinted] from other papers; in general I like the fact that there isn't such empty chatter and whining." Most asked for more information about schools, university entrance exams, etc. and hoped that *Szkoła* could help with their everyday problems, even that "school bathrooms be cleaned, [with] soap by the sinks, mirrors (at least two per school), and toilet paper!" For Niedziewicz's generation, these might be issues with which they would hope to politicize students: today toilet paper, tomorrow political power. For Sokołowska, school issues themselves were what really mattered.

The expectations of *Szkoła's* readers and editors were utterly different from those of the conspiratorial martial-law period. They were at once higher—for a better-quality product—and for a more concrete and local focus. These readers could be called Poland's first true consumers, attentive as much to style as to content. What they knew was that style mattered in their effort to reject the conformity, the resignation, and the distant heroism of their parents' generation. Perhaps because they were a generation raised on television and glossy magazines (sometimes from the West), they found the old opposition just as dull and gray as the regime. The new style they created seemed quite superficial to some, but it introduced a new language of opposition that the communist authorities would find quite difficult to combat.

Professionalization was one of the solutions to the malaise that threatened opposition in all the more liberal communist regimes. In "Power of the Powerless," Václav Havel had shown how powerful, in a repressive society, could be even the smallest gesture, like refusing to display a banal communist slogan in one's store window. But this was not true in the Poland of 1985–86, where the post-Solidarity underground was in its fifth year. One could not still expect society to pay attention to opposition simply because it was brave. Nor should readers have to forgo quality and entertainment to read or listen to the "truth." *Szkoła* and its readers asked what exactly opposition meant. This question had to be answered anew by every generation, for to follow the version laid down by a previous generation would have meant to dilute one's oppositional stance.

GLOOM IN KRAKÓW

The Wrocław prescription for freedom was hardly inevitable, even in Poland. To see how different the streets could be, even in a city known for its opposition, let us turn to Kraków and the disturbing story of Wojciech Polaczek. Born in 1968, he is a year younger than Niedziewicz, and roughly in the middle of the generation of readers of *Szkoła*. His father, an engineer at Nowa Huta, was active in Solidarity in 1980–81; he recalls his mother leading him by the hand to watch the demonstrations during martial law. In 1983 he helped to found the Kraków Youth Resistance Movement, MROK (the acronym means dusk or gloom), later joining the countrywide Federation of Fighting Youth (FMW), of which Wrocław's MKO was also a part. Like Niedziewicz and others, Polaczek became expert in printing and distributing the underground press, painting graffiti, and so on. Also like the editors of *Szkoła*, he and his classmates began to feel frustrated with the adult opposition.

However, MROK's diagnosis was different: Solidarity was not radical enough. Polaczek felt they were hoping that "things would calm down." Polaczek's circle believed the situation could never be resolved peacefully, because this was war. They modeled themselves after the World War II underground and aimed to treat the functionaries of the regime "without mercy." On New Year's Eve, 1984, for example, the group fanned out across Kraków, armed with buckets of paint and names of collaborators culled from the underground press (which often, as a warning to its readers, reported names of informers in various workplaces). They painted the doors and entryways of each target's apartment with slogans like "here lives an *ubek*" and—if the apartment was on a lower floor—broke the windows with rocks. In one case, they painted the wrong door, for which they apologized later in the underground press. But this was a casualty of war; the ultimate aim of Polaczek's FMW was "independence, and the communists six feet under, precisely." There would be a "great uprising," he says, "and we would murder the communists and their families."

As shocking as this sounds nearly two decades later, it is important to remember that the winter of 1984–85, just after the murder of Father Jerzy Popiełuszko, was a frightening, almost apocalyptic moment. Polaczek is rare only in that he has preserved the emotions of that time very faithfully. In Wrocław, the ethos of the war-hardened underground degenerated; Fighting Solidarity ceded the streets to Fredruś, Jakubczak and his guitar, Major Fydrych and his elves. In Kraków, the war continued on.

In the spring of 1987, Pope John Paul II made his third pilgrimage to Poland, and his first in four years. Hundreds of thousands of Krakowians flocked to the mass the pope celebrated on the Błonie fields. MROK went, too—but "we went," says Polaczek, "in order to stage a demonstration, a powerful demonstration. We had everything very carefully divided up— who leads what group, just like in the army. Each group had two backpacks with matériel—with petards, the kind with shrapnel, to wound . . . and smoke bombs. We were going to war." They snuck in with a church group from Nowa Huta. After the mass, various groups began to march out with their banners, toward the police. This would have been the moment of conflict, but students from Freedom and Peace, ahead of MROK, "suddenly just sat down on the ground. And we were prepared," says Polaczek; "there were about two hundred militia there, without helmets, without anything, in civilian clothes, or rather dress uniforms—and we could have started killing them, and there wouldn't have been any problem, in such a hand-to-hand battle. But WiP sat down . . . and they ruined our plan to melt into the crowd after attacking the militia."

The contrast with Wrocław, where just a few days earlier students had celebrated Children's Day with candy and songs for the same police, is chilling. One is tempted to assume that Polaczek simply has a fantastic imagination, but others back up the general outlines of his story. Nor was he the only Kraków activist I interviewed to evoke that era with such hostility. The mood of Orange Alternative was alien to them. Kraków's independent student paper, *Staszek,* dismissed Orange Alternative contemptuously as just a bunch of apolitical hooligans: "It's true, of course: we lack humor and satire, so bravo for Orange Alternative. But there remains one small doubt: graffiti like 'Hands off the Bieszczady Mountains' [an absurdist slogan in Orange style] appear on the walls of Kraków, and they are no different, really, in any way from those like 'Wisła scum, Cracovia #1' [graffiti by hooligan soccer fans]. Supposedly it's something different than those Orange slogans—but still."[20]

Taking the communists lightly—and wasting wall space the same way that *Szkoła* wasted paper—was to this writer a grave mistake. Whatever really happened on the Błonie fields, the Kraków youth opposition's understanding of the streets and the crowd allowed no room for amusement. In this context, Fydrych's account of the October Revolution happening sounds more like a parody of Polaczek's preparations than of official military culture. For MROK, the crowd—of worshippers, or practitioners of nonviolence—could only be a hindrance in the war; it certainly could not participate. Fear and despair were valuable weapons: "the worse things are, the better," is how Polaczek summed up the philosophy of the time. "The more the regime falls apart and things will be worse, with higher prices, then maybe people will wake up." Compare this to the slogan the Twelve popularized at its happenings: "Smile! Tomorrow will be worse." The content is essentially the same, but the latter message breaks with ritual anticommunism and invites participation at its most elemental.

Kraków was the only major city in Poland not to follow Orange Alternative's lead. In the spring of 1988, Orange happenings took place on the streets of Poznań, Gdańsk, Bydgoszcz, Łódź, and even usually quiescent Warsaw. But Wrocław's recipe was not easily transportable to other cities. These happenings lacked the central idea of reaching out to and training the people on the street. Participants in Bydgoszcz's "TUP-TUP Theater" staged complex allegories about the history of socialism. Actors handed out empty candy wrappers to symbolize economic reform, or built a structure using bricks labeled "hunger," "poverty," "alcoholism," etc.[21] One could observe and applaud (and many passersby did), but there was little to laugh about. Or rather, the laughter was the kind that simply reaffirmed one's attitude toward the regime. One could nod one's head—"Yes, that will be the effect of the communists' reforms"—but one did not thus reclaim one's freedom on the streets, or learn how to act in accordance with one's free will.

Another type of happening simply attacked the passivity of the crowd. In Poznań on International Women's Day, March 8, the Mathias Rust Komando* dressed as women (most were men) and marched on the Rynek. They carried banners reading "Polish women support the government's policies," "I'll take any work," "Down with sex segregation" and "[We demand] power and cotton [i.e., sanitary pads]." It seemed that society was almost as much a target as the regime. And when the militia came, these demonstrators did not greet them with flowers but screamed "They're beating women!"[22] The temptation to deliver a finished ideological product, rather than an opportunity for self-liberation and amusement, was strong, and few would-be Majors could resist.

PIETIA'S CRUSADE

The crisis of opposition affected even the nihilist world of the punk subculture, as far from *Szkoła*'s concerns as imaginable. Though punk fans and musicians in a Western society had the liberty to reject the commercialization of music and the entire conformist world, punks (and other

* Named for the young West German who had recently evaded Soviet air defenses to land his light plane on Red Square.

musical subcultures) in Poland couldn't even always get access to their music. The pressure to conform—listening to snatches of Western punk (or metal, or reggae) on state-run Radio Three, or going to officially sanctioned concerts like the annual festival at Jarocin—was thus all the greater. Poland's regime had discovered that (compared to the mainstream political underground) the margins could be more easily normalized. What appeared alternative was no alternative at all, but a production of official culture, with the attendant censorship and control.

Punk's first wave had been a powerful force during the Solidarity revolution, and the second wave had energized martial law. Punk's fate mirrored that of the opposition, though. By mid-decade, the scene was ritualized and dwindling fast, a determined hard core surrounded by a complacent, apolitical mass. The challenge to revive punk seized Piotr "Pietia" Wierzbicki; his solution was not all that different from that of *Szkoła*. In 1986, he became editor-in-chief of *QQRYQ*, a punk 'zine based in Warsaw—the name is a warping of *kukuryku,* the sound of a rooster crowing. There were but a few hundred faithful holdout readers by this time; the few other punk 'zines had at most a few dozen. Within a year, *QQRYQ* doubled its press run. Instead of a more professional product (which would be offensive to punk culture), Pietia offered *QQRYQ*-sponsored concerts across Poland, especially in small towns, and independently produced tapes of new punk bands.

Like his colleagues at *Szkoła*, Pietia aimed both to appeal to a particular audience and to change it, by finding a way out of the impasse of opposition. The answer, oddly enough, was what Pietia called "positivism." First, he advocated "straight edge," a punk subculture whose adherents vowed abstinence from drugs, alcohol, and sex. In a lengthy 1987 interview with Dezerter, Poland's leading punk band, Pietia asked for the band's position on the straight-edge lifestyle, vegetarianism, and so on. Later in that same issue, Pietia confronted the punk scene with brutal honesty, in an editorial entitled "Alcoholism, Sexism, and Idiocy": "Ladies are treated like dirt—which, after all, is often what they desire, but that's another story. . . . There are no girls [in punk jargon], only 'goods' and 'whores.' Of course, sex is great, but I'm talking now about sexism, in other words looking at the world with one's dick. The matter of women in punk rock is a separate topic. They are usually left in the role of subhumans and fucking machines—and often put themselves in that situation." While surprising for a punk 'zine, this was so far a standard diagnosis of a social problem. But Pietia offered a kind of self-governing solution: people should help themselves be free:

> How many punk girls in Poland are putting out 'zines, or organizing concerts, or even just have thought a bit more deeply about the ideas and the music? . . .

How much longer will punk mean alcoholism, filth, helplessness, thoughtlessness? That isn't punk, it's a parody of punk created by the mass media, a youth farce in which we have been assigned the role of fools. I can't listen anymore to those futile moans: "I'm fucking bored," "Nothing's happening," "Let's get wasted, then it'll be fun." Why do you complain that there are so few concerts, since you don't do anything to organize them? Why do you hobble about pointlessly, not trying to do anything positive? . . . I count on people for whom life is a battle, and not just drinking and humping. I count on those who know what to destroy and what to build, who have something more than just a few overheard slogans in their heads and don't run away from a drunken skinhead asking for a light.[23]

Helped by Dezerter's fame, the issue in which this editorial appeared was the one, Pietia recalled, that marked the 'zine's rise to popularity. Where *Szkoła* learned to smuggle in more and more material that was not political, *QQRYQ* slipped in more and more politics along with band interviews and news of the world punk scene. There were short articles on antinuclear protest, and frequent mention of Freedom and Peace and the Animal Liberation Front. The goal was a readership that would both destroy and build, or "think and act positively."[24]

This detour from the core social movements uncovers the depth of rifts in Polish culture in the mid-1980s and suggests how universal was the need for a new, post-Solidarity style that combined positivism and derision. Whether out of fear, a shared ideological past, or belief in the need for negotiation, the opposition in Poland had always accorded the communist regime and the Soviet Union respect. This was something that the post-Solidarity generation was unable to feel. For Pietia (who in one issue styled himself as a Bolshevik commissar), communism was neither positive nor negative, but simply an irrelevant joke. The generation of *Szkoła* might still be required to take Russian, or study Marxism-Leninism, but they knew they'd never need it, and they learned only enough to mock it.

PORNOSLAVIA

Punk was subversive because it did not spare the sacred values of opposition. But this was confusing to the communists, who preferred to tar all resistance with the same brush. The brush of choice, whenever possible, was the label "fascist." In Yugoslavia, where heroic struggle against the Nazis had also faced a native fascist regime, the label was particularly handy, and insidious. Nationalism was, to the Titoists, not far from treason. For better or for worse, this was one of the severest restrictions on Yugoslav public life.

Politicians in Belgrade in the 1980s often spoke of a "Slovene syndrome" and were determined to wipe it out. They meant Slovene tendencies to do things differently, to act out of concert with the other Yugoslav republics. At least since the student movement of 1968–72, when Slovenes had come out on the streets in support of their liberal leaders, the republic had been under suspicion. Though the Croat unrest had been greater at that time, Slovenia shared long borders with noncommunist Austria and Italy and so might (it was thought) be less loyal to Belgrade. The Titoist distrust of national expression increased in the 1980s, even as all republics (led by Serbia) began to rehearse their own interests in preference to those of the country as a whole.

Nationalist ideas are not a destructive genie never to be let out of the bottle. They are also part of modern democratic politics everywhere and were part of democratic opposition in Central Europe, too. But conventional national opposition, rooted in ideas and political process, was vulnerable to attack (as Slovene and Croat nationalists had found in the late 1960s). Nationalism—whether in the guise of a communist leader proposing greater control over his republic's budget, or World War II veterans seeking to honor their fallen comrades—was easy for Belgrade to parse. The communists knew these were dangerous tendencies, smelling of fascism and redolent of the past. By upending the traditional pieties, Slovene counterculture found a way to disarm this weapon with ridicule and so undermine communist ideology thoroughly. What could the Titoists make of punk rockers, who dressed in provocative ways and embraced anarchist slogans, or a heavy metal band whose members dressed in military uniforms and sang in German, and artists who used Nazi imagery to glorify Yugoslavia? Of course, they had to be fascists, every one. In the carnival, though, nothing was as it seemed.

Beginning with the punk scene of the late 1970s, Slovenia became the site of the most vibrant Central European subcultures. Rejecting all of the boring authorities structuring socialist Yugoslavia, the punks carved out a little independence (in bars or clubs, on the streets, at concerts, and in song lyrics), which benefited others as well. Punk rock, in fact, opened up the space for experiment with other movements (including those that contributed to the Peace Movement Working Group).

Gregor Tomc, himself one of punk's pioneers, has described with great irony how the authorities' initial bewilderment soon gave way to simplistic labeling. One punk went to prison for thirty days for wearing a button reading "Nazi punks fuck off" (as well as one with "Crazy governments" written over a swastika and a hammer and sickle); he was presumed to have attacked Yugoslav patriotism. The campaign against so-called Nazi punks—an absurd appellation lumping punks with their sworn enemies—consumed and virtually destroyed the punk scene by 1982.[25]

This was the essence, and the limitation, of the punk style: a basically anarchist attack on authority and ideology, but lacking unifying ideas and communicating in often obscure and ambiguous codes. It was an aesthetic protest more than a political one, despite the often highly political language. The punk scene was virtually defenseless against the police and the larger society. In Poland, Pietia had tried to address this problem. In Slovenia, what punk had started, Laibach would push further.

Laibach, a rock group named for the German translation of "Ljubljana," emerged in 1980. It was less a band than a performance art collective (Laibach is closely tied to the avant-garde art collective Neue Slowenische Kunst, NSK), though Western fans often lump it together with gothic heavy metal. The truth is, Laibach has never been easy to understand. Industrial rhythms accompany German lyrics about blood and the collective will, while vaguely totalitarian images are projected on screens.* This seemed simultaneously a parody of fascism and totalitarianism, and their apogee. The band appeared to glorify the virtues of the collective and of the great Slovene past, yet no careful observer could doubt that they also mocked the concert audience's enthusiasms. The authorities took no chances. The very name Laibach was barred from official media for almost five years, and the group was forbidden to play in Slovenia (though it played elsewhere in Yugoslavia and toured the West frequently, appearing also in Poland).

The Slovene peace community also found Laibach distasteful. Even if it was all an elaborate hoax, symbols of aggression were volatile toys. Laibach could, perhaps inadvertently, arouse the very passions that peace activists hoped to avoid in order to save Europe. There is no evidence that Laibach's listeners became Nazis—and still less did they become adherents of Titoist authoritarianism. Rather, Laibach's attraction, and virtue, was the confusion it spread. Whether one supported Laibach or denounced it, one might be left open to ridicule. To be safe, then, in 1986 the League of Socialist Youth of Slovenia (ZSMS) began calling for Laibach to be rehabilitated.

The pomposity of the Tito cult and the deadening language of Yugoslav bureaucracy cried out for an Orange Alternative, and Laibach and NSK filled that role—though they tended toward the bombastic rather than the entertaining end of the satirical spectrum. A ripe target for ridicule was the Youth Relay. In this annual celebration of the Tito cult and Yugoslavia

---

* Their trademark is a black cross on a white background, painted by Russian artist Kasimir Malevich.

(revived in 1986 after a half-decade dormancy), young runners carried a baton across the country for many weeks, arriving in Belgrade on May 25, Tito's birthday. In 1986 Ljubljana students marked the event with their own ceremony in the city center: while some carved a four-foot baton out of a tree trunk, others circulated a petition against the relay. That same evening, the elaborately painted baton was given funeral rites and discarded.

The next year, according to the complex rotations of the Yugoslav calendar, the relay was scheduled to begin in Slovenia. A competition was announced for a poster to celebrate this honor. The winning design was submitted by NSK: a strapping youth bounds forward with a huge Yugoslav flag in hand, surrounded by a dove and six torches symbolizing the Yugoslav republics. Only after the competition results were announced did the truth leak out: NSK had taken a famous Nazi poster from 1936 and simply switched flags, substituted a dove for an eagle, and replaced "The Third Reich" with "Youth Day."

Who, exactly, were the Nazis here: the authors of the poster, or those who had awarded it first prize? Of course, the former were blamed. Amidst the scandal, however, the relay was quietly shelved. This was the Laibach idea: a strong dose of totalitarian imagery would inoculate society against this disease and make ostensibly antitotalitarian versions of Nazi pageantry impossible.

Punk, not to mention avant-garde performance art, reaches a small audience. Even the subtleties of the poster controversy were probably lost on many Slovenes, who did not have the Poles' long experience with oppositional codes. But Slovenia also boasted the most daring legal media in the communist world, which translated the irreverent style and the specific political and social agenda of the growing Ljubljana opposition into a national language.

Mladina, the youth weekly of ZSMS, had been coming out since 1943 and was once one of the reliable arms of the League of Communists. As of 1981 it was not too different from other youth periodicals in the Communist Bloc (such as *Na przełaj,* where the Polish "I'd Rather Live" movement started): uplifting stories about youth at home and abroad, some profiles of popular rock groups, stories of student life, and a discreet dose of official politics. But the Youth League was looking to become more popular, feeling the pressure of the competition for resources among and within republics in the post-Tito era.

First to go, then, were reverential photos of the recently departed leader. Then there appeared more specifically Slovene articles, like a 1982 issue with Tone Stojko's photos of the demonstrations in Ljubljana in 1970–71. Mile Šetinc, who became editor in 1983, could push even further, as the son of a high communist official. Under his editorship, *Mladina* began to explore military issues, including the problem of military service. The style also became more daring: nude photos on the cover, racy cartoons inside. There was a page in each issue for music news from Radio Študent, the Youth League's other media outlet. The radio station, a few steps ahead of *Mladina*, had publicized (at some risk) the "Nazi punk" affair, even staging a live call-in show during which the regime was subjected to scathing criticism. Radio Študent's page switched *Mladina*'s soundtrack from the Beatles to punk and new-wave rock.

Under Šetinc and his successor Miha Kovač, participants in the Peace Group like Mastnak and Hren, or Jalušič of Lilith, became regular correspondents, writing about Slovenia's ecological crisis, about feminism, peace, and the Cold War. Then in the autumn of 1986, a new editor arrived, straight from Radio Študent. Unlike his predecessors, Franci Zavrl had no connection with the Youth League or the League of Communists. To the communist leaders, he was an enigma. "I don't understand the relationships inside Mladina," complained party leader Milan Kučan during the crisis of the summer of 1988. "What do these guys want? When the editors were [Šetinc, Kovač, and others] it was OK. But these guys are playing games."[26]

Indeed, the rules of the game had changed. Zavrl and his team—mostly young journalists brought over from the radio, like Ali Žerdin—were willing to try anything. The second issue under Zavrl's editorship featured on the cover a black-and-white photograph of Stalin with a bright yellow egg cracked over his nose, the yolk splattering over his chin. Both Laibach and the NSK were frequent subjects and contributors. One of the most famous *Mladina* covers, designed by NSK, showed Tito, looking thoughtful (or maybe threatening) against a Nazi flag. The message was extremely ambiguous: Tito seemed to be condemning fascism, but his pose hinted at a different interpretation.

Mladina pursued serious politics, too: stories on dissident Milovan Djilas, or on the violations of human rights in Kosovo, on strikes in Yugoslavia, or—most famously—a series of articles exposing the corrupt arms deals of Defense Minister Branko Mamula. These are the normal fare of investigative journalism; it is perhaps odd to write about them in the same context as happenings and samizdat. The closest parallel in the communist world was probably the glasnost-era press in the Soviet Union, like the weekly *Ogonyok*. But the context was quite different. *Mladina* was publishing in a provincial capital, far from the centers of real power. Its attacks on Yugoslav corruption had an implicit national tinge, and that is how Belgrade chose to interpret *Mladina*'s attacks.

Before, *Mladina* had often been daring; now, it was frankly aggressive. Zavrl experimented with pornography, like a comic strip called "Pornoslavia." Zavrl wanted to "test the borders of the acceptable." Even he admits *Mladina* may have gone too far sometimes, as when it published a "murder manual" for those wishing to commit a clean and successful crime.

Even the political news could be carnivalesque: in December 1988 *Mladina* published an interview with Prince Alexander, pretender to the Yugoslav throne. From the playful, abrupt questions—"Are you rich?" and "Where is your crown?"—it was impossible to tell if *Mladina* wanted its readers to take the crown prince seriously, or to see him as just another power-hungry politician, ripe for skewering.[27]

Neither *Mladina* and Radio Študent nor Laibach and NSK were social movements themselves. But to quote Laibach's manager Igor Vidmar, they were "detonators" clearing a path for alternative politics. They were more than media: they were provocateurs, insistently raising uncomfortable questions and testing boundaries that were like invisible electric fences, unmarked until someone fell on them. As Slovenes sought for alternatives to the circumscribed official politics, the bombastic, daring style of these groups caught their attention, even if they did not always agree.

GOD, KING, AND COUNTRY IN BOHEMIA

For *Mladina*'s journalists, the idea of a Yugoslav king was something of a joke. Even in Slovenia, though, one could use the joke to explore alternatives to communism. One group took this exploration to its logical extreme and espoused an "Orange" monarchism. The Czech Children's Manifesto appeared in May 1988. In both (slightly archaic) Czech and Latin, Petr Placák (a 24-year-old artist) declared that "the Czech monarchy lives! We are preparing for the coming of a new king—this is our highest goal. . . . The king is the law before which man, tree, animal, earth and forest are equal, and every kind of action by one to the detriment of another is a crime!" He advocated the return to the Czech monarchy of ancestral lands now beyond its borders and promised, "The Royal administration will be just as its people wish. If they want it to be communist, it shall be communist. However, we are convinced that such an administration need not—indeed must not—have any political program; rather, it should be either good or bad."[28]

The manifesto never winks at the reader, never lets the reader in on the joke. This was a happening as disorienting as anything Orange Alternative dreamed up. Though he claims still to be interested in a revival of the Czech monarchy, Placák now explains that monarchism was a way to deny compromise with the regime. After all, a democratic opposition might hope that communism would become more democratic, but no one could seriously believe (the terrible saga of the Ceauşescu regime in Romania aside) that it could be "monarchized." The surrealism of a monarchist in a communist state pointed also to the surrealism of communism. Triumphantly, *Rudé pravo,* the Prague communist daily, published the manifesto to show how ludicrous the opposition was, but the effect was just the opposite. Many who read the manifesto were intrigued (some by the evident humor, others by the prospect of royalty), and the Czech Children gained free publicity.

Most of the roughly thirty original signatories of the Czech Children's Manifesto were not students, but slightly older underground artists and musicians, rather like those in the New Culture Movement in Wrocław. Caught between generations, they abandoned the caution of their elders in Charter 77. Their overarching concern was one not unlike that of the Slovenes (who also lived in a multi-ethnic federal state): how to revive a national pride without unleashing ethnic conflict. A monarchy was a solution to this conundrum. "The monarch symbolizes our unity," explained Placák. "We serve him and he serves us."

Unlike in some other countries (such as Russia or Romania), though, monarchism in Czechoslovakia (or even in the Czech lands) does not have obviously nationalist connotations: there has not been a Czech ruler since the fifteenth century. A royal dynasty in Czechoslovakia would seem almost as unlikely as in the United States. This platform was therefore a way to lampoon nationalist demands—like Laibach, to inoculate the Czechs against the nationalist temptation. The name "Czech Children" hinted at a search for social bonds. It meant, explained participant Anna Hradilková, "that we have inherited something, that we have common roots, a common history. This legacy is given to a person, and one can't be rid of it. . . . It is something in which one grows up, which influences one, which is an integral part of one's being. This is exactly what they had tried to deprive us of for forty years."[29] In other words, the Czech Children tried to find something other than communism (or fear of communism) that would unite society.

Placák kept his distance from the senior opposition. Like most of those in the Independent Peace Association, with whom he worked closely in the fall of 1988, Placák did not sign Charter 77. The Chartists in turn regarded Czech Children as a curiosity at best (though Havel in particular was supportive).

In Polish society, which had already reclaimed an alternative past and identity in nation and Church, Orange Alternative opened up the streets and presented a stark choice to onlookers and police alike: you either beat the elves or join them, but you can hardly be indifferent. In the same way, the Czech Children offered a stark contrast (communism or monarchy) as a way of reopening the question of Czech political identity. Like Major Fydrych, Placák valued not so much the specific political agenda—though he stressed the importance of having a clear program, as opposed to simply having fun on the street—but that people would appear on the streets at all. But the oddity of the program—and the attacks in the communist press—encouraged people to attend demonstrations, if only out of curiosity.

The Czech Children deny any connection to Orange Alternative.* They saw themselves as more serious. "In the Czech Children movement itself there was no joking at all," maintains Lucie Váchová, one of the first of the group to go to jail, for leafleting, in the fall of 1988.

> In essence, the ideas or the aims of the Czech Children were articulated differently, described differently. They had nothing in common, I think, and I would say that no activity which took place before the revolution had any comical nature at all. None. There were no happenings, and the object was never to call attention to oneself in a humorous way, not ever. I think that whenever this [similarity] is presumed, there is a misunderstanding of the Czech Children's Manifesto, simply due to the fact that it is written in a different style.[30]

But it is precisely this different style—and the emphasis on style itself—that links the two movements. Another participant, Luděk Marks, points to the "considerable ironic exaggeration" in the "sarcastic" manifesto,[31] and indeed, the publication of an opposition manifesto in Latin is very much in the vein of Fydrych's writings, differing only in the type of regime whose jargon is being adopted. Content is of course important: for Czech Children, the rejection of compromise with communism, and for Orange Alternative, the ridicule of communism. Ultimately, the political goals were for many in the two movements the same: both Jakubczak and Placák, when asked what the purpose of their activities were, replied instantly, "The overthrow of communism." Nevertheless, the means was nearly as important as the end. To draw people out onto the street, to entertain and engage them for as long as possible with whatever message worked: this was truly the common goal in both cases.

It is not surprising that both Placák and Váchová should emphatically reject the comparison with a movement that was also consistently misunderstood. This misunderstanding is in a way the key to their success, as it was for Orange Alternative. The daring, provocative messages drew people to participation. Once involved, people could experience the freedom that demonstrations, discussions, or happenings offered. From this, in turn, would come political change and the destruction of the communist system. Whether it would be followed by a monarchy, fairyland, or something else was another matter. Both groups were dominated by people who were not (they told themselves) politicians, but artists or musicians. For them, the manner or style of opposition heretofore was almost

---

* Placák, it is true, visited Wrocław in the fall of 1988, but he was almost immediately arrested—with Mirek Jasiński of Polish-Czechoslovak Solidarity—and deported.

as objectionable as the communist system itself. The space separating artistic diversion from political conflict is narrow and is maintained only with a certain sense of irony. The Czech secret police considered the Czech Children dangerous "precisely because its demonstrations were not entirely downright political," explains Váchová.[32] This was the same niche occupied by Orange Alternative.

Given the absence of any obvious alternative model within Czechoslovak culture (after the failure of 1968, and in an essentially agnostic society), the Czech Children needed to propose something consistent and recognizable; advocating monarchy was simpler, and more understandable than, say, Buddhism. I do not mean to suggest the choice was frivolous; only that it met the needs of the moment. In Poland there was instead a surfeit of alternative ideologies: of the Church, of the nation, and of Solidarity (each overlapping with the other, of course). Orange Alternative arose in conflict with all of these, and not their absence. An Orange Alternative was in the end unthinkable in Czechoslovakia, and the Czech Children would have been a marginal curiosity in Poland.

TO BECOME A SMURF

Politics and culture are a volatile combination, not easily mastered. Orange Alternative, which achieved the greatest profile of any movement explored in this chapter, faced great tensions that would eventually tear the movement apart. The main problem was the role of politics. Precisely because of its lack of a guiding ideology, accusations of politicizing the movement today fly from all sides. Definitions are here a bit fuzzy; what was "politics" in the pejorative sense to one participant was simply necessary to another. Everyone agreed that, at one level, every action was political. The question was rather the connection between larger political change and personal freedom. For some, the crowds who flocked out of curiosity to Orange Alternative happenings were a tempting vehicle for pushing a specific political agenda. Like any revolutionaries who suddenly found themselves before a real audience, the students and artists around Orange Alternative knew they could lead the masses somewhere but were not sure where.

Krzysztof Albin, who in early 1988 became the semi-official spokesperson of Orange Alternative, felt that the Western press was trying to force the "political demonstration" label on the happenings. As the commissar of propaganda of the Polish Workers' Party, he issued a communiqué explaining that Orange Alternative was simply a social-artistic movement.[33] But of course, this declaration could itself have been just another absurdist happening. Already in the winter of 1987–88, the happenings began to take on a more political edge. For example, three weeks after the October Revolution happening came one that lampooned the referendum called by General Wojciech Jaruzelski to gather support for economic reform. Leaflets announcing the happening were festooned with dark glasses, a universal reference to Jaruzelski.

The several thousand participants at the Karnawał RIObotniczy (with which this book began) made it the most popular happening yet. As mentioned, the event came on the heels of a government-announced price hike. The happening followed a different agenda from previous ones: when the police began to arrest participants, this crowd did not thank them, wave to those detained, and sing songs, as on Children's Day the previous spring. They attacked the vans, formed human chains to protect those whom the police sought, and chanted "Gestapo!" One of the most famous images of Orange Alternative comes from this happening: a reveler dances, or stomps furiously, on the roof of a police van.

For its part, the police had decided Major was flirting with the most dangerous kind of politics: nothing less than Freedom and Peace must be standing behind him. Referring to Marek Krukowski, a prominent participant in Wrocław's WiP, Waldemar Fydrych's interrogators after Mardi Gras demanded: "Where do you want to work? With whom?—with Mr. Marek, of course. Don't do that, he'll pull you into WiP. Mr. Waldek, you should decide yourself whether Mr. Marek is OK. . . . Mr. Waldek, many have come to this room and sworn, beating their breast, that they have nothing to do with WiP. Then they get mixed up with Mareczek and are swallowed up."[34]

Perhaps, then, the politicization was inevitable; politicians within the movement, outside observers, and the regime were all bound to tip Orange Alternative over the line into mainstream political opposition. Had the communist authorities provoked it into abandoning ridicule for direct protest, they might have destroyed the movement. Instead, fatefully, they pulled back from the brink. In the regime camp, no one rivaled press spokesperson Jerzy Urban as a master of the absurd. His press conferences infuriated television audiences and confounded Western reporters with their audacity. Better than most, Urban understood the language of Orange Alternative. He also spied its political Achilles heel: it needed the regime to remain a distant and impersonal target of ridicule, even while one gave a flower to the policeman standing nearby. In early 1988 Urban proposed to Jaruzelski's Politburo that Urban travel to Wrocław to attend a happening. The most hated man in Poland, whose bald head and large ears made him an easy target of caricature, willing to join in the fun; one can easily imagine him cavorting in a mask, blowing a whistle, maybe even making a comical speech. Urban calculated that his appearance would quickly take the wind out of Orange Alternative's sails. Jaruzelski, however, quickly forbade the idea, and the regime remained an easy target. Nine years later, one could still feel the disappointment of this master manipulator.

For Krzysztof Jakubczak, the greatest threat to Orange Alternative was from Solidarity itself. When Fydrych was sentenced to sixty days in prison that spring, forty intellectuals signed an appeal demanding his release. This should have been another joke, but it wasn't; Orange Alternative was becoming just another movement, and Fydrych, the darling of Warsaw salons.

The logical end of Solidarity's interest was a happening on June 27, 1988, entitled "The People of Wrocław Welcome Pinior and Borowczyk." Józef Pinior, the legendary leader of Wrocław Solidarity and co-founder of the recently revived Polish Socialist Party (PPS), and Czesław Borowczyk, a socialist worker activist, faced the court that day on charges of beating a police officer during a rally at the Dolmel factory in May. Pinior had participated in Orange happenings almost from the beginning; for him, participation felt like liberation from the narrow confines of opposition politics: "I had to throw off that shell, that mask."[35] But when Pinior arrived at the happening in his honor, it was as a politician: he was greeted with shouts of "PPS" and "Solidarity." PPS leaflets fluttered everywhere, and Pinior gave a short speech. As Jakubczak observed, this happening no longer made sense: was Pinior (and his fame) being made fun of, or not? If the demands for his freedom were real, then the line into ordinary politics had been crossed. And if so, then Orange Alternative had outlived its time.

An equally knotty problem was the role of the crowd. The purpose of a happening, again, was both to give participants freedom and to promote certain aesthetic (or political) ideas. Too many happenings, then, would squander spontaneity and excitement and make Orange Alternative routine. But some "happeners" felt they could most efficiently express their ideas in smaller crowds, performing frequently; passersby only got in the way. Practice in using the streets was indeed important; Petr Placák claims that it was precisely the frequency of the Czech Children's protests and open-air discussions that prepared the people of Prague for daily demonstrations during the Velvet Revolution in November 1989. Still, more than one movement has foundered in overexposure.

This problem is illustrated by "Spy Day," a happening in March 1988. For Robert Jezierski, this was one of the most successful, and enjoyable, happenings: each participant (there were about thirty) dressed as a spy of one country or another and darted around downtown pretending to communicate over secret radios and requesting that people show their identity documents; some demanded identification from police officers. Certainly this was something no opposition had ever done before; one ZOMO officer later told Orange Alternative veteran Wiesław Cupała that

Spy Day had been the greatest moment of his life, as he suddenly realized how foolish his work was. But for Jakubczak, Spy Day was a failure. Instead of controlling and shaping the crowd through entertainment, participants in Spy Day pestered the crowd or ignored it, interacting instead with their policers. As Jakubczak put it: "a person, or maybe even a thousand people, come [to a happening] and want to do something"—put on a red cap, sing a song, give a flower to a policeman. A passerby could not join in Spy Day; instead, he or she might be confronted, even attacked, by a participant demanding to see identification. Who, really, was the object of satire here: the officious secret police, or the nervous, hapless citizen?

All these problems would be obvious in 1989. For the moment, Orange Alternative set Poles free to find their own paths back to opposition. An Orange happening, Major Fydrych argued, was a place to learn opposition, to discover more political forms of protest. "The Wrocław street slowly ceases to fear, and through participation in the fun, people learn to support more serious [protest], such as WiP's blizzards (*zadymy*). Fear of detention—usually for a few hours, without serious consequences—evaporated."[36] For Fydrych, then, this was a kind of sociotherapy, allowing people to achieve goals they didn't know they were capable of. A young mother recalls her encounters with Orange Alternative:

> I don't know the Major. Actually, I don't even know any of those who are always at the head of the parade. But I try not to miss any of Orange Alternative's happenings. This is because I want sometimes not to fear the militia and their clubs. I come to convince myself that not every day must be depressing and dirty; I come so that at least once every few months, for a few hours, I can show everyone—and perhaps myself most of all—that I can be just like people somewhere in the ordinary, normal world. I can laugh, have fun, be provocative. I need this for my psychological health. I don't want always to think about the fact that there is no milk for my child. Such a happening, once every few months, is an orange alternative to reality.[37]

She might not have joined Freedom and Peace, but she was more likely to accept and understand WiP's *zadymy,* though the very word "opposition" might once have caused her hurriedly to change the subject.

Beyond the individual sphere, Orange happenings also had a social function. Fydrych again: "The happenings integrate. . . . After every action, new people come to Orange Alternative. Every *zadyma* and detention ends with a gathering that same day. Until recently, everyone knew each other; now there are more unfamiliar faces. And since many also 'blizzard' in other outfits, Orange Alternative is also a way to make contact with the serious opposition."[38] Like *Szkoła,* Czech Children, *Mladina,* and even *QQRYQ,* the Orange happening was a handbook for the would-be young subversive. While throwing candy and singing silly songs, one could easily figure out who had more daring ideas or a specific program—it might be WiP, or the socialists, or perhaps Solidarity.

At the same time, a happening allowed the older generation (like Pinior) to discover the students. The worker opposition, in particular, was quite isolated within the factories. A correspondent for the underground paper of Wrocław's lathe factory saw salvation in the happenings: "I would like to thank the youth of Wrocław, warmly and sincerely, for having helped smiles to bloom on the faces of the people of Wrocław, who can for a moment forget about our communist reality. I appeal to the workers of our factory to participate in these gatherings, which are creating a new climate, unheard of elsewhere; they eliminate generational barriers. These gatherings give us HOPE—because the youth is our hope."[39]

In 1987–88 the *Szkoła* generation took center stage for a moment in Poland. As they did so, the cast of protest changed. Underground leaders were challenged to reinvent themselves with self-irony, and to cast aside the legends of long-ago martial law. The stars of these happenings were not orators nor rock-throwers but artists, script-writers, and the audience (even those who, like those wearing red at the October Revolution happening, did not intend to participate). The symbol of protest, too, was no longer the letter 'S' for Solidarity, but something even more familiar: the Smurf. These popular cartoon characters are blue elves who, week after week on Polish television, performed deeds of brotherly love, kindness, and ordinary bravery to rescue each other, and their home, from evil forces like the giant Gargamel. In the pantheon of protest colors, blue, the color of the police's uniforms and vans, opposed orange. Logically, then, the police were Smurfs—and happening crowds greeted them in this way. But in the carnival world of Orange Alternative, anyone could be anything. When Fydrych, released from prison, appeared at the Children's Day happening of June 1, 1988, he was hailed as "Papa Smurf." As in a Rabelaisian carnival, roles were reversed and one fool, at least, had become king.

Each of the movements discussed in this chapter seems to hover between obvious political definitions—rebellious students, nihilist punks, defiant conservatives, sharp satirists—and the artistic margins, where what seems rebellion is only graffiti, performance art, and loud music. In the terms of the older generation of dissident intellectuals, we might say that these young artists, musicians, and journalists had discovered that all art is political in an ideological dictatorship. But the Orange generation did not seek simply to name Gargamel and expose his perfidy. Instead, they redrew the scenario so that Gargamel ceased to be frightening, and the Smurfs—those on both sides of the barricades—could be free. They bring us out into the streets of revolution, which is where we shall now turn.

Timeline II: 1988–1989

Date	Poland	Czechoslovakia	Hungary	GDR	Slovenia	Ukraine	East/West
I.88				Luxemburg demo; regime crackdown on IFM		Towarystvo Leva inaugurates *vertepy*	
II.88	Price hikes; "Carnival" demo						
III.88		Candlelight demo, Bratislava	March 15 demo draws 10K; **Halozát forms**; **FIDESZ forms**				
IV.88	Nowa Huta strike	**Independent Peace Association forms**				Petition on Ukrainian language circulates	Peace agreement signed in Afghan war
V.88	Gdańsk shipyard strike	**Czech Children forms**	János Kádár removed as party chief		First arrests of *Mladina* editors		
VI.88	2nd Children's Day happening, Wrocław	Abortive East-West seminar, Prague			"Slovene Spring" **Committee for Defense of Human Rights forms**	"Ten Days that Shook Lviv" demos; 1st Dnister expedition	19th Party Conference opens in Moscow
VII.88					*Mladina* trial		
VIII.88	Strikes in Jastrzębie, Gdańsk, Stalowa Wola	Demo marks 20th anniversary of Soviet invasion					
IX.88			Danube Dam demo		*Mladina* Four lose appeal in Belgrade		
X.88	Autumn: negotiations between Solidarity and regime on terms of Round Table	Independence Day demo	More Danube dam demos; October 23 demo commemorates 1956				
XI.88	Wałęsa appears in live TV debate		FIDESZ Workers' Group demo		Calls for sovereignty emerge at Ljubljana demonstration		
XII.88		**John Lennon Peace Club forms**; Human Rights Day demo					At UN, Gorbachev promises troop withdrawals from Eastern Europe
I.89		"Palachiada" demos		Human rights demo, Leipzig		Vertepy in Vilnius	
II.89	Round Table begins		140K sign Danube petition; Party plenum renounces communists' "leading role," proposes multiparty system	First Messedemo in solidarity with Kosovar Albanians	Ljubljana rally supporting *Mladina* Four		

III.89		**Prague Mothers** forms	Huge March 15 demo Opposition Round Table convenes	Émigré groups disrupt Leipzig trade fair		First issue of *Postup* appears	
IV.89	Round Table concludes Solidarity legalized		Demo at Nagymoros			Elections to Congress of People's Deputies begin	
V.89	Demos at Soviet consulate, Kraków	Prague Mothers' protest	Government announces moratorium on dam	Local elections; Opposition protests fraud	New arrests in *Mladina* case spark formal demand for sovereignty	Inaugural congress of **Rukh** in Kyiv	Baltic republics declare sovereignty
VI.89	Solidarity claims victory in Parliamentary election	Green demos, Bratislava	Imre Nagy funeral National Round Table (NRT) begins	Street Music Festival, Leipzig		2nd Dnister expedition	Tiananmen Square massacre
VII.89	General Jaruzelski elected president by Parliament	*Korzo* demos begin in Prague					In Strasbourg, Gorbachev announces that each country can choose its own path to socialism
VIII.89	Solidarity's Tadeusz Mazowiecki chosen to be prime minister	Demo commemorating 1968 Soviet invasion almost sparks revolution Detention of Bratislava Five	Pan-European Picnic FIDESZ members visit Prague	First refugees exit bloc through Hungary		Demos commemorate Molotov–Ribbentrop Pact of 1939	
IX.89	Solidarity-led government takes power	**STUHA** (Student Movement) forms	NRT concludes	Refugee crisis; Hungary lifts border restrictions New Forum, other opposition groups established		Demo for religious freedom draws 150K in Lviv	
X.89		Independence Day demo	Hungarian Socialist Workers' Party disbands	Mikhail Gorbachev visit Monday *Messedemos* reach critical mass	Slovene Parliament amends constitution, asserts right of secession	Police attack Lviv Day demo General strike called	
XI.89	Czech festival in Wrocław	Teplice demo Velvet Revolution Communist government resigns		Berlin Wall opened			
XII.89		Václav Havel chosen president		Round Table opens Helmut Kohl visits Dresden			Romanian revolution ends with execution of Ceauşescus

Independent photographers were very much a part of the opposition scene. Their record of the demonstrations is often the best one we have. To photograph a demonstration was not easy, of course. The police (whose photographs, taken for entirely different reasons, we may someday be able to view) would be swift to confiscate the film of anyone caught photographing a demonstration and might arrest the photographer as well.

Underground photojournalists devised a number of tricks to stay out of harm's way. One older photographer in Warsaw had a sure-fire method: he would dress in suit, tie, and bowler hat as if going to work in a bank. Holding his Olympus camera, already focused,* he would walk straight through the demonstration. When a suitable scene appeared before him, up went the camera hand for a quick shot. Unnoticed, he could photograph an entire demonstration in this way with success.

Another photographer told me of a method he learned from an American *paparazzo* (who was also likely to have his film confiscated, by a movie star's bodyguard): one camera, with a blank roll of film inside, would hang in plain view on his chest. The other was on a long strap to the side, hidden under a long overcoat. Again: up goes the real camera for a quick shot, and then down. When the police demand the film, the unused camera can be surrendered without regret. If taking photographs where a closer search was likely (such as inside a striking factory), an old Soviet camera, cheap even for a Pole, would do the trick. On the way out of the factory, the camera could be chucked into the trash.

Most photographs, of necessity, were taken by amateurs; few professional photographers would risk their careers. But a photojournalist could make a living off underground work, by selling work to Western journalists and news agencies. In Hungary, Ernő Horváth and Éva Kapitány worked this way. Some photos would end up in *Beszélő* or other samizdat. If one were not blackballed by the regime press (much less likely in Hungary than in Poland), one could still work there while keeping opposition work as a hobby. Slovenia's Tone Stojko was in an enviable position, as staff photographer for *Mladina* for many years. As *Mladina* forced Slovenia to become more liberal, more and more of Stojko's work could appear there. Czech opposition appeared to be setting out on the road taken in Poland and Hungary. Student activist Martin Mejstřík mentions photographing every demonstration, and indeed photos begin to appear in samizdat in 1988.

For so many events, there are only the chance photographs of passersby,

---

* The first rule of such photography was to set focus and exposure ahead of time, since it would be too risky to do so at the demonstration itself.

snapped hurriedly and developed at home. These might have great currency, too. A photograph of Fr. Jerzy Popiełuszko's grave, for example, might be copied and passed around to family and friends. And some photos might never see the light of day; one activist suddenly recalled to me that he still had rolls of video film from one demonstration in the back of his refrigerator. Two of the photographs from Czechoslovakia presented here, and the one from Ukraine, are such amateur photos; in some cases, we do not even know the photographer.

Poland's photographic underground was of course the most advanced, with an underground photo agency, Dementi, whose name means roughly "Exposé." The founders, including Tomasz Kizny and Anna Łoś, were not trained photographers at all. Until martial law they had stayed away from Solidarity and politics in general and were part of the hippy community, which was still strong in Wrocław.

Dementi began taking photographs in 1982, moved by an urge to contribute to the struggle in some artistic way. At first, they sold photos through the same underground couriers who sold samizdat. Besides one's favorite underground titles, one could order a package of Dementi photos, which would come handsomely wrapped in black paper. Later some underground journals improved their technology enough to publish photos, and finally Western journalists became clients. Their work was exhibited in underground exhibits (usually in churches) and, since 1985, in the West, too.

Dementi's innovation was that its photographers—mainly Kizny, Andrzej Łuc, and Henryk Prykiel—were everywhere. Like their friends in WiP or Orange Alternative, they would happily travel across Poland to find a demonstration to record. In 1989 they photographed the revolutions in Czechoslovakia and East Germany as well. Later, they took photos in the Soviet Union, too.

In recent years, Kizny has been working on a photographic record of the Soviet Gulag. Others have turned to documenting prisons, the homeless, or other societal margins. Thus, independent photojournalism has a continued role today, and the sensibility of the underground photojournalist pervades the popular press. Indeed, the Central European public seems to accept the idea that a candid photo can uncover truth in ways that no text can.

Each of the photographs in this section is both a record of a particular event and a window on the evolution of opposition media. Looking at these photos, we can see what the opposition saw and examine the differences and similarities in the public face of opposition across the region in the 1980s.

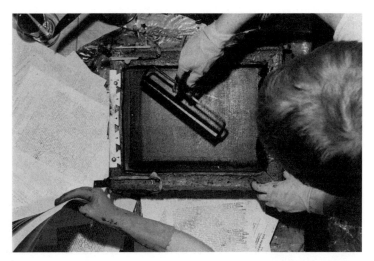

1.

2.

3.

4.

5.

6.

7.

8.

9.

10.

11.

12.

13.

14.

15.

Border Crossings

16.

17.

ALTERNATIVE PATHS

18.

19.

ANNIVERSARIES BECOME STARTING POINTS

20.

21.

POWER OF THE PEOPLE

22.

PHOTOESSAY CAPTIONS

RESOURCES, TRADITIONS

1. The ordinary life of the underground was rarely recorded. This photo, from 1983 or 1984, shows a step in the underground printing process, on a homemade screen. This printing technology was good for producing at most a few hundred copies. It was by this time already being replaced by offset in the largest journals. Photo: Dementi.

2. Pilgrimage, Lower Silesia, August 1984. Pilgrimages in Poland, of which the most important were those to Częstochowa every August, were the main form of independent public expression before the demonstrations of the late 1980s. The people in this photo would not likely have participated in a demonstration until Orange Alternative, or even later, though they probably went to Fatherland Masses. In Slovakia pilgrimages would not have carried flags like these; in fact, there would be no procession at all until participants were in the town where the shrine was located. Photo: Dementi.

EXTRAORDINARY THREATS, ORDINARY PEOPLE

3. Ljubljana, 10 May 1986. The Chernobyl disaster brought people onto the streets all across Central Europe. In Slovenia, concerns about the nuclear plant at Krško intensified protest, organized by the People for Peace Culture/Peace Movement Working Group. Here, Juvan Janez of the People for Peace Culture reads a declaration condemning the recent nuclear accident in Chernobyl. Marko Hren, wearing a mask, shields Janez from nuclear fallout. The sign in the crowd reads, "More Light in the Heads of Slovene Energy Planners!" Photo: Tone Stojko.

4. Wrocław, 8 May 1986. This was Freedom and Peace's second demonstration ever, just two weeks after the Chernobyl incident. It was less a march than an expression of vitality. Strollers with children became a propaganda weapon, as well as a means of security against arrest. The signs read, "Why did we get information about fallout so late?" "We demand powdered milk for all children," "Today Chernobyl, tomorrow Żarnowiec," and "Reaktor." Caution was still in order: the photo was taken from a window above Świdnicka Street. Photo: Dementi.

5. Prague, 29 May 1989. The Prague Mothers' first *korzo*. The tactic of marching with children was by this time widespread across Central Europe. Still, the first time it was employed in a particular country (especially one as repressive as Czechoslovakia was) brought some risk. This was one of the few such mother-child demonstrations in which children actively participated. The children are holding a sign reading, "Let's Protect the Environment for Our Children!" This anonymous photograph was most likely taken by a member of the group. Photo: Nika Archive.

6. Międzyrzecz, September 1987. The Chernobyl demonstrations made the nuclear issue a potent one, even in remote corners of Poland. For a small town, this demonstration was positively huge. Some in the crowd were from Freedom and Peace, but most were locals. The banners read, "We don't want an atomic waste dump," "We don't want to die of radiation sickness," "We want to live," and (half hidden) "Leave the bunkers to the bats!" Notice that this small-town crowd did not swarm across the street, but kept to the sidewalk and crossed at the crosswalk. Photo: Dementi.

THE MAJOR'S TROOPS

7. Wrocław, 1 June 1987. Taking photos from a window was safer, but also a risk: first, the innocent owner of the apartment might get in trouble; second, if the demonstration did not happen to come one's way, there would be no usable photos. This time, Dementi was lucky and captured the first Orange Alternative happening: the Revolution of the Elves. Note the elves' caps on most of the participants. Krzysztof Jakubczak is playing guitar on the left. Photo: Dementi.

8. Wrocław, November 1987. Some photos of the October Revolution happening show that the event was not nearly so well choreographed as Major Fydrych's account (chapter 5) suggests. This one is probably from the beginning of the evening and thus better staged. Major Fydrych, in the center holding a megaphone, leads his Red Guard troops into battle. Photo: Dementi.

9. Wrocław, February 1988. Happenings like the Carnival were truly democratic. Participants dressed as they pleased, and there was only minimal choreography. Visible (among others) are two Ku Klux Klansmen, several skeletons (one cradling a machine gun), and Little Red Riding Hood. The crowd (onlookers and participants) stretched halfway around the Rynek. Photo: Dementi.

10. Gdańsk, August 1988. Orange Alternative on the road, in the striking Lenin Shipyard. This delivery vehicle has been turned into a riot police wagon with styrofoam and paint. Styrofoam was an essential material in a strike. "Styrofoam friends" is today a term of affection in Polish politics: it refers to people with whom one struck (particularly in Gdańsk), spending nights on makeshift styrofoam beds. In August 1988 styrofoam found a new use as the material for Orange Alternative projects like this one. Photo: Dementi.

RIVER CURRENTS

11. Naslavche, Ukraine, summer 1988. The Dnister expedition nears the end of the trip, helping to place the river at the center of Galician (West Ukrainian) consciousness. Before arriving in Naslavche (near the Moldovan border), some members of the expedition changed into folk costumes. The catamarans were decorated with flowers gathered from the river bank. The center catamaran, being brought ashore by Valentyn Stetsiuk, carries the flag of Soviet Ukraine. The one on the right flies an ecology banner, green with a star. Local residents have come out to greet the arrival of the expedition. Photographer unknown. From the archive of Valentyn Stetsiuk.

12. Budapest, September 1988. Though it did not then attract such spectacular expeditions as the Dnister, the Danube is both literally (as it cuts both Hungary and Budapest in two) and figuratively at Hungary's center. It is thus fitting that a breakthrough demonstration in Budapest protested the construction of a dam. Here, the Danube demonstration moves through Kossúth Square. Banners read (among others), "WaterDam/ned" and "Help" (on the fish); Fidesz, Hálózat, and the Hungarian Democratic Forum also have their own banners. Photo: Ernő Horváth.

CHALLENGING THE MILITARY STATE

13. Wrocław, 1 July 1988. This photo shows Freedom and Peace at its most provocative and captures some of its diversity, too. In this demonstration, activists burn their military booklets

(the equivalent of draft cards), on Wrocław's Rynek by the pillory. Leszek Budrewicz (a pacifist) addresses passersby with a megaphone. Wacław Giermek (who wanted to serve, objecting only to the oath) leans over to place a burning booklet in the bucket as Wiesław Mielcarski watches. Photo: Dementi.

14. Ljubljana, 20 July 1988. The trial of Slovene journalists in a military court, where all business was conducted in Serbo-Croatian, galvanized Slovene society. Women of Ljubljana organized strolls across the street from the court but soon ventured closer to engage in gentle confrontation. Flowers, like strollers, became a popular protest device in Central Europe. Photo: Tone Stojko.

15. Ljubljana, 27 July 1988. Victory for the Yugoslavs became defeat, as the *Mladina* Four became national heroes. After their conviction by the military court, Janez Janša (later Slovene defense minister), David Tasić, Ivan Borštner, and Franci Zavrl (wearing a *Mladina* T-shirt) greeted an enthusiastic crowd. Photo: Tone Stojko.

BORDER CROSSINGS

16. Wrocław, April 1987. The demonstration in support of the imprisoned Petr Pospíchal of Brno was the first show of public solidarity—outside the confines of a church—with a foreign prisoner of conscience in the bloc. The large banner reads, "Charter 77—Unity in Strength—Solidarity." The smaller one, held by Mirek Jasiński of Polish-Czechoslovak Solidarity and Zuzanna Dąbrowska, says, "Free Petr Pospíchal." Photo: Dementi.

17. In the Karkonosze/Krkonoše Mountains, January 1989. These Polish-Czechoslovak Solidarity couriers are making a rare winter crossing, as opposition in Prague is heating up and contacts become closer. For the Poles, the risk of being caught had decreased enough to warrant carrying an extra suitcase of samizdat or printing materials. This is the only known photograph of the work of the couriers. Photo: Dementi.

ALTERNATIVE PATHS

18. Kraków, April 1989. Poland's peaceful revolution had a violent underside. This demonstration, in front of the Soviet Consulate, was organized by Freedom and Peace Student Action, the Federation of Fighting Youth, the Independent Students Association, and the youth wing of the Confederation for an Independent Poland. It was condemned by Solidarity and other groups, including most of Freedom and Peace. The air of bravado and adventure is utterly unlike the spirit of the previous half-dozen years. The demonstrators threw rocks at the consulate; the concrete pipes served as barricades. Photo: Andrzej Stawiarski.

19. Budapest, June 1989. To those who rejected the violent path, the Tiananmen Square massacre was a powerful reminder of how fragile nonviolence can be. As similar protests erupted around the world, Hungarians and Chinese staged an impromptu demonstration in front of the Chinese Embassy. Photo: Ernő Horváth.

ANNIVERSARIES BECOME STARTING POINTS

20. Heroes' Square, Budapest, 16 June 1989. The funeral of Imre Nagy was supposed to honor the past and allow communist leaders a taste of national pride. Instead, Fidesz, led by Viktor Orbán's fiery speech, made it an occasion to imagine a state without the communists, as they themselves embodied the future. Here, Gábor Fodor and Tamás Deutsch present a wreath from

Fidesz. The people behind them are mostly veterans of 1956. The Hungarian flags have had the communist symbols in their centers cut out. Photo: Éva Kapitány.

21. Prague, 21 August 1989. The Czechoslovak revolution almost happened in August, as Praguers observed the twenty-first anniversary of the Warsaw Pact invasion that crushed the Prague Spring. As they had the previous year, students and other activists gathered on Václav Square. Hana Marvanová from NMS is third from left. Next to her is Tomáš Dvořák. Leaning down behind the (unidentified) speaker is Stanislav Penc of the John Lennon Peace Club. Photographer unknown.

POWER OF THE PEOPLE

22. Teplice, 11 November 1989. If there is a moment when the trite phrase "people power" fits, it is at this ecological protest in Teplice, a town in Northern Bohemia. The crowd is holding its hands up to show it is defenseless. This move appeared in Prague (with the chant "We have bare hands!") a few weeks earlier (and sporadically at earlier demonstrations); the citizens of Teplice were not as unfamiliar with goings-on in the capital as might have been thought. Still, the faces in the crowd betray a hint of uncertainty; certainly they did not imagine communism would begin to crumble in barely a week. Photograph: Miroslav Vaněk.

✻✻✻✻✻ *PART TWO* ✻✻✻✻✻

A REVOLUTION IN SIXTEEN SCENES

"The Springtime of Peoples, 1988." Nearly a decade and a half later, the slogan seems absurdly misplaced. In 1989 there was an "autumn of peoples"—a phrase invoked frequently then and since, meant to recall the "springtime of peoples" (or nations) in 1848, when revolutionary upsurges swept Central Europe as people demanded national sovereignty and constitutional rights. As 1989 became the 'year of miracles,' the events of the previous year no longer fit the framework of communism's supposedly sudden collapse.

But without the benefit of hindsight, it seemed to some that great changes were in the air. "The fate of the system in which we live hangs in the balance," wrote "Nobelek Rusz-Czkash," a correspondent for *Szkoła,* the Wrocław underground paper, in an article headed by the above slogan. "I think the end of our era is already close at hand."[1] The evidence ranged across the region: Timothy Garton Ash, considering events in Hungary, Czechoslovakia, and Poland, called this a "Pre-Spring."[2] To these, Rusz-Czkash added recent strikes in Romania, peace and ecological demonstrations in the GDR, and massive protests in Armenia. What, the author wondered, might be the connection among these events?

With a focus on Central Europe, that has been the question of this book. In Poland, Hungary, Czechoslovakia, Slovenia, the GDR, and Western Ukraine, I have looked for common themes—youth, concrete action, internal pluralism, irreverence toward politics, and cross-border contacts—to uncover how a carnival of anticommunist opposition spread so enthusiastically across such a wide region.

With this story firmly in mind, it is time to follow the course of the revolutions of 1989. But to do so, we must begin not as is usually done, in 1989 itself, but back in that springtime of 1988, when the two years of revolution began in earnest. The first scene takes place on what once seemed the most unlikely stage, Bratislava.

"I BLINK, AND I SEE ANOTHER WORLD": THE CANDLELIGHT MARCH

BRATISLAVA, MARCH 1988

To risk a religious demonstration in Slovakia, breaking years of fear and secret prayer, was a brainstorm of the vice president of the World Congress of Slovaks, and one-time right wing for the National Hockey League's Quebec Nordiques, Marián Šťastný, who now lived in Switzerland. He envisioned a coordinated protest before Czechoslovak embassies throughout Western Europe and North America. Demonstrators would picket to demand the right for Czechoslovak Catholics to worship, and respect for human rights in general.

Through his mother-in-law, Šťastný smuggled (in a bar of Swiss chocolate) a letter to Ján Čarnogurský in Bratislava. He proposed that Slovak dissidents join the protest, planned for Friday, March 25, 1988. This was a daring idea; there had been nothing of the sort for almost two decades, with the exception of the outburst at Velehrad in 1985. Yet the Navratil petition had energized Slovakia, especially after Cardinal Tomašek had endorsed the campaign. Čarnogurský and František Mikloško sensed that Slovak Catholics were ready for more. On March 6 Mikloško informed a meeting of the secret church, which met every Sunday afternoon, of the letter. "I think," he told the group, "that it wouldn't be right if they were to protest and we here were to be quiet. I believe that we could come up with something similar. Let's say we gather for one half-hour with lighted candles and stand in silence." At first his colleagues were speechless, contemplating the danger. Rudolf Fiby finally spoke up: "I've got a candle."[3]

Mikloško was delegated to apply for permission for the event, which was of course denied. With announcements on Voice of America, Vatican Radio, and others, the march went forward, in the face of intense police surveillance. There would be no speakers—and thus no one whose arrest might derail the demonstration—but only banners, candles, and a half-hour of silence.

The Czechoslovak police counterattacked furiously. Most of the Catholic leaders—Čarnogurský, Mikloško, even Bishop Ján Korec—were detained that day. Police blocked roads into Bratislava and turned back buses from faraway cities. A more subtle technique was for road patrols to discover some technical problem with a car and refuse permission for the driver to proceed until the car was repaired. As six o'clock approached, police closed off Hviezdoslav Square. Water cannons and street sweepers stood nearby; despite the heavy rain, some of these began hosing down the streets, turning parts of the square into a pond.

Nevertheless, several thousand people had already gathered, with as many more beyond the police cordons. At the appointed hour, they began to light candles (hard to see, unfortunately, under the sea of umbrellas) and sang a hymn. As the onslaught of police vans, water cannons, and truncheon-wielding officers began, the crowd fought only to stay on its feet and on the square for thirty minutes. This simple goal gave the demonstration a remarkable clarity.

Until this moment, the normalization of Czechoslovakia had succeeded in keeping Bratislava society divided. The Greens did one thing, the Catholics another, the artists something else entirely. But it was hard to be indifferent to the candlelight demonstration. So environmental activist Mária Filková went, because this was a "just cause." Martin Šimečka— son of Milan, Slovakia's best-known dissident—was not a Catholic and in fact had been brought up in a communist home. He was shocked at how easily one group of resisters could be ignored by everyone else. It would be simple to say to oneself, "Let the Catholics eat what they have cooked for themselves." But these Catholics were his friends. Šimečka cursed his "bad luck": "At five o'clock in the morning they'll drag Mikloško from his home and his worries will be over. They won't think of me, because I'm not a Catholic—so I'll have to crawl out of bed for him, right onto the square!"

Who would be there besides a few fanatics, he wondered? He stopped by a drugstore: sure enough, they hadn't run out of candles. But he found himself at the square nevertheless. Miraculously, he was able to sneak in, through a gap between police vans. "I've never flown in a plane (since there was nowhere to fly to)," he wrote, "but this is how I imagine it: I blink, and I see another world. That's how it was on the other side [of the police cordon]. A colorful roof of umbrellas and a crowd of people where there was supposed to be no one."

Šimečka joined the crowd huddling on the sidewalks. "It was five to six and the square itself was empty. 'What an audience I'll have,' I thought, and stepped off the curb. But the others set off as well. There were well-dressed women and middle-aged ladies; youth of the sort one glimpses in church, and old women with new hairdos. One woman held an umbrella over me; someone handed out candles. People lit their candles from one another. It began to get crowded."[4]

Before Šimečka's eyes, people were teaching themselves how to experience a free space they had just created. And politics made its entrance: elsewhere in the square, Karol Nagy was handing out copies of the law permitting freedom of assembly—until he was arrested and taken away. In all, the police arrested 141 on or near the square; the vast majority of these were under age 40. Dozens—it is difficult to tell how many—were beaten.[5] Yet the crowd remained in place, some singing hymns quietly, and even kept the candles lit, while the high-pressure hoses beat down. Some, at least, made it until 6:30, in quiet triumph.

In peaceful Slovakia, where there had been just a handful of people willing to express disagreement aloud, there was now a new public. Mikloško's call for the demonstration, banners on the square, and Nagy's leaflets had all articulated human rights alongside religious freedom, placing the problems of one group in a universal context. The confusion of the authorities was quite evident. One policeman was arrested three times as he photographed the demonstration. A young man gleefully explained to Šimečka how he had rescued his girlfriend from the police by pretending to be a cop: "There's so many of them that they don't know who is who," he giggled. As was natural in a carnival, all the lines in society, and even those between ruler and ruled, had become blurred. Šimečka felt that, finally, his secret hope, "which had grown feeble, undernourished by a long life without events," had been fulfilled: "The hope that there do exist historical moments."[6]

As the year wore on, the legend of the candlelight demonstration came to signify, not resolute Catholic faith, but "civil courage." Despite the brutal reaction, demonstrators felt they had "experienced personal freedom. . . . We felt that we are free people, and in that atmosphere we acquired a greater taste for freedom. The experience that communism is not all-powerful, and we are not powerless, was very important. . . . The fear that had hold of us began to lose its power."[7]

These are the words of activists in the underground church. But they echoed the thoughts of secular dissidents like Martin Šimečka. Bratislava was not the same after the candlelight demonstration. There would be no further demonstrations until summer 1989; on the other hand, the open display of Catholic faith became an ever more natural thing. And in Prague, the "challenge from Bratislava," as Czech Chartist Václav Benda called it, would soon enough be answered.[8]

Scene Two

A TALE OF TWO LENINS

POLAND, APRIL–MAY 1988

"We came to the conclusion that it is impossible to start a strike, because the people won't come out." Edward Nowak of Nowa Huta had been trying to remobilize his former workmates since leaving prison in 1985.

While he generally favored more educational work, opposing his colleagues in the aboveground opposition, Nowak recognized an opportunity to hoist the banner of worker protest when the government raised
prices on consumer goods in February 1988. The attempt ended in fiasco:
"we wanted to start a strike, even by force . . . [but] we hit an absolute
wall. . . . Nothing happened that February, even though we were not too
badly prepared in one of the plants in the mill." Nowak even feared that
a failed strike would only cause Solidarity to lose what authority it still
had.

Inside the Lenin Steel Mill, things looked slightly different. Underground
Solidarity was no longer alone. Union members in the employees' councils were keeping up pressure on work conditions and pay and became
more visible in the February crisis. The one shop that did strike briefly in
February won a meeting with management, and promises of some material improvements. As the winter passed—without fulfillment of those
promises, but without any sanctions, either—Maciej Mach, head of underground Solidarity in the mill, could feel the tension growing. Solidarity, he believed, was stronger than Nowak or the rest of the "Four" knew;
it was just a matter of time before someone "pushed the red button." He
was planning to bring a sleeping bag to work to prepare for an occupation strike.

But neither Mach nor Nowak nor anyone else knew the man who finally did climb a gantry, on the morning of April 26, to push the button
that automatically stopped the machines in the blooming mill. Andrzej
Szewczuwaniec, 38 years old, had spent the months of Solidarity's first
success in prison, accused of trying to blow up the statue of Lenin in Nowa
Huta's main square. Though he had first worked in the mill in 1971, he
was just one of forty thousand or so workers, with no opposition experience. To this day, many are convinced that he was an agent provocateur,
working for the police, who staged a strike in order to expose and destroy
Solidarity's remnants. Some suggest he was simply unbalanced, as likely
to blow up the factory as to strike.

The truth is more prosaic. Having missed the first Solidarity revolution,
Szewczuwaniec was rather like the students fifteen years his junior, to
whom Solidarity was history, a shell that could not contain one's desire
to stand up against the regime. He was Nowak's age, and five years older
than Mach, but they were as remote to him as the "adult opposition" was
to high school students. He blamed Solidarity for the "seven dead years,
seven years of people living in dread and fear," as he characterized the era
of martial law. Organized structures to him meant nothing, since "people
were unhappy, talked among themselves, but no one saw any possibility
of protest." In thinking about a strike, Szewczuwaniec says, he simply
acted as when he helped organize a protest in prison in 1981: he went

around to talk to the people he knew. "Some were [in Solidarity], but I didn't know anything about that."[9] Even after the strike, when he himself finally joined Solidarity, says Szewczuwaniec, many active strikers stayed away from the union.

As powerful as Solidarity was in 1988, it was probably not capable of organizing a strike. It could take control of a strike quickly, thanks to the experience and the contacts of its leaders at every level. But after the "dead years," the impetus would have to come from elsewhere. The same was true in the other "Lenin," the Lenin Shipyard in Gdańsk. When the news of the strike at Nowa Huta swept Poland, all eyes turned to Lech Wałęsa's former workplace. If the factory where Solidarity was born joined the protest, anything could follow—even the end of communism. "What one Lenin started," went the saying that spring, "two Lenins will finish."

It was almost a week, though, before anything happened. And while the Solidarity organization inside and outside the shipyard was strong, the instigator of the strike, just as in Kraków, was an unknown: 30-year-old Jan Stanecki. Like Szewczuwaniec, he had missed the first Solidarity, in the army, where he spent the first days of martial law patrolling the streets of the city of Kalisz. He came to the shipyard only in the fall of 1987. He had no Solidarity contacts, only his friends from the workers' hostel where he lived, and his immediate workmates. They talked about politics, but mostly about unfair treatment from their foremen: "We talked about these matters in my room in Sopot," he explained. "Sometimes we went for a beer, and by and by a group came together: six people from K-1 [Stanecki's workshop]. We [tried to] gauge who could be trusted, and who not. But on the other hand, [there was a feeling of] helplessness."[10]

On May 2—riding the wave of emotions after the traditional Labor Day clash between riot police and shipyard workers the day before, and responding to a fervent plea from Wałęsa that the shipyard support Nowa Huta—Stanecki stood up in the cafeteria during the breakfast break. He asked everyone to stay—that is, to begin a strike—and to talk about the situation in Nowa Huta. "It looked a little strange," recalled Grzegorz Szrejder of the Solidarity leadership, "because, concretely, he didn't have any precise views. He only said that things are bad, and that Lech Wałęsa will be coming. I figured that if Lech is supposed to come, then the action is organized by the Secret Union Committee [of Solidarity]. But on the other hand, I had leaflets in my pocket [that is, not yet handed out] calling [only] for strike preparations. Damn it, it's embarrassing, I thought. This strike is not coordinated."[11]

Stanecki considered himself a natural organizer; he mentions organizing dances and Ping-Pong tournaments in a workers' hostel at a Silesian coal mine. A university student with a similar bent, feeling the uselessness of formal opposition structures, might find his or her way to Freedom and

Peace. But a worker like Szewczuwaniec or Stanecki would more likely drift from job to job (or to prison, or the army) until the opportunity for mass action presented itself.

Started by outsiders, both strikes quickly became Solidarity protests. Maciej Mach was on the scene at the blooming mill within a few hours of Szewczuwaniec's action. He then took the initiative of forming a strike committee, which included Szewczuwaniec but was dominated by Solidarity activists. Three of the four aboveground leaders eventually entered the plant; Nowak stayed outside to coordinate publicity. In Gdańsk, too, senior union activists took over the strike, coordinating their actions with Wałęsa and others outside the shipyard. If they had their doubts whether this was the right moment to strike, they also knew that Solidarity had to jump aboard or lose control of events.

The strikes were profoundly different from the ones of 1980. They did not spread to many other factories; nor did they get much support from the local population. In 1980 factory gates were the hubs of a free society. Only there could one find out what was "really" happening. Crowds stood before them to wish the occupying strikers well, and to pass them food and other supplies. The gates themselves were festooned with flowers, holy pictures, and dozens of defiant banners. Not so in 1988:

> From the outside, it is hard to tell that something unusual is happening in [the Lenin Steel Works]. There are no decorations on the gates: no flags, no flowers, no images of the Virgin Mary or portraits of the Pope. The gate around the mill looks just the same as on any other day. . . . This is a sad strike. There are no crowds waiting before the gate; no Strike Committee communiqués issued over the factory's public address system; no worker pickets by the entrance.[12]

The Lenin Steel Mill, it is true, is far from the center of Nowa Huta. In Gdańsk, the spirit of 1980 still pulsed, though faintly, at the shipyard gates. But there, too, less than a quarter of the shipyard's roughly twelve thousand workers struck. Elsewhere in the shipyard, work continued as normal, just as across Poland most people continued to work, whether they supported Solidarity or not.

This does not mean that the strikes were a failure. Poland was a different country in 1988. There were now many more ways to manifest one's opposition, beyond signing a petition, writing an essay, or taking part in a strike. With demonstrations, marches, sit-ins, protest fasts, political masses, border crossings, and happenings, the strikers no longer had to carry the whole weight of Poland's anticommunist cause on their shoulders. Nor did one have to make a pilgrimage to the factory gates to experience a free Poland.

In 1980 Poland changed because of the somewhat unexpected fusing of two worlds of opposition, as Tadeusz Mazowiecki and other Warsaw intellectuals came to Gdańsk to help the workers negotiate. In 1988 there was another such convergence. These strikes thrived on the intervention of Freedom and Peace volunteers. And in Gdańsk especially, but also in Nowa Huta, the spirit of Orange Alternative placed the strikes at the center of the carnival in which, until this moment, workers had played only bit parts.

Student activists usually were no more likely to pay attention to a strike than workers were to support a peace march. *A cappella*, WiP's Gdańsk gazette, published a flyer to encourage participation. Next to a large drawing of a masturbating elephant (and the slogan "Don't think only about yourself!") was this appeal, almost apologetically bridging two cultures:

> If you are not at this moment drunk, stoned on grass or television, or exhausted from love, then listen up: The Gdańsk shipyard and a few other factories are on strike. You should give a shit, because WE—your beloved, ever-faithful, loyal friends from WiP—are among those helping out. Victory in this *zadyma* will also be our victory. The strikers are demanding the release of all political prisoners, including those who are in for refusing military service. . . .
>
> From the first day of the strike, there has been a support group at St. Brygida's Church. Show up there. And if the place, or the idea of working in a group, doesn't work for you, then paint walls [with graffiti], shout by the shipyard, vibrate, dance, or play the harmonica—but do it for the STRIKERS."[13]

From the point of view of Freedom and Peace, there was simply a job to be done. When, after the strike had been going for two days, there was still no printing center at St. Brygida's, Freedom and Peace, led by Krzysztof Galiński, showed up with all the necessary equipment—typewriters, mimeograph, silkscreen frames—and set to work. As one of them exclaimed: "I thought that something was happening here, that [this strike] is a serious matter—and what do I see but anarchy!" Anarchy, of course, was something that they understood, since most of Gdańsk WiP came from the anarchist Alternative Society Movement (RSA). "What struck me the most in all of this," recalled another observer, "was that these guys from WiP and the RSA, who were never emotionally attached to Solidarity, who considered it a bunch of worker drones, joined in as soon as the strike situation developed."[14]

This strike was anarchy put into practice. Galiński coordinated the dissemination of information. His printing work was legendary; he had once covered Gdańsk with a blank leaflet, bearing only the words "This is your flyer. Write on it what you want." Wojciech "Jacob" Jankowski (the once-jailed conscientious objector) organized printing within the shipyard itself. Małgosia Gorczewska organized supply, accepting donations of food, medicine, money, and blankets for the strikers. Even Klaudi Wesołek of RSA, who had considered WiP too structured and patriotic (and too close to the Catholic Church) to join, found himself in the St. Brygida's brigade as well. It was the lure of freedom and action, not the worker cause or even the Polish cause, that drew them in. And as a bonus, WiP posters and leaflets were everywhere in the shipyard and across Gdańsk, and their concerns found their way into strikers' demands.

Though from a greater distance, WiP was active in Nowa Huta as well. Grzegorz Surdy coordinated the strike information center in his own apartment with Edward Nowak, relaying information to Warsaw, to Western journalists, and to Radio Free Europe. Bogdan Klich, a doctor, spent the entire strike in the mill itself. He spoke at several rallies there on behalf of WiP and was fortunate to escape arrest at the end. At the "Glass Houses" steelworkers' ministry, Jan Maria Rokita, a recent law graduate, dispensed legal advice to strikers and their families. When the steelworkers were told that their strike was against the law, "we wrote a legal commentary in which we proved the illegality of such statements. That letter got back to the steelworkers, and apparently inspired them a lot."[15]

Meanwhile, two WiP demonstrations were the only examples of public support for the strikers—"saving the honor of the city."[16] Prominent in both demonstrations was Marek Kurzyniec, a relative newcomer to WiP who was a third-year law student and an anarchist with pictures of Bakunin and Che on his dorm walls. He had once been a boy scout and saw his splinter group WiP Student Action as adapting the forest survival skills he had learned there to the streets of Kraków.[17]

If the actions were anarchist, the language was Orange. As in the happenings of Wrocław, the police in Gdańsk now became "smurfs." Reporter Wojciech Giełżyński, a veteran of the 1980 strike, noticed how funereal the songs of the strike were at first. "When May Came," the best known of the songs, had the refrain "Solidarity shall win again," always sung in a "mournful mewing intonation," bringing tears to one's eyes. "Fortunately," he writes, "the Mountain Girl appeared, with her own authentic hit song," the Smurf Song:

> I'll be here on Saturday, and Sunday too,
> But you Gargamels, you're smurfed, you're through!
> Let them smurf away, let them run
> In hell they're expected, every one!
> Boiling water, bubbling tar,
> Smurfs will be frying everywhere!
> Their blue color will boil away
> Red looks better on them anyway.[18]
>
> (Będziem w sobotę, będziem w niedzielę,
> Niech stąd smerfują Gargamele

Niech stąd smerfują, niech uciekają
A w piekle na nich już czekają!
Grzeje się wrzątek, bulgoce smoła
Smażą się smerfy dookoła!
Niebieski kolor odparowuje
Czerwony bardziej im pasuje.)

The song was a hit with the strikers, of course, but also with the riot police. Journalist Anna Majewska saw them carefully writing down the words as the Mountain Girl sang. Then they sang along, even the parts about frying in hell. Lyric sheets, hastily printed up, became valuable currency at the gates. For one "smurf"—a copy of the song—the police might let through someone bearing food or supplies. For two "smurfs," they'd let a whole group through.[19]

Nowa Huta had its own Smurf song, written by Kazimierz Fugiel and Maciej Mach after the riot police attacked the steelworks and cleared out the strikers. The "Ballad of May 5" was not an upbeat song. It began, "On the 5th of May, in that memorable year, the Smurf attacked the mill."[20] But Kraków, as we have seen, was never very hospitable to Orange Alternative, and this was definitely not a merry strike.

The police broke through into the mill at 2:00 A.M. on May 5th and "pacified" the strike in a matter of hours. At least nineteen strikers were beaten, and there were dozens of arrests and fines. Solidarity successfully followed up with an absentee strike, which, with the help of those ministries that had sustained the steelworkers before, lasted for two more weeks. The Strike Committee then turned itself into an Organizational Committee and began acting openly, fighting for recognition like a normal trade union. While not victorious, the strike had ended the era of the underground and begun something new.

The end of the strike in Gdańsk was dramatically different. Of course, the decision to destroy one strike by force while allowing another to end peacefully was in the hands of the Ministry of Internal Affairs and the party. Gdańsk, because of its history, and because the strike was more colorful, was where most Western journalists were. Wałęsa, Mazowiecki, and other Solidarity leaders slipped into the shipyard to join the strikers. An attack on the shipyard would have been a public-relations disaster for General Jaruzelski. In the end, Wałęsa moved first. On May 10, at 8:00 P.M., he led his former workmates in a solemn march out of the shipyard to St. Brygida's Church, where Bishop Tadeusz Gocławski celebrated a mass for the strikers.

It was hard to call this a victory. None of the strikers' demands were met, and a second round of strikes in August (scene 5) would be necessary to force Jaruzelski to pay attention. But if the shipyard workers had avoided the violent reprisals their Kraków colleagues faced and were able to strike again (as Kraków did not), one reason may have been the style of their strike. The riot police could not easily have attacked workers they had sung along with in self-parody. Indeed, one could not really speak of the "failure" of a strike that continually undermined efforts to take it seriously. Gdańsk in 1988 was as much the city of WiP and the anarchists as it was of Solidarity. This new Gdańsk helped strikers conquer fear.

If new movements, and a new style, were so essential to the success of these strikes, an obvious question arises: Why did Wrocław, the birthplace of Orange Alternative and one of WiP's strongholds, not strike? There are a lot of explanations and excuses to be heard in Wrocław today: some key arrests, divisions in Solidarity, failure of nerve. The most succinct and logical answer is that of Jacek Suchorowski, a Solidarity leader at the Hutmen factory, a member of the Polish Socialist Party since its rebirth in 1987, and an eager participant in Orange happenings: "We had the streets, so we didn't need to strike."

In part, the purpose of the strikes was to make the regime acknowledge the opposition of Polish society, and to encourage Poles to think and act bravely once again. This had already occurred in Wrocław, thanks to the vigor of all the groups whose stories have been told in this book. Of course, Wrocław workers could still have struck, as so many hoped; Suchorowski's explanation is also just another excuse.

In some ways, the pluralism of Wrocław's opposition made a coordinated strike impossible. Solidarity's Władysław Frasyniuk tried to organize a strike in one factory, with the help of student leader Paweł Kocięba. At the same time, socialist activists Józef Pinior and Czesław Borowczyk were jumping the fence into another factory to organize there; in a third, strike organization was left to its combative employees' council to organize. The students (led by Kocięba, Orange performer Krzysztof Jakubczak, and Jarosław Obremski, all of the Twelve), in turn, put their energies into organizing a strike at the university. Wrocław was hardly silent in May, but its cacophony of voices was not loud enough to be heard across Poland.

Yet Wrocławians could hear themselves just fine. On June 1, 1988, an estimated ten thousand—the largest crowd in the city since the declaration of martial law—celebrated the first anniversary of Orange Alternative's debut happening. The parade began, in Orange tradition, by the clock on Świdnicka Street. From there, the crowd swarmed to the provincial government offices by the river, then along the Odra River to a massive picnic on Malt Island. The police were helpless to rein in the throng, even when the chanted slogans got a little aggressive. This was more a massive picnic than a demonstration, with thousands of children enjoying the celebration. A countercelebration organized by the city drew anemic attendance.

In late June the Wrocław courts released Pinior and Borowczyk, jailed for their role in the attempted strikes of May. Another Orange Alternative happening (described in chapter 5) welcomed them home. As the happening wore on, the crowd began to notice that something was wrong: the police had not even bothered to show up. They had, in effect, ceded the streets to the people of Wrocław. Almost wistfully, recalling the confrontations that in Wrocław—but not yet in Kraków or Gdańsk—were becoming a thing of the past, the crowd began to chant, "Where are the police? Where are the police?" Surely, when a crowd of ordinary citizens can feel compelled to join in such a chant, fear of the state has evaporated and a revolutionary change has begun. In a festive, free (but still somehow thwarted) mood, the crowd celebrated some more, then gradually broke up to wander around what Major Fydrych declared a "free city." "No one wants to die for Gdańsk, which is not a free city," went a surrealist poem that he read to the crowd.* Wrocław was now free, and no one would have to die there for just that reason.

Scene Three

SLOVENE SPRING

LJUBLJANA, MAY–JULY 1988

"When I grow up, I will be a customs officer on the Kolpa River." Most likely, those who wore this pin on the streets of Ljubljana in 1986 had no intention of growing up, and still less of patrolling a nonexistent Slovene-Croat border. It was a provocation, but also a joke. Two years later, as Belgrade began to treat Slovenia like a breakaway republic, the fantasy began to come true.

Nothing, we have seen, angered the Yugoslav regime more than attacks on the army. The Peace Movement Working Group of Marko Hren, Tomaž Mastnak, and others had opened the attack gently enough with the push for alternative military service. Through *Mladina,* many of the same people could put the military itself under a microscope. Janez Janša was indicted in 1985 by the military prosecutor of the Ljubljana Army District for revealing military secrets in his articles for the weekly. The charges were dropped when *Mladina* threatened to publish the text of the indictment.

The early spring of 1988 brought a new attack (again by Janša, among

---

* Fydrych alluded to the famous slogan of French isolationists in 1939, objecting to a war over German occupation of the Free City of Gdańsk (Danzig).

others) on military corruption: the Yugoslav defense minister, Branko Mamula, was shown to be dealing arms to the Ethiopian Army to be used against the Ethiopian people. At home, he forced soldiers to build him a luxury residence, telling them it was an assignment of great importance for national security. *Mladina* was getting dangerous. It also led a successful campaign against a hard-line candidate for the Slovene presidency. Perhaps most galling of all, Janša was running a strong campaign for the candidacy of the League of Socialist Youth of Slovenia, which he promised to turn into an independent organization.

In response to the Mamula articles, the military prosecutor charged editor Franci Zavrl (and the editor of another magazine) with defamation of the Yugoslav Army. *Mladina*'s response was to publish more exposés of military corruption, and to issue a stirring call (by the "Counterrevolutionary Editorial Board") for freedom of thought, a market economy, "destruction of the monopoly of the League of Communists," and closer relations with noncommunist countries.[21]

To Belgrade, these were all clear signs of the Slovene intention to break up Yugoslavia; Minister Mamula said as much in a published speech. In April and May rumors of an impending military coup began to circulate in Ljubljana. David Tasič, a *Mladina* reporter, acquired notes of a speech by Slovene League of Communists leader Milan Kučan at a closed-door meeting of the national party's Central Committee. It appeared from the text that Kučan was pleading with his comrades to call off the coup. *Mladina* was prevented from publishing these notes, but they soon appeared in papers in Zagreb and Belgrade.* Rumors flew that there was a blacklist of people to be interned, or perhaps executed, during the coup. It was time for a crackdown.

On May 31 security police came to the offices of the Mikro Ada company and arrested Janez Janša (one of the firm's four owners) on charges of receiving military secrets. Tone Stojko, *Mladina*'s photographer, slipped away from Mikro Ada and took several photographs of the arrest from a building across the courtyard. The photographs, showing Janša accompanied by two anonymous-looking young men with briefcases, appeared almost immediately in the Ljubljana press—surely the first time a political arrest had been on display so quickly.

That same day, noncommissioned army officer Ivan Borštner was arrested too. He would eventually be charged with passing a secret document outlining military plans to impose order in Slovenia. David Tasič was arrested a few days later, on the basis of a document (which he

---

* Freedom of speech was no greater in the other republics; that they could publish Kučan's speech simply reflected the naïve Titoist belief that one had only to worry about the "national chauvinism" of individual republics. Thus a report about Slovenia published in Croatia might even be seen as a way to put the Slovenes in their place.

claimed was a plant) discovered on his desk at *Mladina*. At the end of June, editor Franci Zavrl was also indicted. In a foretaste of the military conflict to come, all of these charges were filed not in civilian courts, but by the military prosecutor.

Slovene society responded instantly. The morning after Janša's arrest, eighty-eight intellectuals signed a letter of protest; on June 3, these signers announced the creation of the Committee for the Protection of the Rights of Janez Janša, which later became the Committee for the Defense of Human Rights. Eventually, over one thousand churches, newspapers, social movements, factories, and schools added their collective signatures to the CDHR's declaration, as did over one hundred thousand individuals. Almost all of these were in Slovenia, though there were supporters in Croatia and Serbia, too.

All the activism of the previous five years had come together to create a committee that spoke for all of Slovenia. Igor Bavčar, Janša and Hren's colleague at Mikro Ada, and Mile Šetinc, former editor of *Mladina,* were on the committee's first executive board. The committee shared offices with the People for Peace Culture. The leadership of the committee met almost daily, with larger public meetings every week. It issued national and international appeals for the trial to be held in public, and for respect for the rights of the prisoners, such as access to civilian lawyers.

Radio Student became almost overnight the most listened-to broadcast in Ljubljana, with a daily program called "Free JJ." *Mladina* gave close coverage, too; its circulation, around thirty thousand at the beginning of the year, soared to three times that by July—an almost impossible figure in a republic of less than two million. From these media, listeners could not only follow the trial preparations but even learn about where, when, and how to protest for the release of the three journalists and their alleged contact.

Slovene activists felt the arrests proved that the rumors of impending martial law were true. Soon, they were certain, they would all be detained, just as Solidarity activists in Poland had been six and a half years earlier. The early consensus was that demonstrations were out of the question. Finally Alenka Puhar, one of the editors of the journal *Nova revija* (and the sister of punk sociologist Gregor Tomc), and several other women in the committee organized what was purported to be a "spontaneous" demonstration. Every afternoon from four to five o'clock, between twenty and three hundred women gathered in front of the jail (on the far side of Metelkova Street, to avoid the charge of trespassing on military property). Many of them—just as in Wrocław, Kraków, and later in Prague and Nagymaros—brought their children. Breaking the pretense of spontaneity, some brought flowers to toss at the prison guards' feet.

Marko Hren called for all of Ljubljana to "vibrate" with energy, so that no one could forget the men in prison.[22] So for everyone else, there would be a concert. Slovene opposition had in a way begun with punk music. A musical gathering would be the most direct, safest way to stage a massive national protest. The June 21 concert was organized by rock impresario (and Laibach manager) Igor Vidmar. Gregor Tomc's Bastards had broken up the previous winter, but they came back to headline before thirty-five thousand on Congress Square. For those whose tastes were a bit more traditional, there was classical music, a folk choir, and poetry. Farmers brought their pitchforks; there were flags reading simply "Janša" or "A Military Court? No Thanks. We've got a Civilian One!!!"

The trial began on July 18, on a collision course with Slovenia. The Yugoslav Army committed several fateful errors. As Franci Zavrl put it, the fact that he was denied a civilian lawyer, or that the trial was closed to the public, might be of interest only to human-rights activists. But that the trial was conducted in Serbo-Croatian, denying the defendants the right to use their native language within their own republic: this was enough to trigger a national explosion.

Zavrl was the only defendant not imprisoned during the trial. This was the court's second mistake. Every day after the proceedings, Zavrl staged a sidewalk press conference, explaining the day's events. The defendant became an agent of protest, and the energetic Zavrl was perfect for the role. Meanwhile, the crowds gathered before the prison every afternoon. An impromptu guard of honor, relieved every few minutes, stood before the court holding the Yugoslav flag; at least one elderly guard proudly displayed a copy of *Mladina* as well. Passing cars honked their horns to drown out the court's work.

On the eighth day the trial ended, with guilty verdicts and sentences ranging from five months to four years. Released pending appeal, Janša greeted the crowd of some ten thousand from the back of the truck that had taken him from prison: "With this trial all our dreams of a legal state have died."[23] There followed appeals, retrials, and months in prison before the four were finally released in late 1989.

Ljubljana's carnival came to a close, giving way to the emergence of political parties from out of the CDHR in early 1989, as it became clear that the committee was insufficient if the battle for human rights would move from petitions and rallies to Parliament and beyond. The trial had indeed shown the need for a completely different system. The only question was whether that would be in a radically changed Yugoslavia or in an independent Slovenia.

Looking back at the Ljubljana trial of July 1988, and the activism of the Committee for the Defense of Human Rights, one cannot say that afterward Slovenia's independence (a full three years later) was inevitable. Two things are worth noting, however, and both point to the great importance of the civic movements that Hren, Mastnak, Jalušič, and others had tried to build, and for which *Mladina* had cleared a path.

First, Slovenia was not the only republic to see massive demonstrations in 1988. The Serbs of Kosovo, now joined by the Serbs of Vojvodina, had been protesting what they called discrimination, even genocide, at the hands of Albanians or of Hungarians. These rallies contributed to the triumph of Slobodan Milošević. They could not have been more different from the events in Slovenia. The Slovenes spoke a language of rights and respect cultivated over the previous half-decade. There was no question, for example, of their rights coming at the expense of others. That one hundred thousand individuals signed the declaration of the Committee for the Defense of Human Rights indicates a strong commitment not only to human rights, but also to negotiation as a means of achieving those rights. In republics lacking a similar tradition of organized opposition, protest was divisive and maximalist.

The other difference was that Milan Kučan was a very lucky man. His private speech, smuggled from that March 1988 Central Committee meeting, showed him defending Slovenia and, indirectly, the interests of Slovene civil society against hard-line communist aggression. Had his unguarded words been different, it is unlikely he would be the democratically elected president today. That Kučan, and most of the Slovene leadership, spoke in this way in 1988 was no accident. The Slovene League of Communists, which (through its Youth League) had sponsored the early growth of independent movements, was in turn shaped by the language and attitude of those movements. They had long ago discovered that there was political capital to be made from adopting a language differentiating them from their colleagues in Belgrade.

Similar movements were not so tolerated anywhere else in Central Europe, because only in Slovenia did such movements encounter a communist regime willing to place its bets at home rather than in the capital city. Kučan, again, was fortunate, for when the door to society opened, it would not be to a rock-throwing (or yogurt-throwing, as in Vojvodina) mob, but to a community of activists committed to human rights, democracy, and dialogue.

Scene Four

DAYS THAT SHOOK LVIV

JUNE, 1988

Ihor Melnyk, an engineer at a Lviv construction plant, was by his own description a "passive observer" of the rise of Ukrainian opposition. He attended Lion Society meetings and got to know many of its leaders. He followed closely, on Polish television and Radio Free Europe, the rebirth of Solidarity. But like others of the "lost generation"—born in the 1950s and living their entire adulthood in an atmosphere of national repression—he kept silent, until he read in the newspaper that a leading Ukrainian linguist proposed forming an organization to protect the vitality of the Ukrainian tongue. Such a signal from above inspired Melnyk to explore the same idea from below: he began to collect signatures on a petition to create a "Taras Shevchenko Native Language Society."

The petition circulated at Lion Society meetings and at their public events, such as the auction of black pottery. By mid-April 1988 Melnyk had gathered more than 650 signatures. When, to his surprise, no government office expressed interest in the proposal, Melnyk turned to the Lion Society for advice. Yurko Vynnychuk (of Melnyk's generation; one of the founders of the cabaret group Ne Zhurys) "advised me not to wait for outside assistance, and to organize the society myself."[24] In the end, none of the leading Lion Society activists would play a major role in the new initiative. But at this early juncture, the society's networks and experience allowed Melnyk's idea to take shape.

Several events raised the political temperature in Lviv that spring. First, the Communist Party of the Soviet Union began the selection of delegates to its Nineteenth Conference, expected to begin implementing Gorbachev's political reforms. There were some victories for reformers in Moscow, but in provincial Lviv, party leaders arranged for the selection of the usual faithful bureaucrats. At about the same time, Gorbachev, in cooperation with leaders of the Russian Orthodox Church, participated in the celebrations of Christianity's millennium among the Eastern Slavs, an event that most Ukrainians felt belonged only to them, not to Moscow, since that conversion had come long before a Russian state even existed. Gorbachev's participation was, in hindsight, a major step in the revival of Russian nationalism, but it awakened Ukrainians too.

In the shadow of official ceremonies in Moscow and Kyiv, the clergy and thousands of the faithful of the underground Uniate Church celebrated several masses in Galicia. These were but distractions from the authorities' version of the millennial celebration, which emphasized the unity of the Orthodox Church. Repression was mild, given the international attention that the official ceremonies drew, but it was also clear that Lviv and its traditions were being left out as Gorbachev's revolution gathered speed.*

Meanwhile, Melnyk had obtained reluctant permission from city officials to hold a meeting of the Shevchenko Society on Monday, June 13, at

---

* One outlet was Poland. Many students from Ukraine were able to get permission to attend the millennium celebrations held in Częstochowa in late summer of 1988.

7:00 P.M. "Excusing myself from work," he recalls, "I went over to the Construction Workers' House of Culture on Stefanyk Street at about four in the afternoon, to have time to prepare the stage for the inaugural meeting. The director of the institution informed me that the secretary of the Communist Party City Committee . . . had called him and forbidden him to hold the meeting." For the next three hours, while hundreds arrived only to "kiss the lock" (as the saying goes), Melnyk ran from office to office, desperately seeking permission to meet.[25]

Returning to Stefanyk Street just before seven, he found an outraged crowd of nearly one thousand. Sticking to the approved rituals of Soviet life, some began composing telegrams to Gorbachev, the party conference, the news media, and so forth. Then someone yelled out that they should move to the park by the Ivan Franko monument, a few hundred yards away, and hold the meeting outside. There, before the university, Melnyk read out his draft of the society's statute. Addressing the crowd, Mykhaylo Horyn of the Ukrainian Helsinki Union hailed the new society as "one of the rungs of the ladder by which we will raise our consciousness, which has fallen so low it is difficult to imagine. How many of our children have turned away from their language, how many of our brothers and sisters have forgotten their birthplace? But we are beginning to awaken. I support what has been read out here, but I believe that such a society should set serious goals."[26] Horyn meant political demands: he proposed that the society call for the recognition of Ukrainian as the republic's official language. This would become a focus of the nationalist struggle over the next year.

When the crowd demanded that new delegates be chosen to the party conference, the Lion Society's Orest Sheika was one of the first to be mentioned. The lion cubs had after all whetted the appetite for such a public demonstration. "The meeting of June 13," one participant explained, "was a logical continuation of those processes of rebirth that had been coursing through the souls of hundreds of Lvivians at that time. . . . All across the city, informal groups and organizations formed on the Lion Society's model."[27] The constructive approach of the Lion Society was indeed in the air that June, voiced most clearly by Iryna Kalynets. Her sensible, straightforward call for concrete action was a sharp contrast to the heated rhetoric of some other speakers. "Something doesn't get done just by talking about it," she reminded the crowd. "There are a lot of us here— and let everyone think about what concretely he can do in the [Shevchenko] Society. Who can assemble examination commissions, who can sign up to give cultural performances, who can travel about and give lectures? There should be a statute, and now we must put together a program. Everyone must do something. Go to the villages and inspire the people, go to the factories, talk with people. Do you understand?"[28]

"Lion" Yuriy Voloshchak gave the crowd an example of the concrete work Kalynets had in mind: "Today in the city I met some girls from Poland. I told them about how the Lion Society is taking care of the graves of Polish cultural figures in the Lychakiv cemetery here in Lviv. I asked that they do the same for the neglected graves of well-known Ukrainian cultural figures in Kraków or Przemyśl."[29] From the concrete to the general, as the Lion Society had originally envisioned: the tending of graves established the outlines of national culture and formed a cultural border based upon mutual respect.

Three days later, some eight thousand Lvivians gathered again by Franko's statue. This time, party conference delegates addressed a hostile crowd, in a last-ditch effort to win popularity. Iryna Kalynets, the Horyn brothers, Chornovil, and others challenged the hapless delegates to take up the cause of Ukrainian sovereignty and Ukrainian culture. The following Tuesday, despite flyers warning people not to come, fifty thousand thronged to the soccer stadium to continue this experiment in political pressure.

The Shevchenko Society met quietly on June 20, and local chapters sprang up across Lviv during the summer. Behind the scenes, many of the Lion Society worked on this new initiative. Sheika spoke at the founding conference; Rostyslav Bratun sat on the Executive Council; Ihor Koliushko founded a circle at the university. Aside from the political exhortations at the meetings in Franko Park, the two groups shared a quite concrete approach to culture. For example, one of the first successes of the Shevchenko Society was to force the City Council to change the neon sign above the main bus terminal from the Russian "Lvov" to the Ukrainian "Lviv." One result, in Lviv and across Galicia, was that people began changing signs on their own. Thus an uncompromising position on a sensitive issue (as Ukrainianization certainly was) could be expressed through small, concrete, and seemingly innocuous acts that proved infectious. Since it seemed, to the authorities, a lesser threat than Chornovil's Ukrainian Helsinki Union, the Shevchenko Society could thrive.*

Meanwhile, the object of public meetings became a political confrontation about democratic representation, sovereignty, and respect for Ukrainian heritage. The purposeful, constructive tone disappeared, and with it, the Lion Society's participation. The "Ten Days That Shook Lviv" may have come too early. By the end of the summer, the furor over the party conference had passed, and the city authorities once more controlled the streets. The season that followed would belong again to the Lion Society, and its idea of a Lviv that would put its hopes neither in the vagaries of a party conference, nor in simplistic demands for sovereignty, but would learn to value democracy and national culture for their own sakes.

---

* In February 1989 the society was superseded by a national organization, of which the Lviv organization was now but one component. The name was changed to the Taras Shevchenko Ukrainian Language Society.

Scene Five

STRIKES IN SHADES OF ORANGE

POLAND, AUGUST 1988

There is something about August in Poland. In a country that marks its history by months, and where a farming calendar still echoes faintly, it resonates with victories (1920 and 1980), miracles (the Black Madonna of Częstochowa), and martyrdoms (1944). On August 16, 1988, the Feast of Our Lady of the Harvest, my wife and I were riding in a taxi along the southeast edge of Poland, from Krosno to Nowy Sącz, on our way back from a honeymoon in the Bieszczady Mountains. From the highway, we caught glimpses of religious processions wending through the countryside below us, carrying before them images of the Virgin Mary and the first fruits of the fields. Late that night, we arrived at our destination, a chalet in the Tatra Mountains, to learn that another strike wave had begun.

This time, the instigator was the coal-mining region of Jastrzębie, in the southern part of Silesia. Unlike Kraków, Warsaw, Wrocław, or the Baltic seacoast, Silesia had been quiet ever since the violent confrontation of December 1981. More than elsewhere in Poland, top Solidarity leaders had emigrated or withdrawn from activism; in most mines with a Solidarity organization, a third generation had taken charge. In cities like Jastrzębie, which had mushroomed from nothing in the industrial boom of the 1970s, there was little contact with the national Solidarity leadership. The rest of Poland assumed that the miners were simply enjoying their riches: average pay tended to be higher in the coal mines than in other industries.

But underground, opposition continued. Some miners had contacts with Paweł Gross of the pensioners' group. Closer to Solidarity, some distributed leaflets or printed their own. And Father Czernecki's Fatherland Masses at the "church on the hill" drew faithful from all the mines in the area.

In May Danuta Skorenko of the regional Solidarity leadership came down from Katowice to try to get a strike going. She succeeded only in getting herself arrested. But she did seek out some new blood, too: younger miners who wouldn't fear to create an aboveground Solidarity committee. They included Krzysztof Zakrzewski and Jan Golec of the July Manifesto mine (Golec had just been fired for his strike efforts); Marek "Bartek" Bartosiak, who was not a miner but a printer and a member of the underground Fighting Solidarity; and others. Skorenko called them her kamikazes; they were unafraid, for example, to hold a Solidarity banner at Father Czernecki's masses. They would be Solidarity's new face in Jastrzębie.

August 15, a Monday, was a payday. It was not hard for Golec (who was by far the oldest of the group) and the rest to provoke a protest in the July Manifesto mine on that day, and many miners (who knew that the stories of rich miners were only a myth) readily struck. Keeping the strike going, however, was not so easy. The strikers waited to hear if Radio Free Europe would mention them; if not, they argued, then why strike? And they feared becoming enmeshed in politics: when Skorenko arrived on the second day of the strike to pick up the list of demands (to relay to Warsaw and Radio Free Europe), she found the demand for Solidarity's legalization had been crossed off. She snuck it back in, and eventually the strikers got used to the idea. Then Jan Lityński and Bogdan Lis came from Solidarity leadership in Warsaw, Ryszard Bocian and others came from Kraków, and slowly Solidarity began to feel familiar.

The Jastrzębie strike is a lonely story. By the end of that week, most of the mines in the region were on strike. But most went back to work quickly, and their strike leaders came to join the July Manifesto protest. Because most of a mine is hidden from view below ground, with easily controlled access points, it is very difficult to stage an occupation strike. It is also harder to communicate with the outside world. Accounts of the strike (including the film *Górnicy '88*) portray miners huddled around the radio, seeking proof of their own existence, eking out sustenance from what little food their families or friends could smuggle over the fence. The strikers burned with resentment at the "élites" who sat in the strike co-ordination center at Father Czernecki's church. Day after day, strikers would melt away to slip through the fence and go home, escaping the almost unbearable tension. In the second half of the strike—which would become the longest ever in communist Poland, at twenty days—Golec and Zakrzewski led the strikers underground, where they stayed until the end. When the strike ended on September 3, there were fewer than two hundred strikers left.

This was a strike of desperation, not of hope and creative energy. There were no songs about Smurfs, but dark, painful poetry:

The wind rises and howls
The bandits blink their eyes
Each one has a plan
Each one has his ways
But for what? Why? And what will the storm be like?

Another poem sounds like an Orange Alternative paean to Mothers' Day but was meant with dead seriousness:

Let's rise like one, and say farewell to Mrs. Destitution.
We don't want such a wife, who destroys us from every side.

We demand a divorce, for obvious reasons. We are in love with Freedom.
We must have her for our own, to give birth to Prosperity.[30]

This was not a world where Orange Alternative, or the anarchists, would
be welcome. If the miners feared "politics," they also did not feel themselves part of the carnival that played on elsewhere.

How different was the strike that began in Gdańsk a week later! There,
the strikers were already experienced. Though again only about two thousand struck, the atmosphere was even more festive than in May. The
young radicals who provoked the first strike were no longer strangers to
the old guard—most had joined Solidarity by now—but the irreverence
of the so-called generation of '88 remained. This was truly Orange Alternative's strike.

At the Repair Shipyard (which, though next door to the Lenin Shipyard, had none of the official atmosphere imparted by visiting priests and
writers), strikers built themselves an artillery cannon from styrofoam and
old pipe, painted in camouflage green and brown. They rolled it out on
a lazy Sunday afternoon and aimed it at the riot police on the other side
of the gates. Next, they built a tank: a cart bulked up with styrofoam
panels, adorned with the slogan "Leave your arms at the gate, we want
dialogue!"

The Lenin strikers joined the arms race, building a water cannon, rigged
up with a hose that shot a (not-too-threatening) stream of water. Soon
there were more tanks, a paddywagon, a Pershing missile, and a battleship, all made of styrofoam and various spare parts. On Tuesday, August
30, the Lenin Shipyard staged a happening of which, wrote a local Solidarity reporter, "even Wrocław would not be ashamed." With styrofoam
shields, brandishing styrofoam truncheons, and wearing welder's goggles,
a battalion of "riot police" stormed a crowd waiting inside one gate. The
crowd responded by throwing rocks—also made of styrofoam.[31] It was
a cathartic moment, as the strikers enacted their worst fears in order to
banish them.

Thus the shipyard workers—with the help of Freedom and Peace, the
anarchists, and other young opposition groups—rewrote the terms of
conflict. Just as it became increasingly difficult for the Wrocław police to
arrest the revelers of the Orange Alternative, so it would have been ex-
ceedingly unpleasant for the riot police to attack the shipyard after singing
about smurfs and laughing at styrofoam happenings. Of course, the presence of Lech Wałęsa, a constant stream of foreign guests (including Raymond Flynn, the mayor of Boston, whom I was accompanying around
Poland), and the watchful presence of the archbishop, also made intervention less likely. But the new style of the strikes surely contributed to
their peaceful conclusion.

Freedom and Peace was less in evidence in Gdańsk this time; down the coast in Szczecin, it was at the very center of the shipyard strike. Several WiP participants there had parents active in Solidarity at the shipyard, and they threw themselves into the strike. From Warsaw, Piotr Niemczyk came to coordinate public relations. He discovered that these strikers, too, were hoping for publicity and could not understand why the world was ignoring them. Niemczyk simply called up Radio Free Europe, and suddenly there was news about Szczecin every day. It would be months before Niemczyk, now regarded as something of a media wizard, would be able to get back to Warsaw.

In Nowa Huta, the scene of a brutal "pacification" in May, the steelworkers barely struck in August. Just a few hundred workers walked off the job, for a few days. But like Wrocław in May, Kraków now discovered it did not need to strike in order to be heard. On August 25 (the eleventh day of the strike in Jastrzębie), an International Human Rights Conference opened in Father Jancarz's church at Mistrzejowice. The organizers were Zbigniew Romaszewski's Committee for Intervention and Legality and Freedom and Peace.

Almost sixteen months after WiP's Warsaw peace seminar, the opposition still had to seek the safer confines of a church. But instead of barely a hundred guests, surreptitiously making their way to a cramped basement, here were perhaps a thousand people, invited by regular mail. Few camped out at the church; in fact, the lobby of the Holiday Inn across town was almost as lively a meeting point. There were guests from Guyana, Kazakhstan, and (of course) Afghanistan, as well as most countries of the bloc. Wolfgang Templin came, from his temporary exile. Lane Kirkland of the AFL-CIO was a guest, as was Mayor Flynn, and many Western embassies had observers. Freedom and Peace was there in force; a star presence was Sławomir Dutkiewicz, just out of prison after his long hunger strike. The police, meanwhile, kept their distance, restricting their harassment to anonymous graffiti. "Handzlik, back to work! Gil, back to your plow!" read one spraypainted on the sidewalk, but the Nowa Huta activists in question simply laughed it off.

It was more a festival than a conference. In the church's main hall, hundreds gathered to hear speeches by prominent human rights activists from Poland and the West. Around a long table in a side room, intellectuals hashed out differences and cobbled together joint statements on various human rights issues. In a darkened back room, long-haired students from Hungary, East Germany, and Poland met and shared experiences. Out in the lobby, reporters dashed about after the more famous attendees—Romaszewski himself, Jacek Kuroń, Jan Józef Lipski—often ignoring the younger organizers like Rokita and Czaputowicz (though Rokita's speech praising the United States' invasion of Grenada gained him a lot of shocked attention).

Central Europe had never seen anything like it. The conference had all the formal trappings of, say, a gathering of the World Peace Council, yet it was precisely the opposite. Saša Vondra of Charter 77, the only Czech dissident to make it to Kraków (he was on his way back from a visit to Vilnius) was astonished at the openness of the conference, in spite of the presence of an observer from the Ministry of Internal Affairs. He linked this to a "changing of the guard" in the Polish opposition; in Kraków, he thought, the old opposition was in a "distinct minority."[32]

The sensation of the conference, though, was the arrival of a group of young miners from the July Manifesto and other Jastrzębie mines. As reporters and well-wishers crowded around, they brandished pay slips to prove that they were not paid as well as everyone thought. With a determination that many had not heard since 1980, they talked about working conditions, repression, and the need for Solidarity. This was the real thing, lending the conference discussions a certain urgency and importance. The conference organizers chartered buses to take participants and reporters to the mines two hours away, but the bus drivers refused to make the trip.

This would be the only time in those years that I had enough reporter's sense to follow a story. Deciding I had heard enough of the conference, I followed the directions the young miners had given me and drove down to Jastrzębie (my rental car, I was sure, an easy target of surveillance). Roadblocks at nearly every approach to the city made it almost impossible to get in, but finally I found Father Czernecki's church. There, though it seemed far away to the miners who had now gone down into the shafts to strike till the bitter end, was yet another meeting point between two worlds of opposition. Kraków students, and Freedom and Peace activists from all over Poland, ran the printing presses and coordinated food donations.* But they shared with the workers a generational impatience: the Solidarity of 1980–81, a young miner named Sławek told me, "made a number of little mistakes. They were too deferential to the communists, too tolerant. Martial law left us with a feeling of frustration, of unfulfilled dreams. After that experience, we'll be more radical."[33]

Just like the strikes of 1980, but unlike any other worker protest in the eight years since, these strikes featured unpredictable and potent alliances. They did not promise to bring into being another ten-million-member trade union, though. Given that just a few islands of worker protest kept up the fight, this was an impossible dream. What they augured instead was a new pluralist alliance, uniting the generation of '88: anarchists and nationalists, hardheaded realists and pacifists, students and workers.

* Other WiP activists had gone to help the strike at the steel mill in Stalowa Wola, several hours to the east of Kraków. That strike was the only other significant protest in August beyond the mines and the shipyards.

These alliances might lead in any number of unexpected directions. These would not be the people with whom the regime would sit down at the Round Table talks the following spring. But they certainly helped to make such discussions seem a wise idea.

ᛘᛘᛘᛘᛘ *Scene Six* ᛘᛘᛘᛘᛘᛘ

AN INVASION REMEMBERED

PRAGUE, AUGUST 21, 1988

"Historians, do not forget." This is a warning from the Jazz Section's Karel Srp. "Don't write foolishness about how the time was ripe, about how discontent fermented, and how the nation raised its head. Only two stepped forward: Tomáš Dvořák and Hana Marvanová."[34] Fortunately, the names of the founders of the Independent Peace Association are familiar to us (from chapter 4), so we can without shame accept Srp's admonition, as he stood on the sidewalk on Václav Square on the afternoon of August 21.

If one date symbolized communist control of Czechoslovakia, it was the day Soviet and Warsaw Pact armies crushed the Prague Spring in 1968. The twentieth anniversary is worth observing in its own right, as it marked the moment when the ensuing normalization would come to an end, and the Czechs—next to last, before the East Germans, among the people of Central Europe—took to the streets.

There had always been, as August rolled around, declarations by the Charter condemning the invasion and calling for the withdrawal of Soviet troops from Czechoslovak soil. But as 1988 had brought several new social movements, and new samizdat publications, it seemed time for a more dramatic protest. Most of the prominent figures in Charter 77 thought this a bad idea. A number of them (like Václav Havel) decided it would be safer to spend that weekend out of Prague and went to summer homes. It was easy to guess that the police would not react gently to any show of opposition. Many of the villains of 1968, beginning with President Gustáv Husák himself, were still in power. To question Soviet "fraternal assistance" was to question their right to rule. So there ought to be no confrontation. Petr Uhl of VONS, who also went to his summer cottage, expected only that "the older generation would shed a few tears over the lost chances [of the Prague Spring]: a bit of self-pity with an historical perspective."[35]

Petr Placák of the Czech Children had something else in mind. This would be the moment when all the youth of Czechoslovakia would make themselves heard. On a primitive mimeograph in Lucie Váchová's apartment, the Children cranked out some ten thousand flyers (a far cry from the usual five hundred or so copies of a samizdat publication) announcing a "peaceful manifestation" in front of the monument on Václav Square at 6:00 P.M. "Overcome twenty years of apathy forced on us by the Husák regime, and COME!!"[36]

Meanwhile, Jan Chudomel of NMS called for a "diffuse" demonstration, supplying more specific symbolism to Placák's general invitation. People should simply wear tricolor ribbons, or red, white, and blue clothing, to recall the desecration of the Czechoslovak state and its flag.[37] All during that Sunday morning, NMS members strolled around Prague, showing off their tricolor ribbons. By 1:00 P.M. a few hundred people, mostly young, had gathered before the monument. Though many had brought with them flowers to lay at the foot of the statue, no one seemed to have any plan for what to do next. People stood around in small groups, waiting to see what would happen. "One could sense that people wanted to speak openly," the NMS *Bulletin* reported later. "In this situation, we had the idea that we could explain what our Independent Peace Association is attempting to do."[38]

So Luboš Vydra spoke up, telling those in the crowd near him about the program of NMS. Then he introduced Hana Marvanová and turned to greet a friend. He looked up moments later to discover that a crowd of several hundred had gathered. One thing, apparently, that Marvanová had mastered in law school was how to make a speech. But this was not just any speech: hers was the first public, free voice raised in Prague in twenty years. Whether those in the crowd read samizdat or not, listened to Radio Free Europe or not, this was something they had been missing. More and more onlookers detached themselves from doorways and shop windows on the periphery and joined the crowd. Finally, the time had come to do more than just lay flowers.

Marvanová, Vydra, and Tomáš Dvořák hadn't thought of bringing any NMS literature; Dvořák hopped on the subway and went home to get some. By the time he returned, the demonstration had become a teach-in. Someone suggested drawing up a proclamation of some kind. With Dvořák—a "vigorous and direct" speaker[39]—moderating and Marvanová taking notes, the still-growing crowd debated for several hours before coming up with a nine-point document, calling for the departure of Soviet troops, free multicandidate elections, and respect for human rights. On the spot, over fifteen hundred people signed their names.

As evening began to fall, the crowd marched off to the Old Town Square, urged on by tradition, and perhaps by the need to stretch their legs a bit. Weekenders returning home brought the numbers to over ten thousand. They shouted slogans unheard on Czechoslovak streets for two decades, and they sang the Czechoslovak anthem. A photograph published in *Revolver revue,* the leading samizdat cultural journal (under the caption "Demos . . . a new phenomenon of Czech resistance?"), shows a dense throng, most in their twenties, filling Václav Square and inching toward the Old Town. They may be chanting slogans; one smiling young man flashes 'V' signs at the photographer. But there are no banners (other photos show a few Czechoslovak flags), and no one clutches leaflets. Czechs were only just learning the ways of public demonstration.

Though some had feared a massacre, the police reaction was reserved. Through most of the afternoon, they merely inspected identity cards. As historian Oldřich Tuma puts it: "It was as if the regime could not decide upon intervention, which would concede the very unpleasant (for them) fact that a demonstration is really taking place."[40] Though this was not, as we have seen, the first demonstration in Czechoslovakia, the remarkable turn of events on August 21 marked the beginning of the Czech revolution.

Leading opposition figures sheepishly acknowledged that the face of Czech resistance had changed, and the myth of Czech passivity and apathy had been vanquished. Václav Benda (whose children were in the crowd; he stayed away) had no doubt of the "extraordinary significance" of the demonstration, as "spontaneous forces rose up without any fixed framework." Most surprising of all was the demonstrators' age. After all, mused Karel Srp, they "had felt those deficiencies [of freedom and of living standards] for a relatively short time. I predict the coming generation will be willing to endure what we have endured for an ever shorter period of time."[41] Srp had once advised a younger Martin Mejstřík to stay out of trouble; now Mejstřík was photographing the demonstration for *Kavárna AFFA.*

After the fact, August 21 came to seem almost inevitable (since that will to act had obviously been sleeping within the citizens of Prague) and magical, fueled by what Western observers would later dub "People Power." Tomáš Dvořák, who was at the eye of the storm from the very beginning (and who himself had expected only that "with fear, and with the tricolor in our lapel, we will stroll around Prague"), saw how the breakthrough had really occurred: "Most of all, it came from people's longing to speak openly with one another, without generational divides. To listen to one another. . . . To enter into a dialogue with someone whom I don't know, and who doesn't know me. But we are close to one another in our problems, and we want to solve them. And that determination will remain in us in the future. We won't be satisfied with things as they are. After twenty years, hope rises again in us."[42] Building upon that idea, he and Marvanová proposed to the crowd on Václav Square that they meet regularly, on the last Saturday of every month, for an open discussion. Several hundred showed up at the square on September 24. NMS had found its own constituency and became more than just a samizdat title. They were met by dozens of police, still unsure how to react to this new civil courage. This was another lesson in opposition: some participants tried arguing with the police. Others challenged the police to arrest them, laying on the ground by the police vans, or simply walking up and handing over their identity cards. All those detained were quickly released.

On the edges of the confrontation, meanwhile, the hoped-for discussion began in small groups. Because this was just an ordinary day, with no anniversary to observe, this first NMS discussion was a step deeper into opposition. This was what Tomáš Dvořák had envisioned—and indeed, what Charter 77 had called for over the last year and a half. Discussion, especially when the meetings moved to Peace Square, some distance from the city center, deritualized opposition, even though there were never more than several hundred people involved. One could now participate without flowers and wreaths, without formal declarations or speeches, with only one's ideas, and one's courage.

𝕏𝕏𝕏𝕏𝕏𝕏 *Scene Seven* 𝕏𝕏𝕏𝕏𝕏𝕏

WATERDAM / NED: HUNGARY DEFENDS THE DANUBE

BUDAPEST, SEPTEMBER–OCTOBER 1988

To be a Hungarian, standing amidst a massive crowd—perhaps forty thousand, at least four times anything seen in decades—on Kossuth Square by the Parliament, was an eerie experience. "Here we are again," thought Judit Vasarhelyi of the Danube Circle, feeling that ground beneath her feet on September 12, 1988. Thirty-two years after the Revolution of 1956, the people of Budapest had returned to the center of that protest.

The communists had never dreamed that their proposed dam on the Danube (see chapter 2) would stir up so much trouble. The idea for such a public protest came from discussions among all the groups that had emerged over the last year: the Hungarian Democratic Forum (MDF), the Network of Free Initiatives (Hálózat), and Fidesz. Then, in July, thirteen different environmental groups—of these, the Danube Circle was the best known—came together to form the Nagymaros Committee to coordinate antidam protest. Its first public action was a joint press conference with the Austrian section of the World Wildlife Fund. The September protest, announced at that time, was the second.

Protesters, at first overwhelmingly students, gathered at the university. It was a workday, but the march was scheduled to begin in the late afternoon. Encouraged by the fine late summer weather, many began to arrive after work, picking up their children from school along the way. At 5:30, the crowd began to walk down Museum Boulevard toward the Parliament. Fidesz, Danube Circle, Hálózat, and the MDF all carried banners—the latter's quite professionally painted and standing out from the spray-painted bedsheets the others had brought. The MDF also carried several black flags with white crosses, emblazoned with the names of villages that would be destroyed by the artificial canal, lake, and power plants. One banner took apart the word for "water barrage," turning it into a message of foreboding for the regime: "WaterDam/ned" (*VízLépCsöd*). And above them all swam a yellow fish, with the slogan "Help."

With the government resolutely pressing forward on the Nagymaros project, in fact intensifying work as if to render protest irrelevant, these were powerful slogans. The Hungarian regime had a reputation as the most liberal in the bloc, yet here was a concrete example of discontent it seemed disposed to ignore. Along the parade route, thousands of passersby joined in, until the throng poured into Kossuth Square. The mood was festive, and the crowd wanted more than clean water: "You've lied enough, now get out!" they chanted.

Mária Filková of the Bratislava environmentalists was one of those in the crowd. Filková speaks Hungarian and has some Hungarian ancestry; indeed, a cousin worked in the Hungarian Ministry of the Environment. She had heard about the protest on Hungarian television and had come down by herself to see what Hungarians could do that the Slovaks could not. Gravitating to the Danube Circle banner, she met János Vargha. She marveled at the size of the march and wondered if perhaps the Danube Circle could send a delegation to Bratislava or Gabčikovo to jumpstart protest there. How many of us would you like, Vargha responded. A thousand? two thousand? It would probably have been easy to organize that number, but the repercussions for the Slovaks were still too fearsome to contemplate, as Filková knew from the Candlelight Demonstration in March, so she dropped the idea. But then she met the women of Fidesz's Alice Madzsar Group. Their first and last public action was to stage a march at Nagymaros; they invited Filková to join them.

The little town of Nagymaros* lies just over an hour north of Budapest, directly across the river from the high-perched medieval castle at Vise-

* "Nagy" means great or large in Hungarian, or "gross" in German. Some banners at Danube protests thus renamed it "Grószmaros," in honor of Communist Party chair Károly Grósz.

grad, one of Hungary's most impressive national treasures. The train up to Nagymaros was packed with several hundred protesters, mostly women and children, on the afternoon of September 17 (a Saturday). The mood was festive, like a family picnic. Children of all ages drew pictures of the Danube and its surroundings. Later, the protesters would hand these out to the dam engineers and the rather hostile citizens of Nagymaros.

At the train station, Mária Filková met them with three carloads of women and children from Bratislava. Hungary was not yet a forbidden zone for citizens of communist Czechoslovakia, so for the second time in a week she was able to join a demonstration utterly unlike anything at home. The Slovak delegation sported pins in the blue, red, and white of the Czechoslovak flag. As they marched the few hundred yards to the dam, pushing strollers and leading older children by the hand, the women from Budapest sang songs about nature that the children knew; the Slovaks responded in kind.

The Nagymaros problem had, almost unexpectedly, opened the door to public activism in Hungary. Until the Danube demonstrations, there had been only commemorative moments: March 15, and anniversaries connected with 1956. The former was slowly drawing larger and larger crowds. The latter dates were rather more dangerous; most people preferred to limit their observance to listening to Radio Free Europe or the like. The Danube problem was different: like Chernobyl, the issue was both concrete and immediately comprehensible, while also sufficiently urgent to warrant protest.

There would be two more demonstrations, both in Budapest, before the season was over. A few thousand came together on October 3 to form a human chain embracing the Danube, from the Margit Island Bridge, past Parliament to the Chain Bridge, then up the Buda side of the river to complete the circle. At the end of October, Fidesz took the initiative and gathered thousands of students for a torchlight parade from the Margit Island Bridge to the statue of poet Sandor Petöfi, along the Danube's left bank.

All the while, the Nagymaros Committee was gathering signatures on a new petition demanding a plebiscite on a halt to the project. Not even the Communist-dominated parliament could ignore the some 140,000 signatures delivered in February 1989. In a country of less than ten million, this was nearly as impressive as the response by Slovaks to the petition of Augustin Navratil a year earlier.

After one more demonstration—some fifteen thousand in Nagymaros, in early April—the government capitulated. It announced, on May 13, 1989, a two-month moratorium on dam construction; shortly thereafter, the moratorium was extended to October. By the time October arrived, the political situation had changed completely, and the project became a political hot potato, which successive governments handled at their own peril. Thus the Hungarians, like the Poles, had unexpectedly succeeded: well before revolutionary change, street protest had forced the communist government to change a policy, even in the face of substantial financial loss and an angry Czechoslovak partner. The similarity to the success of Freedom and Peace is not coincidental: both shared a strong nationalist foundation. To change a military oath or to stop a dam, the regime leaders had to feel that the cause was (or could be) theirs, too, as members of the same nation as the protesters. Even so, their decisions would simply expose them to further protest, and ultimately to their downfall.

Scene Eight

INDEPENDENCE DAY AND PALACH WEEK

PRAGUE, OCTOBER 1988–JANUARY 1989

Looking back at the breakthrough demonstration of August, Charter 77 spokesperson Stanislav Devátý believed that society had forced a kind of negotiation with the regime. The subject of this negotiation was perestroika: what did the regime have to offer its citizens? August had "contradicted the lie of a normalized society, which the regime incessantly repeated."[43] And the question of the seventieth anniversary of democratic Czechoslovakia's independence (October 28, 1918) now loomed large. Whatever they thought of bourgeois democracy, the communists would have a hard time suppressing this anniversary, which they had studiously ignored since the last official celebration in 1968. In December 1987 Democratic Initiative had been the first to demand that the national holiday be restored. Emanuel Mandler, for one, felt that his movement had scored a significant victory.[44] For Devátý, the reappearance of the holiday was clear proof that pressure from below worked.

On the other hand, communists in other countries were expert at manipulating national traditions to regime ends. Thus, when President Husák declared that October 28 would be a festive holiday, he threatened to take the initiative away from the rapidly maturing opposition. A bit of flag-waving and nationalist phrases might satisfy most citizens and once again isolate the independent movements. Or worse: the three-day holiday weekend could simply give people a chance for a vacation. How Praguers would respond was crucial.

But the Czechoslovak regime was not nearly as adept at handling national themes as were its neighbors. The official celebration of independence day was inexplicably moved to October 27. In front of the National Museum, the usual suspects—new Prime Minister Ladislav Adamec (who had succeeded a comrade with a slight reformist reputation), Miloslav Stěpan, the hated party chief of Prague, and party *gensek* Miloš Jakeš— gave formal speeches before a solemn crowd of dutiful supporters.

The tactic failed. The next afternoon, some ten thousand people showed up on Václav Square and, later, on Old Town Square. In contrast to August, the crowd was more varied, elderly and middle-aged along with the young protesters. This was so because the demonstration was less spontaneous. Just two weeks earlier, a group of senior opposition leaders calling themselves the Movement for Civic Freedom had issued a manifesto calling for political engagement. In the days before the anniversary, all the major groups—and there were now quite a few, in stark contrast to the monopoly Charter 77 had so recently enjoyed—issued declarations and printed posters (showing a lion ripping free of a leg iron) urging citizens to join in active protest.

October 28 was not unlike a demonstration in martial-law Poland: the police not only guarded the statue of St. Václav but charged the crowd from out of the subway tunnels, and used water cannon to drive people into side streets. So was the crowd more assertive, shouting "Fascists!" or "We want freedom!" or "This is your perestroika!" at the police. There was no drawing up of petitions this time. By five o'clock, after just two hours, the clash was over, with some two hundred people arrested.

"What really happened?" wondered an anonymous student, writing for *Revolver revue*. In the short term, "the organs of state power carried out their mission perfectly. Aside from the number of participants, perhaps, nothing surprised them. They acted in accordance with a precisely arranged plan." Yet he was sure, all the same, that the opposition had succeeded: ten thousand people had seen the regime at its worst and thus would understand things differently now. "People shouted 'We don't believe you!' Slogans which we have known or felt for a long time rang out spontaneously from the crowd of thousands. Society has begun to move."[45]

Michal Dočekal, a colleague of Martin Mejstřík at the Drama Academy, knew that he, at least, had changed that evening: "I had there in my hand a paving stone. . . . This one cop got separated [from the line of police], and the crowd chased him for a moment. And I picked up the paving stone, and did nothing with it. It was a terrible moment for me."[46] Merely to heft a stone in his hand, and to contemplate a state functionary within his reach, was to face the "terrible" question of what he, a theater student, was prepared to do to end communism.

Both sides had drawn lessons from the August demonstration. Six weeks after the independence day clash, the observation of International Human Rights Day, December 10, offered another opportunity to test the limits of negotiated change in communist Czechoslovakia. Because French President François Mitterand was in Prague on a state visit, the authorities gave official permission for a demonstration—but only in a small square in a residential neighborhood a good fifteen-minute walk from "Václavak."

The communists hoped in this way to contain dissent while putting on a show of glasnost. But just as they could not speak the language of nationalism well, nor had they mastered Gorbachevian reform. Rob McRae, the Canadian diplomat, was surprised that only five thousand came to hear Václav Havel, Jana Petrová of NMS, and others speak. "I assumed that if a legal demonstration was permitted the whole city would turn out." He had of course overstated Czech perestroika, which Czechs themselves knew to be window dressing: "Most were not about to lose their jobs over participation in a human rights rally with no chance of affecting the regime."[47] Indeed, Jan Fojtík, the chief party ideologue, condemned the demonstration a few days later and assured the party faithful that it would not happen again.

But it was too late. The threshold had been lowered again, ever so slightly, bringing new faces into the streets. New bridges were connecting the various independent worlds of Prague. One of these was the John Lennon Peace Club, formed on the eighth anniversary of the Beatle's murder, on December 8, 1988. Its founding declaration (see chapter 5) contrasted Lennon's "tireless efforts in the areas of peace, love, and understanding among people and nations" to the repressive policies of the communist regime.[48]

Meanwhile, though Mejstřík and other students still preferred to test the limits within their officially sanctioned student magazines, they were also showing up regularly to demonstrate. "There were plenty of *damaky* (students from the Drama Academy) there, says Pavel Lagner, an editor at *Kavárna,* "and soon they all ended up before the [school's] disciplinary commission, because they were all picked up by the police."[49] The event even drew people from beyond Prague, like Marcel Hájek, a medical student in Plzeň. He had already been going to so-called apartment seminars in Prague; the demonstration cemented his reputation as one of the most dangerous radicals in his city. But even in the provinces, the atmosphere was changing. Socialism was washed up, Hájek believed, and he could tell by the resigned attitude of the security police who brought him in for questioning.

The change had not come thanks to pressure from Gorbachev. With the Czechoslovak Politburo now cleared of reformers, verbal attacks on the opposition escalated. Dozens of new political prisoners (like Marvanová, Vydra, Dvořák, and Tomáš Tvaroch of NMS) spent Human Rights Day in prison. Up close, the supposed liberalization looked quite unimpressive.

What had changed was the opposition. If in August the police had simply failed to respond as they searched the crowd in vain for the Havels and Uhls, in the fall the regime sought a new modus operandi: water cannons? trials of ever-younger opponents? controlled demonstrations? borrowed reformist rhetoric? friendly warnings to recalcitrant students? The communists' uncertainty grew. As in Poland, they could see a new generation coming onstage.

The older opposition, writes Oldřich Tuma, "had on the whole no conception of the strategic exploitation of [the demonstrations]; nor did they give them any concrete political content."[50] The youth were feeling their power. Writing the New Year's editorial for the NMS *Bulletin* in January 1989, editor Radek Zeman admitted: "Just a year ago, I was strongly skeptical about the activism of young people. I saw myself how their spirits were cramped by two decades of decay. But this year I met a whole bunch who smashed my skepticism into bits. Thank you." "In 1989," adds Prague student Pavel Lagner, "we were so attuned to the social situation that now any excuse was good enough to protest."[51]

The game entered a new phase with the "Palachiada," a week-long festival of demonstrations—almost street battles, really—commemorating the death of Jan Palach. Palach was a student who had set himself on fire in Václav Square in January 1969 to call attention to the Soviet occupation of his country.

Celebrating Palach wasn't easy: one could hardly invite others to follow his example. Nor was he exactly a victim of communist repression. It was easy to mock the Chartists' discomfort: both Václav Havel and spokeswoman Dana Němcová received anonymous letters in early January 1989 (presumably from the security police), from people who claimed they would imitate Palach.

But Palach had planned his protest carefully, not from despair. Despite its radical nature, this was "a great ethical act" that deserved respect without emulation, wrote Eva Kantůrková, a former Charter spokeswoman, on the eve of the anniversary.[52] Palach's deed had deeply shaken the nation. Recalling how "we were all struck dumb for a moment" by his protest, and "a crowd one-hundred thousand strong wound through the streets of the Old Town to pay its respects before the casket," the current Charter spokespeople (one of whom, Saša Vondra, had been just seven years old when Palach died) issued a call to action: "This was something fundamental that united us—but it was too little, as the last twenty years have shown. The muddy flood of lies, against which Jan desperately placed his own body, has not yet receded. . . . Jan Palach's sacrifice is not history, but an ever-living challenge for us and for all who appreciate what we owe. Let us then begin to repay our debt today. Let us bow down in his memory—and rise up."[53]

As stirring as the words of the Charter statement were, the observance on Sunday afternoon (January 15) might have ended with a peaceful ceremony. But there is something unnerving in the Palach story, for the regime as well as for the opposition. The Communists' almost pathological fear of uncontrollable protest produced exactly what they had hoped to avoid. It seemed all the police in Prague were on Václav Square; they blocked off the streets and detained most opposition leaders. Indeed, anyone carrying flowers in the general vicinity soon made it into a police van. The police response showed that the regime had now made up its mind, in favor of the hard-line option. Sitting in the city jail that evening, Petr Placák of the Czech Children jotted down a new plan on a piece of paper and passed it around: it was time to "take back Václav Square."[54]

Placák's goal—quickly accepted by other movements—was seemingly modest. He wasn't calling for overthrow of the regime, after all. But, capitalizing on the growing popular animosity toward police actions, he was advocating demonstrations with an avowed political purpose. They would not simply demonstrate, but assert a right. That week, Václav Square was the place to be, and once again the police struggled to respond to the opposition's initiative. Those detained on the January 15 were quickly freed and showed up the next morning to lay flowers again. Several—including Havel, Vondra, Němcová, Placák, Veverka and Penc of the John Lennon Peace Club, and Jana Petrová of NMS—were promptly arrested. Some were released after ten days; others were put on trial and sentenced to up to two years in prison.

The daily papers triumphantly reported the arrests. At another time, this would have had the desired effect of frightening away further demonstration. Now, the result was the opposite: Tuesday saw a spontaneous, indeed leaderless demonstration on the square. Then on Wednesday, as Czechoslovak representatives took part in a meeting in Vienna of the Conference on Security and Cooperation in Europe, the police were nowhere to be found. Rob McRae noted "an amazing feeling of elation, of victory, in the crowd. Speeches were made and there was a new-found sense of dignity from participating in an open political forum."[55] Thursday brought the largest crowd yet, and the police returned, too, with renewed vigor. Demonstrations continued through Saturday, though police turned away pilgrims to Palach's grave.

The absurdist spirit of 1989 was in the air, as the crowds mocked the empty phrases of the regime's reports. "We are but a handful," roared thousands of voices; and: "So where are the 'marginal elements' [živly]?" Havel and Charter 77 were cheered, too, and on Wednesday two Charter signatories were able to speak. Then, with shouts of "Let's go home," the crowd slowly dispersed itself, to return the next afternoon. In that day's peaceful, disciplined crowd, Tomáš Tvaroch of NMS saw the future: "All in all, that evening on Václav Square impressed me as very hopeful; it somewhat balanced out the unpleasant experiences of the previous days."[56]

And the students were out in force, too. "No one made excuses any more," says Martin Mejstřík, "that they were just going to the metro station [and thus only happened to be in the vicinity of the demonstration]." He was stunned to see how the faculty (including the Marxists) and even the rector began openly to support the students.[57] In Brno, meanwhile, Jiří Voráč of *Revue '88* and Vladimir Vyskočil of NMS organized a student petition "to demonstrate that university students are capable of standing up and joining the growing resistance."*

Joining the resistance was exhilarating, but also a little frightening. Classics student Jan Dus (whose father, a Czech Brethren minister, was a prominent Chartist) saw his horizons expand rapidly from the insular world of academic intrigue. He was detained and interrogated that week and soon became active in NMS. "For us, it was important that we believed we were crossing some line," he explains. Even years later, though, the costs of that step have left a "bad feeling" for Dus: a lot of people were beaten up by the police that week—more even than in November 1989, "but somehow we paid no attention." One of the most active students in Dus's circle emigrated that same month, to Austria.[58] The contradictions between working within the system and trying to oppose it had taken their toll.

After January there would be no more large demonstrations until August. A week of clashes with the police may simply have exhausted the people of Prague, and scared them a little, too. But it is also true that, at least for the moment, the "Václavak" demonstration format had achieved all it could. With no more major '68 anniversaries to observe, further demonstrations that winter and spring would likely have drawn smaller numbers. The police would have reclaimed the square, and perhaps the revolution would have looked quite different. Instead, the energy of the Palach festival spread out across the city and the country, spawning ever new ways to resist, and to destabilize, the communist regime.

Scene Nine

ENCIRCLING THE ROUND TABLE

POLAND, FEBRUARY–JUNE 1989

When the last striker left the July Manifesto mine in September 1988, an era came to an end. The miners, and the shipyard workers before them, returned to work with the promise that the government would open ne-

* They gathered some two hundred signatures, mostly from Brno but also from Prague, Olomouc, and Ostrava.

gotiations with Lech Wałęsa. General Czesław Kiszczak and several other Politburo members had given discreet signals that, in return for some measure of "social peace," a round table discussion could begin.

Wałęsa had until recently been ignored by the regime, dismissively referred to as a "private individual" by government spokesman Jerzy Urban. Back in 1980–81, Solidarity had sought dialogue with the regime in order to solve Poland's problems; now they had that dialogue. Was this what Poles had been fighting for over the intervening years?

Perhaps inevitably, a profound sense of disappointment set in. From now on, the actors in the gradual victory of opposition would be veterans of 1980. The key moments would occur indoors: intense private negotiations in the offices of the Episcopate; Wałęsa's televised debate with official trade union head Alfred Miodowicz; and the Round Table negotiations themselves. These provided few photogenic moments. The streets and the factories slowly disappeared from view. This is, of course, a story very different from the one that has been told thus far. In place of colorful demonstration, strikes, and theater, we have solemn negotiations between actors of a much older generation.

The Round Table was not Poland's revolution. That had been under way since at least the previous summer. But it was a transformative moment, shaped by the protest of the previous years while containing seeds of the political developments to come. In a memorable image, Solidarity leaders sat down beside those who had jailed and derided them. Negotiation had generally not been part of the carnival repertoire; this, at least, was a departure. But a focus on what was concrete and achievable—this was now familiar territory.

The communists contrasted what they termed the "constructive opposition" with the extremists who would not or could not sit down to the negotiating table. At first, this latter category specifically included prominent Solidarity thinkers Jacek Kuroń and Adam Michnik; they were accepted only after weeks of negotiation. For the regime, there could be no serious discussion with the "happeners" of Orange Alternative and its clones, with those who refused the patriotic duty of military service, with the radicals of the so-called Kraków group—Wojciech Polaczek's fighters, Marek Kurzyniec's radical wing of WiP, and others (not only in Kraków) who thrived on confrontation—or with those who continued to strike even after the regime compromised. But in a way, these groups performed a valuable service for opposition leaders at that moment. It is not just that this kind of opposition made Wałęsa, or even Kuroń, seem moderate by comparison, but that it empowered and legitimized those who would negotiate. The diversity of opposition made the position of the "constructive opposition," paradoxically perhaps, stronger.

There were many in the young movements who wanted to participate in the Round Table, but the odds were stacked against them. One of the first barriers raised was that of expertise. Senior Solidarity intellectuals and union activists had either the education or the experience (or both) to sit opposite veteran party bureaucrats. Most of the newcomers at the table when formal, public negotiations began on February 8 were symbolic representatives from each of the major striking factories of the previous year. The students, for the most part, had not even been active in 1980; their subsequent experience was not of the type that would be valuable in such negotiations. Or, at least, not on the issues that were on the table. Had foreign relations and the military been under discussion, one can easily imagine what almost anyone from WiP could have contributed. These issues were explicitly not on the table, however; the opposition refrained from raising them, as it was understood these topics might harm relations with the Soviet Union.

The new movements were present at two (of fourteen) "subtables," which convened to debate the resolution of more specialized problems: ecology and youth. Radek Gawlik of WiP participated in the former, as did two activists from recently established green groups close to WiP. Most of the participants on the Solidarity side of that table, however, came from the Polish Ecological Club, an organization comprised largely of scientific experts founded in 1981. The youth subtable—whose main tasks included the relegalization of the Independent Students' Association and the independent Scouting Union—was more varied, with something like a cross-section of youth opposition. There were two young strikers from 1988, representatives of school and university self-governments, and participants in Catholic youth groups. WiP's representative was Jan Maria Rokita. Both subtables remained deep in the background, as the main focus of the plenary discussions was the relegalization of Solidarity as a trade union and the question of elections and reform of the political system.

As little as new movements could do within the Round Table, there was not much more to be accomplished outside, though it may, at least, have been more fun. So the carnival continued, just out of the spotlight. Many of the movements of the previous years were as active as ever in the winter and spring of 1989. Orange Alternative celebrated Carnival for the second year, on the day after the Round Table opened. Several thousand frolicked through Wrocław's center, under the slogan "Socialism in Carnival, Carnival in Socialism!" Participants held aloft little round tables, in mock homage to this new symbol of Polish politics. Somehow, the happening turned also into a demonstration in support of Wałęsa and Solidarity.

This mix of satire and celebration, antipolitics and politics, captured the country's mood during the two months of deliberations. In Gdańsk, nearly every Sunday's mass at St. Brygida's Church was followed by small anti-Wałęsa demonstrations, coordinated by the anarchists of RSA. The WiP Student Action in Kraków demonstrated for legalization of the Independent Students' Association and clashed with police, who responded with water cannons and tear gas. The students declared a twenty-four-hour protest strike but dispersed when the university rector gave them his unexpected support. In Poznań and Gorzów, hundreds marched to protest the planned construction of a nuclear reactor (a companion to that at Żarnowiec) nearby. Warsaw demonstrators arrived by limousine to crash a reception at the Czechoslovak Embassy, and shouted slogans in support of political prisoners in Czechoslovakia. Some forty WiP participants in Katowice staged a hunger strike to protest the imprisonment of Václav Havel; Rinaldo Betkiewicz received a record hundred thousand zloty fine for chaining himself to the fence of the Czechoslovak Consulate.

Even as protesters expanded their reach, then, uncertainty over the limits of the state's tolerance remained. Some demonstrations passed without incident, but others, as in Kraków, or an Orange Alternative happening on the first day of spring, which ended with fifty arrests and some severe beatings, seemed like the old days.

The confusion into which the post-Solidarity opposition had fallen was painfully evident at the Easter Peace March, which WiP organized in Wro-cław on March 22. The object of the march was to follow the tradition in the Western European peace movement of marches at the beginning of spring; marches took place that day in several other European cities. Some one thousand (one estimate reached five thousand) gathered by the clock on Świdnicka Street. The plan was to march to one of the Soviet bases on the north side of the Odra River. Leszek Budrewicz, of WiP and Solidarity's regional leadership, warned the crowd to avoid confrontation. "Whoever throws a stone at a policeman will be thrown out of our demonstration," he said, then turned to the riot police assembled nearby: "Today you have nothing to fear."

Behind a young couple holding a banner reading "We want our child to grow up in a country of peace and freedom," the crowd marched by lines of battle-dressed riot police toward the Rynek. Budrewicz and others threw flowers at the police and urged each other not to test the barricades. Roman Kucharski, a younger WiP participant, grew impatient: "We turn left to avoid a barricade. From afar I can see that Odrzańska Street is also blocked. We chant 'Freedom and Peace' and 'Russians go home,' but apparently we are going too far with that second slogan, because Leszek Budrewicz quiets us with a gesture of his outstretched arms. I wonder why these people have come here, if expressing one's attitude to the presence of Soviet troops in Poland is undesirable. This pleasant little *zadyma* is steadily becoming an irrational stroll around the Rynek," Kucharski continued, and he thought back to WiP's Black Marches, protesting the Siechnice chemical plant. Those marches had made a point of their weakness, proceeding as little as fifty meters before the demonstrators were surrounded and detained. "But that was something completely different, and in another time. Sorry, it isn't, but it was supposed to be. At least that's how I feel."[59]

Times had changed since the Siechnice marches, but WiP found itself unsure how to adapt. Kucharski wondered whether "a flower is too little to fill in the chasm between us and them." But, on the other hand, did it make sense, during the Round Table, to charge the riot police and take a beating, as it were, for the cause of Poland? Thanking the thwarted marchers after their forty-minute circuit, Budrewicz also recalled the Black Marches and hoped that, as in 1987, "'as time goes on, we'll get farther and farther. In a year, we'll march to . . .' 'Holland,' someone suggests"—thinking of the Western peace marches that day. Of course, a year later they could have marched to Holland, but Kucharski was right to sense that WiP's tactics would not find many supporters by then.

The Round Table concluded on April 5, having reached a number of important agreements. Chief among these were the relegalization of Solidarity, permission for the union to publish a weekly and a daily newspaper, and the setting of semi-free elections to parliament (including free elections to a newly created Senate), to be held on June 4. The arena of politics, which had for two months been reduced to Warsaw's Viceroy's Palace, now suddenly expanded again to the entire country.

Solidarity now faced a great challenge to fill this enormous void. The union no longer had ten million members, but perhaps only tens of thousands of active participants. And if Solidarity had enjoyed a virtual monopoly in 1981, there were now many other opposition voices, over which it was not always easy for Solidarity to make itself heard. During the Round Table, Wałęsa spent a great deal of time traveling the country, persuading miners in Jastrzębie, students in Kraków and Wrocław, and many others to support the negotiations. Now, the union had to recreate a unified opposition to stand up to the unified party. Unity was the opposite of carnival, perhaps, but it was also its outcome: dialogue between Solidarity and party had not been possible before 1989. Solidarity could not, on its own, force its voice into the party's monologue. Instead, it cut in when that monologue had already been smashed by the movements of the carnival.

KKKKKK *Scene Ten* **KKKKKKK**

MOTHERS AND CHILDREN

PRAGUE AND BRATISLAVA, MAY–JULY 1989

It began with a cloud: in mid-January, 1989, a dense, foul fog settled upon much of northern Bohemia and southern Poland. Even to citizens who were used to the fumes from coal burning, chemical plants, and the rest of the ills of socialist industrialization, this was worse than usual.

Anna Hradilková (of the Czech Children) and Michaela Valentová, both mothers of young children and familiar with the Prague dissident community (in particular, the circle around the Catholic Church), began to circulate among friends a petition calling on city authorities to provide honest information about daily air pollution, and to take steps to improve air quality. For a year they had been trying politely to get the authorities' attention. Now, calling themselves the Prague Mothers, they acted—and got some five hundred signatures in a month.

As had Chernobyl for Polish women three years earlier, the brown cloud stifling the city in the winter of 1989 impelled the Prague Mothers toward the twin issues of the environment and glasnost. "Accurate and timely information," they wrote, "is the most effective measure against rumors and panic. It is insulting to us, and dangerous for our children, that information about what we breathe is concealed."[60]

In late May, during a much ballyhooed conference on environmental issues hosted by Prime Minister Adamec, the Prague Mothers staged their first protest, repeating the popular tactic of marching with children. It was a Monday morning; dressed in their best clothes, these families (there were about thirty women, and fifty children) were simply strolling the pedestrian zone near Václav Square. Some kids held their mother's hand as they walked; others rode in strollers. A boy and a girl, each about ten, carried a sign reading "Let's Protect Nature for Our Children." It was a happy occasion; everyone was smiling and singing songs (like "The Green Grass," to which all the children knew the words). But this was still a demonstration; in fact, it was a demonstration whose participants could not be shoved into police vans, nor kept at bay with firehoses.*

The environment had become the topic of the moment across Czechoslovakia. That summer there were also demonstrations against a hotel planned near the John Lennon Peace Club's stomping grounds, the Kampa Park. And when several thousand Poles demonstrated in Cieszyń against

---

* Beyond their original petition, the demonstrators also protested the Gabčikovo-Nagymaros Dam, the nuclear power program, and the building of a lift on Sněžka mountain.

the giant Stonava coking plant, in July 1989, they were joined on the Czech side by a small demonstration, too.

The beauty of an environmental demonstration is to appropriate a space usually threatened, and make it one's own. This the Prague Mothers, with the Czech Children (both the ones in strollers and Petr Placák's group), accomplished together in one of the most beloved, and historically significant, spots in Prague: the Arbor, or "Stromovka," a heavily wooded park on a peninsula in the Vltava just north of the city center. A six-lane highway to connect the center to the northern suburbs was to cut right through the park, despite the objections of official ecological and scientific groups. This was a popular area for weekend family excursions and a natural destination for the Mothers and their protesting strollers.

Stromovka was also an issue made to order for the Czech Children: the park had its origins as a royal hunting preserve established in the fourteenth century. It therefore embodied Placák's idea that a true king cared for the land, in the way that a communist state would not. Posters tacked to trees throughout the park announced a demonstration for Wednesday, June 21. As the hour approached, Anna Hradilková found herself sitting on the curb with two banners in her backpack, feeling a long way away from Václav Square:

> Inside, I am resigned to the fact that we are really just a couple of fools, Don Quixotes, who would quickly fall prey to the police. Quite a few of those—in contrast to other people—have turned up. Five o'clock. There's nothing I can do. I would most happily turn around and run, but instead of that I unpack my slogans and reluctantly join the small group of familiar faces. What happens next takes but a few seconds. All at once a crowd forms behind the banners. Those people idly hanging around suddenly step forward, together. The seemingly indifferent couples . . . eagerly join, and the bored-looking families with children create a joyful, optimistic core of the procession, just like that. Before I have time to recover, these people—who a moment before looked as if they were doing nothing—begin to shout the slogans: "We won't give up Stromovka!" and "Let the trees live!"[61]

Thus several hundred people—most of them unfamiliar to the dissident community—gathered in a place where, if they were beaten or arrested, no one would even see. Some may have known that the proposed highway had official opponents, so that protesting it was safer than protesting nuclear power, for example. But the police did turn their dogs on the crowd, frightening the children. They did beat up Petr Placák and a few others, and loaded up the vans. And yet, four hundred showed up the next Wednesday, followed by smaller numbers throughout July. At the last demonstration, in early November on Marian Square in the city center, two or three thousand participated. The highway, incidentally, was never built.

Not surprisingly, the spring of 1989 also awakened the greens of Bratislava. They followed Orange Alternative in making International Children's Day a testing of limits. Ján Budaj and Mária Filková planned a march of children to the mayor's residence, where the children would present him a letter about their wishes for a healthier, happier Bratislava. About fifty marchers, mostly mothers and children (some in strollers), plus a few younger members of SZOPK, gathered. Budaj was arrested as he went to buy paper and markers; Filková (after quickly teaching her six-year-old daughter Katka that if "an officer in green stops us, and they want to take me away in a yellow car," to be sure to come too) managed to stay with the march. Under colorful balloons, and under the watchful gaze of police along the whole route, the children composed a letter asking for clean air, more playgrounds, and trees instead of smokestacks. It was just some children out for a walk, perhaps, but the police who arrested Budaj had not thought so. Once again Filková and the greens had exposed the oddities and weaknesses of the system. "The experience," reported Filková to SZOPK, "will make us stronger for next year."[62]

There was still to come, later that month, the Day of Joy. SZOPK had gotten official approval for this improbably named festival of live music and information about ecological and other movements—including a presentation by Without Barriers, a group that advocated rights for people with disabilities. Despite a steady downpour, hundreds showed up. They didn't get to hear Budaj or a representative of Without Barriers, since both were barred from speaking (and those in wheelchairs were not even allowed on stage). But again, despite police harassment, another public gathering, intended to encourage individual activism, had succeeded. What's more, the SZOPK journal devoted as much space to the police as to the festival itself; this was something no façade or vent would do.

Any illusions about where the Slovak greens really stood were stripped away, and their real purpose revealed: first, get people into the streets, whether to deliver a letter or take part in a festival. From this would come a consciousness about barriers and rights. As the popular actor Milan Kňažko explained, in an interview for SZOPK in which he discussed his reasons for signing the Charter 77 petition "A Few Sentences": "People are waking up slowly. I emphasize: slowly. . . . In their experience, initiative doesn't help, but can even hurt you. They are afraid." Now, people needed to be told "what they could do for their health and for the environment. This "light breeze" would awaken society.[63]

Though ecological demonstrations rarely attract more than a few thousand people—and even then they are often in out-of-the-way places—they lower the bar for political participation. Someone who might (justifiably) fear the consequences of demanding freedom of religion, or for political prisoners, might reasonably wonder what "they" can do to you if you are just protecting some trees (and be outraged enough to risk it any-way). The manageable size of the issue attracts new members, and new organizations, to green politics. In the months between Stromovka and the November revolution in Prague, both official and unofficial green groups expanded and grew bolder. "Every little action then had its own significance," observes Hradilková.[64] Someone who first chants a slogan on Stromovka might, a month later, join the cheering crowd on Václav Square. And in the provinces, or beyond the city center, where it might seem superfluous to copy the political demands of the big demonstrations, an ecological protest might be the pinnacle of opposition to the regime, and just as threatening.

𝔸𝔸𝔸𝔸𝔸𝔸 *Scene Eleven* 𝔸𝔸𝔸𝔸𝔸𝔸

ON THE FOURTH OF JUNE

BEIJING AND CENTRAL EUROPE, JUNE 1989

It is a wonder that the beginning of the end of communism in Europe even made the world's front pages. Solidarity's victory was throughly over-shadowed by the crackdown on prodemocracy demonstrations in Beijing. Since April, Chinese students had moved from Beijing University to Tiananmen Square, where they camped out under hand-lettered signs and a small replica of the Statue of Liberty. In the early morning hours of June 4, Chinese army troops launched an attack on the square. Some five hundred demonstrators were killed, and thousands were imprisoned.

This was the moment at which Central Europe and China went sepa-rate ways. But it was a close call. In East Berlin, new party leader Egon Krenz praised the crackdown as the appropriate response to unrest, as did Romania's Ceauşescu. Other leaders were more prudently silent, but their reticence spoke volumes about their wish to hold power at any cost.

Central European intellectuals reacted with horror. At least in Hungary and Poland (and, to a lesser extent, in Yugoslavia and the Soviet Union), democracy was so close. The sight of communist tanks, such as the ones they had seen crushing opposition in their own countries, was chilling. Leading Chinese oppositionists like Wang Dan had explicitly cited the in-spiration of Poland and Solidarity. Now in Warsaw, Budapest, and Prague there was a sense of responsibility for what had occurred in Beijing. Many Polish activists, as they look back on 1989, are more apt to recall the events in China than those on the same day in Poland. The fear that such a thing could have happened to them was very real. The coincidence of dates neatly illustrated the divergent path that Poland had taken and confirmed the choice of nonviolence that they had made. Those who called for confrontation were wrong. Flowers—the thousands of flowers thrown over the years—had filled in the chasm in Polish society.

For a moment, the language of the carnival returned. Robert Jezierski of Orange Alternative was among those horrified by the feeling of his movement's impotence in the face of state terrorism thousands of miles away, when even the Polish government was at first silent. With people from WiP, the recently concluded students' strike,* and the Inter–School Resistance Committee, he created a "Camp of Living Protest," an occupation of Wrocław's Dzierżyński Square. There were similar protests elsewhere, especially before the Chinese Embassy in Warsaw, but this was the only one that (briefly) featured a memorial, made from treads from a Soviet tank and a mangled bicycle picked up at the junkyard and set in concrete. Probably the first monument in the world built to the victims of Tiananmen, it lasted barely a day before being bulldozed.

The contrast between what could be and what still was moved people across Central Europe. In Prague, the day after Tiananmen, young people (mostly students) gathered to protest on Charles Bridge. There were candles, flowers, and prayers, but also posters reading "Today Peking, Tomorrow Prague." The protesters returned every day that week, even as the police confiscated the petitions they displayed and broke up their gatherings.[65] In Budapest as well as in Warsaw, a makeshift shrine appeared before the Chinese Embassy. Hundreds crowded around to light candles in solidarity with the slain students. On Vörösmarty Square, a Hungarian avant garde art collective constructed a Statue of Liberty out of styrofoam in homage to the one destroyed in Beijing. Then they poured chemicals over it to cause the statue to melt and give off a foul stench. Throughout 1989, Tiananmen remained a reminder of a road not (yet) taken.

But Central Europe, and the world, also had a positive story on June 4. The Polish election was in some ways almost anticlimactic. Solidarity had been allowed, in the Round Table agreement of April 9, to run candidates in 161 seats—35 percent of the total—in the lower house (the Sejm), and for all 100 seats in the new upper house, the Senate. This was easier said than done; preparing for the election was for Solidarity a herculean task. That the election was scheduled for less than two months away put the opposition in a bind, for as popular as Solidarity was, it had no national network, no campaign staff or funds. It did not even have the 261 candi-

---

* Students at most Polish universities had been protesting the authorities' reluctance to allow the Independent Students' Association to register as an official student organization.

dates it needed to contest every seat it could. The communists were clearly planning to place trusted nonparty (and thus ostensibly independent) candidates in races allotted to the opposition. Jerzy Urban, for example, announced he would run for a seat in Warsaw, against Jacek Kuroń.

Three days after the negotiations concluded, Wałęsa's Citizens' Committee, a group composed largely of the Solidarity elite, convened and urged Solidarity supporters in every province to form similar committees to propose candidates. The next two weeks were a frenzy: some regions had almost no one with credible opposition credentials who would stand a chance, so prominent cultural or political figures were loaned from Warsaw. In centers of protest like Wrocław and Kraków, the jockeying was fierce.

For a large part of the new opposition, defeating the communists had been in the end the main goal, whatever the stylistic or strategic differences between them and Solidarity. Many had in fact led double lives for years. Janusz Okrzesik, for example, was two different people: during the week, he was a journalism student at Jagiellonian University in Kraków and a participant in WiP; he joined sit-ins and scaffold-ings, demonstrated against Chernobyl, Stonava, and military service, and helped organize protests against military classes at the university. On weekends, vacations, and in the summer, he was underground in Bielsko-Biała, three hours away: a trusted member of the regional Solidarity leadership and an editor of the underground newspaper. Still others had been openly part of both worlds, like Jacek Czaputowicz in Warsaw, Radek Gawlik and Leszek Budrewicz in Wrocław, or Jan Maria Rokita in Kraków. Others had proved themselves to Solidarity during the strikes of 1988. For all of these, the chance for normal politics had erased the lines between the opposition generations.

The list of candidates eventually chosen included rather fewer workers and students than had been present at the Round Table. Now, intellectuals and professionals dominated. Among the candidates, though, were no fewer than six participants in Freedom and Peace, including Jan Maria Rokita in Kraków (where Grzegorz Surdy narrowly missed being chosen as well); Radek Gawlik in Wrocław (where Leszek Budrewicz and Jarosław Obremski of the Twelve were also considered); Marek Rusakiewicz of Gorzów and the Międzyrzecz protests; and Janusz Okrzesik in Bielsko-Biała (at 24, he was the youngest Solidarity candidate, twelve days younger than Rusakiewicz).* All had, again, strong Solidarity credentials; each of them (as did all the Solidarity candidates) proudly displayed campaign

* Others from movements discussed in this book include Edward Nowak and Mieczysław Gil in Kraków; Stanisław Bożek of Międzyrzecz; Władysław Liwak of the strike at Stalowa Wola; and Andrzej Piszel, leader of the movement of employee councils in Wrocław. Zbigniew Romaszewski was elected to the Senate.

posters that showed them shaking hands with Lech Wałęsa. They, and Solidarity candidates in all the major cities, could count on the support of hundreds of students, from WiP and other movements, who manned tables with campaign literature and collected signatures.

For the election campaign, Freedom and Peace had skills that Solidarity still needed. During the August 1988 strikes the informal information system of the last dozen years finally broke down in Warsaw: the authorities shut off Jacek Kuroń's phone. In the past, they had been reluctant to do so (in order to find out what the opposition knew). Out of this crisis came the idea for a Solidarity Information Service (SIS). Half of the core of SIS was from Freedom and Peace, including Piotr Niemczyk and, from Gorzów, Barbara Hrybacz. With their experience in using and printing underground media, and their strong contacts all across Poland, they were an obvious resource for the revival of Solidarity networks. And as Adam Michnik began to organize Solidarity's national daily, *Gazeta wyborcza*, in April 1989, he too relied in part on the networks of SIS and WiP. Correspondents from Gdańsk, Szczecin, Wrocław, Warsaw, and Gorzów had WiP connections.

One of the candidates running against Solidarity for a Senate seat in Wrocław was none other than Waldemar "Major" Fydrych. Throughout the campaign, he could be seen every day at Orange Alternative's traditional meeting place on Świdnicka Street, promoting his campaign. Legend has it that while Fydrych got few votes, he actually won a majority in one election precinct: that of the riot police barracks. They, more than anyone, appreciated Fydrych's fame.

For Robert Jezierski, June 1989 was the ruin of the Orange revolution. A year earlier, ten thousand Wrocławians had paraded through the streets, celebrating Children's Day. Now, as the election approached, these revelers had given up their initiative. All they had to do, they thought, was vote. Jezierski mocked them: "I take out my soul and put it in the ballot box . . . and I don't have to do or think anything. The senators will do it for me." He hoped to shake them out of this sudden apathy. So when people showed up for the traditional Children's Day happening, just three days before the vote, they found a decidedly unchildlike performance: Orange actors performed an ironic penitential rite, crawling on their knees and beating themselves on the shoulders with canes, while others sprinkled "holy water" on the crowd. This happening appeared to call on the people of Wrocław to atone for their passivity, comparing them to prostrate pilgrims putting power in others' hands. Jezierski wanted the happening to "expose the ignorance" of the crowd, but Orange Alternative no longer spoke a language that reached Polish society

Poland could, in retrospect, have gone in a different direction. If on Tiananmen Square one could see how a revolution could be destroyed, in Kraków Polish revolutionary desires turned briefly violent. The anti-Soviet confrontation that Budrewicz had avoided in Wrocław in March exploded in Kraków in May. On May 16 Marek Kurzyniec's Freedom and Peace Student Action staged the first of its anti-Soviet demonstrations in the main square, from which several hundred demonstrators marched to the Soviet Consulate, chanting "Soviets go home." The next day, demonstrators attempted to storm the building. By the third day, clashes with the police were taking place across the city. Demonstrators threw rocks and attacked police cars; police fired tear gas and used water cannons. Though he did not support the action, candidate Rokita came to speak to the crowd, which included some of his former colleagues in the movement. The choices movements had made for nonviolence and tolerance seemed much less certain as the revolution turned into a democratic political contest.

Ultimately, though, this spring marked Poland's victory. Solidarity won all but one of the seats it contested on June 4 (with a second round of voting on the June 18). This set up a maneuver by which a Solidarity government took power less than three months later. The political maneuvers and negotiations that made the election and the taking of power possible are the story of expertise and experience of another kind of opposition. We have already seen, however, how the negotiation was in part made possible by the tactics of the new opposition, and that opposition's internal pluralism.

🖈🖈🖈🖈🖈🖈 *Scene Twelve* 🏃🏃🏃🏃🏃🏃

HUNGARIANS BURY THE COMMUNISTS

BUDAPEST, MARCH–JUNE 1989

Two pictures of March 15, before the Parliament in Budapest: in one, from 1988, it is not easy to spot an older face, and there are no banners except those at the very front of the demonstration. In the second, from 1989, the same square is full again, but completely different. We see what looks like a cross-section of society, with middle-aged and even elderly faces as common as the younger demonstrators. Dozens of Hungarian flags and banners of all the opposition organizations flutter above the crowd.* Whether

---

* These pictures were shown to me by their author, independent photographer Ernő Horváth. This detail, however, would be difficult to capture reprinted in a book, so I have chosen not to include them.

the second crowd numbered seventy thousand, one hundred thousand, or more is not so important. Hungary was clearly a different place now, where all of society felt it could participate.

What was unthinkable in the fall—when the Fidesz Workers' Group had staged a happening to demand a March 15 holiday, and both Fidesz and the Alliance of Free Democrats (SzDSz) adopted this demand—was now achieved. Parliament had legalized the holiday in December, and everyone could celebrate without fear—and without skipping work.

To achieve the victory was one thing; to make use of it was less easy. The party, now led by Károly Grósz, naturally hoped to use the holiday to shore up its own support, and show that it was faithful to national traditions. And this regime had rather more room to maneuver than the Czechoslovak or Polish regimes, both of which were led by people implicated in the crushing of previous opposition. Nor had the people of Budapest engaged in much protest over previous decades.

That March 15, 1989, was such a giant success, opening up all of society to political engagement, was thanks in part to the impact of the Danube demonstration of the previous September. Over the winter, it became almost commonplace to see thousands of people on the streets. Besides the Danube demonstrations mentioned earlier, there was a student protest for academic freedom and better living standards in November, and a march of students and teachers to Parliament in December. And demonstrations tended to avoid confrontation with the police (with the exception of the demonstration of October 23, 1988). Instead, they became enjoyable and accessible—certainly more so than the ceremonies staged by the party.

The party and the Communist Youth Movement held their rally in front of the National Museum. There were speeches by various political leaders and some live entertainment, for a crowd of some ten thousand. But for the rest of Budapest, the real celebration was farther north on Freedom Square. There, the main attraction was popular actor György Cserhalmi. Accompanied by twelve children holding a banner reading "Free Hungarian television," he led a symbolic seizure of television headquarters (which had been a battleground in 1956). From the building's steps, he read a list of twelve demands, signed by nearly every opposition group in Hungary. The crowd listened to this call for civil and national rights—freedom of speech, independent media, withdrawal of Soviet troops, a rational economic system, respect for 1956—before marching into Kossuth Square, where János Kis of SzDSz and Viktor Orbán spoke. From Parliament, the crowd swarmed over Margit Bridge to the statue of Józef Bem. Polish flags, and the banner of Polish-Hungarian Solidarity (founded the previous month, in the tradition of Polish-Czechoslovak Solidarity) flew above the crowd. A torchlight parade back across the Danube on the Chain Bridge completed the circle.*

Demonstrations the previous year had carved out political positions against the regime, establishing new issues or signaling the power of new opposition groups. Now, they seemed more like a means of negotiation. Since the regime had conceded the March 15 holiday, it was now a matter of dialogue between two demonstrations, or two versions of Hungary. Thus too in Nagymaros in April: the communists had not yet conceded on the question of the dam, but the petition delivered to Parliament had thrown down the gauntlet. The regime thus faced a choice: recognize the petition or try to negotiate with the street, which was in any case no longer restricted just to Budapest.

By early April the party was talking openly about following the Polish precedent and engaging in round table discussions with the opposition. As in Poland, the communists hoped to divide the opposition and find reasonable negotiation partners. But the opposition forestalled this plan; it had already compensated for its lack of cohesion by forming an Opposition Round Table (ORT). Throughout the spring, the ORT negotiated as a body with the communist leadership over the terms of and the participants in any national discussion. Both sides, naturally, claimed the Polish Round Table as a model. And in the end, it was agreed that the National Round Table would address a similar mix of issues, including political reform, the media, and the economic crisis.

Before the National Round Table could even begin, however, it was upstaged by an event that has alone come to symbolize the Hungarian revolution of 1989. This was the ceremonial reburial of Imre Nagy and four of his comrades from 1956, executed together on June 16, 1958, and buried in an unmarked (but well-known) grave. The sequence of events was rather like that leading to the celebration of March 15. The reburial had been an opposition demand for some time; more generally, the restoration of respect for 1956 was something everyone insisted upon. Then the government announced its plans to organize such a reburial and began negotiating with groups of 1956 veterans. Both sides hoped for a respectful, dignified ceremony, to signify the regime's changed relationship with Hungarian society.

Somewhere along the way, it occurred to the veterans that the ceremony ought to include a representative of Hungary's youth. The call went out to Fidesz, which chose Viktor Orbán as its spokesperson. This was a chal-

---

* More than in any other city in Central Europe, Budapest demonstrators follow prescribed routes, in which national symbols (places of past conflict, or important statues, as well as the Danube itself) are visited in turn. The result is quite lengthy marches; this one would have been about 2.5 miles.

lenge nothing like the informal seminars and mass rallies at which Orbán had gained his fame. This national pageant, on national television, was suffused with a historical portent that dwarfed even the triumphant March procession. There would be solemn funeral music, black cloth wrapped around the columns of Heroes' Square, huge national flags (with the communist emblem in the center cut out, just as they had been in 1956), eternal flames, and six coffins: one each for Nagy and his colleagues, plus one symbolizing the "Unknown Insurgent." When Tamás Deutsch and Gábor Fodor stepped forward to present Fidesz's wreath, they looked utterly out of place (future of the nation or not) before the thousands of revolutionary veterans, seated in neat rows, who filled the square. Blond-haired Fodor was 26; Deutsch was just 22, with wild black hair falling over his eyes. Neither wore a tie, but both looked snappy in white shirts and dark suits.

As befit the occasion (and despite the modestly triumphant rhetoric of the first speeches), the crowd was "subdued," noticed British journalist Timothy Garton Ash.[66] What followed next, though, was the crowning performance in the Hungarian carnival. In a three-minute speech, Viktor Orbán proceeded to disrupt the entire ceremony. He gave notice that the generation he was chosen to represent, while full of respect for 1956 and its martyrs, had no interest in observing either convention or the apparent truce between opposition and regime.

He began in conventional terms, praising Nagy and the memory of 1956. Then he threw out an implicit challenge to the crowd:

> We young people fail to understand many things that are obvious to the older generations. We are puzzled that those who were so eager to slander the Revolution and Imre Nagy have suddenly become the greatest supporters of the former Prime Minister's policies. Nor do we understand why the party leaders who saw to it that we were taught from books that falsified the Revolution are now rushing to touch the coffins as if they were good-luck charms. We need not be grateful for their permission to bury our martyrs after thirty-one years; nor do we have to thank them for allowing our political organizations to function.[67]

The pageant was spoiled, but in a way that was crystal clear to the quarter-million assembled. This was a speech of the future, not of the past; the crowd snapped awake. Orbán urged his listeners to take matters into their own hands: "If we trust our souls and our strength, we can put an end to the communist dictatorship; if we are determined enough, we can force the party to submit to free elections; and if we do not lose sight of the ideals of 1956, then we will be able to elect a government that will immediately begin negotiations on the swift withdrawal of Russian troops." For the first and only time that day, the crowd erupted in wild applause.

From one perspective, Orbán's speech was nothing remarkable. After all, the fact that he was allowed to speak was evidence that the rules had already changed a great deal. Orbán was not risking a jail term. As it turned out, what he said was permissible, even if a little impertinent. So Orbán was simply revealing the spirit of the times. And a speech whose most stirring demand was for "negotiations" could not be very revolutionary.

But it was the work of this carnival to show what was possible: to uncover potential, not only to create it. No decree, or newspaper article, or negotiated agreement could make Orbán's point as starkly as could the performer who stepped onto the stage to perform seemingly impossible feats. This was, indeed, both the climactic moment and the conclusion of Hungary's revolution.

Scene Thirteen

KORZOS AND ROAD RACES

CZECHOSLOVAKIA, MAY–AUGUST 1989

"Who controls the horse, controls the square," say veterans of Prague demonstrations. From the base of the statue of St. Václav (and his horse), one can command the square, which drops out below it for about half a mile. Situated on an incline, Václav Square gives the observer or participant an immediate sense of the size of a crowd, and it is the obvious place to come if one hopes to see some action on a contentious anniversary.

If the regime could not confine opposition to Charter 77, it could still hope to confine the newly active public to the square. Important as this spot was, it was just a speck on the Czech map. Then, in the spring and summer of 1989, the virus of Czech opposition found ever new niches, and new hosts in other environments.

The first salvo in the battle for Prague was fired by the communists. Perestroika or no, May 1 remained the holiest day on the official calendar. Parades through every city would express the resolutely proletarian character of communist Czechoslovakia. In Prague the parade was staged as usual on the square: thousands of groups from factories and schools marched by the podium before the National Museum with red flags and proud socialist banners. Most in the opposition wanted nothing to do with this regime ritual, but this was an occasion tailor-made for the Orange Alternative tradition, and thus the Czech Children and the Lennonists were out in force. As the band began to play the national anthem, Charter 77's Devátý unfurled a banner in the midst of the crowd. As the police swarmed to him, other banners appeared, most with names of political prisoners on them. One marcher tore off his windbreaker before the reviewing stand to reveal a T-shirt with the slogan "Free the Political Prisoners." The crowd was full of ancient party veterans, aghast at the treasonous shouts of "Freedom!" To the sound of recorded applause, the police shoved demonstrators and passersby into police vans and ripped up placards—even one with Gorbachev's portrait.[68]

Meanwhile, just a few streets away, the Society for a Merrier Present announced its existence with a foot race down Political Prisoners' Street.* The society—one of whose leaders was Petr Payne of NMS—combined surreal, Orange-style entertainment with straightforward politics. The flyer advertising the race listed fourteen prisoners to whom the runners wanted to call attention and added, with apparent indifference to the inevitable punishment: "Today we race for you. Tomorrow you race for us."[69] The races continued throughout the spring, with over one thousand people eventually participating.

All during the spring, small demonstrations explored the territory beyond Václav Square. In April a few dozen members of NMS paraded through the Old Town with a banner proclaiming "International Day of Solidarity with Freed Political Prisoners and Antifascist Fighters.[†] In Plzeň (which had been liberated by the U.S. Army in 1945 before being ceded to Soviet control), several hundred gathered to honor fallen American soldiers on the anniversary of liberation, May 6; one even waved an American flag.

International Conscientious Objectors' Day, May 15, was a natural occasion for NMS demonstrations. In Prague they gathered on Letenské Park (near the former site of Stalin's statue); in Brno, five women carrying an NMS banner marched down Czech Street with their children, who carried paper doves and blew on whistles. Children participated again two weeks later, when NMS circles in Brno, Liberec, and Prague organized fairs to celebrate Children's Day. They drew chalk pictures on the sidewalk, watched puppet shows, played tug-of-war, or—on Children's Island in Prague—watched a soccer tournament in which NMS took on teams from Czech Children, *Revolver revue,* the John Lennon Peace Club, and the Society for a Merrier Present (which had to sneak onto the island by dinghy). This was utterly unpolitical, to be sure, yet the NMS name and logo was everywhere—as were, in Prague, plainclothes police with videocameras.[70]

At the Polish border the summer brought renewed pilgrimages to the mountaintops, to meet the soon to be victorious Polish opposition. NMS

---

* There really was, and is, such a street, named to honor victims of fascism, of course, not of communism.

† They were stopped, and arrested, before a crowd of German tourists.

and WiP gathered in May; Petr Placák, along with Luboš Rychvalský of the Society for a Merrier Present, joined NMS for a trek in June, bringing along orange vodka to toast Major Fydrych and Orange Alternative. Unfortunately, it was the day before the second round of elections in Poland, and there was no one to meet them. Still, from their perch on the Path of International Friendship they could mock the control the regime still hoped to maintain.

In none of these cases were arrests made, though the police were always evident. None of these happenings shook the republic, to be sure. Cumulatively, though, they created a reality that had not existed a year earlier. The opposition had grown inventive and unpredictable. If before August 1988 it protested on paper and then began mostly to observe anniversaries, now a protest or a happening could occur any time, any place.

Whether opposition participants recognized it or not, there was a certain tension building between the anniversary mass demonstrations of the fall and winter and the diffuse, pluralist actions of the spring. The contrast was starkly evident in August, as the twenty-first anniversary of the invasion (and the first of the inaugural demonstration in 1988) approached.

First, Democratic Initiative applied for permission to hold a human rights rally, in July. Rebuffed, this group and several others* decided to meet anyway and announced a *korzo*, a silent march without banners or leaflets up and down the pedestrian zone at the foot of Václav Square. Some two thousand turned out on July 19; beginning August 1 there was a *korzo* every day in the same place.

A throng of silent marchers was an effective protest, to be sure; it was also hard for the average passerby to read, and certainly it was not entertaining. Something of the momentum of the spring threatened to be lost. The Society for a Merrier Present came to the rescue. On one day in August, they staged their own silent march, entitled "A Fruitless Action": up and down the Charles Bridge they paraded, wearing helmets fashioned from watermelons and holding aloft blank banners. While the banners surely mocked the empty phrases of the regime, they also gently poked fun at the idea that such a march could be a protest. And for their transgression in straying onto the very nerve center of tourist Prague (and the link between the Old Town and the Prague castle, the presidential residence), the marchers were all arrested.

Later that month, in fact on the eve of the invasion anniversary, the Society broke one more barrier, launching a big blue whale down the Vltava River. Flyers informed onlookers that the whale was a "Trojan Horse," and thus the police were justified in going to ridiculous lengths to catch

---

* One of these was NMS, which at this point and in August found itself torn between the two strategies described here.

the floating construction.* Now even the river that divides the city had been breached.

The fierce debate that erupted in the Czech opposition over whether to demonstrate on August 21, 1989, seems almost pathetic now, long after an absurdly easy revolution. Since both Poland and Hungary, now past their revolutions, had already apologized for the invasion, it wouldn't have done to keep silent, but many feared an aggressive counterattack from the regime. A statement signed by Charter 77, NMS, Czech Children, and others announced that they would only stroll, individually, through the center of Prague and other cities. There was no mention even of the tricolor flag. They "would not take advantage of their right to public gathering, and at 5:00 P.M. each [of us] will stand in place and observe a two-minute silent protest."[71]

This was a protest from a bygone era. The intention was to show that society was capable of restraint (as if previous demonstrations were perhaps unseemly), and thus encourage a dialogue like those at the Polish and Hungarian round tables. But society had radicalized since January, thanks to those same demonstrations. There may have been some who followed these instructions for a silent, individual protest; if so, they were lost among the ten thousand or so who crowded the pedestrian zone that day.

The highlight of the demonstration (besides the usual scuffles with police) was the arrival of fifty young Hungarians, mostly from Fidesz. Petr Placák commented: "Not so long ago the word 'Magyar' was a term of abuse!" Now Tamás Deutsch and György Kerenyi unfurled a banner reading: "We have come with flowers, not tanks." Kerenyi then addressed the crowd, in Czech: "Our future must be shared. Thus we must join our forces and drive away fear, so that the living torch of Jan Palach shall never be repeated."[72] The crowd cheered: "Long live the Hungarians!"

Deutsch and Kerenyi were arrested and thrown into prison, where Kerenyi charmed his cellmate, Charter veteran Ladislav Lis. Back home, they became celebrities. During the nine days they were in prison in Czechoslovakia, their friends in Fidesz organized a hunger strike on the street before the Czechoslovak Embassy. Rather than driving them away, Hungarian police kept benevolent watch over this protest, which received enthusiastic television coverage. Upon their release and triumphant return home from Prague, Deutsch and Kerenyi received a heroes' welcome. This Hungarian national drama, in which even the (communist) prime minister lent his support, reminded everyone just how isolated Czechoslovakia was becoming.

---

* Onlookers were probably reminded of Karel Čapek's famous 1937 novel *The War of the Newts,* in which a race of salamanders conquers the world. The land-locked Czechs assume they are safe from invasion—until a giant newt is spotted surfacing in the Vltava.

Looking at the missed opportunity of rebellion in Prague that August, one is reminded, perhaps unfairly, of the Bolsheviks in July 1917: having helped to radicalize the workers of Petrograd, Lenin and his followers held back despite popular pressure for decisive action. In both cases, of course, the revolution took place anyway. But for the forlorn Czechoslovak regime in the summer of 1989—under growing pressure from Poland and Hungary, already bereft of hope for succor from Moscow, and with pesky demonstrators popping up everywhere (whether the opposition planned them or not)—the moment seemed to have arrived. Had events taken a slightly different turn that day, the revolution might have begun in earnest then, three months earlier. Perhaps, though, it would not have been a velvet one.

Scene Fourteen

LVIV PASSES THE BATON

UKRAINE, JANUARY–OCTOBER 1989

The Christmas *vertepy* in Lviv were such a success that in January 1989 the Ukrainian community of Vilnius invited one of the processions to come perform in Lithuania. There, the students from Lviv saw a level of freedom they had not glimpsed before: national flags (Lithuanian, not Soviet) everywhere, and a sense of fearlessness fostered by Sajudis, the Lithuanian national movement founded the previous summer. The carnival in Vilnius was in full swing, and the Christmas revelers from the Lion Society joined in, waving the blue and gold Ukrainian flag, for which one could still be arrested back home.

In retrospect, the contacts between the Baltic and Ukrainian social movements—Olisevych's trip to Riga in 1987, the attempted participation of Baltic activists at the Lion Society meeting in October, and the *vertepy* in Vilnius—were emblematic of the loss of control by Soviet leaders, beginning with the country's internal borders. And Ukraine, the most populous of the non-Russian republics and once a reliable anchor of Soviet power, rapidly became one of the empire's weakest links. Lviv was one of the cities where the revolution in the Soviet Union began.

The Sajudis contacts that the Lion Society made soon came in handy, as the Ukrainians prepared to publish their own samizdat gazette, *Postup* (Progress). The editors brought prepared layouts to Vilnius, where the more experienced Lithuanian printers helped them turn out several hundred copies. The first issue appeared in Lviv in late March, in time for the Lion Society to join the election campaign for the USSR's Congress of People's Deputies.

This election was a cornerstone of Gorbachev's program of democratization and proved a stunning reversal for the communist nomenklatura. For the first time, there were some multicandidate races (modeled in part on the Hungarian elections a few years earlier), and secret ballots. Gorbachev hoped to increase public trust in the political system, and thus gain more support for perestroika. Instead, the impetus for change now burst through the relatively narrow channels that had contained it so far. Gorbachev and the communist reformers began to lose control of their revolution from above.

The Lion Society's candidate was Rostyslav Bratun, the 62-year-old poet who had from the beginning been one of the society's strongest supporters and elder statesmen. Like Iryna Kalynets, Bratun exemplified the society's idea of tolerance and national diversity: he was himself Orthodox, but he actively supported the revival of Uniate Catholicism. He had close ties to Lviv's Polish and Jewish communities, too. Even getting Bratun on the ballot, however, was daunting. The system was rigged so that the party still had great control over the nomination process; this was especially true in Lviv, far from the reformist strongholds like Moscow.

Back in January at the Kineskop factory, Orest Sheiko and Ihor Hryniw, along with Ihor Melnyk of the Shevchenko Society, interrupted a ritual election meeting to propose Bratun as a candidate. They were unsuccessful. The official media now confronted his supporters with materials purporting to show that Bratun had cooperated with the fascists during the war (though Bratun had been just 14). These attempts backfired: in the first round of voting, many officially backed candidates, though running unopposed, failed to win enough votes to gain seats. Massive support from several nomination meetings (held, as traditional in the proletarian state, at workplaces), and a signature drive by the Lion Society, finally forced the authorities to accept Bratun as a candidate in the second round of voting.

Postup's first issue trumpeted Bratun's program, which called for "economic independence and political sovereignty" and the preservation of individual rights, the standard of living, and the environment. Bratun, wrote the editors, "has become a symbol of the awakening of the people of Lviv to independent participation in civic and political life."[73]

Through the spring and into the second round of voting in May, Lion Society members were everywhere in Lviv, rallying support for Bratun and other independent candidates. Alik Olisevych and Doviria were there, too. The Ukrainian Helsinki Union, meanwhile, called for an election boycott, arguing that the results were known in advance. They were not, of course; Bratun (and many other independent candidates across Ukraine and the USSR) won a seat in the Congress. In the months to come, Bratun would be one of the more vocal proponents of sovereignty for Ukraine. The Congress of People's Deputies, while never an effective legislative body, became a focal point for glasnost, as the independent deputies, though outnumbered still by party appointees, used their parliamentary immunity to raise previously taboo issues, often on live television.

That story takes us far from Lviv, where the impetus for change, in Ukraine at least, had begun. The next few months were euphoric ones for the Lion Society. A few weeks after Bratun's election, the society (and several other independent groups) staged a demonstration in front of City Hall marking the third anniversary of the Chernobyl disaster. There, for the first time in nearly fifty years, the banned blue and yellow Ukrainian flag appeared, hoisted by Lion Society member Yuriy Voloshchak during a speech by the mayor. The mayor showed no reaction to a symbol his party had often denounced as reactionary, even fascistic. Soon—at the May 1 parade that same week, and at the Lion Society's festive *haivka* later in May—the flag was everywhere in Lviv, and eventually across Ukraine.

The second Dnister expedition set off a month later, in the same spirit. As before, the expedition began by walking along the upper reaches of the river, followed by a solemn ceremony as the boats were launched lower down. But if the previous year riverbank residents were suspicious of a flotilla of students and scientists, 1989 brought a new awareness and openness. Whole villages now came out to greet the expedition. People wept when they saw the blue and yellow flags on the catamarans; some yelled, "Lend us your flag!"[74] This time also, the rafters were ready to discuss politics, history, and religion as well as the environment.

Local authorities hesitated to respond; what had been an officially sponsored expedition the year before was now being advertised on Radio Free Europe. Their initial confusion gave way to anger, especially because of the flags. But if the police on one side of the river confiscated the flags—as they did in Zaleshchyky—the expedition needed only send to Lviv for more flags and keep to the other side of the river, where the police seemed not to care. By now, Soviet television was bringing radical parliamentary speeches into even the remotest hamlets. Bratun and other nationalists were prevented from addressing the Congress. But the Dnister expedition brought similar ideas, wrapped in a national and environmental package, to broad areas of rural Ukraine that had been beyond the reach of Gorbachev's revolution.

Even as the society gained its widest renown, the torch of revolution was passing to groups more focused on a nationalist agenda. For two full years, from the first expedition to the Lychakiv cemetery to the end of the second Dnister expedition, Lviv had reveled in the Central European carnival—or, as Yuriy Vinnychuk called it, the "cabaret." But events were building toward a climax on another stage entirely. Though it would be another two years yet before the Soviet Union broke up, the emphasis now shifted to the formation of national fronts, to weighty congresses of nationalist intellectuals, and to emerging political parties. The impetus for the formation of the Popular Movement of Ukraine for Perestroika, or Rukh, came over the winter of 1988–89, an outgrowth of the demonstrations in Lviv the previous summer (as well as, again, the model provided by Sajudis). Though many of the drafters of Rukh's charter were from Lviv—including Chornovil and Horyn of the Ukrainian Helsinki Union—the natural focus of such a movement would be the capital, Kyiv.

Kyiv began to wake up. The blue and yellow flag flew there for the first time on May 22, at a postelection rally. Rukh's inaugural congress took place in Kyiv in September. Here, the debt to Poland was repaid. Visiting Poland that summer, for a festival of Ukrainian Culture in Sopot, Bohdan Horyn had given a speech linking the fates of independent Poland and an independent Ukraine. Now Adam Michnik, Bogdan Borusewicz, and the Polish-Ukrainian activist Włodzimierz Mokry—all Solidarity members of Parliament—came to congratulate Rukh. Michnik got a standing ovation for his cry, "Long live a democratic, just, free Ukraine."[75]

As they had before, Lion Society activists looked on uncomfortably at this political transformation. A more radical Rukh, they believed, might actually forfeit its chance to radicalize society. Writing in *Postup,* R. Matsyuk worried that Rukh was isolating itself from society. The movement's charter praised recent actions of the Communist Party and referred "obsessively" to perestroika. But perestroika was not the creation of one person, Matsyuk wrote: "Each one of us has paid a high price for it" in wasted lives and in suffering. He saw Rukh attempting to play the same role as the Communist Party, supplanting popular initiative and becoming just a "puppet" in the party's hands.[76] In the next issue, *Postup*'s editors warned that the Congress revealed a movement abandoning social and economic questions in favor of the simple slogan of sovereignty—a slogan that communist leader Leonyd Kravchuk, who would later become Ukraine's first president, had already deftly snatched up. Markiian Ivashchyshyn of the Student Brotherhood summed up the Lviv perspective: "We all know that we need a sovereign Ukraine, [but] we must fight for democracy."[77] Or as each issue of *Postup* proclaimed from above the title in the words of the poet Ivan Franko: "More sweat, less blood!"

The march toward an independent Ukraine reminds one of parallel events in Yugoslavia. There, too, the movements that had stirred public activism now expressed misgivings as the ideas and goals of the movements were overwhelmed by the prerogatives of national sovereignty. Marko Hren had dreamed of making Slovenia a demilitarized zone, without any military or weapons. But in the context of Serb aggression, which culminated in the seven-day war following Slovenia's declaration of independence in June 1991, few Slovenes felt confident enough to follow this path. Tomaž Mastnak watched with dismay as the victorious Demos coalition, made up of parties and individuals who had not been much in evidence before 1988, arrogated to itself the mantle of anticommunism and backed it up with the only program it could offer: nationalism.[78] This was a language of certainty, comforting for a people who feared losing everything. It promised a Central Europe that was not the same as the one of which the movement activists had dreamed.

Meanwhile, Lviv, where the public appetite for political expression had long been whetted, remained an incubator of Ukrainian national politics. August 1989 saw demonstrations across Ukraine to mark the fiftieth anniversary of the Molotov-Ribbentrop Pact (which had reunified Ukraine, as Poland lost land to the Soviet Union, but had, tragically, thus brought communist rule to Western Ukraine). Three weeks later, on September 17 (the date of the Soviet invasion of what was then Eastern Poland, in 1939), 150,000—the largest crowd ever in Lviv—gathered to demand relegalization of the Uniate Church. City authorities were powerless as the massive crowd paraded through the city streets and then convened for an open-air mass, holding candles in mourning for the victims of Soviet occupation.

To the regime, Lviv was still the place where "the nationalists have stupefied the population, and Lviv propagates the nationalist virus all over Ukraine," as Taras Stetskiw observed sarcastically.[79] And thus the regime struck back, on October 1. This was Lviv Day; all the unofficial groups staged events. The Lion Society held a concert in front of City Hall, while another group marched in the streets wearing historic soldiers' uniforms. "All these festivities, celebrations, and carnivalesque parades through the city's Old Town," wrote one observer, "made the holiday especially attractive."[80] But in the evening the police attacked, forcing crowds of revelers into darkened alleys where they were beaten mercilessly.

In response to this "pogrom,"[81] the more radical groups in Lviv, such as the Ukrainian Helsinki Union, organized a strike committee. Over the next few months the committee called several protests, including a one-day general strike on October 27. *Postup* again warned against radical, hasty steps: if the police had hoped to provoke violence to show that Lviv was dangerous, now they would have proof. Would the result thus be "more blood"?

The Lion Society offered instead more sweat. That same week "Chervona Ruta,"* a festival of "Ukerock," kicked off in the town of Chernivtsy, about 130 miles southeast of Lviv. The idea had come up during the Lion Society's first ever television interview earlier that year. Bands from all over Ukraine, Central Europe, and the Ukrainian diaspora played to an enthusiastic crowd. With this concert, the Lion Society returned to its roots, advancing Ukrainian culture and language not through protest and resistance, but through patience and entertainment.

Lviv's carnival had come to an end. If it did not achieve its own victory, as in other countries, it had run its leg of the race well. A symbolic end to Lviv's dominance came in January 1990, when Rukh—along with the Shevchenko Society, which provided thousands of flags and ribbons in blue and yellow—organized a human chain to celebrate the unification of a (briefly) independent Ukraine in 1919. Some three-quarters of a million people reached from Kyiv to Lviv and beyond through Galicia. If the chain delineated the central artery of Ukrainian nationalism, the source of its power was now at the Kyiv end, where the struggle would continue in parliaments and diplomatic negotiations.

Scene Fifteen

THE MOSQUITO AND THE *MESSEDEMOS*

EAST GERMANY, JANUARY–NOVEMBER 1989

After the expulsions of IFM activists in January 1988, the initiative in East Germany (and the informal center of the opposition) passed to Leipzig. Here, as Wolfgang Templin put it, there were "normal people"—*konkretny* activists who did not overintellectualize dissent. Ludwig Mehlhorn, in turn, pointed to the harsher conditions in the provincial city, coupled with a tradition of student protest (most recently in 1968).[82] Indeed, Leipzig's relationship to Berlin is not unlike that of Wrocław to Warsaw, or Brno to Prague, or even Ljubljana to Belgrade. There were things possible in a large provincial university town, actions difficult to imagine in the capital.

By the end of 1988, Leipzig had given birth to an infant network of opposition groups—most of them not quite movements yet, and hard sometimes to tell apart. In addition to the Working Group for Justice (AKG), there was a Working Group of the Solidarity Church, a Working Group

---

* From the title of a famous song by the young Lviv composer Volodymyr Ivasiuk, who was killed in mysterious circumstances (suggesting KGB execution) in 1979.

for Human Rights, a Working Group for Peace Service, and the Initiative Group for Life, which promoted environmental causes. The names themselves betray a certain caution, or perhaps distance from the usual terms of opposition. In action, though, the groups' persistence began to have effect. One local samizdat publication portrayed Leipzig in 1988 as "The Mosquito," buzzing in the ear of the regime.

Throughout 1988 Leipzig activists staged one demonstration after another. By Thomas Rudolph's count, there were no less than thirty-five from September 1987 to September 1989, with anywhere from 35 to 1,500 participants. There was no question of joining an official rally; they struck out on their own, over and over, trying to change the culture of Leipzig's streets.

The demonstration of January 15, 1989, was a real breakthrough. Based on the contacts Rudolph and Rainer Müller had made in Czechoslovakia, it was timed to coincide with the beginning of the *Palachiada* in Prague, and with the meeting of the Conference for Security and Cooperation in Europe opening in Vienna. As many as eight hundred Leipzigers marched through the old town, demanding civil rights; fifty-three were detained. To Rudolph's surprise and pride, all the East German protesters were let out in just six days, while some of the Czechs faced stiff prison terms. Templin, too, noticed the contrast with his fate after the Luxemburg demonstration a year earlier. Leipzig's persistence had forced a subtle change in the way the regime treated opposition.

The young activists of Leipzig espoused the internal pluralism often lacking in Berlin. They did not shy away from the would-be émigrés, as did so many others—especially those who were socialists. Unlike the intellectuals of Berlin, with whom Templin and a few others in the IFM had had to argue to get any recognition for emigration groups, the Leipzig attitude was tolerant: "Of course we had would-be emigrants in our group," recalled an activist in the Initiative Group for Life. "We did not think much about it. This was a human right, so what the heck . . . I myself might have left for the West, if all my friends would have left with me."[83]

In return, Thomas Rudolph and the others in Leipzig opposition expected that would-be émigrés support the broader cause of human rights. The emigration activists supplied a broad base of people with nothing to lose, while the AKG and the others supplied the concrete ideas and networks that made Leipzig the center of attention. Leipzigers thus brought into collaboration two usually antithetical kinds of protest strategies: one that looked to change the system, and another that did not care what the system looked like as long as one could escape it. They had a common denominator, though, for the right to leave (or to travel) was, after all, a human right, too.

Emigration activists, in the terms of this book, are supremely pragmatist and *konkretny*, even though their goals were so personal. Any means to achieve their aims, regardless of content, was appropriate. Many joined whatever protest they calculated would get them expelled most quickly. In Leipzig, they turned to the church, specifically the peace seminars held every Monday in St. Nicholas Church. And when the church administrator banned their evidently utilitarian participation in the fall of 1988, they simply gathered outside. The younger opposition continued to support them, though, and the space before the church became a public forum for both kinds of opposition. February 1989 saw the first *Messedemo*: the Monday peace prayers gave way to a march through the city center. By March these were substantial demonstrations of several hundred, taking place weekly. As Petr Placák had noted in Prague, demonstrations that became ritual were also more accessible and safer.

Confrontation with the regime escalated with every month through 1989. In March emigration activists in the *Messedemo* disrupted the Leipzig trade fair, chanting "We Want Out!" when the police moved in— the first time a silent protest turned vocal. In April the AKG sponsored an alternative forum on education, entitled "A School in Motion." Participants discussed the dangers of Marxist-Leninist indoctrination. In May opposition across East Germany monitored local elections. The regime claimed near-total approval, as usual, but it was easy to prove the results were falsified, and the opposition denounced the regime with renewed vigor. Leipzig saw a rally of fifteen hundred in front of City Hall.

Besides the *Messedemos*, Leipzig opposition found other ways to welcome people on the streets. Jochen Lässig, a 27-year-old theology student, tried musical protest. When he and Silke Krasulsky of AKG paraded in the street in March, they were quickly arrested and fined. So in May Lässig formally requested from city officials permission for a "Street Music Festival." "The spontaneous making of music without amplifiers can have a pleasant effect on the streets and squares of a city such as Leipzig," he wrote. "To demonstrate this, some groups of street musicians will gather on June 10 in a small music festival." He already had at least twenty groups ready to sing, dance, or perform skits at various points throughout the downtown. This would be a democratic festival: no one would be excluded because of ability or the type of music he or she wished to play.[84]

Not surprisingly, City Hall rejected this proposal to enact a Central European carnival in Leipzig. But Lässig went ahead anyway. Coming six days after the Tiananmen massacre, the festival, which attracted around a thousand onlookers and participants (and surely thousands more who heard the music and kept their distance), became an observance of that event, as well as of the anniversary of the East German uprising of June

17, 1953. While eighty-four participants were arrested, the music had been unleashed onto Leipzig streets; Lässig and the AKG had made the point that one could make public statements that appeared apolitical. Also in June, the Initiative Group for Life staged its second Pleisse Pilgrimage, as some five hundred marched to call attention to the polluted state of a Leipzig river.

With every protest, march, and festival, the population of Leipzig became more and more familiar with this very un–East German style of protest. Rudolph and the AKG were following a dictum of their counterparts in the rest of Central Europe: most important was to be out on the street, whatever the ostensible purpose of the protest. Only repeated public action would both wear down the indifference of the public and routinize the repression, until finally something would break. Then Leipzig would really come alive.

The break came, unexpectedly, in Hungary. The first waves of refugees from East Germany appeared in Budapest in June. At first they were summer vacationers, mostly young professionals with their families; Hungary (especially Lake Balaton) had always been a favorite destination. As Budapest (still in the hands of the Hungarian Socialist Workers' Party) began to dismantle the Cold War's landmines and electric fences at the Austrian border, these families decided to try their luck as refugees rather than return home to a country that offered less and less hope. This was an uncomfortable situation for the Hungarian regime, though, for good relations with Erich Honecker still mattered. When the regime proposed expelling German refugees, the SzDSz announced a campaign laden with irony: "Hide a German!" Would the communists dare follow the path the Nazi occupiers of Europe had once taken and search homes for refugees? In consternation, the authorities rescinded the extradition policy, and the flood of Germans began in earnest.

By mid-August there were some three thousand in Budapest, and many more waiting near the border. Still, the communists hoped that a symbolic border opening could suffice. In the city of Sopron, on the Austrian border, local members of the Hungarian Democratic Forum (with the help of local Fidesz and SzDSz activists, in the spirit of the Opposition Round Table) planned a "Pan-European Picnic" for August 19: they would celebrate Hungary's "return to Europe" with a symbolic opening of a long-disused border crossing and a brief visit across the border. Otto von Habsburg, heir to the throne of the Austro-Hungarian Empire, and Imre Pozsgay, a reform-minded communist then still touted as the leading candidate for president, were invited as patrons of the celebration.

It was shortly after three in the afternoon, and the official press conference was running late. Pozsgay had sent his secretary, and Otto Habsburg, his daughter. The most prominent figure there was the dissident writer György Konrád. Outside, the festive crowd, reaching perhaps twenty thousand, awaited the ceremonial opening of the gate. Suddenly, several hundred East Germans charged the border, heading for Austria. The Austrian officials were prepared, having been tipped off by Hungarians working with the refugees; a fleet of buses waited to take them to Vienna. Almost inadvertently, the Iron Curtain melted away. Three weeks later, Hungary lifted all restrictions on traveling West; the last of the barbed wire between Hungary and Austria disappeared.

Eventually, over twenty thousand East Germans would simply walk across that border as if the Iron Curtain had never existed. In response, the communist leaders in East Berlin imposed restrictions on travel to Hungary, which was, after all, a Warsaw Pact ally. Perhaps most East Germans had at one time at least contemplated emigration. Now it was both more imaginable and more cruelly denied than ever before. Mass discontent spread across East Germany. The regime's cynical treatment of these refugees angered those who wanted to follow them out.

The dynamics of opposition in Leipzig changed abruptly. At the beginning of September, the AKG's carefully constructed alliance seemed to be falling apart, no doubt to the joy of the security police. A Monday demonstration on September 4—after the peace prayers, which resumed following a summer break—turned into two rival demonstrations, with rival messages: "We Want Out!" versus "We're Staying!"

Perhaps at this point Leipzig could have gone the way of Berlin, where the intellectual opposition was still becoming more isolated from society. When, in the following week, Hungary completely opened its Austrian border, the emigration groups disappeared as a political ally. Instead of demonstrating for freedom to leave, they packed up and headed for Hungary; when that was impossible, they chose Czechoslovakia.

But the Leipzig opposition did not fall apart. To those who wanted to stay and change their country, the news of the border opening was a catalyst. It removed the huge distraction that was the emigration issue and suddenly made the GDR seem worth fighting for. The new repression thus provoked opposition to grow stronger, even as it remained divided. The September 25 Monday protest was the first large demonstration, in which some five thousand marched through the city. In place of demands for open borders came demands for change.

Meanwhile, the opposition in Berlin reorganized. Bärbel Bohley had returned from Britain as soon as she was let in. In mid-September she brought together some thirty prominent dissidents for a weekend-long meeting that led to the creation of New Forum, which became the most vocal proponent of political change. Ludwig Mehlhorn founded Democracy Now—slightly more insistent in its demands, as the name indicates—days later, followed by Rainer Eppelmann's Democratic Awakening. Each of these opened up political participation in ways that had been absent before. At the grass roots, the initiative was still in the hands of Leipzig.

The following week, October 2, the Monday crowd was three to five times larger. "The people of Leipzig were," writes Christian Joppke, "on the brink of reclaiming their city."[85] Both police and citizens expected that the next Monday, October 9, would result in a confrontation, perhaps violent. The police planned to use force, to open fire if necessary. Things had happened too quickly for a softening of police attitudes, as had occurred in Poland. Behind-the-scenes appeals from prominent figures (like the conductor Kurt Masur) and from the Soviet Embassy convinced some party leaders to change tactics. Remarkably, though an estimated seventy thousand Leipzigers flooded the streets, the police held their fire, and Leipzig avoided a massacre. "Erich," a senior party leader, explained to an irate Honecker at a Politburo meeting the next morning, "we can't beat up hundreds of thousands of people."[86]

This was the turning point of the East German revolution. The slogan of the revolution, "We Are the People," was heard and seen for the first time that day. That same week, Gorbachev visited Berlin to celebrate the fiftieth anniversary of the creation of the German Democratic Republic. Wherever he went, thousands of Berliners demonstrated for "Gorbi's" support. They sensed, perhaps, that the Soviet leader's presence gave them immunity from repression, making the streets safe and free. And indeed, as soon as Gorbachev was gone the riot police moved in. But that weekend, East Germans saw for the first time that they too might achieve what their neighbors in Central Europe had. The decision not to use force in Leipzig on October 9 was followed by increasingly conciliatory signals from the Politburo, and a wave of energy from below. The crowd in Leipzig on October 16 was double the previous week, and it doubled again the following week. Honecker was forced to resign, and a desperate leadership reshuffling began.

Before September only a small group of dissidents were as willing as the emigration groups to risk everything. Now, they had been joined by "the people." Traditions of street protest were so much fainter than elsewhere in Central Europe. Most East Germans had no experience on the streets, except in the ubiquitous official marches on May Day and various communist anniversaries. But in Leipzig, at least, there was a small group that regularly ventured out into public. The Church of St. Nicholas had become a recognizable landmark of free protest. When the occasion arose, Leipzigers would know that they would not be alone in public. They had someone to join and somewhere to go, and thus the protests in Leipzig grew.

East Germany, however, would not be reformed or changed. The fate of the revolution was not decided on the streets. The abrupt decision to open the Berlin Wall on November 9—in the wake of a half-million-strong demonstration in East Berlin on November 4—was, we now know, almost an accident. Gorbachev had told the new East German leaders he had nothing against new travel regulations. No one, the opposition least of all, expected the wall to be opened. A regime desperately trying to keep ahead of the crowds decided to open the border in some limited way. When a government spokesman misread the bulletin announcing this, and a confused checkpoint guard blinked before eager Berliners crowding his post, the gate opened and the Wall began to fall.

In a way, the night of November 9 was the largest show of the carnival of Central Europe. Germans East and West dancing in the streets, popping champagne corks, carousing on top of the Wall—these have become the most familiar images of 1989. Provoked by a decision from above, though, they are really a separate story from the carnival we have followed elsewhere, and it is at this point that the experience of East Germany diverges completely from that of Central Europe. Within a month of the fall of the Wall, the loudest slogans in East Germany were for re-unification of Germany: "We Are One People." In early 1990 West German Chancellor Helmut Kohl made it clear that his government was prepared to pick up the tab for reunification on his terms.

The year that followed was one of politics even farther removed from the street than had been the round tables. Negotiations over every aspect of political, legal, and economic reunification (actually, the annexing of the East German lands into Germany) pushed the social movements to the margins. New Forum and the other social movements barely registered in the elections of spring 1990. But let us return to that autumn of 1989, when the sight of massive crowds taking over a city, and literally overwhelming the borders, played a necessary role in the revolutions of Central Europe. Thanks in part to new ties stretching across their common border, they were an important catalyst for what followed in Czechoslovakia.

Scene Sixteen

BRING A FLOWER WITH YOU! THE VELVET REVOLUTION

Czechoslovakia, October–November 1989

After the improbable opening of the Berlin Wall, the fall of communism began to feel inexorable. Central Europeans turned their eyes now to

Czechoslovakia. Change took place in barely a week, and the instigators, surprisingly to some, were the students. Though they had seemed to keep the burgeoning public opposition at arm's length, Czech students had an illustrious tradition of resistance to authoritarian regimes. Even more than 1968—redolent, after all, of the now-discarded dream of "socialism with a human face"—the shining example of student resistance was November 1939. Students had put up the most vigorous opposition to the Nazi takeover; one medical student, Jan Opletal, was shot during a demonstration on Independence Day, October 28, 1939, and died two weeks later. The November 15 funeral turned into a citywide anti-Nazi demonstration, in which students clashed with police and sang patriotic songs. Two days later, the Germans arrested over a thousand students, deported them to concentration camps, and closed the universities. Under the communists, November 17 had become International Students' Day, and Opletal, the Nazis' first victim, its symbol.

An official student demonstration on the fiftieth anniversary was not only expected, but obligatory. A year earlier, independent students had thought about organizing a student demonstration on that day, to show they too were ready for opposition. "I had the idea," says Martin Mejstřík, "that we could attempt some kind of demonstration or manifestation—have all the students gathered together—and see how it turns out. . . . In the end we abandoned that idea, because we felt that the situation in the schools is not right, and we don't yet have that kind of strength."[87]

In 1989 the students were fully prepared. The authorities approved a march, but only a short one, away from the city center. Beginning at the medical school in the Albertov neighborhood, students (guided by the Union of Socialist Youth [SSM]) would proceed to the grave of the romantic poet Karel Mácha on the Vyšehrad hill. Students rejected this plan, however, and forced the SSM to support a route to Václav Square, then down Opletal Street (past Political Prisoners' Street, where the Society for a Merrier Present was still racing), to lay flowers at a monument to fallen students. "We don't want just to recall with reverence those tragic events," read the flyer that appeared all over the university a few days before, "but we want to show our active support for the ideals of freedom and truth, for which those students gave their lives. For even today, those ideals are seriously threatened. We don't want to be ashamed before our university colleagues who so bravely rose up in their name fifty years ago."[88]

The SSM, meanwhile, took the precaution of getting senior opposition leaders to promise they would not manipulate the march, nor let foreign broadcasting (i.e., Radio Free Europe) know about the new route. Independent student leaders were determined at any rate to organize this one themselves. It was a question of honor for these relative novices to show what they could accomplish without the "professional revolutionaries."[89] The students sensed that Jan Opletal was their Otto Schimek or Janez Janša, a symbol of resistance to authority who could mobilize students as they had not been before.

At four o'clock that chilly afternoon, as darkness began to fall, some ten thousand students gathered to hear one of the student heroes of 1939 speak. There were several more speeches, and then Martin Klíma rose, to read the appeal quoted above. "We have to fight for freedom and against totalitarian lawlessness," he declared. By the time Klíma was done, the crowd was quite whipped up. They marched off to Vyšehrad for the official ceremonies, chanting, "We want a new government" and other slogans against the communist leadership. One could also hear the names of Havel, Masaryk, and Alexander Dubček. As if offering insurance for what was to come, organizers handed out a second leaflet, this one signed by student leaders at most of the faculties and institutes of Prague.[90]

By 6:30 the official ceremonies on Vyšehrad were over. Now the crowd, growing ever larger, streamed out toward the city center. They knew where they were headed, and what it meant: to the repertoire of slogans they added, "Václav Square!" as well as "Czechs, come with us!" Somehow, the crowd took a path completely different from the one the flyer had proposed: less direct, but more symbolically potent. Along the river they went to the National Theater (where Havel had waved to Gorbachev), then along National Avenue. Shortly before 8:00 P.M., they approached a cordon of riot police. Those at the front of the crowd sat down, chanting a slogan that had appeared frequently over the last few months: "We have bare hands!" A makeshift shrine, with candles and flowers, appeared in the street between the police and the crowd. For about forty minutes, the two sides stared at each other. Not for the first time that year, young Central Europeans wondered: could a flower fill the chasm between them?

Then the police attacked, closing off escape routes and beating students mercilessly. When it was over, some five hundred had been hurt, and twenty-four hospitalized. There were widespread reports, later revealed to be a police fabrication, that a student (Martin Šmíd of NMS) had been killed.*

Nothing, in other words, had gone according to plan. Neither the stu-

---

* There are many conspiracy theories concerning November 17. It is possible the crowd was steered toward National Avenue. But if one considers the growing experience of student opposition leaders, the unpredictable nature of earlier demonstrations (such as August 21, in both 1988 and 1989), and the fact that the crowd moved slowly enough in any case for the police to react, then the conspiracy theory proves to be not so much impossible as irrelevant. Moreover, even if the events of November 17 were controlled, those on subsequent days certainly were not.

dents nor the police had expected such a huge crowd, nor that the march would head in the direction it did. Martin Klíma experienced the jubilant community Poles had discovered years before, at the masses of Pope John Paul II and in Solidarity demonstrations:

> We were always just a handful of revolutionaries, a handful just waiting to be swept up. Our meetings were always very proper. We tried hard not to provoke; we stopped at red lights. That crowd, on the other hand, was something else. It was aware of its own power, as it poured down the streets, ignoring traffic, ignoring the lights. It just went on. . . . It was a beautiful feeling of mutual harmony. People finally understood that they are not alone anymore, that we all think the same way, and that when we are all together, nothing can happen because we are so strong.[91]

Such a crowd, and such a demonstration, was anything but inevitable. Even though communism may have been doomed by November, the particular path its fall took was not foreordained—neither by the regime nor by Charter 77. To understand this crowning moment of the Revolution of 1989, we must instead look back at the paths Central Europe had taken over the previous year, and pull out the threads that lead us to National Avenue.

Five important events occurred in the two months prior to November 17. Three of these took place in Prague: the formation of a student self-government, the arrival of waves of East German refugees, and new examples of regime arrogance. Two others took place farther away but were nonetheless of crucial importance in Prague as well: the festival of Czech culture in Wrocław and, just days before the Opletal anniversary, a large ecological demonstration in Teplice, in northern Bohemia. Together, these events allowed the Czechs, finally, to create their own revolution.

The students who formed STUHA (Ribbon, but also "Student Movement" [Studentské hnutí]) had all been involved in independent activity (as the euphemism goes) for some time. The idea of a student self-government was to create something new, focused on student needs and clearly oppositional, too. In late September (anticipating the beginning of the school year in October), they began meeting on Slovanský Island, then moved in later meetings to the Petřín Gardens on the hill overlooking the river. Through October the group grew ever larger, to as many as fifty, from nearly all the academies and universities of Prague. From their individual experiences—some with NMS, or the Democratic Initiative; others from their dissident parents, or independent culture; and all in one or another student magazine—a common movement emerged, stretching across Prague, above any one circle of friends.

STUHA's main task was to plan the Opletal anniversary demonstration and to write the appeal to be read there. But they found time, too, for a

happening, an early November protest under the windows of the Pedagogical Institute where a disciplinary committee was examining Michal
Semín and several other students. They were accused of engaging in political activity: ostensibly Democratic Initiative, but the authorities were
probably concerned about STUHA as well. For two hours a crowd of
some two hundred students sang songs, chanted the students' names, and
blew soap bubbles, which drifted up past the window where their friends
were being interrogated.

"The reaction of passersby surprised me," wrote Marek Benda later.
"Some of them stopped and sang with us, others at least asked what was
going on, and one woman even brought us a huge bag of doughnuts. We
were, of course, under police supervision, but it took my breath away
when I saw that one of the patrols, walking back and forth by us, sang
along with us and waved to us in time to the beat."[92] This was their only
happening (and they used the word popularized by Orange Alternative),
but it had the same effect on police, passersby, and the participants themselves and taught the same lessons about humor and nonviolence as those
happenings in Wrocław.

One of the slogans chanted during the Opletal march would have been
quite confusing (perhaps in an Orange way) to uninformed observers.
"We want a new hundred!" students chanted, and "Gottwald equals
Stalin!" This cryptic slogan reflected the Czech passion for national symbols, and anger at their desecration. Perhaps only the Czechs could have
become so angry over a new hundred-crown banknote. But only the
Czech communists would have dared to issue a bill with the face of Kle-
ment Gottwald, whose Stalinist rule of show trials and executions had
been one of Czechoslovakia's darkest hours. It was an act worthy of Romania's Ceaușescu. Unlike the routine propaganda in the daily newspaper or on the radio, or the discipline of an official parade, the bill forced
itself into every citizen's hands, in restaurants, at the train station, in the
grocery store, provoking "millions of little shocks, and bitter laughs."[93]

The scandal was tailor-made for the Czech Children, who called for a
demonstration on the pedestrian zone at the base of Václav Square for
October 25, under the slogan "Away with Gottwald and the Stalinists!"
Three days later, Czechs observed Independence Day with bitter rage, a
stark contrast to the buoyant mood of earlier demonstrations. The citizens of Prague—screaming at the police, angry tears running down their
cheeks—had had enough. The Gottwald banknote was a very small straw
indeed, but it was one of the last ones.

The battle lines, then, were hardening. We should not be surprised, not
in November 1989. But the cast of characters was still changing. In the
final weeks before the November 17 march, the people of Prague were
joined by their neighbors. The first of these were the East Germans. After

mid-September Hungary was closed to refugees from the GDR; Poland had been virtually off-limits for a decade already (though some East Germans would swim the Odra or Nysa rivers into Poland). This left hardline Czechoslovakia as the only accessible country for those determined to escape.

Within a few weeks, nearly six thousand East Germans—once again, mostly young families—had swarmed into Prague. At first they camped out on the narrow, hilly streets of the Malá Strana district near the West German Embassy; when the embassy allowed them through the gate and onto the lawn while their fate was negotiated, thousands more came to take their place on the streets. While Czechoslovakia was still a staunch ally of the GDR, no communist regime had ever been faced with such a crowd of foreigners on its streets. There was no precedent for arresting and deporting them (especially after Hungary had backed down from its deportation plans), so the refugees were left in peace.

East Germany was a country many Czechs were familiar with from vacations and official visits. It was a shock for Praguers to see so many people, just like them, risking their freedom and livelihood for a chance to lead a normal life elsewhere. When the GDR's Erich Honecker agreed to allow the refugees safe passage to West Germany (by sealed train across East Germany), Czechs didn't know what to think. Věra Krincvájová, a journalism student active in the student movement, decided to fulfill a school assignment by filming the Germans. "It made an awfully great impression on us," she recalled, "when we saw those people getting into a bus and driving away . . . somewhere to something normal. . . . Our professor didn't know what to tell us."[94]

Others traveled to East Germany to see the demonstrations in Leipzig and Berlin for themselves. What had begun as small demonstrations in early September had reached the tens of thousands by early October. Slogans about the refugees had given way to demands for democracy. Michaela Valentová of the Prague Mothers took her seven-year-old daughter Kristina to visit friends in Dresden and Leipzig, and then Berlin. It didn't seem as if anything was happening in Czechoslovakia yet, she thought, but she ended up missing November 17.

In the university town of Olomouc, two friends decided to go to Leipzig as well. To see a demonstration one hundred thousand strong; to sit in a café and chat with the participants; to visit the church where the opposition was coordinated; to grab a copy of Adam Michnik's *Gazeta wyborcza* to follow events back in Prague—this was to realize just how quickly things could change. Watching one demonstration, Martin Šteiner noticed "the most curious thing, which really shocked us, that the police stood at the edge of the road and made way for the march. De facto they were on the [people's] side, or at least they were not definitely on the side of the regime. I said to myself, here's a peaceful demonstration, where people express their thoughts freely."[95] Perhaps he would have expected such a thing in Poland, but East Germany had seemed the country most like Czechoslovakia politically.

By early November the waves of East Germans through Prague had stopped. The Berlin Wall came down, almost by accident, on November 9. "Normality" was now sweeping east, not waiting for refugees to jump fences or board trains to find it. Just a week later, students like Šteiner and Krincvájová would take the memory of the Germans' determination and calm with them as they marched and organized.

Other students had seen a different kind of resistance, in the distinctive carnival traditions of Wrocław. Since at least the June elections, Mirek Jasiński of Polish-Czechoslovak Solidarity had been planning his biggest undertaking yet: a four-day festival of Czech culture in Wrocław, to take place November 2–5. To this liberated city, where cultural expression had become the core of public opposition, he invited scores of distinguished exiled Czech singers, poets, novelists, and essayists.

He also invited his friends from Czechoslovakia. But crossing that barrier was considerably more difficult than coming from the West to a now-free Poland. Hundreds were stopped at the border, in cars and on trains. Their passports were confiscated, and they were sent home. None of the singers or artists made it; a planned exhibit of independent art was replaced by empty frames hung on the wall, notes inside describing the work and its artist.

The only leading dissident to make it was Petruška Šustrová, a former spokesperson of Charter 77. Her poor knowledge of geography saved her, she claims: this was only her second trip outside Czechoslovakia (after a concert in Budapest that summer). Not realizing how far away it was from Wrocław, she bought a plane ticket to Warsaw; the police had not bothered to look for anyone taking such a roundabout route. When she arrived in Wrocław, into a typical Silesian November fog, she felt she had entered another world: everywhere the Czech language was spoken, but the conversation was utterly different, free.

Šustrová got used to casual greetings in stores or on the street: "Oh, you're from Czechoslovakia! Don't worry, ma'am, communism will fall there too!" In a passionate letter published just days before the Czechoslovak revolution began, she recalled her shame that the Czechs had done so little to fight for freedom in "the last immovable island of totalitarianism in Central Europe." But instead of reproach from the Poles, she had heard encouragement: "Here, too, it looked for a long time as if the regime would not give in and the people had completely lost interest. Don't you dare give in to that!"[96]

Besides Šustrová, several thousand other Czechs did make it to the festival. The vast majority of these were young; most students, after all, would not be on any police lists of suspect dissidents. They also had the energy to find more obscure crossing points. Some of them hiked across the trails blazed by Polish-Czechoslovak Solidarity couriers. In Wrocław they lived in student dormitories, sharing space with veterans of Orange Alternative, Freedom and Peace, and the student movements. They thronged to readings, concerts—such as exiled singer Karel Kryl's two standing-room-only shows at the Polish Theater—and showings of long-banned Czech films. Like Lion Society performers in Vilnius, or Tamás Fellegi's young law students visiting Gdańsk, they had wandered into a zone of freedom, where they could think and do as they pleased.

Returning home, they brought some of this irreverent freedom with them. In Plzeň, a week after the festival, Marcel Hájek and Luboš Smatana stood up at a Union of Socialist Youth meeting and began to tell what they had seen and heard. In the audience, Jaroslav Straka was amazed to see two ordinary students ignoring threats from secret police officers in the room, carrying on as if what they had done was normal.

This tone of normality and confidence, new to Czechoslovakia, was what the trips to Wrocław, or to East Germany, or even the passionate speech of Fidesz's György Kerenyi at the August 21 demonstration, had given Czechs: a sense that elsewhere there were people who knew how to be free. Why, then, could it not happen here? "Those thousands of people, mostly young," wrote Šustrová, "will bring home more than just impressions from a concert and from a beautiful gathering. I think that the optimism of our Polish friends has infected them. And then, when you see with your own eyes that something can be accomplished, it stimulates you. . . . The hope we have brought home is a great foundation for the future."[97]

The Czechoslovak communists had seen so many lines of defense fall over the last year. No longer did they have the support of their neighbors, as even East Germany had turned away. But still, one could look at the ten or twenty thousand demonstrators in August or October and shrug: compared to the 1.5 million in Prague or the 15 million in the entire country, all was not lost. Students and intellectuals were not impossible to control, no matter what the signals from Moscow might be. Beyond Prague, there were a handful of letter writers, underground publishers, and participants at seminars, plus the pesky greens and Catholics of Bratislava. This was so until Teplice, when the regime's luck ran out.

The cause was the weather. Northern Bohemia was one of the most polluted places in Europe, and November's damp, cold air sent pollution levels soaring. When a poster appeared on the streets of the small city of Teplice calling for a November 11 protest on Nejedlý Square, it reached people who had never demonstrated before and had no connection at all with existing opposition groups. The author was not a signer of Charter 77, nor a member of any group, but 16-year-old Zbyšek Jindra: "Friends, maybe you have recently noticed various minor health problems, especially problems with respiratory passages." Jindra blamed industry, and "the apathy of humanistic organizations [i.e., the Communist Party], which supposedly do everything for the good of humanity." He asked that people come wearing gas masks to protest the foul air.

That Saturday some six to eight hundred demonstrators, mostly high school students or students from the teachers' college in nearby Ústí nad Labem, came to chant, "We want clean air!" and "Oxygen!" The next day there were even more demonstrators; the police responded with water-cannon and nightsticks. But the following day, after meeting with a group of local intellectuals who presented a petition, the provincial party leader promised an angry crowd to hold a public meeting on the ecological situation, to be held in one week at the indoor stadium.[98]

As Czech historian (and Teplice native) Miroslav Vaněk observes, this was "the first breakthrough," the Czechoslovak regime's one attempt at dialogue. The news reached a stunned Prague through Radio Free Europe, and between the lines of somewhat sympathetic newspaper reports. The students, groups like NMS, and the Chartists had all been seeking dialogue for a long time; the hope that the regime was finally ready to talk may have spurred participation in the demonstration of November 17.

Not for a few days would the events in Prague—and still less those in Teplice—reach the ears of Bratislava; nevertheless, the Slovaks were also ready for revolution. The regime greatly helped the different strands of opposition to come together by arresting, in August, five Bratislava activists, including Ján Čarnogurský and Miroslav Kusý, one of the few Slovak signers of the Charter. There could not have been a neater way to unite Bratislava behind a common cause. Slovaks across the political spectrum signed petitions demanding the release of the "Bratislava Five." Early in November Ján Budaj convened a gathering—for a concert and discussion—of most of the independent scene at Archa. It was organized by another group Budaj was close to: Without Barriers, surely the first disabled activists in the communist world, who had been thwarted in their first attempted debut at the "Day of Joy." The theme of barriers, says Budaj, became a general idea, as the discussion turned to Havel, to the "Few Sentences" petition, and so on: "The idea of destroying barriers, all across the political and social sphere," he insists, "appeared first there."[99]

Finally, Bratislava students—again, Catholic and non-Catholic alike, united as never before—staged their own march on the very day before the revolution in Prague began; they marched to the Ministry of Education, demanding discussion of the crisis in the educational system. As in

Teplice, the police decision not to intervene changed the way many thought about the possibility of change.

Each of the events described above, while they did not directly cause the revolution in Czechoslovakia, was on participants' minds. Still, the events of November 17 stand alone. Neither the participants nor the police knew that this demonstration would have a more dramatic conclusion, and greater impact, than all previous demonstrations. And no one knew what would happen now.

The morning after the assault on National Avenue, students gathered to figure out what to do next. The first reaction had been sorrow and exhaustion rather than anger, but determination to act quickly took over. Dialogue, they realized, was now impossible. As if in shock themselves, the police were almost invisible that day; the initiative briefly shifted to the students, as it had in Teplice four days earlier. By St. Václav's horse, Petr Placák read out a statement on the events of the previous night. In the coming days, "Václavak" would become the public center of the revolution.

At the Drama Academy, students declared a strike and announced their demands to an audience in the Realistic Theater, where many of Prague's actors had gathered to plan a similar protest. Through these two networks, of students and actors, news of the strikes spread across the country. By November 20, most universities and theaters in the country were on strike and calling for a general strike on November 27. Especially beyond Prague, these became centers of information for Czechs and Slovaks. Thus were ready-made networks—students in the provinces, for example, had learned to listen to Prague—now used for the purposes of political change. They filled the spaces where there had been no organized opposition at all and made information, and influence, available to everyone. They enabled the emergence of a revolution both peaceful and nationwide. The Velvet Revolution—no more, and no less, velvet than the others of Central Europe—had finally occurred, and Central Europe was free.

Timeline III: 1990–1991

Date	Poland	Czechoslovakia	Hungary	GDR	Slovenia	Ukraine	East/West
I.90	Leszek Balcerowicz introduces "shock therapy". Communist party dissolves, reforms	Communists cede control of Parliament	USSR agrees to withdraw troops	Honecker arrested. Anti-Stasi riot	League of Communists of Yugoslavia (LSY) collapses as Slovenes walk out of Congress. Opposition parties form Demos coalition	"Human chain" from Kyiv to Lviv	
II.90		Soviet Army begins withdrawing troops		New Forum demo against "capitalist unification"	Slovene League of Communists declares independence from LSY		
III.90			In first free elections in region, MDF is victorious	CDU wins election. Communists get 16%		Elections to Ukrainian Supreme Soviet	Lithuania declares independence from USSR
IV.90		Czechoslovakia renamed: Czech and Slovak Federative Republic. Pope John Paul II visits	Árpád Göncz chosen president		Demos wins election. Milan Kučan elected president		
V.90	Local elections held						
VI.90		Civic Forum (OF) and Public Against Violence (VPN) win parliamentary election	Parliament votes to withdraw from Warsaw Pact	Unification treaty ratified			
VII.90	Solidarity begins to divide into separate parties	Havel reelected President		German monetary union established	Slovene parliament declares sovereignty	Ukraine declares sovereignty	28th Party Congress opens in Moscow; ends party's monopoly on political power
VIII.90	Privatization begins						
IX.90				Four Allied powers sign treaty ending occupation			
X.90		Václav Klaus chosen Civic Forum leader		Unification of Germany			Mikhail Gorbachev receives Nobel Peace Prize
XI.90		Free local elections won by OF and VPN					CSCE summit in Paris declares end to European conflict
XII.90	Lech Wałęsa elected president			First All-German election	Referendum on independence. Slovenia declares sovereignty		

Month						
I.91						Soviet forces kill 13 in assault on Vilnius TV station
II.91		Splits emerge in OF and VPN; Political parties begin to emerge			Parliament declares that Slovene laws supersede Yugoslavia's		Agreement signed to dissolve Warsaw Pact
III.91							Referendum on fate of Soviet Union
IV.91		Vladimír Mečiar dismissed as prime minister in Bratislava; succeeded by Ján Čarnogurský	First Soviet troops withdraw				
V.91							
VI.91		Last Soviet troops leave	Last Soviet troops leave	Parliament votes to move capital to Berlin	Slovenia and Croatia declare independence		
VII.91					Ten-day war with Yugoslavia ends with Yugoslav Army's withdrawal	Soviet Republics negotiate new union treaty; Ukraine declares independence	Warsaw Pact dissolves
VIII.91			Pope visits				Attempted coup in Moscow
IX.91				Soviet Union announces schedule for troop withdrawal			
X.91	First free national elections	Voucher-based privatization begins					
XI.91		Gustáv Husák dies				Independence referendum	
XII.91							Soviet Union ceases to exist

EPILOGUE: NO MORE PICNICS,

AFTER THE REVOLUTION

THIS book ends at the very beginning of an era, and we must spend a moment thinking about what came next. The aftermath of revolution, though, sometimes bears little relationship to the struggle itself. While Central Europeans, like the veterans of other revolutions before them, dissect the present era, the historian is left to ponder whether the brave new world owes something to its turbulent origins.

The carnival of the 1980s may have faded away, yet something of its spirit has lived on. Dimitrij Rupel, independent Slovenia's first foreign minister, writes of his country leaving the Balkans and moving to Central Europe.[1] The Central Europe Rupel has in mind was the product not only of national traditions linking Slovenia to Austria and Italy, but also of the social activism linking Slovenia to Hungary, Poland, and the rest of the region explored here. If we define who we are by what we do, then we can say that the carnival participants, as they developed new strategies and styles of opposition—sometimes in parallel, sometimes interacting—created a new Central Europe.

Before we try to assess the revolution, though, the story of communism's fall needs to be brought to a close. To begin where the carnival ended first: The peaceful voting in Poland of June 4 was the logical outcome of the happenings and campaigns described in this book. They empowered people not to fear their own beliefs and desires, and to take a realistic yet hopeful view of their own ability to influence politics. If only 62 percent of the population voted, that is still more than half who had come to believe they had the right and the power to express themselves publicly, and did so. Even as the moment passed, and the carnival departed Poland for other countries, still it left its stamp on the Polish revolution. And, of course, the Polish revolution, in myriad ways, would catalyze all those that came after. Almost as soon as they were blessed with parliamentary immunity—and especially after Tadeusz Mazowiecki formed a Solidarity-led government in September—Solidarity members of Parliament fanned out across Central Europe to encourage their dissident colleagues. In Prague, Kyiv, Budapest, and Berlin, they proudly shared their experience and offered what support they could.

The Hungarian National Round Table concluded in September 1989. Binding commitments assured Hungary of free elections and major changes in the constitution. The Free Democrats and Fidesz refused to sign the agreement, however, in protest over the means by which the president would be elected.* In the end, a referendum was held on this point, and the opposition won handily. In October the country was renamed the Hungarian Republic ("Socialist" was dropped), and the party dissolved itself, eventually to spawn two smaller parties. And changes at the border had begun to do their part to precipitate change in East Germany and Czechoslovakia.

The most memorable image of the parliamentary elections, finally held in March 1990, was a Fidesz campaign poster. It juxtaposed two photographs: above, the Soviet troglodyte General Secretary Leonid Brezhnev kissing his East German counterpart Erich Honecker on the mouth. Below, a young couple, kissing on a park bench. Between, the simple slogan: "Fidesz. You choose." But of course, the people had already chosen. Contrasted with the fresh yet unthreatening campaign of the newly visible opposition, the communists already seemed painfully obsolete. While Fidesz itself received only 9 percent of the vote, and nearly one hundred thousand votes less than the renamed Hungarian Socialist Party, the latter had been resoundingly defeated and had just thirty-three seats in the new Parliament.

For the moment, at least, Fidesz would take a backseat in Parliament to its elders from the opposition, the Hungarian Democratic Forum and the Free Democrats. Voters may have liked the young couple on the bench, but they were not prepared to turn the country over to them just yet. Still, just as in Poland the previous June, the victory had been achieved not only by those whose expertise and experience drove the bargain with the regime and drew the votes, but also by those who had shown how to reimagine freedom. Following the small steps of Dialogue, and of the Danube Circle, and Zsolt Keszthelyi, Fidesz had opened the way. And in 1998 Viktor Orbán led Fidesz into power, becoming prime minister at the age of 34.

In the elections of March 1990, many *Rukh* activists were elected to the Parliament of the Ukrainian Soviet Socialist Republic; the movement swept all twenty-four seats in the Lviv region. Independent activists swept City Council elections, too. Lviv essentially ceased to be run by the Communist Party. The communist daily paper was shut down, replaced by an independent paper. Even Lenin's statue disappeared shortly thereafter. Outside of the Baltic Republics, Lviv had become the only free city in the Soviet Union, following the rhythms not of Moscow and Kyiv, but of Central Europe.

It would be over a year before Ukraine won its independence, in the aftermath of the failed attempt by Soviet hardliners to oust Mikhail Gor-

---

* They preferred that the president be elected (by Parliament) after free parliamentary elections and not before, as the latter would assure a communist—most assuredly Imre Pozsgay (see scene 15)—in that office.

bachev in August 1991. By that time, old communists like Leonid Kravchuk, once the chief ideologist of the Communist Party of Ukraine, had
adopted nationalist demands and prolonged their political careers. The
dissolution of the Soviet Union was most certainly not a part of the Central European carnival, any more than the unification of Germany in 1990
was; Lviv activists would also find that Kyiv was not necessarily an easier master than Moscow had been.

The key issue of 1989 in Yugoslavia was not Slovene independence, but
solidarity with the Albanians of Kosovo. When miners there announced
a hunger strike to protest Milošević's destruction of their region's autonomy, the CDHR organized a mass "public meeting"—not a demonstration, its organizers carefully emphasized—for February 27. The day after,
Belgrade authorities organized a counterrally. Soon Milošević was loudly
condemning Slovene "fascists." And as the situation in Kosovo worsened,
Slovenes saw there a reflection of the dangers they too faced. The "Ljubljana Four" went off to prison in May, their appeals exhausted. Rumors
of an invasion of Slovenia seemed entirely credible. When Slovene authorities prevented a Serb-sponsored rally against Slovene separatism from
taking place, Serbia responded with an economic boycott of Slovenia.

The only remaining question, as Slovenia headed toward a referendum
on national sovereignty in December 1990, was what kind of Slovenia
would emerge from Yugoslavia. Multiparty elections in April 1990 (the
first in Yugoslavia) brought victory to presidential candidate Kučan (who
had led his party out of the Yugoslav League of Communists in January)
and, in Parliament, the Demos coalition of five parties. Meanwhile, the
Youth League reformed itself (keeping the same initials, ZSMS) as "For
the Freedom of the Thinking World"; later it would become the Liberal
Party. Defense minister in the new government was *Mladina*'s Janez
Janša—an irony that surely matched any of the marvelous role reversals
that the revolutions of 1989 produced.

In Prague, finally, as the strikes and demonstrations became a revolution, students and actors would not be enough. The men and women who
gathered in Prague and in Bratislava on November 19 to found Civic
Forum and Public Against Violence (VPN), respectively, brought with
them two kinds of authority. People like Václav Havel, other Chartists,
and Catholic activists in Slovakia had been articulating ideas of opposition and freedom for years, even decades, and could draw on that experience and moral authority both when negotiating with the regime and
when addressing the crowds. But they also drew upon the peculiar paths
of mobilization over the past year or so. Some had been directly involved:
in Slovakia, Ján Budaj of *Bratislava/nahlas* became the spokesperson of
VPN, while Mária Filková was among other Bratislava greens in the activist core of the group. Independent artists and writers predominated.

In Prague, where opposition was more diverse, Civic Forum included representatives of many different movements: Hana Marvanová, Jana Petrová, and Jan Chudomel of NMS, Petr Plácak of Czech Children, and Emanuel Mandler of Democratic Initiative were members, as were a number of students, including Tomáš Drábek, Martin Mejstřík, Martin Benda, and Šimon Pánek. More important than the actual roster of participants, though, is that Civic Forum (like the Polish Round Table) drew upon the authority of the protests these groups had engineered. Both they and the regime, when they sat down to negotiate what would become a "Velvet" transfer of power, were aware that they spoke for, and could speak thanks to, those who had ventured out into the streets in ever-greater numbers since March 1988.

Just as in Poland, Czech and Slovak senior opposition veterans came together to form a coalition to represent society versus the communist regime. This is not to suggest that they somehow usurped the revolution. The fact that the same process occurred in every case does suggest a natural progression to the revolutions that toppled communism. After the street phase had finally won the humbled attention of the regime and the allegiance of society, it was time for experts to manage political change.

Even as the discussions of Civic Forum were continuing in the basement of the Theater of the Magic Lantern, British writer Timothy Garton Ash whimsically suggested to Václav Havel that, in contrast to the ten years it took Poles to topple communism (reckoning from the visit of Pope John Paul II in 1979); the ten months (perhaps from the first Danube demonstration to the Round Table) in Hungary; and the ten weeks of demonstration in the GDR before the wall fell, "perhaps in Czechoslovakia it will take ten days!"[2]

This remark spread like wildfire, becoming one of the most popular slogans of the revolution. It captured neatly the Czech desire to catch up with their neighbors and to expiate the shame that Petruška Šustrová had felt during her visit to Wrocław. And indeed, on the eighth day the party leadership resigned; on the eleventh, half the country's workers joined a two-hour general strike; and on the twenty-fourth day (December 10), a new government dominated by Civic Forum was appointed, and President Gustáv Husák resigned. It had all gone by much faster than the fall of communism anywhere else to date. Finally, the Czechoslovak revolution offered a fitting gracenote to the revolutionary year, when Václav Havel addressed a crowd gathered before the Prague Castle on New Year's Day, 1990, as their new president (chosen by a still-communist Parliament).

But Garton Ash's quip, as he surely knew, conflated two things, revolution in the sense of civic mobilization, which had been going on in Czechoslovakia for over two years, and revolution as political settlement.

This endgame was quick (as it was nonviolent) everywhere in Central Europe. In Poland the comparable period was perhaps just February to August 1989. The Czechs and Slovaks found it easy to forget that behind the all-too-brief "ten days" stretched long months, even years, of slow mobilization, on so many different stages. Without those hundreds of days, Czechs would never have been able to stand there on Václav Square in late November. But most had not witnessed that long struggle, and so they would give the name "Velvet Revolution" to what they knew best. The carnival began to recede from memory.

Concluding the story of each country's revolutionary moment, let's replace Garton Ash's impromptu sorting of revolutions with a different one. To begin, recall some of the things we would expect to find in a successful and stable democratic state: a vigorous nongovernmental sphere; openness to or tolerance of different political perspectives and different cultures (both of minorities and of neighboring states); and a willingness to compromise and to build coalitions. None of these skills is innate to any society, and it is difficult to believe they could be passed down from distant democratic pasts (such as the interwar era), either.

Central Europe's training was more recent: the intellectual ferment of the 1970s and 1980s and, especially, the new movements of the carnival. This was not a crash course. Poland's ten (or perhaps thirteen, since KOR) years of opposition seems about right, in fact. Next in our hierarchy would be Hungary and Slovenia, each of which could claim credit for revolutionary training stretching back almost a decade to Dialogue and punk protests; Slovakia (thanks to the Catholic underground) comes just after them, with the Czech lands just a bit behind.* East Germany and Western Ukraine are the relative latecomers to this revolutionary course, but far ahead of those societies, like Romania, that begin their study only at the end of 1989, as the carnival was already coming to a close.

Observers of postcommunist Central Europe will perhaps object that this ranking does not fit the region much better. Poland has certainly seen as many sudden political shifts—and even a near-coup, in 1992—as any other country, if not more. The historian must respond, though, that it is far too soon to label these regimes with any sense of finality. At different times since the revolution, conventional wisdom has labeled each country as anything from dangerously dysfunctional to a model of stability. Each can boast, though, that it graduated with distinction from the school of concrete, public anticommunist opposition.

---

* Czechs would probably find this order a bit unfair, as it overlooks the long struggle of Charter 77. But the Slovak effort to build networks and communities should rank a bit higher than the very important and courageous work of Czech intellectuals, who did not aim to organize society until quite late.

JACOB'S RETREAT

Worn out by eight years of opposition, Wojciech "Jacob" Jankowski needed a vacation. He had led a frenetic existence for so long: underground courier, printer, anarchist, and peace activist. He had spent long nights writing essays for the underground press until dawn, on a typewriter wrapped in blankets to keep down the noise; taken endless trips on slow trains across Poland to join in demonstrations in Wrocław, or on pilgrimages to the Schimek grave in Machowa; and endured over a year in jail. He was disgusted by the return of the "old-style" opposition at the May 1988 shipyard strike, crowned by the almost religious procession out of the shipyard that brought the strike to an end. Where was the place for the improvisation and the happenings, and for the energy of the new generation—without which, he was sure, that strike would never have happened?

So when a friend told him of a bit of land deep in the Mazurian lakes region, and a house that needed tending, Jankowski was off. Before long, he had built himself a tepee and began the life of a semi-hermit, teaching classes on wilderness survival to kids at a nearby summer camp. The marijuana he grew among his garden vegetables would eventually land him, briefly, in jail again; he likened the criminalization of this "harmless" hobby to the persecution of the underground press in an earlier time.

Jankowski missed the August strikes completely. He was invited to join both the Round Table and Adam Michnik's *Gazeta wyborcza* but declined both, with some regret and misgivings. By the time I met him, in the summer of 1997, he was living in an old cottage in the mountains near the Slovak border, without running water or electricity. The cottage, behind a fence adorned with deer skulls, sits in a breathtakingly beautiful valley, empty except for the shrines left behind by earlier residents when their houses were torn down and they were deported in the 1940s. It was about as far from public life as this very politically engaged man (who lived off essays he still wrote for a variety of newspapers) could be. His harsh, even scandalous views of Wałęsa, the Catholic Church, and Solidarity had mellowed. The inner life of meditation and deep ecology was now more important to him than the fate of the Polish revolution.[3]

This retreat, though perhaps extreme, illuminates the fate of the carnival in the revolutionary moments of 1989 (that is, during those moments that captured world attention) and in the subsequent decade. It reminds us that the new movements did not always achieve their goals, and that the moment of revolution was not precisely what they had anticipated (if they imagined the end of communism at all). Some, indeed, were profoundly disappointed by what occurred.

The reader will have already noticed that few of the movements portrayed here played a significant role in the actual transfers of power in 1989. Freedom and Peace was not a party to the Polish Round Table; nor was Orange Alternative, nor any other group besides Solidarity. In Czechoslovakia the Independent Peace Association, the Czech Children, or the environmentalists were not contestants in the Velvet Revolution. Neither the Lion Society nor the People for Peace Culture were themselves leaders of the national fronts that emerged in Ukraine or Slovenia, respectively. And though some of these movements still exist today, their influence does not begin to approach that which they enjoyed before 1989.

There are a number of reasons for this disappearance. One is suggested by the story of "Jacob": as events approached critical confrontations or negotiations, younger activists—better known for their particular styles of protest and focus on specific issues, and lacking any seniority in the opposition—were elbowed aside or ignored. It was not surprising that the bishop of Gdańsk, and Solidarity leaders, should conduct the procession to St. Brygida's Church. The message of dignified retreat that Wałęsa wanted to convey to the leaders of communist Poland and the world would hardly have been intelligible had young workers and anarchist printers led the procession. It is hard not to wish that the anarchists had been given a chance to speak for the Gdańsk strike, or that Wojciech Jankowski had accepted the invitation to the Round Table. Perhaps the revolution would have looked quite different if he had. But at such moments, opposition pluralism simply became, to those who would lead negotiations, a hindrance.

Civic Forum, Public Against Violence, Solidarity, Rukh, Demos: each spoke (or claimed to speak) with the voice of "the nation"; for the moment, that would be one voice.* During negotiations or elections, meanwhile, the new groups were unlikely to offer serious competition. Few could pretend to the kinds of expertise that seemed to be necessary now. Some would argue, of course, that this cult of expertise, which simply reinforced old habits and foreclosed real revolutionary change, was precisely the problem. At any rate, Jankowski—whose movement had helped to bring about one of the few significant concessions the communist regime made between 1981 and 1989 (the change in the military oath and the introduction of alternative military service, both in 1988)—was invited to join the subtable on youth, and not on, say, the judiciary system, the political system, or the media.

But of course, such participation was not what he, or so many others

---

* In East Germany, by contrast, the triumphant voice would not be any movement of East Germans, though New Forum pretended to that role, but the West German Christian Democratic Union and its leader, Helmut Kohl.

like him, had been looking for. Whether their goal was the complete destruction of the communist system, some kind of genuine total democracy, or an alternative lifestyle based on rejection of traditional authority, many activists refused, or did not seek, participation in the political transformations of 1989. Krzysztof Jakubczak of Wrocław's happenings felt that the new political process (which he had helped to set in motion) "was not for me," and somehow dirty; he did not even vote in the negotiated election in June. To raise awareness of human rights, or to use music or theater to provoke people into activism, was one thing; to leave the streets for parliamentary offices, or even for the voting booths, was quite another.*

Still others, perhaps, had something to contribute but were purposefully ignored as opposition leaders pursued a different agenda. This sense of neglect has hit workers most painfully. Researching the August 1988 strike in the Jastrzębie coal mines was a wrenching experience, each interview an encounter with bitterness and regret. One story in particular still haunts: Two years after the Jastrzębie strike, Krzysztof Zakrzewski, the strike's local leader, hanged himself. Some who knew him saw a link to the disappointments of 1988. Indeed, when I encountered Warsaw politicians and journalists who had come to know Zakrzewski during the strike, I found that not one had been aware of his death. I also found, though, that while one could write of the workers' tragedy, there was another story of success: often, when I went in search of a participant in the employees' councils, I would find him or her now working as a consultant, or running a small business, or immersed in trade union work. The game had changed entirely, and these activists had adapted.

This book is not meant to be a record of paths not taken, but a map of the paths that led to revolutionary change, whether or not they continue on after 1989. Still, it is a difficult task to link the transnational festival of opposition to the formal politics that followed. There are two ways in which the stories join. First, it should be clear by now that negotiations would have been quite unlikely without the active opposition of the previous half-decade. In place of the apathy and resignation of the urban majority, and the hermetic underground militancy of a tiny minority, there arose a much broader social commitment to concrete, open engagement. The regime did not agree to negotiate because this or that opposition leader showed indefatigable determination (nor, of course, simply due to economic decline and Western pressure, both of which had been the case for a long time). The catalyst to dialogue was the broad social unrest on dozens of stages. Resistance had spread beyond the usual large cities to

---

* Jakubczak has since had a change of heart. In 1998 he ran for and won a seat on Wrocław's City Council, currently headed by his old Twelve colleague Jarosław Obremski.

places like Międzyrzecz, Teplice, and Nagymaros, and from workers and young intellectuals to retirees and high school students. It was harder to pin down, too, as the new opposition traveled easily from issue to issue, from city to city, over the fences into striking factories, and across international borders.

There is a second contribution of the carnival as well, if we recall the idea of internal pluralism raised in the introduction. The new opposition moved freely across the activist landscape, devoting less time to programmatic statements and more time to opposing communism by any (nonviolent, mostly) means possible. If there could be a pluralism of issues, there could also be a diversity of paths. Later, some embraced the ordinary politics of postcommunist democracy. Even those who turned away would agree, with few exceptions, that the negotiations and the subsequent transfers of power ushered in an era of normality, in which anyone could do what he or she desired. That, naturally, included the freedom to sell out or to desert politics altogether.

The new movements shared a commitment to concrete goals and could often point to tangible achievements. This orientation could easily be compatible with participation in ordinary parliamentary politics, but also with leaving the stage entirely. Thinking about why she is no longer involved, former Polish high school activist Barbara Widera asserted the privileges of a pioneer: "now there are lots of willing volunteers, so I can take care of myself." That there would one day be many volunteers: was not this, in the end, one of the purposes of their activism?

A logical continuation of their drive to awaken society has been, for many, the media. Among Freedom and Peace activists, there are editors of at least two major city dailies, as well as numerous television, magazine, and newspaper reporters. Orange Alternative is, not surprisingly, the background of several web designers. Franci Zavrl of Slovenia's *Mladina* runs a PR firm, whose offices are adorned with a series of large oil paintings depicting the boss's travails in prison in 1988–89. He is not the only one in public relations: Piotr Niemczyk of WiP and Jaromir Piskoř of the Czechoslovak greens are other examples. In Ukraine a Lion Society activist edits a leading political weekly. The 1989 publications of both the Lion Society and Fidesz in Hungary have transformed into important journals of opinion. Public mobilization continues, then, but in a form more adapted to a free society.

For other activists, the causes they championed continued to engage them after 1989. The offices of Amnesty International in each country are home to many participants of the late-communist opposition. Where there has been a campaign against the military draft, as in Poland, or against the war, as in Yugoslavia, it has been a direct outgrowth of the movements of the 1980s. In the former military jail on Metelkova Street in Ljubljana, Marko Hren of the Peace Group now holds sway in the Peace Institute, as does Vlasta Jalušič. The entire complex, in fact, has been turned over to alternative movements, underground bands, artists, and museums. Another example is feminist movements across Central Europe, which, like their counterparts in the United States in the 1970s, often draw their energy from women who felt they were pushed to the margins in the antiregime opposition.

The most visible continuities have been green movements. In 1989–90 Tomasz Burek of the Gdańsk WiP circle pushed for a regional referendum on the Żarnowiec plant, as it became clear the Solidarity government of Tadeusz Mazowiecki was not going to shelve the project. The referendum was successful, and Poland's nuclear power program, for all practical purposes, was over. Several years later, Jarema Dubiel of Warsaw's WiP organized a similar referendum against a trash incinerator; he, too, was successful. Both of these campaigns are dwarfed by the ongoing struggle against the Gabčikovo-Nagymaros Dam in Hungary. There, it also turned out that the fall of communism was just the beginning of the struggle. It would take years of continued pressure to defeat the dam. While the Hungarian government canceled the dam agreement in 1992, the legal battles with Slovakia, and with the momentum created by the pre-1989 construction, rage on today.*

What of those who entered politics? Whether the subject is Jan Maria Rokita of WiP, now one of the leaders of the Catholic right in his Conservative People's Party; or Janez Janša, Defense Minister from 1990 to 1994; or Jana Petrová and Hana Marvanová, once of NMS and until 1998 members of the Czech Parliament in Václav Klaus's center-right Civil Democratic Party; or the boys from Fidesz who now head the Hungarian government, it is easy to encounter vituperative accusations of betrayal from former colleagues. Most scandalous of all, to some, have been the careers that several participants in WiP have made in the Ministry of Internal Affairs and the Bureau for State Defense. Their activism in the communist era, some say, was just a cynical mask to be discarded as soon as political power was in sight. At best, their naiveté led them to be co-opted into the very corridors of power they once opposed.

The politicians in question will themselves talk of coincidence, personal decisions, and even patriotic duty. But in the end, they point to the essentially political work they did before 1989. Opposition for them was not antipolitical, but ruthlessly political. Ideology had taken a back seat to goals before 1989, and that would still be so afterward. There is not so

* While Hungarian opposition to the dam became a matter of national honor, in Slovakia the opposite happened. Most people came to believe that to oppose the dam was to belittle Slovakia's capabilities; thus the dam (improbably enough, without Hungary's cooperation) moves forward.

much, really, separating these politicians from their former colleagues. Just as one could be an anarchist, or a hippy, or a performance artist and yet engage in oppositional politics, so too the line between, say, peace activism and peace-based oppositional politics was blurry indeed. To join the new establishment after the old one was defeated was not necessarily a cynical move, but a logical one. "There are many volunteers now," they might say, paraphrasing Barbara Widera, "so now I can be the politician I was meant to be."

As I conducted interviews with those from Freedom and Peace or NMS who had gone into Parliament in 1989 or 1990, I often wondered whether they had formed a caucus of any kind within the Civic Parliamentary Club of Solidarity or the Civic Forum. Each interviewee seemed genuinely perplexed by my question. Of course, they greeted each other in the corridors and occasionally worked together on legislation (for example, rewriting laws on military service), but it had never occurred to any of them that they constituted a faction or pressure group. The peace movements were not so much of the past as they were from a different arena. In the arena of Parliament, there was no place for a movement. Elsewhere, of course, others might continue the movement, and the two might even be in contact with one another. But for them, the era of normal politics had at last arrived, and they could leave the politics of the street behind.

A careful study of postcommunist Central Europe would most likely reveal that the issues of the 1980s have a continuing impact on the rhetoric and practice of politics. Green politics, or feminist politics, or peace issues hardly dominate, but they all have their advocates, probably to a greater extent than might have been otherwise. More generally, the question of political access for disadvantaged groups, and especially of minorities, is a constant source of tension. And surely the average age of parliamentary deputies—and even prime ministers—is much lower than in Western Europe. As the "generation of '88" reaches into its forties over the next decade, it is likely that its styles and ways of thinking will only increase in impact.

Remembering 1989

Coming home to Wrocław after the conclusion of the Round Table in April 1989, Władysław Frasyniuk knew that Solidarity had scored an impressive victory. Even with the election two months away, he could see that, at the least, communism would never be the same again. This was a moment to show the regime just how powerful and united Polish society was, and to celebrate the end of the underground years. "We should have had a picnic," he said later with regret, "found some orchestra to play, some beer, and said 'OK, pick your dance partner.'" But there was so much to be done to prepare for the election. He and others in the opposition were used to working around the clock, producing leaflets, discussing strategy, and taking care of the union. So they buckled down to work again, to try to win the election. Who had time for a picnic?

That picnic could have helped Poles feel that they, too, had participated in the Round Table. Instead, much of society would come to the conclusion that the Round Table, and everything that took place in 1989, was merely an élite affair, to which the nation as a whole was not a party. And as there were no celebrations then, so there are no commemorations today. The participants of the Polish Round Table celebrated the tenth anniversary of that remarkable gathering far from home in Ann Arbor, Michigan. Back in Warsaw, April 5, 1999, passed without much fanfare at all.

The lack of catharsis is one of the reasons 1989 has faded so quickly in people's memories. Among the countries where 1989 marked the actual change, only the Czechs have November 17 to celebrate, and the East Germans, the Wall's fall of November 9. Not only the Poles, but also the Hungarians do not celebrate 1989 at all. For Slovenes and Ukrainians, independence in 1991 is a far more commemorable moment. For the same reason, Western observers have also had a hard time calling 1989 a revolution, unless there is an adjective like "negotiated" attached. Revolutions are supposed to have dramatic confrontations where people are tossed out of windows or have their heads stuck on pikes. The negotiations of 1989 are indeed moments that lack vivid imagery, until we widen our vision just a bit. Then we can see that these revolutions were made up of a long series of smaller confrontations, over a period of several years, even a decade, before they culminate in the negotiations and committees that bring about the actual fall of communism. It is difficult now to find the moment of revolution, and thus to know what to celebrate. An opportunity was lost, in 1989, to create such a moment.

For individual activists, the uncertainty is no less. At the end of an intense, two-hour interview with an old friend, an underground journalist in Wrocław, I reluctantly turned off the tape recorder and prepared to pack up. Suddenly our conversation changed; there was something unspoken nagging my friend, brought to the surface by these reminiscences. She was just finishing her law degree, had a nice apartment in the center of the city, and could afford to travel all over the world. But had her opposition been worth it? It had taken her years of study to make up the time lost to underground pursuits. She thought of her friends from high school (three of whom, for example, started a very successful computer firm): "While we were busy with leaflets and other foolish stuff," she complained, "they were studying." This was true. I met a number of college dropouts, and even high school dropouts, during my travels. Some were happy on the fringes of society; others were not so sure. They wondered whether the excitement of the carnival had been worth the price of admission.

In some ways, it is too early to realize just how important those years were. Most of the participants are even now still at the beginning of their professional careers. The cities and towns where they live and where they created new forms of opposition are today, almost without exception, teeming with civic life. As they shape the media, the civic organizations, the more radical opposition, and politics both local and national, the imprint of the carnival will be ever more visible.

And what of the revolution itself? One of the most common criticisms of the revolutions of 1989—even of the very idea that these were revolutions—is that 1989 produced no great new idea or form of government (unlike, say, the American, Russian, or French revolutions). Instead, it simply produced states whose leaders and citizens aspire to be like Western free-market democracies.[4] This fact has made the changes after 1989 seem rather inevitable, and the excitement before 1989 a bit unnecessary.

But let me propose an alternative definition of revolution, one perhaps more suited to a revolutionary age quite unlike those that have come before. A revolution is a relatively sudden rupture in the normal or familiar practices of politics and society. I have called that rupture a carnival, which destroys the regime's monologue and lays the foundation for a later dialogue. During that rupture, an infinite number of possibilities open up, and imaginations are set loose. These might be ideas about radical political change—a "third way," or a "Europe without borders," or radical democracy. But they might also be more fundamental and personal than this: people can perform on the streets, or design their own protests, or write what they please, or retreat from society, or negotiate with leaders and sit in Parliament. They can embrace socialism, or deep ecology, or reinvent national traditions. The Church will change, the old opposition will change, people's mindsets and prejudices will change, the very nature of politics will change.

Much, maybe even most, of this comes to pass only briefly, if at all. The inertia of tradition and example, and the pressures of everyday concerns, turn revolutionaries back into ordinary people with jobs and families. The threat of defeat or annihilation—so important in earlier revolutions, but in 1989 relevant mainly in the Slovene case with the specter of Beijing also ever present—pushes more unusual ideas to the margins. This may be cause for regret, but it seems to be natural. What is more, it does not destroy that moment when all of the imaginings of a society (or its most active core) were laid bare. This is the more so when those ideas belong largely to a generation that expresses them just at the beginning of adulthood. The revolutions of 1989 did not lack for this dynamism, any more than did previous revolutions. And just as in those other revolutionary eras, it is likely that the memory and experience of unlimited potential will remain one of the lasting legacies of the carnival of Central Europe.

ACKNOWLEDGMENTS

WHAT was once a modest investigation of social movements in Poland's decade of Solidarity became a huge project in which I interviewed over three hundred people in twelve countries and read sources in half a dozen languages. Stretching beyond familiar territory, I have incurred a lot of debts that I cannot even begin to repay. I am grateful that so many people, in Central Europe, Western Europe, and the United States, took time to answer questions, to open their address books and supply further contacts, and to give me access to hard-to-find sources. I hope that I have done their stories justice.

In the Sources section, I provide a list of the interviews used in this book; there were many, many others whose stories I was unable to make use of. I have put a star next to the names of those activists who were particularly generous with their time or their archives.

When I traveled beyond Poland, I needed guides—and I found them, everywhere. Exceptionally helpful were Mirek Jasiński, Mirek Vaněk, Petr Uhl, and Petr Jehlička in Prague; Mark Pittaway, Miklós Haraszti, and Wojciech Maziarski in Budapest; Gregor Tomc and Jill Benderly in Ljubljana; Ihor Markov in Lviv; Stefan Troebst and Helena Flam in Leipzig; and Patrick Burke in London. Some of the time, I was fortunate enough to have translators assist me in interviews: Andriy Poritko in Lviv, Eva Nekolová in Prague, Thea Jacob in Leipzig, and Robert Fidrich in Budapest. Lászlo Benczö, Luka Fornazarič, Katalin Lustyik, Christopher Flacke, and Katharina Vester helped me translate documents. Zala Volčič and Krystyna Lenczowska went out of their way to collect materials for me. I am especially indebted to the research assistance of Izabella Bień, who annotated dozens of interviews and also provided helpful suggestions. As I traveled, I enjoyed the warm hospitality of my parents-in-law, Krystyna and Marian Ziółkowski, Marek and Krystyna Czapliński in Wrocław, Maria Drobiszewska in Kraków, the late Halina Lachendro in Jastrzębie, John and Tamsin Slyce in London, and Fruzsina Albert and her family in Budapest. The staff at Central European University in Budapest has always made me feel at home.

I cannot begin to list the scholars, far more expert on particular countries than I, who listened patiently to my ideas or steered me onto fruitful paths. It goes without saying that they are not responsible for the interpretation they will find here. I should recognize, however, colleagues whose work and encouragement have influenced me more than they know: Roman Szporluk, Konstanty Gebert, Andrzej Paczkowski, and Wojciech Wrzesiński. A number of friends have read and critiqued parts of the manuscript at various stages, among them Paulina Bren, Patrick Burke, Zsuzsa Gille, Warren Morishige, and John Slyce. I am grateful to the anonymous readers for Princeton University Press for their timely advice. Most of all, though, I thank the perceptive and unsparing readers in my family: my wife, Izabela, and my parents, Michael and Sara.

I thank Waldemar Fydrych for permission to quote at length from his inimitable account of the October Revolution happening in chapter 5. Parts of chapter 2 appear in "Perceived Political Opportunities in Repressive Regimes: A Case Study of Poland's Freedom and Peace Movement," *Mobilization: An International Journal* 6 (2) (2001): 171–88. My account of protest in Ukraine and Slovenia appeared first as "The Habsburg Empire (Re)Disintegrates: The Roots of Opposition in Lviv and Ljubljana, 1988," in *Cultures and Nations of Central and Eastern Europe,* ed. Zvi Gitelman, Lubomyr Hajda, John-Paul Himka, and Roman Solchanyk (Cambridge: Harvard Ukrainian Research Institute, 2000), 329–42. I am especially grateful to all the photographers and graphic artists whose work appears in this book, for their kind permission. In particular, the book cover is based upon a 1987 Orange Alternative poster stencilled by Jacek "Ponton" Jankowski. David Underwood prepared the map.

The University of Colorado, and specifically the Graduate Council on Arts and Humanities and the Committee on Research and Creative Work, was supportive of this project from the very beginning, funding several research trips. The bulk of the research was done on a grant from the National Council for Soviet (now Eurasian) and East European Research, under contract #811-24, and a Research Fellowship at the Woodrow Wilson International Center for Scholars. Writing was completed with sabbatical support from the University of Colorado, and a fellowship from the Research Support Program of the German Marshall Fund. Colorado's Institute of Behavioral Science provided a pleasant retreat for that year.

I would be remiss if I did not thank one foundation that did *not* fund this project (in fact, it rejected two applications). In 1986 I received a Language Training Grant from the International Research and Exchanges Board (IREX), to spend a year in Poland. The idea was that I would learn Polish while beginning research on an eventual topic for a dissertation. Sending a very early graduate student on a fishing expedition to communist Poland, IREX expressed a belief that putting promising scholars into sustained contact with an unfamiliar culture would be a worthwhile investment. I do believe that had it not been for that wonderful year I spent in Wrocław, I could not have conceived of this book.

As I complete this project, I cannot help but feel an odd sort of nostalgia for a time that was not my own, even though I was fortunate enough to catch a glimpse or two of the carnival. To my friends—those I made then, and those I have made in the course of this research—I offer this book as a window back into a younger time. For my daughters Maia (born the year the Soviet Union disappeared) and Karolina, I offer postcards from a vanished world, one that is also part of their heritage. And to Izabela, I offer an account, of sorts, of our wonderful years together. Thank you all.

NOTES

INTRODUCTION: STREET THEATER, CONCRETE POETRY

1. Waldemar Fydrych and Bogdan Dobosz, *Hokus-pokus, czyli Pomarańczowa Alternatywa* (Wrocław: Kret, 1989), 74.
2. *Z dnia na dzień* 4 (460), 4.
3. Jacek Kuroń, "Przed tym, co może się zdarzyć," *Tygodnik mazowsze* 240, 24 February 1988, 1.
4. J. F. Brown, *Surge to Freedom: The End of Communist Rule in Eastern Europe* (Durham: Duke University Press, 1991), ix; Michael Randle, *People Power: The Building of a New European Home* (Stroud, UK: Hawthorn Press, 1991); Raymond Pearson, *The Rise and Fall of the Soviet Empire* (New York: St. Martin's Press, 1997); William Echikson, *Lighting the Night: Revolution in Eastern Europe* (New York: W. Morrow, 1990). The best accounts are Timothy Garton Ash, *The Magic Lantern: The Revolution of '89 Witnessed in Warsaw, Budapest, Berlin and Prague* (New York: Random House, 1990); Vladimir Tismaneanu, *Reinventing Politics: Eastern Europe from Stalin to Havel* (New York: Free Press, 1993); Gale Stokes, *The Walls Came Tumbling Down: The Collapse of Communism in Eastern Europe* (New York: Oxford University Press, 1993); and Mark Frankland, *The Patriots' Revolution: How Eastern Europe Toppled Communism and Won Its Freedom* (Chicago: Ivan R. Dee, 1992).
5. I am drawing here on the ideas of Ukrainian philosopher Vladimir Zviglyanich (*The Morphology of Russian Mentality: A Philosophical Inquiry into Conservatism and Pragmatism* [Lewiston, NY: Edwin Mellen Press, 1993]), who describes Gorbachev's perestroika as a Bakhtinian carnival. Thanks to an anonymous reader for pointing out Zviglyanich's work.

CHAPTER ONE: EATING THE CROCODILE WITH A SPOON

1. "Oświadczenie TKK NSZZ 'S'," *Tygodnik mazowsze* 107, 22 November 1984.
2. "'Iść pod prąd!'," *Gazeta akademicka,* Wrocław, 5–6 (November 1986).
3. "Zamierzam działać jawnie. Rozmowa z Zbigniewem Romaszewskim," *Tygodnik mazowsze* 102, 18 October 1984.
4. Padraic Kenney, "Young Workers Fuel Solidarity," *The Boston Globe,* 4 September 1988.
5. František Mikloško, *Nebudete ich môct' rozvrátit'. Z osudov katolickej cirkvi na Slovensku v rokoch 1943–89* (Bratislava: Archa, 1991), 130.
6. Ján Šimulčik, *Svetlo z podzemia. Z kroniky katolíckeho samizdatu 1969–1989* (Prešov: Vydavatel'stvo Michala Vaška, 1997), 111.
7. Ján Šimulčik, *Čas svitania. Sviečková manifestaciá 25. marec 1988* (Prešov: Vydavatel'stvo Michala Vaška, 1998), 24–25. Also Timothy Garton Ash, *The Uses of Adversity: Essays on the Fate of Central Europe* (New York: Vintage, 1990), 218.

8. Quoted in Paweł Skrzywanek, "Historia 'Dwunastki'," ms. in possession of author, 8.

9. Quoted in Piotr Buzar, "Realizacja funkcji czasu wolnego poprzez uczestników Duszpasterstwa Akademickiego 'Dominik,'" M.A. thesis, Pedagogy, Wrocław University, 1989, 37–38.

10. Szymon Jakubowicz, "Wstęp, czyli kilka uwag o niezależności samorządów pracowniczych," in *Niezależne samorządy pracownicze*, ed. Jakubowicz (Warsaw: Instytut Socjologii, Uniwersytet Warszawski, 1989), 11. Also Jakubowicz, "Geneza i początki samorządu pracowniczego w latach osiemdziesiątych," in ibid., esp. 309–20.

11. *U nas* 60, 5 November 1984.

12. Letter from Przemysław Bogusławski to Komisja Wyborcza Przedsiębiorstwa, 12 November 1984; copy in possession of author.

13. Employees' Council, Polar, resolution 74/88, 31 August 1988; copy in possession of author.

14. Employees' Council, Coking Plant, Lenin Steelworks, resolution 21/III, 16 January 1988.

15. Ms. in possession of the author; dated 14–15 June 1986.

16. Marcin Przybyłowicz, "Dlaczego Otrzeźwienie," *Tygodnik powszechny*, 24 May 1987.

17. Jackson Diehl, "Poland's Month of Solidarity, Down the Hatch," *Washington Post National Weekly Edition*, 23 September 1985, 19.

18. "W celi. Rozmowa z Magdą Góralską, działaczką Bractwa Otrzeźwienia im. Maksymiliana Kolbe," *KOS* 21 (128), 6 December 1987.

19. Gabriel Szum, "Dotykalny fundament zwycięstwa," ms., n.d. (1985?), copy in possession of author.

20. Cited in Ks. Jan Śledzianowski, *Towarzystwo Pomocy im. Św. Brata Alberta a bezdomność* (Wrocław: Towarzystwo Pomocy im. Św. Brata Alberta, 1995), 12.

21. "Odezwa do polskich emerytów, rencistów i inwalidów," Katowice, August 1985. Copy in possession of author.

22. Open letter to Jan Dobraczyński, 13 October 1985. Copy in possession of author.

CHAPTER TWO: COME WITH US!

1. "Rota przysięgi wojskowej," Ustawa z dn. 22.XI.52, *Dziennik ustaw* 46, poz. 310.

2. "Ballada o Marku Adamkiewiczu," printed in untitled folder issued during the fast, in Ossolineum Library, Wrocław, Dział Dokumentacji Społecznej, Wolność i Pokój collection (uncatalogued). Hereafter Ossolineum collection.

3. Maciej Śliwa, "Ruch 'Wolność i Pokój' 1985–1989," M.A. thesis, History, Jagiellonian University, 1992, 9–10.

4. Wacław Giermek, "Dlaczego odmówiłem złożenia przysięgi wojskowej?" June 1986, Ossolineum collection.

5. Wojciech Jankowski, letter from Zwartowo prison, 13 August 1986, in Ossolineum collection.

6. *Szaniec. Biuletyn informacyjny Ruchu Młodzieży Niezależnej* 13/61, 7 April 1986.

7. *A cappella* 2, 16 December 1986.

8. Małgorzata Świerzewska, "Komunikat No. 1," Podkowa Leśna, 17 March 1986, Ossolineum collection.

9. *Biuletyn WiP* 6, 14 March 1987.

10. Julia, "Czernobyle—pomnik Matki Polki," *Gazeta. Pismo 'Solidarności' Świdnik—Chełm—Tomaszów—Zamość—Lublin* 5, 21 May 1986.

11. *Gazeta Akademicka* 4 (May 1986).

12. "'Najtrudniej było nam przekroczyć własną śmieszność . . .' o Międzyrzeczanach Międzyrzeczanki opowieść z taśmy spisana," *Pismo ruchu "Wolność i Pokój"* 4 (June 1988), 19.

13. Miroslav Vaněk, *Nedalo se tady dýchat* (Prague: Maxdorf, 1996), 89, 90.

14. *Charta 77 očima součastníků. Po dvaceti letech* (Prague: Doplněk, 1997), 238.

15. Charter document 2/87, in *Charta 77, 1977–1989. Od moralní k demokratické revoluci. Dokumentace,* ed. Vílem Prečan (Bratislava: Archa, 1990), 301–4.

16. "Ekologické fórum Charty 77," *Informace o Chartě* 10 (1987), 9.

17. Ivan Dejmal, "Začít, začít, ale jak?" *Ekologický bulletin* 3 (March 1988).

18. Pavel Křivka, "Kdo se bude radovat?" *Ekologický bulletin* 11 (March 1989), 1–3.

19. Edward K. Snajdr, "Green Mask, Green Mirror: Environmentalism, Culture and Politics in Slovakia's Transition from Socialism (1985–1995)," Ph.D. diss., University of Pittsburgh, 1998, 61.

20. "Odezwa programowa," *Na przełaj* 27, 1 July 1984.

21. Anna Wyka, "Ruch ekologiczno-pokojowy 'Wolę być'—spojrzenia socjologa," in *Ruchy i organizacje ekologiczne w Polsce,* ed. Piotr Czajkowski (Warsaw: Ośrodek Spraw Międzynarodowych PAX, 1990), 69.

22. Ibid., 71–72.

23. Quoted in Anna Wyka, "Ruch 'Wolę być'," *Państwo i kultura polityczna* 4 (1988), 63.

24. Ibid., 94.

25. *Na przełaj* 11, 15 March 1987.

26. In addition to an interview with Katarzyna Terlecka, this section is based upon Eryk Mistewicz, "Kajka. Reportaż dedykowany Tobie," *Wolę być. Pismo ogólnopolskiego ruchu ekologiczno-pokojowego* 1 (1991), 2–4.

27. "Oświadczenie w sprawie formuły działania Ruchu 'Wolność i pokój'," *Dezerter* 15 (61), 17 April 1988.

28. "Wokół 'Oświadczenia,' formuły działania i przyszłości 'WiP-u'. Dyskusja podczas głodówki we Wrocławiu," *Dezerter* 19/20 (65/66), 20 June 1988.

29. Władysław Frasyniuk, "Dobra rada dla WiP-u," *WiP,* Wrocław, 3, 17 November 1986.

CHAPTER THREE: AS IF IN EUROPE

1. Reprinted in *Protest and Survive* (New York: Monthly Review Press, 1981),

165. Thompson did not write the entire document, but he drafted this part of the appeal. See interview with Thompson, "The Peace Movement and Eastern Europe," *Labour Focus on Eastern Europe* 5 (5/6) (Winter 1982–83), 7.

2. Václav Havel, "Anatomy of a Reticence," in Havel, *Open Letters: Selected Writings 1965–1990* (New York: Vintage, 1991), 292.

3. Kavan interview in Randle, *People Power,* 157, 162.

4. E. P. Thompson, "The 'Normalisation' of Europe," a lecture delivered in a private apartment in Budapest, 23 September 1982, in Ferenc Köszegi and E. P. Thompson, *The New Hungarian Peace Movement* (London: Merlin Press, 1983), 44.

5. Quoted in E. P. Thompson, "Foreword," in ibid., 1.

6. Köszegi, "The Making of the New Peace Movement in Hungary," in ibid., 13–14, 10.

7. "Dialogue Continues," trans. Bill Lomax, *Peace News* 2222, 15 June 1984, 11.

8. Ibid.

9. E. P. Thompson, "Healing the Wound," *END Journal* 1 (December 1982–January 1983), 11.

10. E. P. Thompson, "Letter to Prague," in *Voices from Prague: Documents on Czechoslovakia and the Peace Movement,* ed. Jan Kavan and Zdena Tomin (London: Palach Press, 1983), 21.

11. "Message from the Delegates to the First Congress of the Independent Self-Governing Trade Union Solidarity," reprinted in *Communist Affairs* 1 (2) (April 1982), 538.

12. Quoted in John C. Torpey, *Intellectuals, Socialism, and Dissent: The East German Opposition and Its Legacy* (Minneapolis: University of Minnesota Press, 1995), 87.

13. Ludwig Mehlhorn interview, in Dirk Philipsen, *We Were the People: Voices from East Germany's Revolutionary Autumn of 1989* (Durham: Duke University Press, 1993), 77–78.

14. Christian Joppke, *East German Dissidents and the Revolution of 1989: Social Movement in a Leninist Regime* (New York: New York University Press, 1995), 102.

15. Björn, "Reiseimpressionen aus Polen oder Eine Lektion Zivilcourage," *Grenzfall* 3/86. Reprinted in Initiative Frieden & Menschenrechte, *Grenzfall: Vollständiger Nachdruck aller in der DDR erscheinenen Ausgaben (1986/87) Erstes unabhängiges Periodikum* (Berlin: Self-published, 1989), 14–15.

16. Lynne Jones, "Time for a Change," *END Journal* 28/29 (Summer 1987), 19.

17. Ibid.

18. *END Journal* 30 (October–November 1987), 11.

19. Joanne Landy, "To Defend END's Non-Alignment, We Must Oppose Admission of the Hungarian Peace Council to the Liaison Committee," *Bulletin of the European Network for East-West Dialogue,* trial issue (September 1987), 57–58.

20. *Serwis informacyjny Ruchu WiP* 43, 26 July 1987.

21. Quoted in *Tygodnik mazowsze* 211, 13 May 1987.

22. Polly Duncan, "A New Generation of Opposition," *Sojourners* 16 (9) (October 1987), 15.

23. Stanisław Puzyna, "Szósta konwencja ruchu Europejskiego Rozbrojenia Nuklearnego: Coventry 15–19 lipiec 1987r.," *Czas przyszły* 1, 1 September—15 December 1987, 38.

24. Jan Maria Rokita, "Wolność i pokój, czyli jak zwiększyć szanse pokoju w Europie," *Czas przyszły* 1, 1 September–15 December 1987, 20–21.

25. Ruch 'Wolność i Pokój', *Seminarium pokojowe w Warszawie 7–9.V.87. Dokumenty* (Warsaw, 1987), 31.

26. "Independent Voices, East and West, Speak Out Against Reagan's Nicaragua Policy," *Peace and Democracy News* 2 (2) (Summer–Fall 1986), 14–15.

27. Janusz Onyszkiewicz, quoted in Duncan, "A New Generation," 18. See "Bezpieczeństwo uparte na solidarności—projekt do dyskusji," in *Seminarium*, 22–23.

28. Quoted in Gillian Wylie, "Social Movements and International Change: The Case of Détente from Below," *International Journal of Peace Studies* 4 (2) (July 1999), 72.

CHAPTER FOUR: THE NEW POLITICS OF THE *KONKRETNY* GENERATION

1. Václav Havel, "Meeting Gorbachev," in Havel, *Open Letters*, 352.

2. Ibid., 353.

3. "Dopis Michailu Gorbačovovi" (statement 20/87), 23 March 1987, in *Charta 77, 1977–1989. Od moralní k demokratické revoluci*, 324–26.

4. Adam Michnik, Józef Tischner, and Jacek Żakowski, *Między panem a plebanem* (Kraków: Znak, 1996); Havel, "Meeting Gorbachev," 354.

5. *Biuletyn WiP* 7–8, 26 April 1987, 9–11.

6. Viacheslav Chornovil, in *Ukrainskyi Visnyk* 9–10 (October–November 1987) (reprint: Baltimore: Smoloskyp Press, 1988), 313.

7. T. Stetskiw, "Predtecha Tovarystva," *Postup* 12 (October 1989), 2.

8. Valentyn Stetsiuk, "Istoriia Tovarystva Leva," ms., 1999, 3.

9. Ibid., 5.

10. Ibid.

11. Valentyn Stetsiuk and Myron Kolodko, "Ekologichna karta Dnistra," in *Na varti Dnistra* (Lviv: Tovarystvo Leva, 1996), 75–96.

12. Stetsiuk, "Istoriia Tovarystva Leva." 8.

13. Gregor Tomc, "Militarization of Society," *Information Booklet: Peace Movement in Yugoslavia* 2 (3) (August 1986), 17–18.

14. Slavenka Drakulić, *The Balkan Express: Fragments From the Other Side of the War* (New York: Harper Collins, 1993), 12.

15. Mastnak, e-mail correspondence, 11 July 2000.

16. *Information Booklet* 2 (3) (August 1986), 7–8.

17. Marko Hren, "Action: Give Children a Chance," *Information Booklet* 2 (1) (January 1986), 11–13.

18. Vlasta Jalušič, "The Proposal for Obligatory Military Training for Women to Be Withdrawn," *Information Booklet* 2 (1) (January 1986), 6–8.

19. "What Is on with the Conscientious Objection to Military Service (CO)

Recognition in Yugoslavia?" *Information Booklet* 3 (1) (January 1987), 39–41.

20. Tomc, "Alternative Politics: Example of the Initiative for Civil Service," *Information Booklet* 3 (2) (June 1987), 22.

21. Gregor Tomc, "AC/BC," *Information Booklet* 2 (3) (August 1986), 30.

22. Interview with Kövér in Katalin Bossányi, *Szólampróba. Beszélgetések az alternatív mozgalmakról* (Budapest, 1989), 68; interview with Orbán in *Ellenzéki karakasztal. Portrévázlatok,* ed. Anna Richter (Budapest, 1990), 77.

23. Kövér interview in *Szólampróba, 69.*

24. Viktor Orbán, "Recapturing Life," *Across Frontiers* 4 (2–3) (Spring–Summer 1988), 34–35.

25. István Kovács, "Kontakty węgierskie Wacława Felczaka w latach siedemdziesiątych i osiemdziesiątych," in *Polskie lato, węgierska jesień. Polsko-węgierska solidarność w latach 1956–1990,* ed. Csaba Kiss Gy. and Konrad Sutarski (Budapest, 1997), 147.

26. Reprinted in *Fidesz News* 1 (1) (1989), 4–5. Emphasis in original.

27. *Revolver revue* 11 (1988), n.p.

28. *Informace o Chartě* 10 (5) (1987), 9–13. The Charter 77 document is 27/87.

29. *Bulletin Nezávislé mírové sdružení—Iniciativa za demilitarizaci společnosti* (hereafter *Bulletin NMS)* 1 (May 1988), 2–4.

30. Ibid., 7–8.

31. Rudolf Vévoda, "Nezávislá mírová sdružení," ms., 22.

32. *Bulletin NMS* 5 (January 1989), 9–10; Vévoda, "Nezávislá mírová sdružení," 58, n. 41.

33. "Pomoc lesům v Jizerských horách," *Bulletin NMS* 4 (November 1988), 18.

34. *Bulletin NMS* 19 (June 1989), 16–17.

35. Rob McRae, *Resistance and Revolution: Vaclav Havel's Czechoslovakia* (Ottawa: Carleton University Press, 1997), 97.

36. Milan Otáhal and Miroslav Vaněk, *Sto studentských revolucji: Studenti v období pádu komunismu—životopisná vyprávěni* (Prague: Lidové Noviny, 1999), 565–66.

37. Quoted in ibid., 133.

38. Ibid., 406.

39. Ibid., 135, 623.

40. Ibid., 281, 286.

41. Šimon Pánek, quoted in ibid., 641.

42. Ibid., 842.

43. Ibid., 801.

44. Ibid., 285.

45. Ibid., 803.

46. Mejstřík, quoted in ibid., 149.

CHAPTER FIVE: HOW THE SMURFS CAPTURED GARGAMEL

1. Reprinted in Alicja Grzymalska, "Pomarańczowa Alternatywa, czyli jak śmiechem można zabić przeciwnika," M.A. thesis, History, Wrocław University 1993.

2. Tomasz Jerz, "Młody Wrocław," *Most* 18 (April 1988).

3. "Rozmowa z Krzyśkiem Jakubczakiem (Jakubem): Nie lubię uczniów najlepszych ze wszystkiego," *Szkoła* 6 (43), 15–30 February 1988.

4. Fydrych and Dobosz, *Hokus-Pokus*, 48.

5. Ibid., 66–69.

6. Slavenka Drakulić, *How We Survived Communism and Even Laughed* (New York: Harper Collins, 1993), 66–75, 124.

7. Timothy Ryback, *Rock Around the Bloc: A History of Rock Music in Eastern Europe and the Soviet Union* (New York: Oxford University Press, 1990), 112.

8. Oleg Olisewicz [Oleh Olisevych], "Listy ze Lwowa," *Czas przyszły* 3–4 (Autumn 1988–Winter 1989), 9.

9. Ibid., 5.

10. P. S., "'Pogulyaite, khloptsi, do travnya,'" *Ukrainskyi visnyk* 9–10 (reprint, New York, 1987), 527.

11. Olisewicz, "Listy ze Lwowa," 11.

12. Otáhal and Vaněk, *Sto studentských revolucji*, 279–80.

13. Mírová demonstrace mládeže k 5. výročí smrti J. Lennona," *Infoch* 9 (1), 4 December 1985–7 January 1986, 8–10.

14. Ota Veverka, "Do zobaczenia za rok," *Biuletyn informacyjny Solidarności Polsko-Czeskosłowackiej* 10–12 (1989), 17.

15. Základní prohlášení Mirového Klubu Johna Lennona," *Bulletin NMS* 6 (February 1989), 15.

16. *Szkoła* 2 (28), 1–15 December 1986.

17. "Rozmowa z Krzyśkiem Jakubczakiem."

18. *Szkoła*, special edition, n.d. (September 1988).

19. Ján Šimulčík, *Zápas o nadej. Z kroniky tajných kňazov 1969–1989* (Prešov: Vydavateľstvo Michala Vaška, 2000), 78.

20. *Staszek*, 3, 7 (19), 22 April 1988.

21. *Wolne związki. Pismo NSZZ 'Solidarność'*, Bydgoszcz, 27, 28 June 1988, and 29, 19 October 1988.

22. *Obserwator wielkopolski*, Poznań, 119 (March 1988).

23. *QQRYQ*, 10, n.d. (late 1987).

24. *QQRYQ*, 12, n.d. (1988).

25. Gregor Tomc, "The Politics of Punk," in *Independent Slovenia: Origins, Movements, Prospects*, ed. Jill Benderly and Evan Kraft (New York: St. Martin's Press, 1994), 121.

26. Ali Žerdin shared with me these quotes from a diary kept by Igor Bavčar, published in *Mladina* in 1989.

27. Reprinted in *South Slav Journal* 11 (2–3) (40–41) (Summer–Autumn 1988), 116–30.

28. *Koruna* 1 (1989); reprinted in Jana Svobodová, ed., *Nezávislá skupina České děti (1988–1989). Dokumenty. Česká společnost v období normalizace a revoluce 1969–1989. Materiály, studie, dokumenty* 3 (Prague: USD AVČR, 1995), 74–76.

29. Interview with Anna Hradilková, in ibid., 12.

30. Interview with Lucie Váchová, in ibid., 27.

31. Interview with Luděk Marks, in ibid., 29, 36.

32. Interview with Lucie Váchová, in ibid., 22–23.

33. Krzysztof Albin, "Ostatnia faza każdej epoki jest komedią," *Przegląd akademicki* 13 (July–August 1992), 34.

34. Fydrych and Dobosz, *Hokus-Pokus,* 77.

35. Grzymalska, "Pomarańczowa Alternatywa," 24.

36. Anonymous [Waldemar Fydrych], "Pomarańczowa Alternatywa," *Kultura* 3 (486) (March 1988), 33.

37. Hanna Bałtyn, "Jak pewien major dostał przepustkę do historii," *Przegląd akademicki* 13 (July–August 1992), 31.

38. Anonymous [Waldemar Fydrych], "Pomarańczowa Alternatywa," 34.

39. *Fatamorgana. Pismo pracowników Fabryki Automatów Tokarskich* 4 (124), 23 February 1988.

PART TWO: A REVOLUTION IN SIXTEEN SCENES

1. Nobelek Rusz-Czkash, "Wiosna ludów 1988," *Szkoła* 46/47 (15 May–June 1988) 13–14.

2. Garton Ash, *The Uses of Adversity,* 214–27.

3. Quoted in Šimulčík, *Čas svitania,* 31.

4. Martin M. Šimečka, "Sviatky jari," *Fragment K* 2 (1988), 26–27.

5. Šimulčík, *Čas svitania,* 137–38.

6. Šimečka, "Sviatky jari," 29.

7. Július Bročka and Ladislav Stromček, quoted in Šimulčík, *Čas svitania,* 154.

8. Benda, "Výzva z Bratislavy," *Bratislavské listy,* January 1989, 5.

9. Unpublished interview, collected by a research team headed by Jerzy Wertenstein-Żuławski, IfiS PAN, 2, 5.

10. Tomasz Tabako, *Strajk '88* (Warsaw: NOWa, 1992), 65.

11. Ibid., 71.

12. Paweł Smoleński, "A na hucie strajk . . . ," in *Robotnicy '88* (London: Aneks, 1989), 7–8.

13. Reprinted in *A cappella* 10 (1988), 9.

14. Wojciech Giełżyński, "Gdańsk, maj 88," in *Robotnicy '88,* 116.

15. *Dezerter* 17, 16 May 1988, 2.

16. Smoleński, "A na hucie strajk . . . ," 80.

17. Paweł Chojnacki, "Grupa krakowska. Szkic o młodej opozycji," *Promieniści* 16 (127) (1989).

18. Giełżyński, "Gdańsk, maj 88," 142–43.

19. Ibid., 143–44.

20. Smoleński, "A na hucie strajk . . . ," 87.

21. Quoted in Jan Lundin, "Slovenia 1988: Pluralism and Reaction," *Working Papers,* Uppsala University, Department of Soviet and East European Studies, 1 (1989), 12.

22. Tone Stojko, *Slovenska pomlad/Slovenian Spring,* text by Ali Žerdin (Ljubljana: Prodok, 1992), 31.

23. Ibid., 51.

24. Ihor Melnyk, "Desiat rokiv tomu," *Postup* 106 (115), 13 June 1998, 3.

25. Ibid. Also Vsevolod Iskiw, quoted in Oleh Stetsyshyn, "Mityng, iakyj zakhvytav pidvalyny rezhymu," *Tyzhden* (Lviv), 12–18 June 1998.

26. *Desiat dniv, shcho skolykhnuly Lviv . . .* (Kyiv-Lviv, 1988; reprint New York: Zakordonnyi predstavnytstva Ukraïnskoï helsinskoï spilki, 1989), 12–13.

27. Petro Marko, quoted in Stetsyshyn, "Mityng."

28. *Desiat dniv,* 14.

29. Ibid., 18.

30. Pejot, "Koledzy!" and untitled verse, from typescripts distributed at the July Manifesto mine and found in the archive of the mine's Solidarity office. Pejot published several similar poems in the strike bulletins as well.

31. "Wyścig zbrojeń," in Tabako, *Strajk '88,* 293–94.

32. Saša Vondra, "Akreditační číslo 1019," *Infoch* 11 (16) (1988), 17.

33. Kenney, "Young Workers Fuel Solidarity."

34. Karel Srp, *Výjimečné stavy. Povolání Jazzová Sekce* (Prague: Pragma, 1994), 137.

35. *Revolver revue* 11 (1988), n.p.

36. Oldřich Tuma, *Zitra zase tady! Protirežimní demonstrace v předlistopadové Praze jako politický a socjální fenomén* (Prague: Maxdorf, 1994), 80.

37. *Infoch* 11 (15) (1988), 7.

38. *Bulletin NMS* 2 (September 1988), 9.

39. McRae, *Resistance and Revolution,* 4.

40. Tuma, *Zitra zase tady!,* 22.

41. *Revolver revue* 11 (1988), n.p.

42. Ibid.

43. Ibid.

44. See documents 4 and 27 in *Čas Demokratické iniciativy 1987–1990 (Sborník dokumentů)* (Prague: Nadace Demokratické iniciativy pro kulturu a politiku, 1993), 28–29, 72.

45. MH, "Udalosti 28 října 1988," *Revolver revue* 11 (1988), n.p.

46. Otáhal and Vaněk, *Sto studentských revolucji,* 149.

47. McRae, *Resistance and Revolution,* 13.

48. Reprinted in *Infoch* 12 (1) (1989), 14–15; and *Bulletin NMS* 6 (February 1989), 15–16.

49. Otáhal and Vaněk, *Sto studentských revolucji,* 497.

50. Tuma, *Zitra zase tady!,* 37.

51. Radek Zeman, "Místo úvodníku," *Bulletin NMS* 5 (January 1989), 1; Otáhal and Vaněk, *Sto studentských revolucji,* 498.

52. Eva Kantůrková, "On the Ethics of Palach's Deed," in *Good-bye Samizdat: Twenty Years of Czechoslovak Underground Writing,* ed. Marketa Goetz-Stankiewicz (Evanston: Northwestern University Press, 1992), 180.

53. Charter document 4/89, "Vzpomínka na Jana Palacha," in *Horký leden 1989 v Československu,* ed. Jan Vladislav and Vilem Prečan (Prague: Noviná, 1990), 67, 69.

54. Tuma, *Zitra zase tady!,* 37.

55. McRae, *Resistance and Revolution,* 22.

56. *Horký leden,* 123–24, 93, 95.

57. Otáhal and Vaněk, *Sto studentských revolucji,* 567. See also 497–98 (interview with Pavel Lagner).

58. Ibid., 302.

59. Roman Kucharski, "Spacer po rynku," *WiPek* 3 (1989), 2.

60. Originally published in *Ekobulletin* 15 (July 1989), 25; reprint *Přes Prah* 9 (3) (March 1999), 25–26.

61. A. H., "Královská obora," *Koruna* 3 (1989), in *Nezávislá skupina České děti,* ed. Svobodová, 92–93.

62. Mária Filková, "MDD očami účastníka," *Ochranca prírody. Spravodaj MV SZOPK Bratislava* 3–4 (1989), 30–31.

63. Interview in ibid., 43.

64. Interview with Anna Hradilková, in *Nezávislá skupina České děti,* ed. Svobodová, 13.

65. Pavel Jegl, "Týden solidarity s čínským lidem w Praze," *Bulletin NMS* 10 (June 1989), 20; *Infoch* 12 (13) (1989), 15; JM, "Čina," *Koruna* 2 (1989), in *Nezávislá skupina České děti,* ed. Svobodová, 80–81.

66. Garton Ash, *The Magic Lantern,* 51.

67. *Uncaptive Minds* 2 (4) (August–October 1989), 26.

68. J. Grygar, "1 maj: Ty na tribune to muselo prastit do oci!" *Koruna* 2 (1989), in *Nezávislá skupina České děti,* ed. Svobodová, 77–78. Jiří Všetečka and Jiří Doležal, *Rok na náměstích. Československo 1989* (Prague: Academia, 1990), 36.

69. McRae, *Resistance and Revolution,* 39.

70. *Bulletin NMS* 9 (May 1989), 7–8, 10–11.

71. "Slovo k srpnovému vyročí," *Bulletin NMS* 11 (July–August 1989), 21.

72. *Bulletin NMS* 11 (July–August 1989), 23; Petr Placák, "21 srpen," *Koruna* 3 (1989), in *Nezávislá skupina České děti,* ed. Svobodová, 96. See also interview with Ladislav Lis in *Zpravodaj HOS* 7 (September 1989), in *Hnutí za občanskou svobodu, 1988–1989. Sborník dokumentů* (Prague: Maxdorf, 1994), 176.

73. "I znovu, vybory!" *Postup* 1 (April 1989), 1.

74. K. Darmograj, "Tyzhden v ekspedytsiy," *Postup* 8 (August 1989), 8.

75. Bohdan Nahaylo, *The Ukrainian Resurgence* (Toronto: University of Toronto Press, 1999), 217.

76. R. Matsyuk, "Na zustrichi zizdu NRU," *Postup* 10 (September 1989), 1, 3.

77. Quoted in *Postup* 11 (October 1989), 2.

78. Mastnak, "Civil Society in Slovenia: From Opposition to Power," in *The Tragedy of Yugoslavia: The Future of Democratic Transformation,* ed. Jim Seroka and Vukasin Pavlovic (Armonk, NY: M. E. Sharpe, 1992), 62–63.

79. Quoted in Taras Kuzio and Andrew Wilson, *Ukraine: From Perestroika to Independence* (New York: St. Martin's Press, 1994), 116.

80. *Spadshchyna* 1 (October 1989), 2.

81. Taras Stetskiw, "Strayk, strayk, strayk!" *Postup* 14 (November 1989), 7.

82. In Philipsen, *We Were the People,* 213.

83. Quoted in Joppke, *East German Dissidents,* 146.

84. Quoted in *Heute vor 10 Jahren. Leipziger MenschenRechtsgruppen 1989,* 4 (4–10 June 1999).

85. Joppke, *East German Dissidents,* 152.

86. Quoted in Craig Whitney, "How the Wall Was Cracked—a Special Report; Party Coup Turned East German Tide," in *The Collapse of Communism,* ed. Bernard Gwertzman and Michael T. Kaufman (New York: Random House, 1991), 219.

87. Otáhal and Vaněk, *Sto studentských revolucji,* 563–64.

88. *Deset pražských dnů (17.-27. listopad 1989). Dokumentace* (Prague: Academia, 1990), 15.

89. Interview with Martin Klíma, in *Deset pražských dnů,* 593.

90. Marek Benda et al., *Studenti psali revoluce* (Prague: Univerzum, 1990), 16–20; "Jak to bylo doopravdy," *Lidove noviny,* 17 November 1999.

91. Quoted in Otáhal and Vaněk, *Sto studentských revolucji,* 24.

92. Benda et al., *Studenti psali revoluci,* 18–19. Also Otáhal and Vaněk, *Sto studentských revolucji,* 148.

93. Martin Šmíd, "V oběhu Gottwald mimozemšťan . . . ," *Bulletin NMS* 12 (January 1990), 30.

94. Quoted in Otáhal and Vaněk, *Sto studentských revolucji,* 190.

95. Ibid., 758.

96. Petruška Šustrová, "Polské dojmy," *Sport* 4 (1989), 26.

97. Ibid.

98. Miroslav Vaněk, "Předehra k 17. listopadu 1989: Ekologické demonstrace w Teplicích," in *Historické studie. K sedmdesátinam Milana Otáhala* (Prague: Maxdorf, 1998), 225.

99. *Verejnosť proti násiliu 1989–1991. Svedectvá a dokumenty* (Bratislava: Nadácia Milana Šimečku, 1998), 31.

EPILOGUE: NO MORE PICNICS

1. Dimitrij Rupel, "Slovenia's Shift from the Balkans to Central Europe," in *Independent Slovenia,* 182–200.

2. Garton Ash, *The Magic Lantern,* 78.

3. Wojciech Jankowski, *Dumki Jakoba* (Warsaw: Tu, 1999).

4. See, for example, Ralf Dahrendorf, *Reflections on the Revolution in Europe* (New York: Random House, 1990).

SOURCES

ARCHIVES

Budapest: Open Society Archives
Prague: Libri Prohibiti
Wrocław: Oddział Życia Społecznego, Ossolineum Library

SAMIZDAT PERIODICALS (SELECTED)

Poland

A cappella. Nieregularnik Ruchu "Wolność i Pokój." Gdańsk.
Ad vocem. Dwutygodnik informacyjny WiP. Szczecin.
Agnus. Pismo Ruchu "Wolność i Pokój." Bydgoszcz.
Akademik. Wrocław.
Amazonka—Kobiece pismo niezależne "Solidarności." Bydgoszcz.
Bajtel. Pismo młodzieży solidarnej. Katowice.
Bez przemocy. Pismo Ruchu "Wolność i Pokój." Gorzów Wlkp.
Biuletyn informacyjny Solidarności Polsko-Czeskosłowackiej. Wrocław.
Biuletyn Strajkowy Komitetu Strajkowego Huty Stalowa Wola.
Biuletyn WiP. Warsaw.
BIUST. Biuletyn Informacyjny Uczniów Szkół Technicznych. Wrocław.
Czas przyszły. Warsaw.
Dezerter. Serwis informacyjny Ruchu "Wolność i Pokój." Warsaw.
Dialogi. Biuletyn polsko-ukraiński.
Gazeta akademicka. Wrocław—Warsaw.
Gazeta jastrzębska. Pismo Polskiej Partii Socjalistycznej. Jastrzębie Zdrój.
Głos Hutmenu. Pismo TKZ NSZZ "Solidarność" Hutmen. Wrocław.
Głos śląsko-dąbrowski. Katowice.
Grizzly. Pismo studentów i absolwentów. Warsaw.
Hej. Informator uczniowski MKO FMW. Wrocław.
Homek. Pismo Ruchu Społeczeństwa Alternatywnego. Gdańsk.
Hutnik. Pismo członków NSZZ "S" HiL. Kraków.
Jutrzenka. Pismo TKZ Solidarność Pafawag. Wrocław.
Kablowiec. Pismo członków NSZZ "Solidarność" przy KFK i MK. Kraków.
Katatymia. Kwartalnik nieregularny. Warsaw.
KOS. Warsaw.
Kronika małopolska. Kraków.
*Manifeściak. Zakładowy informator Kopalni Węgla Kamiennego "Manifest Lip-
    cowy."* Jastrzębie.
*Nasz głos. Biuletyn informacyjno-kulturalny młodzieży walczącej NSZZ "S" szkół
    średnich woj. krakowskiego.* Kraków.
*Nowohucki biuletyn Solidarności. Pismo Komitetu Organizacyjnego NSZZ "Sol-
    idarność" KM HiL.* Kraków.

Obecność. Niezależne pismo literackie. Wrocław.
Obserwator wielkopolski. Poznań.
Odrodzenie. Niezależne pismo Tajnej Komisji Zakładowej NSZZ "Solidarność" w DZWMB Dolmel. Wrocław.
Ość. Biuletyn Informacyjny Jastrzębskiej Delegatury RKW NSZZ Solidarność.
Pismo Ruchu "Wolność i Pokój." Szczecin.
Promieniści. Kraków.
Przegląd wiadomości agencyjnych. Warsaw.
QQRYQ. Warsaw.
Region. Dwutygodnik RKW NSZZ "Solidarność" Dolny Śląsk. Wrocław.
Robotnik. Pismo Międzyzakładowego Robotniczego Komitetu "Solidarności."
Samorządna Rzeczpospolita. Dwutygodnik NSZZ "Solidarność." Warsaw.
Serwis Informacyjny Ruchu "WiP." Warsaw.
Solidarność ELWRO. Wrocław.
Solidarność Hutników. Biuletyn Informacyjnej Tajnej Komisji Robotniczej Hutników NSZZ Solidarność Kombinatu Metalurgicznego. Kraków.
Spotkania. Niezależne pismo młodych katolików. Kraków-Lublin-Warsaw.
Stan Cywilny. Pismo krakowskiego garnizonu Ruchu "Wolność i Pokój."
Staszek. Pismo uczniów szkół ponadpodstawowych. Kraków.
Sumienie. Dwumiesięcznik. Wrocław.
Szaniec. Gorzów Wlkp.
Szkoła. Wrocław.
Towarzystwo Gospodarcze w Warszawie. Biuletyn.
Trzynaście. Kraków.
Tu i teraz. Warsaw.
Tygodnik mazowsze. Warsaw.
U nas. Pismo NSZZ Solidarność Polar. Wrocław.
W Brew. Pismo ruchu "Wolność i Pokój" oraz krewnych i przyjaciół krolika. Wrocław.
Wipek. Organ kilku uczestników Ruchu "Wolność i Pokój" z Wrocławia.
"Wolność i Pokój." Pismo ruchu "Wolność i Pokój." Kraków.
Wrocławski student.
Z dnia na dzień. Wrocław.

Czechoslovakia

Alternativa. Prague.
Bratislavské listy. Bratislava.
Bulletin NMS. Prague.
Ekologický bulletin. Prague.
Fragment K. Bratislava.
Informace o Chartě. Prague.
Kontakt. Bratislava.
Koruna. Prague.
Lidové noviny. Prague.
Magazyn SPUSA. Zlín.
Naboženstvo a súčasnost. Bratislava.
Nezávislé mírové sdružení. Bulletin. Liberec.
Protějši chodník. Opava.

Revolver revue. Prague.
Sport. Prague.
Spravozdaj HOS. Prague.
Střední Europa. Prague.
Ze zasuvky i z bloku. Prague.

Ukraine

Postup. Lviv.
Sal'tseson. Lviv.
Spadshchyna. Lviv.
Ukrainskyi visnyk. Lviv.
Ukrainskyi visnyk-Ekspres. Lviv.
Z dnem na den'. Moscow.

German Democratic Republic

Grenzfall. Berlin.

NONSAMIZDAT PERIODICALS

Across Frontiers. Berkeley.
East European Reporter. London.
END Journal. London.
Federal Broadcast Information Service. Eastern Europe.
Gazeta wyborcza. Warsaw.
Heute vor 10 Jahren. Leipziger MenschenRechtsgruppen 1989. Leipzig.
Information Booklet: Peace Movement in Yugoslavia/Independent Voices from Yugoslavia. Ljubljana.
Kultura. Paris.
Labour Focus on Eastern Europe. Oxford.
Listy. Rome.
Mladina. Ljubljana.
Na przełaj. Warsaw.
Peace and Democracy News. New York.
Peace News. London.
Samizdat Bulletin. San Mateo CA.
Smoloskyp. Ellicott City MD.
Ukrainian Review. London.
Uncaptive Minds. Washington, DC.
Uncensored Poland. London.

INTERVIEWS

☆ *Stars indicate interviewees who also provided me with primary documents or other special assistance.*

Czechoslovakia

Pavol Benko, Bratislava, 9 June 2000.
Ján Budaj, Bratislava, 2 June 1998 and 9 June 2000.

Ján Čarnogurský, Bratislava, 1 June 1998. ☆
Mariá Filková, Bratislava, 1 June 1998 and 9 June 2000. ☆
Yvonna Gailly and Jan Hollan, Brno, 31 May 1998.
Anna Hradilková, Washington, 12 May 2000.
Jolana Kusá, Bratislava, 2 June 1998.
Ivan Lamper, Prague, 18 November 1999.
Emanuel Mandler, Prague, 15 November 1999.
Hana Marvanová, Prague, 27 May 1998.
František Mikloško, Bratislava, 2 June 1998. ☆
Petr Payne, by letter.
Jana Petrová-Marcová, Prague, 28 May 1998.
Jaromir Piskoř, Prague, 27 May 1998.
Petr Placák, Prague, 28 May 1998.
Kamil Prochazká, Bratislava, 1 June 1998.
Michal Šaman, Jaroslav Straka, and Leoš Motl, Prague, 16 November 1999.
Ruth Šormová, Soběslav, 29 May 1998.
Petruška Šustrová, Prague, 16 November 1999.
Petr Uhl, Prague, 24 May 1998.
Michaela Valentová, Prague, 18 November 1999.
Alexander Vondra, Washington, DC, 12 May 2000.
Jiří Voráč, Brno, 30 May 1998.
Luboš Vydra, Prague, 17 November 1999.

German Democratic Republic

Ludwig Mehlhorn, Berlin, 21 June 1999.
Bernd Oehler, Wermsdorf, 26 June 1999.
Thomas Rudolph, Leipzig, 25 June 1999. ☆
Wolfgang Templin, Berlin, 23 June 1999. ☆

Hungary

Béki Gabriella, Budapest, 4 June 1998.
Bozóki András, Budapest, 8 June 1998. ☆
Bruszt László, Budapest, 8 June 1998.
Csaba Ivan and Vardi Katalin, Budapest, 15 June 1998.
Csapody Tamás, Budapest, 9 June 1998. ☆
Deutsch Tamás, Budapest, 8 June 2000.
Diószegi Olga, Budapest, 8 June 1998.
Enyedi Zsolt, Budapest, 8 June 1998.
Fellegi Tamás, Budapest, 8 June 2000.
Fodor Gábor, Budapest, 16 June 1998.
Gille Zsuzsa, Champaign, IL, 17 February 2000. ☆
Haraszti Miklós, Budapest, 3 June 1998 and 12 June 2000. ☆
Hegedűs István, Budapest, 12 June 2000. ☆
Honecz Agnesz, by e-mail.
Keszthelyi Zsolt, Baja, 6 June 1998. ☆
Köszeg Ferenc, Budapest, 24 October 1996.
Mattrai Juliana, Budapest, 13 June 2000.

Merza József, Budapest, 22 October 1996.
Miszlivetz Ferenc, Budapest, 8 June 2000. ✩
Molnár Peter, Budapest, 9 June 1998.
Rékvenyi Zsolt, Budapest, 5 June 1998.
Rozgonyi Zoltán, Budapest, 15 June 1998. ✩
Stumpf István, Budapest, 13 June 2000.
Vasarhelyi Judit, Budapest, 7 June 2000.
Vargha Janos and Droppa György, Budapest, 22 October 1996.

Poland

Bogdan Aniszczyk, Wrocław, 9 January 1997.
Marek Bartosiak and Lech Osiak, Jastrzębie, 22 February 1997.
Ryszard Bocian, Kraków, 15 January 1997.
Przemysław Bogusławski and Krzysztof Zadrożny, Wrocław, 24 January 1997. ✩
Adam Borysławski, Kraków, 27 May 1997. ✩
Stanisław Bożek, Międzyrzecz, 17 July 1997.
Tomasz Burek, Karwia, 6 July 1997. ✩
Leszek Budrewicz, Wrocław, 5 November 1996.
Małgorzata Calińska and Urszula Mika, Wrocław, 7 January 1997.
Paweł Chmiel, by e-mail.
Jan Ciesielski, Kraków, 13 January 1997.
Wiesław Cupała, Wrocław, 11 February 1997.
Jacek Czaputowicz, Warsaw, 31 January 1997, 20 June 1997, and by e-mail. ✩
Mirosław Czech, Warsaw, 21 June 2000.
Fr. Bernard Czernecki, Jastrzębie, 22 February 1997.
Zuzanna Dąbrowska and Piotr Ikonowicz, Warsaw, 1 February 1997.
Sławomir Dutkiewicz, Sopot, 6 July 1997.
Henryk Feliks, Wrocław, 11 December 1996.
Zbigniew Ferczyk, Kraków, 23 June 1998.
Grzegorz and Krystyna Francuz, Wrocław, 20 February 1997.
Władysław Frasyniuk, Wrocław, 29 January 1997.
Kazimierz Fugiel, Kraków, 16 January 1997.
Waldemar Fydrych, Wrocław, 17 June 2000.
Anna Gawlik and Anna Koczut, Wrocław, 9 December 1996.
Radosław Gawlik, Wrocław, 25 November 1996.
Katarzyna Gierełło and Anna and Ewa Szynkaruk, Warsaw, 1 February 1997.
Wacław Giermek, Wrocław, 4 December 1996 and 12 June 1997. ✩
Jan Golec, Racibórz, 13 May 1997. ✩
Małgorzata Gorczewska, Gdańsk, 6 July 1997.
Paweł Gross, Jastrzębie, 22 February 1997.
Stanisław Handzlik, Kraków, 14 January 1997.
Barbara Hrybacz, Warsaw, 19 June 1997, and by phone.
Radosław Huget, Kraków, 11–12 January 1997. ✩
Adam Jagusiak, New York, 8 April 2000.
Krzysztof Jakubczak, Wrocław, 18 December 1996.
Marek and Ewa Jakubiec, Wrocław, 10 May 1997. ✩
Zbigniew Janas, Ann Arbor MI, 10 April 1999.

Wojciech Jankowski, Czarne k/Gładyszowa, 29 June 1997. ☆
Mirosław Jasiński, Wrocław, 25 November 1996 and 6 June 1997. ☆
Robert Jezierski, Wrocław, 22 January 1997.
Andrzej Kamiński, Jastrzębie, 21 February 1997. ☆
Marian Kania, Kraków, 15 January 1997, and by e-mail.
Krzysztof Kawalec, Wrocław, 2 January 1997. ☆
Tomasz Kizny and Anna Łoś, Wrocław, 15 June 2000.
Bogdan Klich, Kraków, 15 January 1997.
Paweł Kocięba, Wrocław, 16 December 1996. ☆
Anastazja Konieczna, Wrocław, 3 January 1997.
Stanisław Kosek, Jastrzębie, 21 February 1997. ☆
Zbigniew Kostecki, Wrocław, 11 March 1997 and 9 June 1997. ☆
Andrzej Kowalski, Wrocław, 29 April 1997.
Grzegorz Kozakiewicz, Kraków, 20 June 2000.
Stanisław Kracik, Kraków, 22 June 1998.
Marek Krukowski, Wrocław, 6 February 1997.
Wiesław Krupiński, Jastrzębie, 21 February 1997. ☆
Zygmunt Łenyk, Kraków, 12 January 1997.
Jan Lityński, Ann Arbor, MI, 10 April 1999.
Maciej Mach, Kraków, 16 January 1997.
Ryszard Majdzik, Kraków, 28 May 1997.
Sławomira Malczewska, Kraków, 15 January 1997.
Andrzej Marciniak, Janusz Pura, and Marek Szczupak, Kraków, 28 May 1997. ☆
Agata Michałek-Budzicz, Kraków, 17 January 1997.
Eryk Mistewicz, Warsaw, 1 February 1997.
Marek Muszyński, Wrocław, 12 March 1997.
Robert Naklicki, Szczecin, 5 July 1997.
Marek Niedziewicz, Wrocław, 29 November 1996.
Piotr Niemczyk, Warsaw, 2 February 1997 and 21 June 2000. ☆
Edward Nowak, Wrocław, 4 March 1997.
Urszula Nowakowska, Warsaw, 6 May 1997.
Jarosław Obremski, Wrocław, 23 January 1997.
Marek Oktaba, Wrocław, 13 June 1997.
Janusz Okrzesik, Bielsko-Biała, 22 February 1997. ☆
Dariusz Paczkowski, Bielsko-Biała, 22 February 1997.
Józef Pinior, Wrocław, 20 December 1996/30 January 1997.
Andrzej Piszel, Wrocław, 19 December 1996 and 11 March 1997.
Wojciech Polaczek, Kraków, 11–12 January 1997.
Krystyna Politacha, Wrocław, 25 April 1997.
Marcin Przybyłowicz, Warsaw, 20 June 1997.
Konstanty Radziwiłł, Warsaw, 18 June 1997.
Jan Maria Rokita, Kraków, 26 May 1997.
Marek Rusakiewicz, Gorzów, 17 July 1997.
Agata Saraczyńska, Wrocław, 28 January 1997. ☆
Iwona Sienkiewicz, Wrocław, 23 January 1997.
Jolanta Skiba, Wrocław, 30 April 1997.
Danuta Skorenko, Katowice, 23 February 1997.
Leopold Sobczyński, Jastrzębie, 22 February 1997.

Sławomir Sobieszek and Paweł Kieruzal, Wrocław, 9 January 1997. ☆
Benita Sokołowska, Wrocław, 2 December 1996. ☆
Kazimierz Sokołowski, Gorzów, 17 July 1997.
Jacek Suchorowski, Wrocław, 7 January 1997.
Grzegorz Surdy, Kraków, 14 January 1997.
Katarzyna Terlecka, Kraków, 23 June 1998.
Bazyli Tyszkiewicz, Ruda Śląska, 13 May 1997.
Bogumiła Tyszkiewicz, Wrocław, 22 May 1997.
Jerzy Urban, Warsaw, 17 June 1997.
Jarosław Wardęga, Wrocław, 9 June 1997.
Barbara Widera, Wrocław, 27 January 1997.
Piotr Wierzbicki, Warsaw, 17 June 1997. ☆
Fr. Ludwik Wiśniewski, Małe Ciche, 30 June 1997.
Piotr Wojciechowski, Warsaw, 19 June 1997. ☆
Tomasz Wójcik, Wrocław, 7 January 1997.
Henryk Wojtała, Wodzisław Śląski, 22 February 1997. ☆
Wojciech Woźniak, Szczecin, 5 July 1997.
Mariusz Zieliński, Wrocław, 24 April 1997.
Stanisław Zubek, Kraków, 14 January 1997 and 26 May 1997. ☆
Jerzy Żurko, Wrocław, 23 November 1996 and 6 June 1997. ☆

Slovenia

Marko Hren, Ljubljana, 11 June 1998, and by e-mail. ☆
Vlasta Jalušič and Tonči Kuzmanič, Golnik, 11 June 1998, and by e-mail.
Tomaž Mastnak, Ljubljana, 12 June 1998, and by e-mail. ☆
Alenka Puhar, Ljubljana, 12 June 1998. ☆
Gregor Tomc, Ljubljana, 13 June 1998. ☆
Igor Vidmar, Ljubljana, 10 June 1998.
Franci Zavrl, Ljubljana, 12 June 1998, and by e-mail.
Ali Žerdin, Ljubljana, 10 June 1998. ☆

Ukraine

Taras Batenko, Lviv, 19 June 1998, and by e-mail.
Ihor Copestynskyi and Orest Drul, Lviv, 18 June 1998.
Markiian Ivashchyshyn, Lviv, 18 June 1998.
Iryna Kalynets, Lviv, 20 June 1998.
Ihor Koliushko, Lviv, 20 June 1998.
Ihor Melnyk, Lviv, 19 June 1998.
Oleh Olysevych, Lviv, 19 June 1998, and by e-mail. ☆
Aleksander Starovoit, Lviv, 19 June 1998.
Valentyn Stetsiuk, by e-mail. ☆
Yuri Vynnychuk, Lviv, 18 June 1998.
Lev Zakharchyshyn, Lviv, 18 June 1998.

Western Europe

Paul Anderson, London, 7 June 1999.
Marko Bojcun, London, 8 June 1999.
Patrick Burke, Brighton, 11 June 1999. ☆

Bruno Coppetiers, Brussels, 14 June 1999. ☆
Luc Deliens, Brussels, 13 June 1999.
Dieter Esche, Berlin, 22 June 1999. ☆
Mient-Jan Faber, The Hague, 16 June 1999.
Ruth Henning, Berlin, 23 June 1999.
Lynne Jones, by e-mail.
Neil Finer, London, 12 June 1999. ☆
Mary Kaldor, London, 7 June 1999.
Joanne Landy, New York, 18 September 1999. ☆
Sylvie Mantrant, Brussels, 14 June 1999.
Jan Minkiewicz, Amsterdam, 17 June 1999.
Mark Thompson, Oxford, 9 June 1999. ☆
Ton van Eck and Martin Abma, Amsterdam, 15 June 1999.
Paul Wilson, Toronto, September 1999.
Nancy Wood, Brighton, 11 June 1999. ☆

INDEX